Mastering Linux Security and Hardening

Secure your Linux server and protect it from intruders, malware attacks, and other external threats

Donald A. Tevault

BIRMINGHAM - MUMBAI

Mastering Linux Security and Hardening

Commissioning Editor: Vijin Boricha
Acquisition Editor: Rohit Rajkumar
Content Development Editor: Devika Battike
Technical Editor: Mohd Riyan Khan
Copy Editors: Safis Editing, Dipti Mankame
Project Coordinator: Judie Jose
Proofreader: Safis Editing
Indexer: Pratik Shirodkar
Graphics: Tania Dutta
Production Coordinator: Deepika Naik

First published: January 2018

Production reference: 1090118

Published by Packt Publishing Ltd.
Livery Place
35 Livery Street
Birmingham
B3 2PB, UK.

ISBN 978-1-78862-030-7

www.packtpub.com

`mapt.io`

Mapt is an online digital library that gives you full access to over 5,000 books and videos, as well as industry leading tools to help you plan your personal development and advance your career. For more information, please visit our website.

Why subscribe?

- Spend less time learning and more time coding with practical eBooks and Videos from over 4,000 industry professionals

- Improve your learning with Skill Plans built especially for you

- Get a free eBook or video every month

- Mapt is fully searchable

- Copy and paste, print, and bookmark content

PacktPub.com

Did you know that Packt offers eBook versions of every book published, with PDF and ePub files available? You can upgrade to the eBook version at `www.PacktPub.com` and as a print book customer, you are entitled to a discount on the eBook copy. Get in touch with us at `service@packtpub.com` for more details.

At `www.PacktPub.com`, you can also read a collection of free technical articles, sign up for a range of free newsletters, and receive exclusive discounts and offers on Packt books and eBooks.

Contributors

About the author

Donald A. Tevault—but you can call him *Donnie*—got involved with Linux way back in 2006, and has been working with it ever since. He holds the Linux Professional Institute Level 3—Security certification, and the GIAC Incident Handler certification. Donnie is a professional Linux trainer, and thanks to the magic of the internet, teaches Linux classes literally the world over from the comfort of his living room.

> *First, I'd like to thank the good folk at Packt, who were most delightful to work with on this project. I'd also like to thank my cats, who so graciously allowed me to use their names in the demos.*

About the reviewer

Salman Aftab has 10+ years of experience in Linux and 7+ years of experience in networks and security. He authored the book *Linux Security and Unified Threat Management System*.

Salman is an owner of the Linux Zero To Hero project, where he teaches Linux from very basic to advanced level free of cost. He is skilled in Linux, AWS, Networks and Security, and VOIP. He is RHCE trained and holds NCLA, SCNS, CEH, 3 X CCNA, CCNA Security, CCNA Voice, CCNP Security, CCNP, and OSCP is in progress.

Packt is searching for authors like you

If you're interested in becoming an author for Packt, please visit authors.packtpub.com and apply today. We have worked with thousands of developers and tech professionals, just like you, to help them share their insight with the global tech community. You can make a general application, apply for a specific hot topic that we are recruiting an author for, or submit your own idea.

Table of Contents

Preface

In this book, we'll cover security and hardening techniques that apply to any Linux-based server or workstation. Our goal is to make it harder for the bad guys to do nasty things to your systems.

Who this book is for

We're aiming this book at Linux administrators in general, whether or not they specialize in Linux security. The techniques that we present can be used on either Linux servers or on Linux workstations.

We assume that our target audience has had some hands-on experience with the Linux command line, and has the basic knowledge of Linux Essentials.

What this book covers

Chapter 1, *Running Linux in a Virtual Environment*, gives an overview of the IT security landscape, and will inform the reader of why learning Linux security would be a good career move. We'll also cover how to set up a lab environment for performing hands-on exercises. We'll also show how to set up a virtualized lab environment for performing the hands-on labs.

Chapter 2, *Securing User Accounts*, covers the dangers of always using the root user account, and will introduce the benefits of using sudo, instead. We'll then cover how to lock down normal user accounts, and ensure that the users use good-quality passwords.

Chapter 3, *Securing Your Server with a Firewall*, involves working with the various types of firewall utilities.

Chapter 4, *Encrypting and SSH Hardening*, makes sure that important information—both at rest and in transit—are safeguarded with proper encryption. For data-in-transit, the default Secure Shell configuration is anything but secure, and could lead to a security breach if left as is. This chapter shows how to fix that.

Chapter 5, *Mastering Discretionary Access Control*, covers how to set ownership and permissions on files and directories. We'll also cover what SUID and SGID can do for us, and the security implications of using them. We'll wrap things up by covering Extended File Attributes.

Chapter 6, *Access Control Lists and Shared Directory Management*, explains that normal Linux file and directory permissions settings aren't very granular. With Access Control Lists, we can allow only a certain person to access a file, or we can allow multiple people to access a file with different permissions for each person. We're also going to put what we've learned together in order to manage a shared directory for a group.

Chapter 7, *Implementing Mandatory Access Control with SELinux and AppArmor*, talks about SELinux, which is a Mandatory Access Control technology that is included with Red Hat-type Linux distros. We'll give a brief introduction here about how to use SELinux to prevent intruders from compromising a system. AppArmor is another Mandatory Access Control technology that is included with Ubuntu and Suse-type Linux distros. We'll give a brief introduction here about how to use AppArmor to prevent intruders from compromising a system.

Chapter 8, *Scanning, Auditing, and Hardening*, discusses that viruses aren't yet a huge problem for Linux users, but they are for Windows users. If your organization has Windows clients that access Linux fileservers, then this chapter is for you. You can use auditd to audit, which accesses either files, directories, or system calls. It won't prevent security breaches, but it will let you know if some unauthorized person is trying to access a sensitive resource. SCAP, the Security Content Application Protocol, is a compliance framework that's promulgated by the National Institute of Standards and Technology. OpenSCAP, the open source implementation, can be used to apply a hardening policy to a Linux computer.

Chapter 9, *Vulnerability Scanning and Intrusion Detection*, explains how to scan our systems to see if we've missed anything since we've already learned how to configure our systems for best security. We'll also take a quick look at an intrusion detection system.

Chapter 10, *Security Tips and Tricks for the Busy Bee*, explains that since you're dealing with security, we know that you're a busy bee. So, the chapter introduces you to some quick tips and tricks to help make the job easier.

To get the most out of this book

To get the most out of this book, you don't need much. However, the following things would be quite helpful:

1. A working knowledge of basic Linux commands, and of how to navigate through the Linux filesystem.
2. A basic knowledge about tools such as less and grep.
3. Familiarity with command-line editing tools, such as vim or nano.
4. A basic knowledge of how to control systemd services with systemctl commands.

For hardware, you don't need anything fancy. All you need is a machine that's capable of running 64-bit virtual machines. So, you can use any host machine that runs with almost any modern CPU from either Intel or AMD. (The exception to this rule is with Intel Core i3 and Core i5 CPUs. Even though they're 64-bit CPUs, they lack the hardware acceleration that's needed to run 64-bit virtual machines. Ironically, Intel Core 2 CPUs and AMD Opteron CPUs that are much older work just fine.) For memory, I'd recommend at least 8 Gigabytes.

You can run any of the three major operating systems on your host machine, because the virtualization software that we'll be using comes in flavors for Windows, MacOS, and Linux.

Download the color images

We also provide a PDF file that has color images of the screenshots/diagrams used in this book. You can download it here: `http://www.packtpub.com/sites/default/files/downloads/MasteringLinuxSecurityandHardening_ColorImages.pdf`.

Conventions used

There are a number of text conventions used throughout this book.

`CodeInText`: Indicates code words in text, database table names, folder names, filenames, file extensions, pathnames, dummy URLs, user input, and Twitter handles. Here is an example: "let's use `getfacl` to see if we have any Access Control Lists already set on the `acl_demo.txt` file."

A block of code is set as follows:

```
[base]
     name=CentOS-$releasever - Base
     mirrorlist=http://mirrorlist.centos.org/?
     release=$releasever&arch=$basearch&repo=os&infra=$infra
       #baseurl=http://mirror.centos.org/centos/
         $releasever/os/$basearch/
     gpgcheck=1
     gpgkey=file:///etc/pki/rpm-gpg/RPM-GPG-KEY-CentOS-7
     priority=1
```

Any command-line input or output is written as follows:

```
[donnie@localhost ~]$ tar cJvf new_perm_dir_backup.tar.xz new_perm_dir/ --
acls
new_perm_dir/
new_perm_dir/new_file.txt
[donnie@localhost ~]$
```

Bold: Indicates a new term, an important word, or words that you see onscreen. For example, words in menus or dialog boxes appear in the text like this. Here is an example: "Click the **Network** menu item, and change the **Attached to** setting from **NAT** to **Bridged Adapter**."

 Warnings or important notes appear like this.

 Tips and tricks appear like this.

Get in touch

Feedback from our readers is always welcome.

General feedback: Email feedback@packtpub.com and mention the book title in the subject of your message. If you have questions about any aspect of this book, please email us at questions@packtpub.com.

Errata: Although we have taken every care to ensure the accuracy of our content, mistakes do happen. If you have found a mistake in this book, we would be grateful if you would report this to us. Please visit www.packtpub.com/submit-errata, selecting your book, clicking on the Errata Submission Form link, and entering the details.

Piracy: If you come across any illegal copies of our works in any form on the Internet, we would be grateful if you would provide us with the location address or website name. Please contact us at copyright@packtpub.com with a link to the material.

If you are interested in becoming an author: If there is a topic that you have expertise in and you are interested in either writing or contributing to a book, please visit authors.packtpub.com.

Reviews

Please leave a review. Once you have read and used this book, why not leave a review on the site that you purchased it from? Potential readers can then see and use your unbiased opinion to make purchase decisions, we at Packt can understand what you think about our products, and our authors can see your feedback on their book. Thank you!

For more information about Packt, please visit packtpub.com.

1
Running Linux in a Virtual Environment

So, you may be asking yourself, *"Why do I need to study Linux security? Isn't Linux already secure? After all, it's not Windows."* But, the fact is, there are many reasons.

It's true that Linux has certain advantages over Windows when it comes to security. These include:

- Unlike Windows, Linux was designed from the ground up as a multiuser operating system. So, user security tends to be a bit better on a Linux system.
- Linux offers a better separation between administrative users and unprivileged users. This makes it a bit harder for intruders, and it also makes it a bit harder for a user to accidentally infect a Linux machine with something nasty.
- Linux is much more resistant to virus and malware infections than Windows is.
- Certain Linux distributions come with built-in mechanisms, such as **SELinux** in Red Hat and CentOS and **AppArmor** in Ubuntu, which prevents intruders from taking control of a system.
- Linux is a free and open source software. This allows anyone who has the skill to audit Linux code to hunt for bugs or backdoors.

But, even with those advantages, Linux is just like everything else that's been created by mankind. That is, it isn't perfect.

Here are the topics that we'll cover in this chapter:

- Why every Linux administrator needs to learn about Linux security
- A bit about the threat landscape, with some examples of how attackers have, at times, been able to breach Linux systems
- Resources for keeping up with IT security news
- How to set up Ubuntu Server and CentOS virtual machines with VirtualBox, and how to install the EPEL repository in the CentOS virtual machine
- How to create virtual machine snapshots
- How to install Cygwin on a Windows host so that Windows users can connect to a virtual machine from their Windows hosts

The threat landscape

If you've kept up with IT technology news over the past few years, you'll likely have seen at least a few articles about how attackers have compromised Linux servers. For example, while it's true that Linux isn't really susceptible to virus infections, there have been several cases where attackers have planted other types of malware on Linux servers. These cases have included:

- **Botnet malware**: It causes a server to join a botnet that is controlled by a remote attacker. One of the more famous cases involved joining Linux servers to a botnet that launched *denial-of-service* attacks against other networks.
- **Ransomware**: It is designed to encrypt user data until the server owner pays a ransom fee. But, even after paying the fee, there's no guarantee that the data can be recovered.
- **Cryptocoin mining software**: It causes the CPUs of the server on which it's planted to work extra hard and consume more energy. Cryptocoins that get mined go to the accounts of the attackers who planted the software.

And, of course, there have been plenty of breaches that don't involve malware, such as where attackers have found a way to steal user credentials, credit card data, or other sensitive information.

 Some security breaches come about because of plain carelessness. Here's an example of where a careless Adobe administrator placed the company's private security key on a public security blog: `https://www.theinquirer.net/inquirer/news/3018010/adobe-stupidly-posts-private-pgp-key-on-its-security-blog`.

So, how does this happen?

Regardless of whether you're running Linux, Windows, or whatever else, the reasons for security breaches are usually the same. They could be security bugs in the operating system, or security bugs in an application that's running on that operating system. Often, a bug-related security breach could have been prevented had the administrators applied security updates in a timely manner.

Another big issue is poorly-configured servers. A standard, out-of-the-box configuration of a Linux server is actually quite insecure and can cause a whole ton of problems. One cause of poorly-configured servers is simply the lack of properly-trained personnel to securely administer Linux servers. (Of course, that's great news for the readers of this book, because, trust me, there's no lack of well-paying, IT security jobs.)

As we journey through this book, we'll see how to do business the right way, to make our servers as secure as possible.

Keeping up with security news

If you're in the IT business, even if you're not a security administrator, you want to keep up with the latest security news. In the age of the internet, that's easy to do.

First, there are quite a few websites that specialize in network security news. Examples include *Packet Storm Security* and *The Hacker News*. Regular tech news sites and Linux news websites, such as *The INQUIRER, The Register, ZDNet*, and *LXer* also carry reports about network security breaches. And, if you'd rather watch videos than read, you'll find plenty of good YouTube channels, such as *BeginLinux Guru*.

Finally, regardless of which Linux distribution you're using, be sure to keep up with the news and current documentation for your Linux distribution. Distribution maintainers should have a way of letting you know if a security problem crops up in their products.

Links to security news sites are as follows:

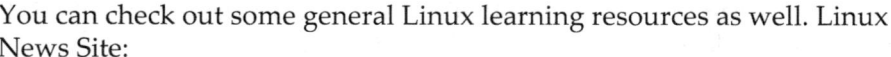

- Packet Storm Security: https://packetstormsecurity.com/
- The Hacker News: http://thehackernews.com/

Links to general tech news sites are as follows:

- The INQUIRER: https://www.theinquirer.net/
- The Register: http://www.theregister.co.uk/
- ZDNet: http://www.zdnet.com/

You can check out some general Linux learning resources as well. Linux News Site:

- LXer: http://lxer.com/
- *BeginLinux Guru* on YouTube: https://www.youtube.com/channel/UC88eard_2sz89an6unmlbeA

(Full disclosure: I am the *BeginLinux Guru*.)

One thing to always remember as you go through this book is that the only operating system you'll ever see that's totally, 100% secure will be installed on a computer that never gets turned on.

Introduction to VirtualBox and Cygwin

Whenever I write or teach, I try very hard not to provide students with a cure for insomnia. Throughout this book, you'll see a bit of theory whenever it's necessary, but I mainly like to provide good, practical information. There will also be plenty of step-by-step hands-on labs.

The best way to do the labs is to use Linux virtual machines. Most of what we'll do can apply to any Linux distribution, but we will also do some things that are specific to either Red Hat Enterprise Linux or Ubuntu Linux. (Red Hat Enterprise Linux is the most popular for enterprise use, while Ubuntu is most popular for cloud deployments.)

 Red Hat is a billion-dollar company, so there's no doubt about where they stand in the Linux market. But, since Ubuntu Server is free-of-charge, we can't judge its popularity strictly on the basis of its parent company's worth. The reality is that Ubuntu Server is the most widely-used Linux distribution for deploying cloud-based applications.

See here for details: `http://www.zdnet.com/article/ubuntu-linux-continues-to-dominate-openstack-and-other-clouds/`.

Since Red Hat is a fee-based product, we'll substitute CentOS 7, which is built from Red Hat source code and is free-of-charge. There are several different virtualization platforms that you can use, but my own preferred choice is VirtualBox.

VirtualBox is available for Windows, Linux, and Mac hosts, and is free of charge for all of them. It has features that you have to pay for on other platforms, such as the ability to create snapshots of virtual machines.

Some of the labs that we'll be doing will require you to simulate creating a connection from your host machine to a remote Linux server. If your host machine is either a Linux or a Mac machine, you'll just be able to open the Terminal and use the built-in Secure Shell tools. If your host machine is running Windows, you'll need to install some sort of Bash shell, which we'll do by installing Cygwin.

Installing a virtual machine in VirtualBox

For those of you who've never used VirtualBox, here's a quick how-to to get you going:

1. Download and install VirtualBox and the VirtualBox Extension Pack. You can get them from: `https://www.virtualbox.org/`.

2. Download the installation `.iso` files for Ubuntu Server and CentOS 7. You can get them from: `https://www.ubuntu.com/` and `https://www.centos.org/`.

3. Start VirtualBox and click the **New** icon at the top of the screen. Fill out the information where requested. Increase the virtual drive size to 20 GB, but leave everything else as the default settings:

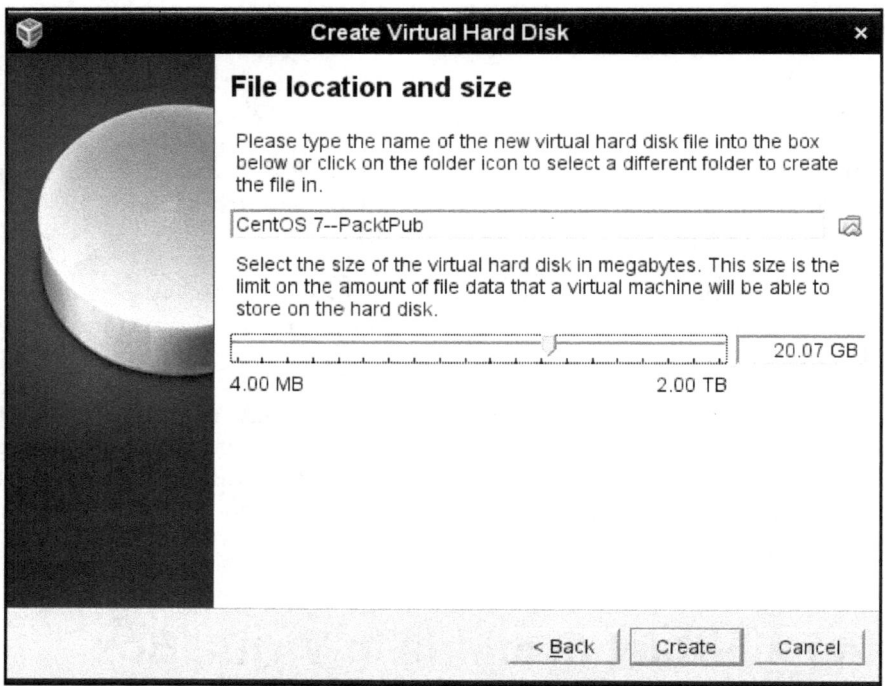

4. Start the new virtual machine. Click on the folder icon at the bottom-left corner of the dialog box and navigate to the directory where you stored the .iso files that you downloaded. Choose either the Ubuntu .iso file or the CentOS .iso file as shown in the following screenshot:

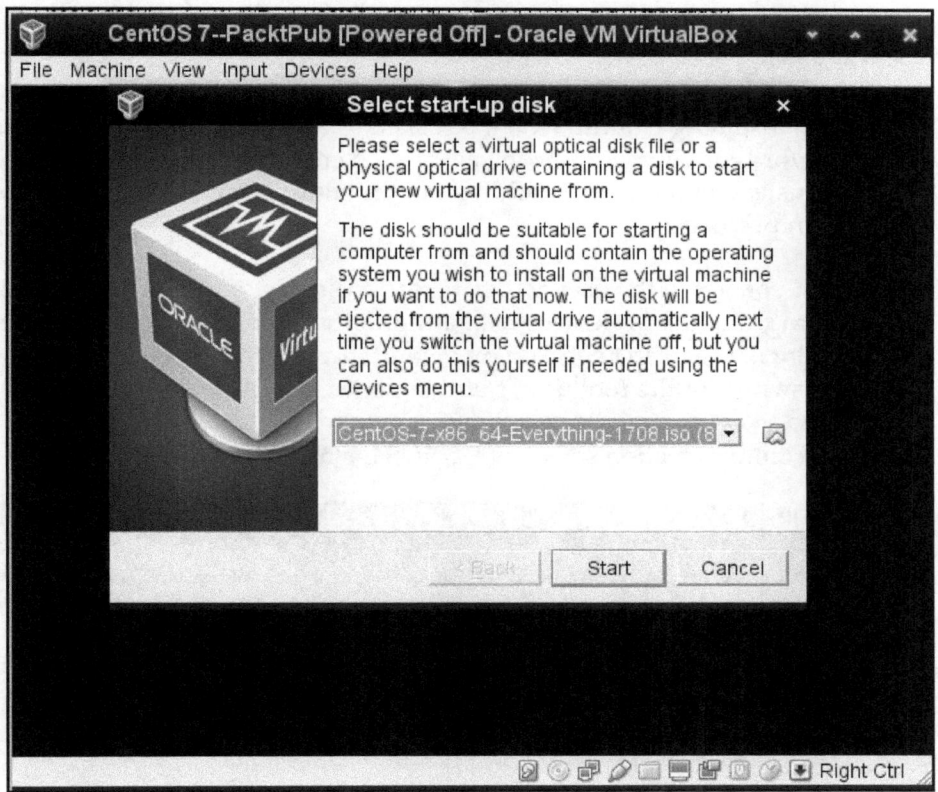

5. Click the **Start** button on the dialog box to start installing the operating system. Note that, for Ubuntu Server, you won't be installing a desktop interface. For the CentOS virtual machine, choose either the KDE desktop or the Gnome desktop, as you desire. (We'll go through at least one exercise that will require a desktop interface for the CentOS machine.)

6. Repeat the procedure for the other Linux distribution.

7. Update the Ubuntu virtual machine by entering:

```
sudo apt update
sudo apt dist-upgrade
```

8. Hold off on updating the CentOS virtual machine because we'll do that in the next exercise.

When installing Ubuntu, you'll be asked to create a normal user account and password for yourself. It won't ask you to create a root user password, but will instead automatically add you to the sudo group so that you'll have admin privileges.

When you get to the user account creation screen of the CentOS installer, be sure to check the **Make this user administrator** box for your own user account, since it isn't checked by default. It will offer you the chance to create a password for the root user, but that's entirely optional—in fact, I never do.

The user account creation screen of CentOS installer is shown as follows:

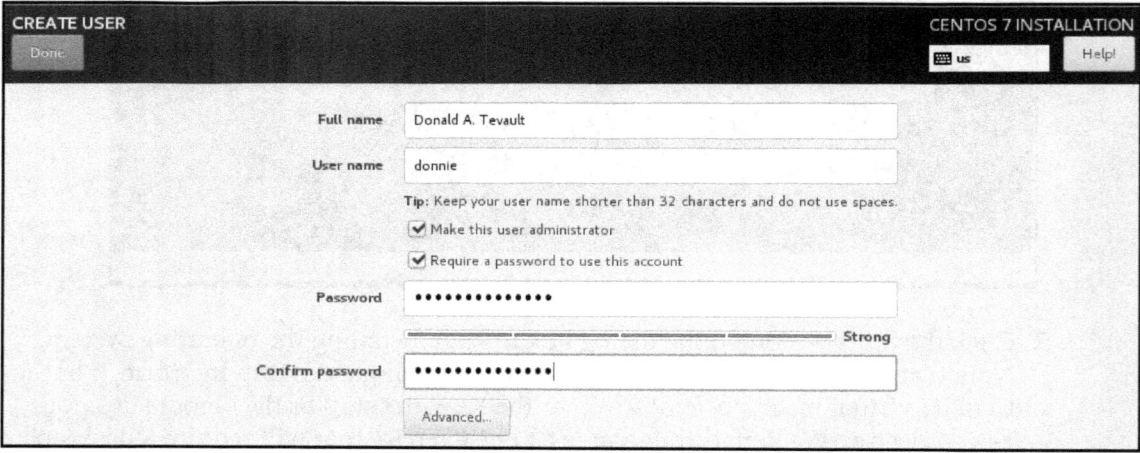

The EPEL repository on the CentOS virtual machine

While the Ubuntu package repositories have pretty much everything that you need for this course, the CentOS package repositories are—shall we say—lacking. To have the packages that you'll need for the CentOS hands-on labs, you'll need to install the **EPEL** (**Extra Packages for Enterprise Linux**) repository. (The EPEL project is run by the Fedora team.) When you install third-party repositories on Red Hat and CentOS systems, you'll also need to install a `priorities` package, and edit the `.repo` files to set the proper priorities for each repository. This will prevent packages from the third-party repository from overwriting official Red Hat and CentOS packages if they just happen to have the same name. The following steps will help you install the required packages and edit `.repo` file:

1. The two packages that you'll need to install EPEL are in the normal CentOS repositories. Run the command:

   ```
   sudo yum install yum-plugin-priorities epel-release
   ```

2. When the installation completes, navigate to the `/etc/yum.repos.d` directory, and open the `CentOS-Base.repo` file in your favorite text editor. After the last line of the `base`, `updates`, and `extras` sections, add the line, `priority=1`. After the last line of the `centosplus` section, add the line, `priority=2`. Save the file and close the editor. Each of the sections that you've edited should look something like this (except with the appropriate name and priority number):

   ```
   [base]
   name=CentOS-$releasever - Base
   mirrorlist=http://mirrorlist.centos.org/?
   release=$releasever&arch=$basearch&repo=os&infra=$infra
     #baseurl=http://mirror.centos.org/centos/
       $releasever/os/$basearch/
   gpgcheck=1
   gpgkey=file:///etc/pki/rpm-gpg/RPM-GPG-KEY-CentOS-7
   priority=1
   ```

3. Open the `epel.repo` file for editing. After the last line of the `epel` section, add the line, `priority=10`. After the last line of each remaining section, add the line, `priority=11`.

4. Update the system and then create a list of the installed and available packages by running:

```
sudo yum upgrade
sudo yum list > yum_list.txt
```

Configuring a network for VirtualBox virtual machines

Some of our training scenarios will require you to simulate creating a connection to a remote server. You would do this by using your host machine to connect to a virtual machine. When you first create a virtual machine on VirtualBox, the networking is set to **NAT** mode. In order to connect to the virtual machine from the host, you'll need to set the virtual machine's network adapter to **Bridged Adapter** mode. Here's how you can do this:

1. Shut down any virtual machines that you've already created.
2. On the VirtualBox manager screen, open the **Settings** dialog for a virtual machine.
3. Click the **Network** menu item, and change the **Attached to** setting from **NAT** to **Bridged Adapter**:

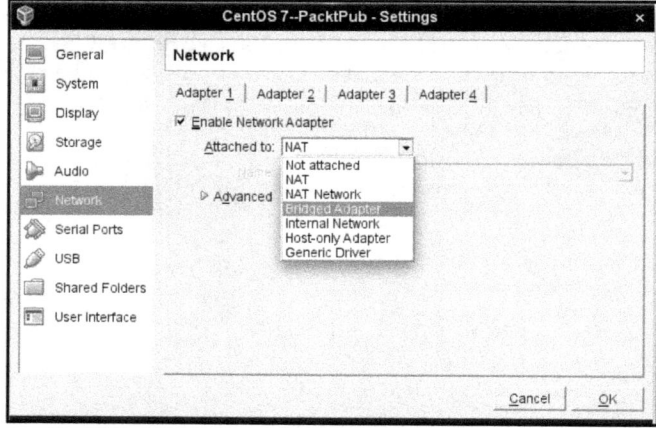

4. Expand the **Advanced** item, and change the **Promiscuous Mode** setting to **Allow All**:

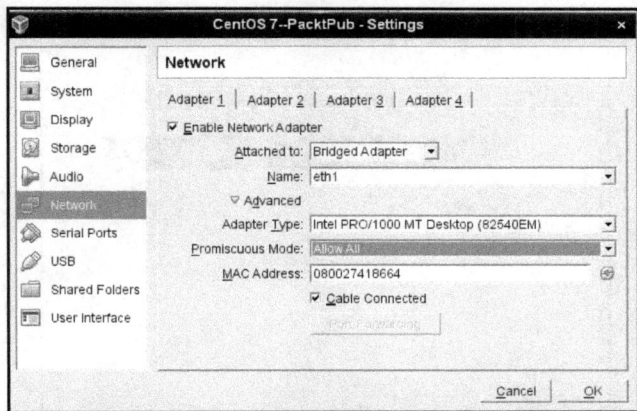

5. Restart the virtual machine and set it to use a static IP address.

 If you assign static IP addresses from the high end of your subnet range, it will be easier to prevent conflicts with low-number IP addresses that get handed out from your internet gateway.

Creating a virtual machine snapshot with VirtualBox

One of the beautiful things about working with virtual machines is that you can create a snapshot and roll back to it if you mess something up. With VirtualBox, that's easy to do.

1. At the top, right-hand corner of the VirtualBox manager screen, click the **Snapshots** button:

2. Just left of mid-screen, you'll see a camera icon. Click on that to bring up the snapshot dialog box. Either fill in the desired **Snapshot Name**, or accept the default name. Optionally, you can create a description:

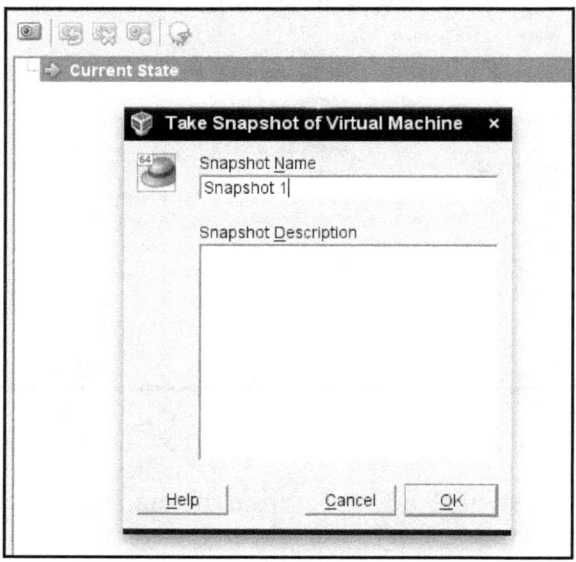

3. After you've made changes to the virtual machine, you can roll back to the snapshot by shutting down the virtual machine, then right-clicking on the snapshot name, and selecting the proper menu item:

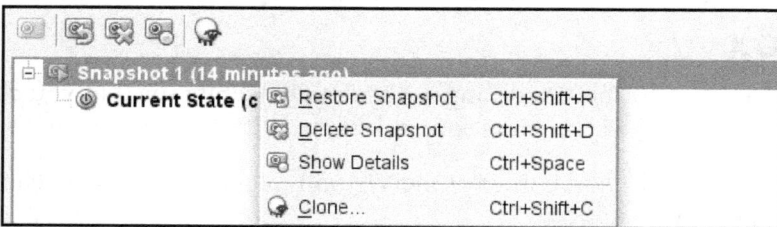

Using Cygwin to connect to your virtual machines

If your host machine is either a Linux or Mac machine, you'll simply open the host's Terminal and use the tools that are already there to connect to the virtual machine. But, if you're running a Windows machine, you'll want to install some sort of Bash shell and use its networking tools. Windows 10 Pro now comes with a Bash shell that's been provided by the Ubuntu folk and you can use that if you desire. But, if you don't have Windows 10 Pro, or if you prefer to use something else, you might consider Cygwin.

Cygwin, a project of the Red Hat company, is a free open source Bash shell that's built for Windows. It's free-of-charge, and easy to install.

Installing Cygwin on your Windows host

Here's a quick how-to to get you going with Cygwin:

1. In your host machine's browser, download the appropriate `setup*.exe` file for your version of Windows from: `http://www.cygwin.com/`.

2. Double-click on the setup icon to begin the installation. For the most part, just accept the defaults until you get to the package selection screen. (The one exception will be the screen where you select a download mirror.)

3. At the top of the package selection screen, select **Category** from the **View** menu:

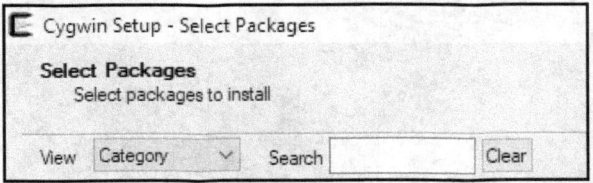

4. Expand the **Net** category:

5. Scroll down until you see the openssh package. Under the **New** column, click on **Skip**. (This causes a version number to appear in place of the **Skip**.):

Skip	n/a	n/a	1,898k	openldap-server: Lightweight Directory Access Protocol suite (server)
Skip	n/a	n/a	750k	openssh: The OpenSSH server and client programs
Skip	n/a	n/a	570k	openssl: A general purpose cryptography toolkit with TLS implementation
Skip	n/a	n/a	4,693k	openssl-devel: A general purpose cryptography toolkit with TLS implementation (development)

6. After you have selected the proper package, your screen should look like this:

Skip	n/a	n/a	1,898k	openldap-server: Lightweight Directory Access Protocol suite (server)
7.5p1-1	☒	☐	750k	openssh: The OpenSSH server and client programs
Skip	n/a	n/a	570k	openssl: A general purpose cryptography toolkit with TLS implementation
Skip	n/a	n/a	4,693k	openssl-devel: A general purpose cryptography toolkit with TLS implementation (development)

7. In the bottom right-hand corner, click **Next**. If a **Resolving Dependencies** screen pops up, click **Next** on it as well.

8. Keep the setup file that you downloaded, because you'll use it later to either install more software packages, or to update Cygwin. (When you open Cygwin, any updated packages will show up on the **Pending** view on **View** menu.)

9. Once you open Cygwin from the Windows Start menu, you can resize it as you desire, and use either the *Ctrl + +* or *Ctrl + -* key combinations to resize the font:

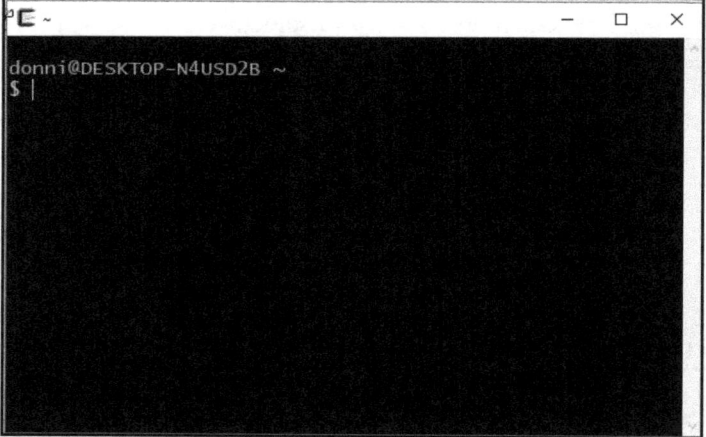

Summary

So, we've made a good start to our journey into Linux security and hardening. In this chapter, we looked at why it's just as important to know about securing and hardening Linux systems as it is to know how to secure and harden Windows systems. We provided a few examples of how a poorly-configured Linux system can be compromised, and we mentioned that learning about Linux security could be good for your career. After that, we looked at how to set up a virtualized lab environment using VirtualBox and Cygwin.

In the next chapter, we'll look at locking down user accounts, and ensuring that the wrong people never get administrative privileges. I'll see you there.

2
Securing User Accounts

Managing users is one of the more challenging aspects of IT administration. You need to make sure that users can always access their stuff and that they can perform the required tasks to do their jobs. You also need to ensure that users' stuff is always secure from unauthorized users and that users can't perform any tasks that don't fit their job description. It's a tall order, but we aim to show that it's doable.

In this chapter, we'll cover the following topics:

- The dangers of logging in as the root user
- The advantages of using sudo
- How to set up sudo privileges for full administrative users and for users with only certain delegated privileges
- Advanced tips and tricks to use sudo
- Locking down users' home directories
- Enforcing strong password criteria
- Setting and enforcing password and account expiration
- Preventing brute-force password attacks
- Locking user accounts
- Setting up security banners

The dangers of logging in as the root user

A huge advantage that Unix and Linux operating systems have over Windows is that Unix and Linux do a much better job of keeping privileged administrative accounts separated from normal user accounts. Indeed, one reason that older versions of Windows were so susceptible to security issues, such as **drive-by** virus infections, was the common practice of setting up user accounts with administrative privileges, without having the protection of the **User Access Control** that's in newer versions of Windows. (Even with User Access Control, Windows systems still do get infected, just not quite as often.) With Unix and Linux, it's a lot harder to infect a properly configured system.

You likely already know that the all-powerful administrator account on a Unix or Linux system is the root account. If you're logged in as the root user, you can do anything you want to do to that system. So you may think, *"Yeah, that's handy, so that's what I'll do."* However, always logging in as the root user can present a whole load of security problems. Consider the following. Logging in as the root user can:

- Make it easier for you to accidentally perform an action that causes damage to the system
- Make it easier for someone else to perform an action that causes damage to the system

So if you always log on as the root user or even if you just make the root user account readily accessible, you could say that you're doing a big part of attackers' and intruders' work for them. Also, imagine if you were the head Linux administrator at a large corporation, and the only way to allow users to perform admin tasks was to give them all the root password. What would happen if one of those users were to leave the company? You wouldn't want for that person to still have the ability to log in to the systems, so you'd have to change the password and distribute the new one to all of the other users. And, what if you just want for users to have admin privileges for only certain tasks, instead of having full root privileges?

What we need is a mechanism that allows users to perform administrative tasks without incurring the risk of having them always log on as the root user and that would also allow users to have only the admin privileges they really need to perform a certain job. In Linux and Unix, we have that mechanism in the form of the sudo utility.

The advantages of using sudo

Used properly, the sudo utility can greatly enhance the security of your systems, and it can make an administrator's job much easier. With sudo, you can do the following:

- Assign certain users full administrative privileges, while assigning other users only the privileges they need to perform tasks that are directly related to their respective jobs.
- Allow users to perform administrative tasks by entering their own normal user passwords so that you don't have to distribute the root password to everybody and his brother.
- Make it harder for intruders to break into your systems. If you implement sudo and disable the root user account, would-be intruders won't know which account to attack because they won't know which one has admin privileges.
- Create sudo policies that you can deploy across an entire enterprise network even if that network has a mix of Unix, BSD, and Linux machines.
- Improve your auditing capabilities because you'll be able to see what users are doing with their admin privileges.

In regards to that last bullet point, consider the following snippet from the secure log of my CentOS 7 virtual machine:

```
Sep 29 20:44:33 localhost sudo: donnie : TTY=pts/0 ; PWD=/home/donnie ;
USER=root ; COMMAND=/bin/su -
Sep 29 20:44:34 localhost su: pam_unix(su-l:session): session opened for
user root by donnie(uid=0)
Sep 29 20:50:39 localhost su: pam_unix(su-l:session): session closed for
user root
```

You can see that I used su - to log in to the root command prompt and that I then logged back out. While I was logged in, I did several things that require root privileges, but none of that got recorded. What did get recorded though is something that I did with sudo. That is, because the root account is disabled on this machine, I used my sudo privilege to get su - to work for me. Let's look at another snippet to show a bit more detail about how this works:

```
Sep 29 20:50:45 localhost sudo: donnie : TTY=pts/0 ; PWD=/home/donnie ;
USER=root ; COMMAND=/bin/less /var/log/secure
Sep 29 20:55:30 localhost sudo: donnie : TTY=pts/0 ; PWD=/home/donnie ;
USER=root ; COMMAND=/sbin/fdisk -l
Sep 29 20:55:40 localhost sudo: donnie : TTY=pts/0 ; PWD=/home/donnie ;
USER=root ; COMMAND=/bin/yum upgrade
Sep 29 20:59:35 localhost sudo: donnie : TTY=tty1 ; PWD=/home/donnie ;
```

```
USER=root ; COMMAND=/bin/systemctl status sshd
Sep 29 21:01:11 localhost sudo: donnie : TTY=tty1 ; PWD=/home/donnie ;
USER=root ; COMMAND=/bin/less /var/log/secure
```

This time, I used my sudo privilege to open a log file, to view my hard drive configuration, to perform a system update, to check the status of the Secure Shell daemon, and to once again view a log file. So, if you were the security administrator at my company, you'd be able to see whether or not I'm abusing my sudo power.

Now, you're asking, *"What's to prevent a person from just doing a sudo su - to prevent his or her misdeeds from being detected?"* That's easy. Just don't give people the power to go to the root command prompt.

Setting up sudo privileges for full administrative users

Before we look at how to limit what users can do, let's first look at how to allow a user to do everything, including logging into the root command prompt. There are a couple of methods for doing that.

Method 1 – adding users to a predefined admin group

The first method, which is the simplest, is to add users to a predefined administrators group and then, if it hasn't already been done, to configure the sudo policy to allow that group to do its job. It's simple enough to do except that different Linux distro families use different admin groups.

On Unix, BSD, and most Linux systems, you would add users to the wheel group. (Members of the Red Hat family, including CentOS, fall into this category.) When I do the groups command on my CentOS machine, I get this:

```
[donnie@localhost ~]$ groups
donnie wheel
[donnie@localhost ~]$
```

This shows that I'm a member of the wheel group. By doing `sudo visudo`, I'll open the sudo policy file. Scrolling down, we'll see the line that gives the wheel group its awesome power:

```
## Allows people in group wheel to run all commands
%wheel ALL=(ALL) ALL
```

The percent sign indicates that we're working with a group. The three ALLs mean that members of that group can perform any command, as any user, on any machine in the network on which this policy is deployed. The only slight catch is that group members will be prompted to enter their own normal user account passwords in order to perform a sudo task. Scroll down a bit more, and you'll see the following:

```
## Same thing without a password
# %wheel ALL=(ALL) NOPASSWD: ALL
```

If we were to comment out the `%wheel` line in the former snippet and remove the comment symbol from in front of the `%wheel` line in this snippet, then members of the `wheel` group would be able to perform all of their sudo tasks without ever having to enter any password. That's something that I really don't recommend, even for home use. In a business setting, allowing people to have passwordless sudo privileges is a definite no-no.

To add an existing user to the `wheel` group, use `usermod` with the `-G` option. You might also want to use the `-a` option as well, in order to prevent removing the user from other groups to which he or she belongs. For our example, let's add Maggie:

`sudo usermod -a -G wheel maggie`

You can also add a user account to the `wheel` group as you create it. Let's do that now for Frank:

`sudo useradd -G wheel frank`

Note that with my usage of `useradd`, I'm assuming that we're working with a member of the Red Hat family, which comes with predefined default settings to create user accounts. For non-Red Hat-type distros that use the `wheel` group, you'd need to either reconfigure the default settings or use extra option switches in order to create the user's home directory and to assign the correct shell. Your command then would look something like:

```
sudo useradd -G wheel -m -d /home/frank -s /bin/bash
frank
```

For members of the Debian family, including Ubuntu, the procedure is the same, except that you would use the sudo group instead of the wheel group. (This kind of figures, considering that the Debian folk have pretty much always marched to the beat of a different drummer.)

One way in which this technique would come in handy is whenever you need to create a virtual private server on a cloud service, such as Rackspace, DigitalOcean, or Vultr. When you log in to one of those services and initially create your virtual machine, the cloud service will have you log in to that virtual machine as the root user. (This even happens with Ubuntu, even though the root user account is disabled whenever you do a local installation of Ubuntu.)

The first thing that you'll want to do in this scenario is to create a normal user account for yourself and give it full sudo privileges. Then, log out of the root account and log back in with your normal user account. You'll then want to disable the root account with the command:

```
sudo passwd -l root
```

You'll also want to do some additional configuration to lock down Secure Shell access, but we'll cover that in Chapter 4, *Encrypting and SSH Hardening.*

Method 2 – creating an entry in the sudo policy file

Okay, adding users to either the wheel group or the sudo group works great if you're either just working with a single machine or if you're deploying a sudo policy across a network that uses just one of these two admin groups. But what if you want to deploy a sudo policy across a network with a mixed group of both Red Hat and Ubuntu machines? Or what if you don't want to go around to each machine to add users to an admin group? Then, just create an entry in the sudo policy file. You can either create an entry for an individual user or create a user alias. If you do sudo visudo on your CentOS virtual machine, you'll see a commented-out example of a user alias:

```
# User_Alias ADMINS = jsmith, mikem
```

You can uncomment this line and add your own set of usernames, or you can just add a line with your own user alias. To give members of the user alias full sudo power, add another line that would look like this:

```
ADMINS ALL=(ALL) ALL
```

It's also possible to add a `visudo` entry for just a single user, and you might need to do that under very special circumstances. For example:

```
frank ALL=(ALL) ALL
```

But for ease of management, it's best to go with either a user group or a user alias.

 The sudo policy file is the `/etc/sudoers` file. I always hesitate to tell students that because every once in a while I have a student try to edit it in a regular text editor. That doesn't work though, so please don't try it. Always edit `sudoers` with the command, `sudo visudo`.

Setting up sudo for users with only certain delegated privileges

A basic tenet of IT security philosophy is to give network users enough privileges so that they can get their jobs done, but no privileges beyond that. So, you'll want as few people as possible to have full sudo privileges. (If you have the root user account enabled, you'll want even fewer people to know the root password.) You'll also want a way to delegate privileges to people according to what their specific jobs are. Backup admins will need to be able to perform backup tasks, help desk personnel will need to perform user management tasks, and so on. With sudo, you can delegate these privileges and disallow users from doing any other administrative jobs that don't fit their job description.

The best way to explain this is to have you open `visudo` on your CentOS virtual machine. So, go ahead and start the CentOS VM and enter the following command:

```
sudo visudo
```

Unlike Ubuntu, CentOS has a fully commented and well-documented `sudoers` file. I've already shown you the line that creates the ADMIN user alias, and you can create other user aliases for other purposes. You can, for example, create a BACKUPADMINS user alias for backup administrators, a WEBADMINS user alias for web server administrators, or whatever else you desire. So, you could add a line that looks something like this:

```
User_Alias SOFTWAREADMINS = vicky, cleopatra
```

That's good, except that Vicky and Cleopatra still can't do anything. You'll need to assign some duties to the user alias.

If you look at the example user alias mentioned later, you'll see a list of example Command Aliases. One of these examples just happens to be SOFTWARE, which contains the commands that an admin would need to either install or remove software or to update the system. It's commented out, as are all of the other example command aliases, so you'll need to remove the hash symbol from the beginning of the line before you can use it:

```
Cmnd_Alias SOFTWARE = /bin/rpm, /usr/bin/up2date, /usr/bin/yum
```

Now, it's just a simple matter of assigning the SOFTWARE command alias to the SOFTWAREADMINS user alias:

```
SOFTWAREADMINS ALL=(ALL) SOFTWARE
```

Vicky and Cleopatra, both members of the SOFTWAREADMINS user alias, can now run the rpm, up2date, and yum commands with root privileges.

All but one of these predefined command aliases are ready to use after you uncomment them and assign them to either a user, group, or user alias. The one exception is the SERVICES command alias:

```
Cmnd_Alias SERVICES = /sbin/service, /sbin/chkconfig, /usr/bin/systemctl
start, /usr/bin/systemctl stop, /usr/bin/systemctl reload,
/usr/bin/systemctl restart, /usr/bin/systemctl status, /usr/bin/systemctl
enable, /usr/bin/systemctl disable
```

The problem with this SERVICES alias is that it also lists the different subcommands for the systemctl command. The way sudo works is that if a command is listed by itself, then the assigned user can use that command with any subcommands, options, or arguments. So, in the SOFTWARE example, members of the SOFTWARE user alias can run a command such as:

```
sudo yum upgrade
```

But, when a command is listed in the command alias with a subcommand, option, or argument, that's all anyone who's assigned to the command alias can run. With the SERVICES command alias in its current configuration, the systemctl commands just won't work. To see why, let's set Charlie and Lionel up in the SERVICESADMINS user alias and then uncomment the SERVICES command alias, as we've already done earlier:

```
User_Alias SERVICESADMINS = charlie, lionel
SERVICESADMINS ALL=(ALL) SERVICES
```

Now, watch what happens when Lionel tries to check the status of the Secure Shell service:

```
[lionel@centos-7 ~]$ sudo systemctl status sshd
[sudo] password for lionel:
Sorry, user lionel is not allowed to execute '/bin/systemctl status sshd'
as root on centos-7.xyzwidgets.com.
[lionel@centos-7 ~]$
```

Okay, so Lionel can run sudo systemctl status, which is pretty much useless, but he can't do anything meaningful, like specifying the service that he wants to check. That's a bit of a problem. There are two ways to fix this, but there's only one way that you want to use. You could just eliminate all of the systemctl subcommands and make the SERVICES alias look like this:

```
Cmnd_Alias SERVICES = /sbin/service, /sbin/chkconfig, /usr/bin/systemctl
```

But, if you do that, Lionel and Charlie will also be able to shut down or reboot the system, edit the services files, or change the machine from one systemd target to another. That's probably not what you want. Because the systemctl command covers a lot of different functions, you have to be careful not to allow delegated users to access too many of those functions. A better solution would be to add a wildcard to each of the systemctl subcommands:

```
Cmnd_Alias SERVICES = /sbin/service, /sbin/chkconfig, /usr/bin/systemctl
start *, /usr/bin/systemctl stop *, /usr/bin/systemctl reload *,
/usr/bin/systemctl restart *, /usr/bin/systemctl status *,
/usr/bin/systemctl enable *, /usr/bin/systemctl disable *
```

Now, Lionel and Charlie can perform any of the systemctl functions that are listed in this command alias, for any service:

```
[lionel@centos-7 ~]$ sudo systemctl status sshd
[sudo] password for lionel:
● sshd.service - OpenSSH server daemon
   Loaded: loaded (/usr/lib/systemd/system/sshd.service; enabled; vendor
preset: enabled)
```

```
    Active: active (running) since Sat 2017-09-30 18:11:22 EDT; 23min ago
      Docs: man:sshd(8)
            man:sshd_config(5)
  Main PID: 13567 (sshd)
    CGroup: /system.slice/sshd.service
            └─13567 /usr/sbin/sshd -D

Sep 30 18:11:22 centos-7.xyzwidgets.com systemd[1]: Starting OpenSSH server
daemon...
Sep 30 18:11:22 centos-7.xyzwidgets.com sshd[13567]: Server listening on
0.0.0.0 port 22.
Sep 30 18:11:22 centos-7.xyzwidgets.com sshd[13567]: Server listening on ::
port 22.
Sep 30 18:11:22 centos-7.xyzwidgets.com systemd[1]: Started OpenSSH server
daemon.
[lionel@centos-7 ~]$
```

Keep in mind that you're not limited to using user aliases and command aliases. You can also assign privileges to either a Linux group or to an individual user. You can also assign individual commands to a user alias, Linux group, or individual user. For example:

```
katelyn ALL=(ALL) STORAGE
gunther ALL=(ALL) /sbin/fdisk -l
%backup_admins ALL=(ALL) BACKUP
```

Katelyn can now do all of the commands in the STORAGE command alias, whereas Gunther can only use fdisk to look at the partition tables. The members of the backup_admins Linux group can do commands in the BACKUP command alias.

The last thing we'll look at for this topic is the host aliases examples that you see preceding the user alias example:

```
# Host_Alias     FILESERVERS = fs1, fs2
# Host_Alias     MAILSERVERS = smtp, smtp2
```

Each host alias consists of a list of server hostnames. This is what allows you to create one sudoers file on one machine, and deploy it across the network. For example, you could create a WEBSERVERS host alias, a WEBADMINS user alias, and a WEBCOMMANDS command alias with the appropriate commands.

Your configuration would look something like this:

```
Host_Alias    WEBSERVERS = webserver1, webserver2
User_Alias    WEBADMINS = junior, kayla
Cmnd_Alias    WEBCOMMANDS = /usr/bin/systemctl status httpd,
/usr/bin/systemctl start httpd, /usr/bin/systemctl stop httpd,
/usr/bin/systemctl restart httpd

WEBADMINS    WEBSERVERS=(ALL) WEBCOMMANDS
```

Now, when a user types a command into a server on the network, sudo will first look at the hostname of that server. If the user is authorized to perform that command on that server, then sudo allows it. Otherwise, sudo denies it. In a small to medium-sized business, it would probably work just fine to manually copy the master sudoers file to all the servers on the network. But, in a large enterprise, you'll want to streamline and automate the process. For this, you could use something like Puppet, Chef, or Ansible. (These three technologies are beyond the scope of this book, but you'll find plenty of books and video courses about all three of them at the Packt website.)

All of these techniques will work on your Ubuntu VM as well as on the CentOS VM. The only catch is, Ubuntu doesn't come with any predefined command aliases, so you'll have to type them in yourself.

Anyway, I know that you're tired of reading, so let's do some work.

Hands-on lab for assigning limited sudo privileges

In this lab, you'll create some users and assign them different levels of privileges. To simplify things, we'll use the CentOS virtual machine.

1. Log in to the CentOS virtual machine and create user accounts for Lionel, Katelyn, and Maggie:

```
sudo useradd lionel
sudo ueradd katelyn
sudo useradd maggie
sudo passwd lionel
sudo passwd katelyn
sudo passwd maggie
```

2. Open `visudo`:

```
sudo visudo
```

Find the STORAGE command alias and remove the comment symbol from in front of it.

3. Add the following lines to the end of the file, using tabs to separate the columns:

```
lionel    ALL=(ALL)    ALL
katelyn  ALL=(ALL) /usr/bin/systemctl status sshd
maggie  ALL=(ALL) STORAGE
```

Save the file and exit `visudo`.

4. To save time, we'll use `su` to log into the different user accounts. You won't need to log out of your own account to perform these steps. First, log in to Lionel's account and verify that he has full sudo privileges by running several root-level commands:

```
su - lionel
sudo su -
exit
sudo systemctl status sshd
sudo fdisk -l
exit
```

5. This time, log in as Katelyn and try to run some root-level commands. (Don't be too disappointed if they don't all work, though.)

```
su - katelyn
sudo su -
sudo systemctl status sshd
sudo systemctl restart sshd
sudo fdisk -l
exit
```

6. Finally, log in as Maggie, and run the same set of commands that you ran for Katelyn.

7. Keep in mind that although we only had three individual users for this lab, you could just as easily have handled more users by setting them up in user aliases or Linux groups.

Since sudo is such a great security tool, you would think that everyone would use it, right? Sadly, that's not the case. Pretty much any time you look at either a Linux tutorial website or a Linux tutorial YouTube channel, you'll see the person who's doing the demo logged in at the root user command prompt. In some cases, I've seen the person remotely logged in as the root user on a cloud-based virtual machine. Now, if logging in as the root user is already a bad idea, then logging in across the internet as the root user is an even worse idea. In any case, seeing everybody do these tutorial demos from the root user's shell drives me absolutely crazy.

Having said all this, there are some things that don't work with sudo. Bash shell internal commands, such as cd don't work with it, and injecting kernel values into the /proc filesystem also doesn't work with it. For tasks such as these, a person would have to go to the root command prompt. Still though, make sure that only users who absolutely have to use the root user command prompt have access to it.

Advanced tips and tricks for using sudo

Now that we've looked at the basics of setting up a good sudo configuration, we're confronted with a bit of a paradox. That is, even though sudo is a security tool, certain things that you can do with it can make your system even more insecure than it was. Let's see how to avoid that.

The sudo timer

By default, the sudo timer is set for 5 minutes. This means that once a user performs one sudo command and enters a password, he or she can perform another sudo command within 5 minutes without having to enter the password again. Although this is obviously handy, it can also be problematic if users were to walk away from their desks with a command terminal still open. If the 5 minute timer hasn't yet expired, someone else could come along and perform some root-level task. If your security needs require it, you can easily disable this timer by adding a line to the Defaults section of the sudoers file. This way, users will have to enter their passwords every time they run a sudo command. You can make this a global setting for all users, or you can just set it for certain individual users.

Hands-on lab for disabling the sudo timer

For this lab, you'll disable the sudo timer on your CentOS VM.

1. Log in to the same CentOS virtual machine that you used for the previous lab. We'll be using the user accounts that you've already created.
2. At your own user account command-prompt, enter the following commands:

```
sudo fdisk -l
sudo systemctl status sshd
sudo iptables -L
```

   You'll see that you only needed to enter the password once to do all three commands.

3. Open visudo with:

```
sudo visudo
```

   In the Defaults specification section of the file, add the following line:

```
Defaults        timestamp_timeout = 0
```

   Save the file and exit visudo.

4. Perform the commands that you performed in *Step 2*. This time, you should see that you have to enter a password every time.
5. Open visudo and modify the line that you added so that it looks like this:

```
Defaults:lionel        timestamp_timeout = 0
```

   Save the file and exit visudo.

6. From your own account shell, repeat the commands that you performed in *Step 2*. Then, log in as Lionel and perform the commands again.
7. Note that this same procedure also works for Ubuntu.

Preventing users from having root shell access

Let's say that you want to set up a user with limited sudo privileges, but you did so by adding a line like this:

```
maggie      ALL=(ALL)      /bin/bash, /bin/zsh
```

I'm sorry to say that you haven't limited Maggie's access at all. You effectively gave her full sudo privileges with both the Bash shell and the Zsh shell. So, don't add lines like this to your sudoers because it will get you into trouble.

Preventing users from using shell escapes

Certain programs, especially text editors and pagers, have a handy *shell escape* feature. This allows a user to run a shell command without having to exit the program first. For example, from the command mode of the Vi and Vim editors, someone could run the ls command by doing :!ls. Executing the command would look like this:

```
# useradd defaults file
GROUP=100
HOME=/home
INACTIVE=-1
EXPIRE=
SHELL=/bin/bash
SKEL=/etc/skel
CREATE_MAIL_SPOOL=yes


~
~
:!ls
```

The output would look like this:

```
[donnie@localhost default]$ sudo vim useradd
[sudo] password for donnie:

grub nss useradd

Press ENTER or type command to continue
grub nss useradd

Press ENTER or type command to continue
```

Now, imagine that you want Frank to be able to edit the `sshd_config` file and only that file. You might be tempted to add a line to your sudo configuration that would look like this:

```
frank     ALL=(ALL)     /bin/vim /etc/ssh/sshd_config
```

This looks like it would work, right? Well, it doesn't because once Frank has opened the `sshd_config` file with his sudo privilege, he can then use Vim's shell escape feature to perform other root-level commands, which would include being able to edit other configuration files. You can fix this problem by having Frank use `sudoedit` instead of vim:

```
frank     ALL=(ALL)     sudoedit /etc/ssh/sshd_config
```

`sudoedit` has no shell escape feature, so you can safely allow Frank to use it.

Other programs that have a shell escape feature include the following:

- emacs
- less
- view
- more

Preventing users from using other dangerous programs

Some programs that don't have shell escapes can still be dangerous if you give users unrestricted privileges to use them. These include the following:

- cat
- cut
- awk
- sed

If you must give someone sudo privileges to use one of these programs, it's best to limit their use to only specific files. And, that brings us to our next tip.

Limiting the user's actions with commands

Let's say that you create a sudo rule so that Sylvester can use the `systemctl` command:

```
sylvester       ALL=(ALL)  /usr/bin/systemctl
```

This allows Sylvester to have full use of the `systemctl` features. He can control daemons, edit service files, shutdown or reboot, and every other function that `systemctl` does. That's probably not what you want. It would be better to specify what `systemctl` functions that Sylvester is allowed to do. Let's say that you want him to be able to control just the Secure Shell service. You can make the line look like this:

```
sylvester       ALL=(ALL)  /usr/bin/systemctl * sshd
```

Sylvester can now do everything he needs to do with the Secure Shell service, but he can't shut down or reboot the system, edit service files, or change systemd targets. But, what if you want Sylvester to do only certain specific actions with the Secure Shell service? Then, you'll have to omit the wild card and specify all of the actions that you want for Sylvester to do:

```
sylvester       ALL=(ALL)  /usr/bin/systemctl status sshd, /usr/bin/systemctl
restart sshd
```

Now, Sylvester can only restart the Secure Shell service or check its status.

When writing sudo policies, you'll want to be aware of the differences between the different Linux and Unix distros on your network. For example, on Red Hat 7 and CentOS 7 systems, the `systemctl` binary file is located in the `/usr/bin` directory. On Debian/Ubuntu systems, it's located in the `/bin` directory. If you have to roll out a `sudoers` file to a large enterprise network with mixed operating systems, you can use host aliases to ensure that servers will only allow the execution of commands that are appropriate for their operating systems.

Also, be aware that some system services have different names on different Linux distros. On Red Hat and CentOS systems, the Secure Shell service is `sshd`. On Debian/Ubuntu systems, it's just plain `ssh`.

Letting users run as other users

In the following line, (ALL) means that Sylvester can run the systemctl commands as any user:

```
sylvester      ALL=(ALL) /usr/bin/systemctl status sshd, /usr/bin/systemctl
restart sshd
```

This effectively gives Sylvester root privileges for these commands because the root user is definitely any user. You could, if desired, change that (ALL) to (root) in order to specify that Sylvester can only run these commands as the root user:

```
sylvester      ALL=(root) /usr/bin/systemctl status sshd, /usr/bin/systemctl
restart sshd
```

Okay, there's probably not much point in that because nothing changes. Sylvester had root privileges for these systemctl commands before, and he still has them now. But, there are more practical uses for this feature. Let's say that Vicky is a database admin, and you want her to run as the database user:

```
vicky     ALL=(database)     /usr/local/sbin/some_database_script.sh
```

Vicky could then run the command as the database user by entering the following code:

```
sudo -u database some_database_script.sh
```

This is one of those features that you might not use that often, but keep it in mind anyway. You never know when it might come in handy.

Okay, this wraps it up for our discussion of sudo. Let's now turn our attention to ensuring the security of our regular users.

Locking down users' home directories the Red Hat or CentOS way

This is another area where different Linux distro families do business differently from each other. As we shall see, each distro family comes with different default security settings. A security administrator who oversees a mixed environment of different Linux distros will need to take this into account.

One beautiful thing about Red Hat Enterprise Linux and all of its offspring, such as CentOS, is that they have better out-of-the-box security than any other Linux distro. This makes it quicker and easier to harden Red Hat-type systems because much of the work has already been done. One thing that's already been done for us is locking down users' home directories:

```
[donnie@localhost home]$ sudo useradd charlie
[sudo] password for donnie:
[donnie@localhost home]$

[donnie@localhost home]$ ls -l
total 0
drwx------. 2 charlie charlie 59 Oct 1 15:25 charlie
drwx------. 2 donnie donnie 79 Sep 27 00:24 donnie
drwx------. 2 frank frank 59 Oct 1 15:25 frank
[donnie@localhost home]$
```

By default, the useradd utility on Red Hat-type systems creates user home directories with a permissions setting of 700. This means that only the user who owns the home directory can access it. All other normal users are locked out. We can see why by looking at the /etc/login.defs file. Scroll down towards the bottom of the file, and you'll see:

```
CREATE_HOME      yes
UMASK 077
```

The login.defs file is one of two files where default settings for useradd are configured. This UMASK line is what determines the permissions values on home directories as they get created. Red Hat-type distros have it configured with the 077 value, which removes all permissions from the *group* and *others*. This UMASK line is in the login.defs file for all Linux distros, but Red Hat-type distros are the only ones that have UMASK set to such a restrictive value by default. Non-Red Hat distros usually have a UMASK value of 022, which creates home directories with a permissions value of 755. This allows everybody to enter everybody else's home directories and access each others' files.

Locking down users' home directories the Debian/Ubuntu way

Debian and its offspring, such as Ubuntu, have two user creation utilities:

- useradd on Debian/Ubuntu
- adduser on Debian/Ubuntu

useradd on Debian/Ubuntu

The useradd utility is there, but Debian and Ubuntu don't come with the handy preconfigured defaults as Red Hat and CentOS do. If you were to just do sudo useradd frank on a default Debian/Ubuntu machine, Frank would have no home directory and would be assigned the wrong default shell. So, to create a user account with useradd on a Debian or Ubuntu system, the command would look something like:

```
sudo useradd -m -d /home/frank -s /bin/bash frank
```

In this command:

- -m creates the home directory.
- -d specifies the home directory.
- -s specifies Frank's default shell. (Without the -s, Debian/Ubuntu would assign to Frank the /bin/sh shell.)

When you look at the home directories, you'll see that they're wide open, with execute and read privileges for everybody:

```
donnie@packt:/home$ ls -l
total 8
drwxr-xr-x 3 donnie donnie 4096 Oct 2 00:23 donnie
drwxr-xr-x 2 frank frank 4096 Oct 1 23:58 frank
donnie@packt:/home$
```

As you can see, Frank and I can get into each other's stuff. (And no, I don't want Frank getting into my stuff.) Each user could change the permissions on his or her own directory, but how many of your users would know how to do that? So, let's fix that ourselves:

```
cd /home
sudo chmod 700 *
```

Let's see what we have now:

```
donnie@packt:/home$ ls -l
total 8
drwx------ 3 donnie donnie 4096 Oct 2 00:23 donnie
drwx------ 2 frank frank 4096 Oct 1 23:58 frank
donnie@packt:/home$
```

That looks much better.

To change the default permissions setting for home directories, open `/etc/login.defs` for editing. Look for the line:

```
UMASK       022
```

Change it to:

```
UMASK       077
```

Now, new users' home directories will get locked down on creation, just as they do with Red Hat.

adduser on Debian/Ubuntu

The `adduser` utility is an interactive way to create user accounts and passwords with a single command, which is unique to the Debian family of Linux distros. Most of the default settings that are missing from the Debian implementation of `useradd` are already set for `adduser`. The only thing wrong with the default settings is that it creates user home directories with the wide-open `755` permissions value. Fortunately, that's easy to change. (We'll see how in just a bit.)

Although `adduser` is handy for just casual creation of user accounts, it doesn't offer the flexibility of `useradd` and it isn't suitable for use in shell scripting. One thing that `adduser` will do that `useradd` won't is to automatically encrypt a user's home directory as you create the account. To make it work, you'll first have to install the `ecryptfs-utils` package. So, to create an account with an encrypted home directory for Cleopatra, you do:

```
sudo apt install ecryptfs-utils

donnie@ubuntu-steemnode:~$ sudo adduser --encrypt-home cleopatra
[sudo] password for donnie:
Adding user `cleopatra' ...
Adding new group `cleopatra' (1004) ...
Adding new user `cleopatra' (1004) with group `cleopatra' ...
Creating home directory `/home/cleopatra' ...
Setting up encryption ...

***************************************************************************
YOU SHOULD RECORD YOUR MOUNT PASSPHRASE AND STORE IT IN A SAFE LOCATION.
  ecryptfs-unwrap-passphrase ~/.ecryptfs/wrapped-passphrase
THIS WILL BE REQUIRED IF YOU NEED TO RECOVER YOUR DATA AT A LATER TIME.
***************************************************************************
```

```
Done configuring.

Copying files from `/etc/skel' ...
Enter new UNIX password:
Retype new UNIX password:
passwd: password updated successfully
Changing the user information for cleopatra
Enter the new value, or press ENTER for the default
    Full Name []: Cleopatra Tabby Cat
    Room Number []: 1
    Work Phone []: 555-5556
    Home Phone []: 555-5555
    Other []:
Is the information correct? [Y/n] Y
donnie@ubuntu-steemnode:~$
```

The first time that Cleopatra logs in, she'll need to run the `ecryptfs-unwrap-passphrase` command that's mentioned in the preceding output. She'll then want to write her passphrase down and store it in a safe place:

```
cleopatra@ubuntu-steemnode:~$ ecryptfs-unwrap-passphrase
Passphrase:
d2a6cf0c3e7e46fd856286c74ab7a412
cleopatra@ubuntu-steemnode:~$
```

We'll look at the whole encryption thing more in detail when we get to the encryption chapter.

Hands-on lab for configuring adduser

For this lab, we'll be working with the `adduser` utility, which is peculiar to Debian/Ubuntu systems:

1. On your Ubuntu virtual machine, open the `/etc/adduser.conf` file for editing. Find the line that says:

   ```
   DIR_MODE=0755
   ```

   Change it to:

   ```
   DIR_MODE=0700
   ```

---

[44]

Save the file and exit the text editor.

2. Install the `ecryptfs-utils` package:

   ```
   sudo apt install ecryptfs-utils
   ```

3. Create a user account with encrypted home directory for Cleopatra and then view the results:

   ```
   sudo adduser --encrypt-home cleopatra
   ls -l /home
   ```

4. Log in as Cleopatra and run the `ecryptfs-unwrap-passphrase` command:

   ```
   su - cleopatra
   ecryptfs-unwrap-passphrase
   exit
   ```

Note that some of the information that `adduser` asks for is optional, and you can just hit the *Enter* key for those items.

Enforcing strong password criteria

You wouldn't think that a benign-sounding topic such as *strong password criteria* would be so controversial, but it is. The conventional wisdom that you've undoubtedly heard for your entire computer career says:

- Make passwords of a certain minimum length
- Make passwords that consist of a combination of uppercase letters, lowercase letters, numbers, and special characters
- Ensure that passwords don't contain any words that are found in the dictionary or that are based on the users' own personal data
- Force users to change their passwords on a regular basis

But, using your favorite search engine, you'll see that different experts disagree on the details of these criteria. For example, you'll see disagreements about whether passwords should be changed every 30, 60, or 90 days, disagreements about whether all four types of characters need to be in a password, and even disagreements on what the minimum length of a password should be.

The most interesting controversy of all comes from—of all places—the guy who invented the preceding criteria to begin with. He now says that it's all bunk and regrets having come up with it. He now says that we should be using passphrases that are long, yet easy to remember. He also says that they should be changed only if they've been breached.

Bill Burr, the former National Institutes of Standards and Technology engineer who created the strong password criteria that I've outlined earlier, shares his thoughts about why he now disavows his own work.

Refer to: `https://www.pcmag.com/news/355496/you-might-not-need-complex-alphanumeric-passwords-after-all`.

However, having said all that, there is the reality that most organizations are still wedded to the idea of using complex passwords that regularly expire, and you'll have to abide by their rules if you can't convince them otherwise. And besides, if you are using traditional passwords, you do want them to be strong enough to resist any sort of password attack. So now, we'll take a look at the mechanics of enforcing strong password criteria on a Linux system.

I have to confess that I had never before thought to try creating a passphrase to use in place of a password on a Linux system. So, I just now tried it on my CentOS virtual machine to see if it would work.

I created an account for Maggie, my black-and-white tuxedo kitty. For her password, I entered the passphrase, `I like other kitty cats`. You may think, "*Oh, that's terrible. This doesn't meet any complexity criteria, and it uses dictionary words. How is that secure?*" But, the fact that it's a phrase with distinct words separated by blank spaces does make it secure and very difficult to brute-force.

Now, in real life, I would never create a passphrase that expresses my love for cats because it's not hard to find out that I really do love cats. Rather, I would choose a passphrase about some more obscure part of my life that nobody but me knows about.

In any case, there are two advantages of passphrases over passwords. They're more difficult to crack than traditional passwords, yet they're easier for users to remember. For extra security though, just don't create passphrases about a fact of your life that everybody knows about.

Installing and configuring pwquality

We'll be using the pwquality module for **PAM (Pluggable Authentication Module)**. This is a newer technology that has replaced the old cracklib module. On a Red Hat 7 or CentOS 7 system, pwquality is installed by default, even if you do a minimal installation. If you cd into the /etc/pam.d directory, you can do a grep operation to see that the PAM configuration files are already set up. The retry=3 means that a user will only have three tries to get the password right when logging into the system:

```
[donnie@localhost pam.d]$ grep 'pwquality' *
password-auth:password      requisite      pam_pwquality.so try_first_pass
local_users_only retry=3 authtok_type=
password-auth-ac:password      requisite      pam_pwquality.so try_first_pass
local_users_only retry=3 authtok_type=
system-auth:password      requisite      pam_pwquality.so try_first_pass
local_users_only retry=3 authtok_type=
system-auth-ac:password      requisite      pam_pwquality.so try_first_pass
local_users_only retry=3 authtok_type=
[donnie@localhost pam.d]$
```

For your Ubuntu system, you'll need to install pwquality yourself. You'll do that with the command:

```
sudo apt install libpam-pwquality
```

We'll now cd into the /etc/pam.d directory and perform the same grep command that we did before. We'll see that installing the libpam-pwquality modules automatically updates the PAM configuration files:

```
donnie@packt:/etc/pam.d$ grep 'pwquality' *
common-password:password          requisite
pam_pwquality.so retry=3
donnie@packt:/etc/pam.d$
```

The rest of the procedure is the same for both operating systems and consists of just editing the /etc/security/pwquality.conf file. When you open this file in your text editor, you'll see that everything is commented out, which means that no password complexity criteria are in effect. You'll also see that it's very well-documented because every setting has its own explanatory comment.

You can set password complexity criteria however you want just by uncommenting the appropriate lines and setting the proper values. Let's take a look at just one setting:

```
# Minimum acceptable size for the new password (plus one if
# credits are not disabled which is the default). (See pam_cracklib
manual.)
# Cannot be set to lower value than 6.
# minlen = 8
```

The minimum length setting works on a credit system. This means that for every different type of character class in the password, the minimum required password length will be reduced by one character. For example, let's set the minlen to a value of 19 and try to assign Katelyn the password, turkeylips:

```
minlen = 19
```

```
[donnie@localhost ~]$ sudo passwd katelyn
Changing password for user katelyn.
New password:
BAD PASSWORD: The password is shorter than 18 characters
Retype new password:
[donnie@localhost ~]$
```

Because the lowercase characters in turkeylips count as credit for one type of character class, we're only required to have 18 characters instead of 19. If we try this again with TurkeyLips, we'll get:

```
[donnie@localhost ~]$ sudo passwd katelyn
Changing password for user katelyn.
New password:
BAD PASSWORD: The password is shorter than 17 characters
Retype new password:
[donnie@localhost ~]$
```

This time, the uppercase T and uppercase L count as a second character class, so we only need to have 17 characters in the password.

Just below the minlen line, you'll see the credit lines. Let's say that you don't want lowercase letters to count toward your credits. You would find this line:

```
# lcredit = 1
```

Also, you would change the 1 to a 0:

```
lcredit = 0
```

Then, try assigning Katelyn `turkeylips` as a password:

```
[donnie@localhost ~]$ sudo passwd katelyn
Changing password for user katelyn.
New password:
BAD PASSWORD: The password is shorter than 19 characters
Retype new password:
[donnie@localhost ~]$
```

This time, the `pwquality` really does want 19 characters. If we set a credit value to something higher than one, we would get credit for multiple characters of the same class type up to that value.

We can also set the credit values to negative numbers in order to require a certain number of characters types in a password. We have the following example:

```
dcredit = -3
```

This would require at least three digits in a password. However, it's a really a bad idea to use this feature because someone who's doing a password attack would soon find the patterns that you require, which would help the attacker to more precisely direct the attack. If you need to require that a password has multiple character types, it would be better to use the `minclass` parameter:

```
# minclass = 3
```

It's already set to a value of three, which would require characters from three different classes. To use this value, all you have to do is to remove the comment symbol.

The rest of the parameters in `pwquality.conf` work pretty much the same way, and each one has a well-written comment to explain what it does.

 If you use your sudo privilege to set someone else's password, the system will complain if you create a password that doesn't meet complexity criteria, but it will let you do it. If a normal user were to try to change his or her own password without sudo privileges, the system would not allow a password that doesn't meet complexity criteria.

Hands-on lab for setting password complexity criteria

For this lab, you can use either the CentOS or Ubuntu virtual machine, as desired. The only difference is that you won't perform *Step 1* for CentOS:

1. For Ubuntu only, install the `libpam-pwquality` package:

    ```
    sudo apt install libpam-pwquality
    ```

2. Open the `/etc/security/pwquality.conf` file in your preferred text editor. Remove the comment symbol from in front of the `minlen` line and change the value to `19`. It should now look like this:

    ```
    minlen = 19
    ```

    Save the file and exit the editor.

3. Create a user account for Goldie and attempt to assign her the passwords, `turkeylips`, `TurkeyLips`, and `Turkey93Lips`. Note the change in each warning message.

4. In the `pwquality.conf` file, comment out the `minlen` line. Uncomment the `minclass` line and the `maxclassrepeat` line. Change the `maxclassrepeat` value to `5`. The lines should now look like:

    ```
    minclass = 3
    maxclassrepeat = 5
    ```

    Save the file and exit the text editor.

5. Try assigning various passwords that don't meet the complexity criteria that you've set to Goldie's account and view the results.

     In the `/etc/login.defs` file on your CentOS machine, you'll see the line:

    ```
    PASS_MIN_LEN        5
    ```

    Supposedly, this is to set the minimum password length, but in reality, `pwquality` overrides it. So, you could set this value to anything at all, and it would have no effect.

Setting and enforcing password and account expiration

Something you never want is to have unused user accounts remain active. There have been incidents where an administrator set up user accounts for temporary usage, such as for a conference, and then just forgot about them after the accounts were no longer needed. Another example would be if your company were to hire contract workers whose contract expires on a specific date. Allowing those accounts to remain active and accessible after the temporary employees leave the company would be a huge security problem. In cases like these, you want a way to ensure that temporary user accounts aren't forgotten about when they're no longer needed. If your employer subscribes to the conventional wisdom that users should change their passwords on a regular basis, then you'll also want to ensure that it gets done.

Password expiration data and account expiration data are two different things. They can be set either separately or together. When someone's password expires, he or she can change it, and everything will be all good. If somebody's account expires, only someone with the proper admin privileges can unlock it.

To get started, take a look at the expiry data for your own account. (Note that you won't need sudo privileges to look at your own data, but you will still need to specify your own username.)

```
donnie@packt:~$ chage -l donnie
[sudo] password for donnie:
Last password change : Oct 03, 2017
Password expires : never
Password inactive : never
Account expires : never
Minimum number of days between password change : 0
Maximum number of days between password change : 99999
Number of days of warning before password expires : 7
donnie@packt:~$
```

You can see here that no expiration data have been set. Everything here is set according to the out-of-box system default values. Other than the obvious items, here's a breakdown of what you see:

- **Password inactive**: If this were set to a positive number, I would have that many days to change an expired password before the system would lock out my account.

- **Minimum number of days between password change**: Because this is set to 0, I can change my password as often as I like. If it were set to a positive number, I would have to wait that number of days after changing my password before I could change it again.
- **Maximum number of days between password change**: This is set to the default value of 99999, meaning that my password will never expire.
- **Number of days warning before password expires**: The default value is 7, but that's rather meaningless when the password is set to never expire.

With the chage utility, you can either set password and account expiration data for other users or you use the -l option to view expiration data. Any unprivileged user can use chage -l without sudo to view his or her own data. To either set data or view someone else's data, you need sudo. We'll take a closer look at chage a bit later.

Before we look at how to change expiration data, let's first look at where the default settings are stored. We'll first look at the /etc/login.defs file. The three relevant lines are:

```
PASS_MAX_DAYS 99999
PASS_MIN_DAYS 0
PASS_WARN_AGE 7
```

You can edit these values to fit your organization's needs. For example, changing PASS_MAX_DAYS to a value of 30 would cause all new user passwords from that point on to have a 30 day expiration data. (By the way, setting the default password expiry data in login.defs works for both Red Hat or CentOS and Debian/Ubuntu.)

Configuring default expiry data for useradd – for Red Hat or CentOS only

The /etc/default/useradd file has the rest of the default settings. In this case, we'll look at the one from the CentOS machine.

Ubuntu also has this same useradd configuration file, but it doesn't work. No matter how you configure it, the Ubuntu version of useradd just won't read it. So, the write-up about this file only applies to Red Hat or CentOS.

```
# useradd defaults file
GROUP=100
```

```
HOME=/home
INACTIVE=-1
EXPIRE=
SHELL=/bin/bash
SKEL=/etc/skel
CREATE_MAIL_SPOOL=yes
```

The EXPIRE= line sets the default expiration date for new user accounts. By default, there is no default expiration date. INACTIVE=-1 means that user accounts won't be automatically locked out after the users' passwords expire. If we set this to a positive number, then any new users will have that many days to change an expired password before the account gets locked. To change the defaults in the useradd file, you can either hand-edit the file or use useradd -D with the appropriate option switch for the item that you want to change. For example, to set a default expiration date of December 31, 2019, the command would be:

```
sudo useradd -D -e 2019-12-31
```

To see the new configuration, you can either open the useradd file or just do sudo useradd -D:

```
[donnie@localhost ~]$ sudo useradd -D
GROUP=100
HOME=/home
INACTIVE=-1
EXPIRE=2019-12-31
SHELL=/bin/bash
SKEL=/etc/skel
CREATE_MAIL_SPOOL=yes
[donnie@localhost ~]$
```

You've now set it so that any new user accounts that get created will have the same expiration date. You can do the same thing with either the INACTIVE setting or the SHELL setting:

```
sudo useradd -D -f 5
sudo useradd -D -s /bin/zsh

[donnie@localhost ~]$ sudo useradd -D
GROUP=100
HOME=/home
INACTIVE=5
EXPIRE=2019-12-31
SHELL=/bin/zsh
SKEL=/etc/skel
CREATE_MAIL_SPOOL=yes
[donnie@localhost ~]$
```

Now, any new user accounts that get created will have the Zsh shell set as the default shell and will have to have expired passwords changed within five days to prevent having the account automatically locked out.

 useradd doesn't do any safety checks to ensure that the default shell that you've assigned is installed on the system. In our case, Zsh isn't installed, but useradd will still allow you to create accounts with Zsh as the default shell.

So, just how useful is this useradd configuration feature in real life? Probably not that much, unless you need to create a whole bunch of user accounts at once with the same settings. Even so, a savvy admin would just automate the process with a shell script, rather than messing around with this configuration file.

Setting expiry data on a per-account basis, with useradd and usermod

You might find it useful to set the default password expiry data in login.defs, but you probably won't find it too useful to configure the useradd configuration file. Really, what are the chances that you'll want to create all user accounts with the same account expiration date? Setting password expiry data in login.defs is more useful because you'll just be saying that you want new passwords to expire within a certain number of days, rather than to have them all expire on a specific date.

Most likely, you'll want to set account expiry data on a per-account basis, depending on whether you know that the accounts will no longer be needed as of a specific date. There are three ways that you can do this:

- Use useradd with the appropriate option switches to set expiry data as you create the accounts. (If you need to create a whole bunch of accounts at once with the same expiry data, you can automate the process with a shell script.)
- Use usermod to modify expiry data on existing accounts. (The beautiful thing about usermod is that it uses the same option switches as useradd.)
- Use chage to modify expiry data on existing accounts. (This one uses a whole different set of option switches.)

You can use `useradd` and `usermod` to set account expiry data, but not for setting password expiry data. The only two option switches that affect account expiry data are:

- `-e`: Use this to set an expiration date for the account, in the form YYYY-MM-DD
- `-f`: Use this to set the number of days after the user's password expires that you want for his or her account to get locked out

Let's say that you want to create an account for Charlie that will expire at the end of 2020. On a Red Hat or CentOS machine, you could enter the following:

```
sudo useradd -e 2020-12-31 charlie
```

On a non-Red Hat or CentOS machine, you'd have to add the option switches that create the home directory and assign the correct default shell:

```
sudo useradd -m -d /home/charlie -s /bin/bash -e 2020-12-31 charlie
```

Use `chage -l` to verify what you've entered:

```
donnie@ubuntu-steemnode:~$ sudo chage -l charlie
Last password change : Oct 06, 2017
Password expires : never
Password inactive : never
Account expires : Dec 31, 2020
Minimum number of days between password change : 0
Maximum number of days between password change : 99999
Number of days of warning before password expires : 7
donnie@ubuntu-steemnode:~$
```

Now, let's say that Charlie's contract has been extended, and you need to change his account expiration to the end of January, 2021. You'll use `usermod` the same way on any Linux distro:

```
sudo usermod -e 2021-01-31 charlie
```

Again, verify that everything is correct with `chage -l`:

```
donnie@ubuntu-steemnode:~$ sudo chage -l charlie
Last password change : Oct 06, 2017
Password expires : never
Password inactive : never
Account expires : Jan 31, 2021
Minimum number of days between password change : 0
Maximum number of days between password change : 99999
Number of days of warning before password expires : 7
donnie@ubuntu-steemnode:~$
```

Optionally, you can set the number of days before an account with an expired password will get locked out:

```
sudo usermod -f 5 charlie
```

But, if you were to do that now, you wouldn't see any difference in the `chage -l` output because we still haven't set an expiration data for Charlie's password.

Setting expiry data on a per-account basis, with chage

You would only use `chage` to modify existing accounts, and you would use it for setting either an account expiration or a password expiration. Here are the relevant option switches:

-d	If you use the -d 0 option on someone's account, you'll force the user to change his or her password on their next login.
-E	This is equivalent to the lower-case -e for `useradd` or `usermod`. It sets the expiration date for the user account.
-I	This is equivalent to -f for `useradd` or `usermod`. It sets the number of days before an account with an expired password will be locked out.
-m	This sets the minimum number of days between password changes. In other words, if Charlie changes his password today, a -m 5 option will force him to wait five days before he can change his password again.
-M	This sets the maximum number of days before a password expires. (Be aware though that if Charlie last set his password 89 days ago, using a -M 90 option on his account will cause his password to expire tomorrow, not 90 days from now.)
-W	This will set the number of warning days for passwords that are about to expire.

You can set just one of these data items at a time or you can set them all at once. In fact, to avoid frustrating you with a different demo for each individual item, let's set them all at once, except for the -d 0, and then we'll see what we've got:

```
sudo chage -E 2021-02-28 -I 4 -m 3 -M 90 -W 4 charlie

donnie@ubuntu-steemnode:~$ sudo chage -l charlie
Last password change : Oct 06, 2017
Password expires : Jan 04, 2018
```

```
Password inactive : Jan 08, 2018
Account expires : Feb 28, 2021
Minimum number of days between password change : 3
Maximum number of days between password change : 90
Number of days of warning before password expires : 4
donnie@ubuntu-steemnode:~$
```

All expiration data have now been set.

For our final example, let's say that you've just created a new account for Samson, and you want to force him to change his password the first time he logs in. There are two ways to do that. Either way, you would do it after you've set his password initially. We have the following code:

```
sudo chage -d 0 samson
```

or

```
sudo passwd -e samson
```

```
donnie@ubuntu-steemnode:~$ sudo chage -l samson
Last password change                      : password must be changed
Password expires                          : password must be changed
Password inactive                         : password must be changed
Account expires                           : never
Minimum number of days between password change        : 0
Maximum number of days between password change        : 99999
Number of days of warning before password expires     : 7
donnie@ubuntu-steemnode:~$
```

Hands-on lab for setting account and password expiry data

In this lab, you'll create a couple of new user accounts, set expiration data, and view the results. You can do this lab on either the CentOS or the Ubuntu virtual machine. (The only difference will be with the useradd commands.)

1. Create a user account for Samson with the expiration date of June 30, 2023, and view the results.

    For CentOS:

    ```
    sudo useradd -e 2023-06-30 samson
    sudo chage -l samson
    ```

For Ubuntu:

```
sudo useradd -m -d /home/samson -s /bin/bash -e 2023-06-30
sudo chage -l samson
```

2. Use `usermod` to change Samson's account expiration date to July 31, 2023:

```
sudo usermod -e 2023-07-31
sudo chage -l samson
```

3. Assign a password to Samson's account, then force him to change his password on his first login. Log in as Samson, change his password, then log back out to your own account:

```
sudo passwd samson
sudo passwd -e samson
sudo chage -l samson
su - samson
exit
```

4. Use `chage` to set a 5 day waiting period for changing passwords, a password expiration period of 90 days, an inactivity period of 2 days, and a warning period of 5 days:

```
sudo chage -m 5 -M 90 -I 2 -W 5 samson
sudo chage -l samson
```

5. Keep this account because you'll be using it for the lab in the next section.

Preventing brute-force password attacks

Amazingly enough, this is another topic that engenders a bit of controversy. I mean, nobody denies the wisdom of automatically locking out user accounts that are under attack. The controversial part concerns the number of failed login attempts that we should allow before locking the account.

Back in the stone age of computing, so long ago that I still had a full head of hair, the early Unix operating systems only allowed users to create a password with a maximum of eight lowercase letters. So in those days, it was possible for early man to brute-force someone else's password just by sitting down at the keyboard and typing in random passwords. That's when the philosophy started of having user accounts get locked out after only three failed login attempts. Nowadays, with strong passwords, or better yet, a strong passphrase, setting a lockout value of three failed login attempts will do three things:

- It will unnecessarily frustrate users
- It will cause extra work for help desk personnel
- If an account really is under attack, it will lock the account before you've had a chance to gather information about the attacker

Setting the lockout value to something more realistic, like 100 failed login attempts, will still provide good security, while still giving you enough time to gather information about the attackers. Just as importantly, you won't cause undue frustration to users and help desk personnel.

Anyway, regardless of how many failed login attempts your employer allows you to allow, you'll still need to know how to set it all up. So, let's dig in.

Configuring the pam_tally2 PAM module

To make this magic work, we'll rely on our good friend, the PAM module. The pam_tally2 module comes already installed on both CentOS and Ubuntu, but it isn't configured. For both of our virtual machines, we'll be editing the /etc/pam.d/login file. Figuring out how to configure it is easy because there's an example at the bottom of the pam_tally2 man page:

```
EXAMPLES
        Add the following line to /etc/pam.d/login to lock the account after
4 failed logins. Root account will be locked as well. The accounts will be
automatically unlocked after 20 minutes. The module does not have to be
called in the account phase because the login calls pam_setcred(3)
correctly.

            auth required pam_securetty.so
            auth required pam_tally2.so deny=4 even_deny_root
unlock_time=1200
            auth required pam_env.so
            auth required pam_unix.so
            auth required pam_nologin.so
            account required pam_unix.so
            password required pam_unix.so
            session required pam_limits.so
            session required pam_unix.so
            session required pam_lastlog.so nowtmp
            session optional pam_mail.so standard
```

In the second line of the example, we see that `pam_tally2` is set with:

- `deny=4`: This means that the user account under attack will get locked out after only four failed login attempts
- `even_deny_root`: This means that even the root user account will get locked if it's under attack
- `unlock_time=1200`: The account will get automatically unlocked after 1200 seconds or 20 minutes

Now, if you look at the actual `login` file on either of your virtual machines, you'll see that they don't look exactly like this example login file that's in both of their man pages. That's okay, we'll still make it work.

Once you've configured the `login` file and have had a failed login, you'll see a new file created in the `/var/log` directory. You'll view information from that file with the `pam_tally2` utility. You can also use `pam_tally2` to manually unlock a locked account if you don't want to wait for the timeout period:

```
donnie@ubuntu-steemnode:~$ sudo pam_tally2
Login Failures Latest failure From
charlie 5 10/07/17 16:38:19
donnie@ubuntu-steemnode:~$ sudo pam_tally2 --user=charlie --reset
Login Failures Latest failure From
charlie 5 10/07/17 16:38:19
donnie@ubuntu-steemnode:~$ sudo pam_tally2
donnie@ubuntu-steemnode:~$
```

Note how after I did the reset on Charlie's account, I received no output from doing another query.

Hands-on lab for configuring pam_tally2

Configuring `pam_tally2` is super easy because it only requires adding one line to the `/etc/pam.d/login` file. To make things even easier, you can just copy and paste that line from the example in the `pam_tally2` man page. In spite of what I said earlier about bumping the number of failed logins up to 100, we'll keep that number at 4 for now. (I know that you don't want to have to do 100 failed logins in order to demo this.)

1. On either the CentOS or the Ubuntu virtual machine, open the `/etc/pam.d/login` file for editing. Look for the line that invokes the `pam_securetty` module. (That should be around line 32 on Ubuntu and around line 2 on CentOS.)

Beneath that line, insert the following line:

```
auth required pam_tally2.so deny=4
even_deny_root unlock_time=1200
```

Save the file and exit the editor.

2. For this step, you'll need to log out of your own account because `pam_tally2` doesn't work with `su`. So, log out, and while purposely using the wrong password, attempt to log in to the `samson` account that you created in the previous lab. Keep doing that until you see the message that the account is locked. Note that when the `deny` value is set to `4`, it will actually take five failed login attempts to lock Samson out.

3. Log back in to your own user account. Run this command and note the output:

```
sudo pam_tally2
```

4. For this step, you'll simulate that you're a help desk worker, and Samson has just called to request that you unlock his account. After verifying that you really are talking to the real Samson, enter the following line:

```
sudo pam_tally2 --user=samson --reset
sudo pam_tally2
```

5. Now that you've seen how this works, open the `/etc/pam.d/login` file for editing, and change the `deny=` parameter from `4` to `100` and save the file. (This will make your configuration a bit more realistic in terms of modern security philosophy.)

Locking user accounts

Okay, you've just seen how to have Linux automatically lock user accounts that are under attack. There will also be times when you'll want to be able to manually lock out user accounts. Let us look at the following example:

- When a user goes on vacation and you want to ensure that nobody monkeys around with that user's account while he or she is gone
- When a user is under investigation for questionable activities
- When a user leaves the company

In regard to the last point, you may be asking yourself, "*Why can't we just delete the accounts of people who are no working here?*" And, you certainly can, easily enough. However, before you do so, you'll need to check with your local laws to make sure that you don't get yourself into deep trouble. Here in the United States, for example, we have the Sarbanes-Oxley law, which restricts what files that publicly traded companies can delete from their computers. If you were to delete a user account, along with that user's home directory and mail spool, you just might be running afoul of Sarbanes-Oxley or whatever you may have as the equivalent law in your own home country.

Anyway, there are two utilities that you can use to temporarily lock a user account:

- Using `usermod` to lock a user account
- Using `passwd` to lock user accounts

Using usermod to lock a user account

Let's say that Katelyn has gone on maternity leave and will be gone for at least several weeks. We can lock her account with:

```
sudo usermod -L katelyn
```

When you look at Katelyn's entry in the `/etc/shadow` file, you'll now see an exclamation point in front of her password hash, as follows:

```
katelyn:!$6$uA5ecH1A$MZ6q5U.cyY2SRSJezV000AudP.ckXXndBNsXUdMI1vPO8aFmlLXcbG
V25K5HSSaCv4RlDilwzlXq/hKvXRkpB/:17446:0:99999:7:::
```

This exclamation point prevents the system from being able to read her password, which effectively locks her out of the system.

To unlock her account, just follow this:

```
sudo usermod -U katelyn
```

You'll see that the exclamation point has been removed so that she can now log in to her account.

Using passwd to lock user accounts

You could also lock Katelyn's account with:

```
sudo passwd -l katelyn
```

This does the same job as usermod -L, but in a slightly different manner. For one thing, passwd -l will give you some feedback about what's going on, where usermod -L gives you no feedback at all. On Ubuntu, the feedback looks like this:

```
donnie@ubuntu-steemnode:~$ sudo passwd -l katelyn
[sudo] password for donnie:
passwd: password expiry information changed.
donnie@ubuntu-steemnode:~$
```

On CentOS, the feedback looks like this:

```
[donnie@localhost ~]$ sudo passwd -l katelyn
Locking password for user katelyn.
passwd: Success
[donnie@localhost ~]$
```

Also, on the CentOS machine, you'll see that passwd -l places two exclamation points in front of the password hash, instead of just one. Either way, the effect is the same.

To unlock Katelyn's account, just do:

```
sudo passwd -u katelyn
```

In versions of Red Hat or CentOS prior to version 7, usermod -U would remove only one of the exclamation points that passwd -l places in front of the shadow file password hash, thus leaving the account still locked. No big deal, though, because running usermod -U again would remove the second exclamation point.

In Red Hat or CentOS 7, it has been fixed. The passwd -l command still places two exclamation points in the shadow file, but usermod -U now removes both of them. (That's a shame, really, because it ruined a perfectly good demo that I like to do for my students.)

Locking the root user account

The cloud is big business nowadays, and it's now quite common to rent a virtual private server from companies such as Rackspace, DigitalOcean, or Microsoft Azure. These can serve a variety of purposes, as follows:

- You can run your own website, where you install your own server software instead of letting a hosting service do it
- You can set up a web-based app for other people to access
- Recently, I saw a YouTube demo on a crypto-mining channel that showed how to set up a Proof of Stake master node on a rented virtual private server

One thing that these cloud services have in common is that when you first set up your account and the provider sets up a virtual machine for you, they'll have you log in to the root user account. (It even happens with Ubuntu, even though the root account is disabled on a local installation of Ubuntu.)

I know that there are some folk who just keep logging in to the root account of these cloud-based servers and think nothing of it, but that's really a horrible idea. There are botnets, such as the Hail Mary botnet, that continuously scan the internet for servers that have their Secure Shell port exposed to the internet. When the botnets find one, they'll do a brute-force password attack against the root user account of that server. And yes, the botnets sometimes are successful in breaking in, especially if the root account is set with a weak password.

So, the first thing that you want to do when you set up a cloud-based server is to create a normal user account for yourself and set it up with full sudo privileges. Then, log out of the root user account, log into your new account, and do the following:

```
sudo passwd -l root
```

I mean, really, why take the chance of getting your root account compromised?

Setting up security banners

Something that you really, really don't want is to have a login banner that says something to the effect, "*Welcome to our network*". I say that because quite a few years ago, I attended a mentored SANS course on incident handling. Our instructor told us the story about how a company took a suspected network intruder to court, only to get the case thrown out. The reason? The alleged intruder said, "*Well, I saw the message that said 'Welcome to the network', so I thought that I really was welcome there.*" Yeah, supposedly, that was enough to get the case thrown out.

A few years later, I related that story to the students in one of my Linux admin classes. One student said, "*That makes no sense. We all have welcome mats at our front doors, but that doesn't mean that burglars are welcome to come in.*" I have to confess that he had a good point, and I now have to wonder about the veracity of the story.

At any rate, just to be on the safe side, you do want to set up login messages that make clear that only authorized users are allowed to access the system.

Using the motd file

The /etc/motd file will present a message banner to anyone who logs in to a system through Secure Shell. On your CentOS machine, an empty motd file is already there. On your Ubuntu machine, the motd file isn't there, but it's a simple matter to create one. Either way, open the file in your text editor and create your message. Save the file and test it by remotely logging in through Secure Shell. You should see something like:

```
maggie@192.168.0.100's password:
Last login: Sat Oct 7 20:51:09 2017
Warning: Authorized Users Only!

All others will be prosecuted.
[maggie@localhost ~]$
```

 motd stands for Message of the Day.

Using the issue file

The issue file, also found in the /etc directory, shows a message on the local terminal, just above the login prompt. A default issue file would just contain macro code that would show information about the machine. Look at the following example:

```
Ubuntu 16.04.3 LTS \n \l
```

Or, on a CentOS machine:

```
\S
Kernel \r on an \m
```

On an Ubuntu machine, the banner would look something like this:

```
Ubuntu 16.04.3 LTS ubuntu-steemnode tty1

ubuntu-steemnode login: _
```

On a CentOS machine, it would look something like this:

```
CentOS Linux 7 (Core)
Kernel 3.10.0-693.2.2.el7.x86_64 on an x86_64

localhost login: _
```

You could put a security message in the issue file, and it would show up after a reboot:

```
Warning!  Authorized Users Only!

CentOS Linux 7 (Core)
Kernel 3.10.0-693.2.2.el7.x86_64 on an x86_64

localhost login: _
```

In reality, is there really any point in placing a security message in the issue file? If your servers are properly locked away in a server room with controlled access, then probably not.

Using the issue.net file

Just don't. It's for telnet logins, and anyone who has telnet enabled on their servers is seriously screwing up. However, for some strange reason, the `issue.net` file still hangs around in the `/etc` directory.

Summary

We covered a lot of ground in this chapter, and hopefully you found some suggestions that you can actually use. We started out with showing you the dangers of always logging in as the root user and how you should use sudo, instead. In addition to showing you the basics of sudo usage, we also looked at some good sudo tips and tricks. We moved on to user management, by looking at how to lock down users' home directories, how to enforce strong password policies, and how to enforce account and password expiration policies. Then, we talked about a way to prevent brute-force password attacks, how to manually lockout user accounts, and set up security banners.

In the next chapter, we'll look at how to work with various firewall utilities. I'll see you there.

3
Securing Your Server with a Firewall

Security is one of those things that's best done in layers. *Security-in-depth*, we call it. So, on any given corporate network, you will find a firewall appliance separating the internet from the **demilitarized zone** (**DMZ**), where your internet-facing servers are kept. You will also find a firewall appliance between the DMZ and the internal LAN, and firewall software installed on each individual server and client. We want to make it as tough as possible for intruders to reach their final destinations within our networks.

Interestingly though, of all the major Linux distros, only the SUSE distros and the Red Hat-type distros come with firewalls already set up and enabled. When you look at your Ubuntu virtual machine, you'll see that it's wide open, as if it were extending a hearty welcome to any would-be intruder.

Since the focus of this book is on hardening our Linux servers, we'll focus this chapter on that last level of defense, the firewalls on our servers and clients.

In this chapter, we'll cover:

- An overview of iptables
- Uncomplicated Firewall for Ubuntu systems
- firewalld for Red Hat systems
- nftables, a more universal type of firewall system

An overview of iptables

A common misconception is that iptables is the name of the Linux firewall. In reality, the name of the Linux firewall is **netfilter** and every Linux distro has it built-in. What we know as iptables is just one of several command-line utilities that we can use to manage netfilter. It was originally introduced as a feature of Linux kernel, version 2.6, so it's been around for a long time. With iptables, you do have a few advantages:

- It's been around long enough that most Linux admins already know how to use it
- It's easy to use iptables commands in shell scripts to create your own custom firewall configuration
- It has great flexibility, in that you can use it to set up a simple port filter, a router, or a virtual private network
- It comes preinstalled on pretty much every Linux distro, although most distros don't come with it preconfigured
- It's very well documented, with free of charge, book-length tutorials available on the internet

But, as you might know, there are also a few disadvantages:

- IPv4 and IPv6 require their own special implementation of iptables. So, if your organization still needs to run IPv4 while in the process of migrating to IPv6, you'll have to configure two firewalls on each server, and run a separate daemon for each (one for IPv4, the other for IPv6).
- If you need to do Mac bridging that requires **ebtables**, which is the third component of iptables, with its own unique syntax.
- arptables, the fourth component of iptables, also requires its own daemon and syntax.
- Whenever you add a rule to a running iptables firewall, the entire iptables ruleset has to be reloaded, which can have a huge impact on performance.

Until recently, iptables was the default firewall manager on every Linux distro. It still is on most distros, but Red Hat Enterprise Linux 7 and all of its offspring now use a newer technology called **firewalld**. Ubuntu comes with **Uncomplicated Firewall (ufw)**, an easy-to-use frontend for iptables. An even newer technology that we'll explore at the end of the chapter is **nftables**.

For the purposes of this chapter, we'll only look at the IPv4 component of iptables. (The syntax for the IPv6 component would be very similar.)

Basic usage of iptables

iptables consists of four tables of rules, each with its own distinct purpose:

- **Filter table**: For basic protection of our servers and clients, this is the only table that we would normally use
- **NAT table**: **Network Address Translation** (**NAT**) is used to connect the public internet to private networks
- **Mangle table**: This is used to alter network packets as they go through the firewall
- **Security table**: The security table is only used for systems that have SELinux installed

Since we're currently only interested in basic host protection, we'll only look at the filter table. Each table consists of chains of rules, and the filter table consists of the INPUT, FORWARD, and OUTPUT chains. Since our CentOS 7 machine uses Red Hat's firewalld, we'll look at this on our Ubuntu machine.

While it's true that Red Hat Enterprise Linux 7 and its offspring do come with iptables already installed, it's disabled by default so that we can use firewalld. It's not possible to have both iptables and firewalld running at the same time, because they're two totally different animals that are completely incompatible. So, if you need to run iptables on a Red Hat 7 system, you can do so, but you must disable firewalld first.

However, if your organization is still running its network with version 6 of either Red Hat or CentOS, then your machines are still running with iptables, since firewalld isn't available for them.

We'll first look at our current configuration with sudo iptables -L command:

```
donnie@ubuntu:~$ sudo iptables -L
[sudo] password for donnie:
Chain INPUT (policy ACCEPT)
target prot opt source destination

Chain FORWARD (policy ACCEPT)
target prot opt source destination

Chain OUTPUT (policy ACCEPT)
target prot opt source destination
donnie@ubuntu:~$
```

And remember, we said that you need a separate component of iptables to deal with IPv6. Here we will use `sudo ip6tables -L` command:

```
donnie@ubuntu:~$ sudo ip6tables -L
Chain INPUT (policy ACCEPT)
target      prot opt source              destination

Chain FORWARD (policy ACCEPT)
target      prot opt source              destination

Chain OUTPUT (policy ACCEPT)
target      prot opt source              destination
donnie@ubuntu:~$
```

In both cases, you see that there are no rules, and that the machine is wide open. Unlike the SUSE and Red Hat folk, the Ubuntu folk expect you to do the work of setting up a firewall. We'll start by creating a rule that will allow the passage of incoming packets from servers to which our host has requested a connection:

```
sudo iptables -A INPUT -m conntrack --ctstate ESTABLISHED,RELATED -j ACCEPT
```

Here's the breakdown of this command:

- `-A INPUT`: The `-A` places a rule at the end of the specified chain, which in this case is the `INPUT` chain. We would have used a `-I` had we wanted to place the rule at the beginning of the chain.
- `-m`: This calls in an iptables module. In this case, we're calling in the `conntrack` module for tracking connection states. This module allows iptables to determine whether our client has made a connection to another machine, for example.
- `--ctstate`: The `ctstate` or connection state, portion of our rule is looking for two things. First, it's looking for a connection that the client established with a server. Then, it looks for the related connection that's coming back from the server, in order to allow it to connect to the client. So, if a user were to use a web browser to connect to a website, this rule would allow packets from the web server to pass through the firewall to get to the user's browser.
- `-j`: This stands for *jump*. Rules jump to a specific target, which in this case is `ACCEPT`. (Please don't ask me who came up with this terminology.) So, this rule will accept packets that return from the server with which the client has requested a connection.

Our new ruleset looks like this:

```
donnie@ubuntu:~$ sudo iptables -L
Chain INPUT (policy ACCEPT)
target prot opt source destination
ACCEPT all -- anywhere anywhere ctstate RELATED,ESTABLISHED

Chain FORWARD (policy ACCEPT)
target prot opt source destination

Chain OUTPUT (policy ACCEPT)
target prot opt source destination
donnie@ubuntu:~$
```

We'll next open up port 22 in order to allow us to connect through Secure Shell. For now, we don't want to open any more ports, so we'll finish this with a rule that blocks everything else:

```
sudo iptables -A INPUT -p tcp --dport ssh -j ACCEPT
sudo iptables -A INPUT -j DROP
```

Here's the breakdown:

- `-A INPUT`: As before, we want to place this rule at the end of the INPUT chain with a `-A`.
- `-p tcp`: The `-p` indicates the protocol that this rule affects. This rule affects the TCP protocol, of which Secure Shell is a part.
- `--dport ssh`: When an option name consists of more than one letter, we need to precede it with two dashes, instead of just one. The `--dport` option specifies the destination port on which we want this rule to operate. (Note that we could also have listed this portion of the rule as `--dport 22`, since 22 is the number of the SSH port.)
- `-j ACCEPT`: Put it all together with `-j ACCEPT`, and we have a rule that allows other machines to connect to this one through Secure Shell.
- The DROP rule at the end silently blocks all connections and packets that aren't specifically allowed in by our two ACCEPT rules.

There are actually two ways in which we could have written that final blocking rule:

- `sudo iptables -A INPUT -j DROP`: It causes the firewall to silently block packets, without sending any notification back to the source of those packets.

- `sudo iptables -A INPUT -j REJECT`: It would also cause the firewall to block packets, but it would also send a message back to the source about the fact that the packets have been blocked. In general, it's better to use `DROP`, because we normally want to make it harder for malicious actors to figure out what our firewall configuration is.

Either way, you always want to have this rule at the end of the chain, because any `ALLOW` rule that comes after it will have no effect.

Finally, we have an almost complete, usable ruleset for our `INPUT` chain:

```
donnie@ubuntu:~$ sudo iptables -L
Chain INPUT (policy ACCEPT)
target     prot opt source               destination
ACCEPT     all  --  anywhere             anywhere             ctstate
RELATED,ESTABLISHED
ACCEPT     tcp  --  anywhere             anywhere             tcp dpt:ssh
DROP       all  --  anywhere             anywhere

Chain FORWARD (policy ACCEPT)
target     prot opt source               destination

Chain OUTPUT (policy ACCEPT)
target     prot opt source               destination
donnie@ubuntu:~$
```

It's almost complete, because there's still one little thing that we forgot. That is, we need to allow traffic for the loopback interface. That's okay, because it gives us a good chance to see how to insert a rule where we want it, if we don't want it at the end. In this case, we'll insert the rule at `INPUT 1`, which is the first position of the `INPUT` chain:

```
sudo iptables -I INPUT 1 -i lo -j ACCEPT
```

When we look at our new ruleset, we'll see something that's rather strange:

```
donnie@ubuntu:~$ sudo iptables -L
Chain INPUT (policy ACCEPT)
target prot opt source destination
ACCEPT all -- anywhere anywhere
ACCEPT all -- anywhere anywhere ctstate RELATED,ESTABLISHED
ACCEPT tcp -- anywhere anywhere tcp dpt:ssh
DROP all -- anywhere anywhere

Chain FORWARD (policy ACCEPT)
target prot opt source destination

Chain OUTPUT (policy ACCEPT)
target prot opt source destination
donnie@ubuntu:~$
```

Hmmm...

The first rule and the last rule look the same, except that one is a DROP and the other is an ACCEPT. Let's look at it again with the -v option:

```
donnie@ubuntu:~$ sudo iptables -L -v
Chain INPUT (policy ACCEPT 0 packets, 0 bytes)
 pkts bytes target      prot opt in      out      source
destination
    0      0 ACCEPT     all  --  lo      any      anywhere
anywhere
  393  25336 ACCEPT     all  --  any     any      anywhere
anywhere             ctstate RELATED,ESTABLISHED
    0      0 ACCEPT     tcp  --  any     any      anywhere
anywhere             tcp dpt:ssh
  266  42422 DROP       all  --  any     any      anywhere
anywhere

Chain FORWARD (policy ACCEPT 0 packets, 0 bytes)
 pkts bytes target      prot opt in      out      source
destination

Chain OUTPUT (policy ACCEPT 72 packets, 7924 bytes)
 pkts bytes target      prot opt in      out      source
destination
donnie@ubuntu:~$
```

Now, we see that `lo`, for loopback, shows up under the `in` column of the first rule, and `any` shows up under the `in` column of the last rule. This all looks great, except that if we were to reboot the machine right now, the rules would disappear. The final thing that we need to do is make them permanent. There are several ways to do this, but the simplest way to do this on an Ubuntu machine is to install the `iptables-persistent` package:

```
sudo apt install iptables-persistent
```

During the installation process, you'll be presented with two screens that ask whether you want to save the current set of iptables rules. The first screen will be for IPv4 rules, and the second will be for IPv6 rules:

```
┤ Configuring iptables-persistent ├
 Current iptables rules can be saved to the configuration file /etc/iptables/rules.v4. These rules will then be loaded automatically during system startup.
 Rules are only saved automatically during package installation. See the manual page of iptables-save(8) for instructions on keeping the rules file up-to-date.
 Save current IPv4 rules?
                              <Yes>                              <No>
```

You'll now see two new rules files in the `/etc/iptables` directory:

```
donnie@ubuntu:~$ ls -l /etc/iptables*
total 8
-rw-r--r-- 1 root root 336 Oct 10 10:29 rules.v4
-rw-r--r-- 1 root root 183 Oct 10 10:29 rules.v6
donnie@ubuntu:~$
```

If you were to now reboot the machine, you'd see that your iptables rules are still there and in effect.

Hands-on lab for basic iptables usage

You'll do this lab on your Ubuntu virtual machine.

1. Shut down your Ubuntu virtual machine, and create a snapshot.

 You'll roll back to this snapshot for the lab in the next section.

2. Look at your iptables rules, or lack thereof, with:

   ```
   sudo iptables -L
   ```

3. Create the rules that you need for a basic firewall, allowing for Secure Shell access but denying everything else:

   ```
   sudo iptables -A INPUT -m conntrack
                           --ctstate ESTABLISHED,RELATED
                -j ACCEPT
   sudo iptables -A INPUT -p tcp --dport ssh -j ACCEPT
   sudo iptables -A INPUT -j DROP
   ```

4. View the results with:

   ```
   sudo iptables -L
   ```

5. Oops, it looks like you forgot about that loopback interface. Add a rule for it at the top of the list:

   ```
   sudo iptables -I INPUT 1 -i lo -j ACCEPT
   ```

6. View the results with these two commands. Note the difference between the output of each:

   ```
   sudo iptables -L
   sudo iptables -L -v
   ```

7. Install the `iptables-persistent` package, and choose to save the IPv4 and IPv6 rules when prompted:

   ```
   sudo apt install iptables-persistent
   ```

8. Reboot the virtual machine and verify that your rules are still active.
9. End of lab.

Now, I know you're thinking, "*Wow, that's a lot of hoops to jump through just to set up a basic firewall.*" And yeah, you're right. So, give me a moment to get rid of what I just did with iptables, and I'll show you what the Ubuntu folk came up with to make things simpler.

 You can get the whole scoop on how to do iptables on Ubuntu here: `https://help.ubuntu.com/community/IptablesHowTo`.

Uncomplicated Firewall for Ubuntu systems

The Uncomplicated Firewall is already installed on your Ubuntu machine. It still uses the iptables service, but it offers a vastly simplified set of commands. Perform just one simple command to enable it, and you have a good, preconfigured firewall. There's a graphical frontend for use on desktop machines, but since we're learning about server security, we'll just cover the command-line utility here.

Basic usage of ufw

ufw is disabled by default, so you'll need to enable it:

```
donnie@ubuntu:~$ sudo ufw enable
Command may disrupt existing ssh connections. Proceed with operation (y|n)?
y
Firewall is active and enabled on system startup
donnie@ubuntu:~$
```

To do this, I logged in to the virtual machine remotely from a terminal of my trusty OpenSUSE workstation. It gave me a warning that my Secure Shell connection could be disrupted, but that didn't happen. (It could be because of connection tracking rules, or it could be that I just got lucky.) I'll leave it up to you to do a `sudo iptables -L`, because ufw creates a very large default ruleset that would be impossible to display in this book.

Next, let's add a rule that will allow us to remotely connect through Secure Shell in the future:

```
sudo ufw allow 22/tcp
```

Do a `sudo iptables -L`, and you'll see that the new rule shows up in the `ufw-user-input` chain:

```
Chain ufw-user-input (1 references)
target     prot opt source               destination
ACCEPT     tcp  --  anywhere             anywhere             tcp dpt:ssh
```

In the preceding `sudo ufw allow 22/tcp` command, we had to specify the TCP protocol, because TCP is all that we need for Secure Shell. We can also open a port for both TCP and UDP just by not specifying a protocol. For example, if you're setting up a DNS server, you'll want to have port 53 open for both protocols (you'll see the entries for port 53 listed as `domain` ports):

```
sudo ufw allow 53

Chain ufw-user-input (1 references)
target      prot opt source               destination
ACCEPT      tcp  --  anywhere             anywhere             tcp dpt:ssh
ACCEPT      tcp  --  anywhere             anywhere             tcp
dpt:domain
ACCEPT      udp  --  anywhere             anywhere             udp
dpt:domain
```

If you do `sudo ip6tables -L`, you'll see that a rule for IPv6 also got added for both of the two preceding examples.

Hands-on lab for basic ufw usage

You'll do this lab on a clean snapshot of your Ubuntu virtual machine:

1. Shut down your Ubuntu virtual machine and restore the snapshot. (You want to do this to get rid of all of the iptables stuff that you just did.)
2. When you've restarted the virtual machine, verify that the iptables rules are now gone:

   ```
   sudo iptables -L
   ```

3. View the status of ufw, enable it, and view the results:

   ```
   sudo ufw status
   sudo ufw enable
   sudo ufw status
   sudo iptables -L
   sudo ip6tables -L
   ```

4. Open port `22/tcp` to allow Secure Shell access:

   ```
   sudo ufw allow 22/tcp
   sudo iptables -L
   sudo ip6tables -L
   ```

5. This time, open port `53` for both TCP and UDP:

```
sudo ufw allow 53
sudo iptables -L
sudo ip6tables -L
```

6. End of lab.

firewalld for Red Hat systems

So far, we've looked at iptables, a generic firewall management system that's available on all Linux distros, and ufw, which is only available for Ubuntu. For our next act, we turn our attention to **firewalld**, which is specific to Red Hat Enterprise Linux 7 and all of its offspring.

Unlike ufw for Ubuntu, firewalld isn't just an easy-to-use frontend for iptables. Rather, it's an entirely new way of doing your firewall business, and it isn't compatible with iptables. Understand, though, that iptables still comes installed on the Red Hat 7 family, but it isn't enabled, because you can't have iptables and firewalld enabled at the same time. If you have to use older shell scripts that leverage iptables, you can disable firewalld and enable iptables.

The reason that iptables and firewalld are incompatible is that iptables stores its rules in plain text files in the `/etc/sysconfig` directory, and firewalld stores its rules files in `.xml` format files in the `/etc/firewalld` directory and in the `/usr/lib/firewalld` directory. Also, iptables doesn't understand the concepts of zones and services the way that firewalld does, and the rules themselves are of a completely different format. So, even if you could have both iptables and firewalld running at the same time, you'd just end up confusing the system and breaking the firewall.

The bottom line is, you can run either iptables or firewalld on your Red Hat or CentOS machine, but you can't run both at the same time.

If you're running Red Hat or CentOS on a desktop machine, you'll see in the applications menu that there is a GUI frontend for firewalld. On a text-mode server, though, all you have is the firewalld commands. For some reason, the Red Hat folk haven't created an ncurses-type program for text-mode servers, the way they did for iptables configuration on older versions of Red Hat.

A big advantage of firewalld is the fact that it's dynamically managed. That means that you can change the firewall configuration without restarting the firewall service, and without interrupting any existing connections to your server.

Verifying the status of firewalld

Let's start by verifying the status of firewalld. There are two ways to do this. We can use the `--state` option of `firewall-cmd`:

```
[donnie@localhost ~]$ sudo firewall-cmd --state
running
[donnie@localhost ~]$
```

Or, if we want a more detailed status, we can just check the daemon, the same as we would any other daemon on a systemd machine:

```
[donnie@localhost ~]$ sudo systemctl status firewalld
● firewalld.service - firewalld - dynamic firewall daemon
   Loaded: loaded (/usr/lib/systemd/system/firewalld.service; enabled;
vendor preset: enabled)
   Active: active (running) since Fri 2017-10-13 13:42:54 EDT; 1h 56min ago
     Docs: man:firewalld(1)
 Main PID: 631 (firewalld)
   CGroup: /system.slice/firewalld.service
           └─631 /usr/bin/python -Es /usr/sbin/firewalld --nofork --nopid

Oct 13 13:42:55 localhost.localdomain firewalld[631]: WARNING: ICMP type
'reject-route' is not supported by the kernel for ipv6.
Oct 13 13:42:55 localhost.localdomain firewalld[631]: WARNING: reject-
route: INVALID_ICMPTYPE: No supported ICMP type., ignoring for run-time.
Oct 13 15:19:41 localhost.localdomain firewalld[631]: WARNING: ICMP type
'beyond-scope' is not supported by the kernel for ipv6.
Oct 13 15:19:41 localhost.localdomain firewalld[631]: WARNING: beyond-
scope: INVALID_ICMPTYPE: No supported ICMP type., ignoring for run-time.
Oct 13 15:19:41 localhost.localdomain firewalld[631]: WARNING: ICMP type
'failed-policy' is not supported by the kernel for ipv6.
Oct 13 15:19:41 localhost.localdomain firewalld[631]: WARNING: failed-
policy: INVALID_ICMPTYPE: No supported ICMP type., ignoring for run-time.
Oct 13 15:19:41 localhost.localdomain firewalld[631]: WARNING: ICMP type
```

```
'reject-route' is not supported by the kernel for ipv6.
Oct 13 15:19:41 localhost.localdomain firewalld[631]: WARNING: reject-
route: INVALID_ICMPTYPE: No supported ICMP type., ignoring for run-time.
[donnie@localhost ~]$
```

firewalld zones

firewalld is a rather unique animal, in that it comes with several preconfigured zones and services. If you look in the /usr/lib/firewalld/zones directory of your CentOS machine, you'll see the zones files, all in .xml format:

```
[donnie@localhost ~]$ cd /usr/lib/firewalld/zones
[donnie@localhost zones]$ ls
block.xml dmz.xml drop.xml external.xml home.xml internal.xml public.xml
trusted.xml work.xml
[donnie@localhost zones]$
```

Each zone file specifies which ports are to be open, and which ones are to be blocked for various given scenarios. Zones can also contain rules for ICMP messages, forwarded ports, masquerading information, and rich language rules.

For example, the .xml file for the public zone, which is set as the default, looks like this:

```
<?xml version="1.0" encoding="utf-8"?>
<zone>
  <short>Public</short>
  <description>For use in public areas. You do not trust the other
computers on networks to not harm your computer. Only selected incoming
connections are accepted.</description>
  <service name="ssh"/>
  <service name="dhcpv6-client"/>
</zone>
```

In the service name lines, you can see that the only open ports are for Secure Shell access and for DHCPv6 discovery. Look at the home.xml file, and you'll see that it also opens the ports for Multicast DNS, and the ports that allow this machine to access shared directories from either Samba servers or Windows servers:

```
<?xml version="1.0" encoding="utf-8"?>
<zone>
  <short>Home</short>
  <description>For use in home areas. You mostly trust the other computers
on networks to not harm your computer. Only selected incoming connections
are accepted.</description>
  <service name="ssh"/>
```

```
<service name="mdns"/>
<service name="samba-client"/>
<service name="dhcpv6-client"/>
</zone>
```

The `firewall-cmd` utility is what you would use to configure firewalld. You can use it to view the list of zone files on your system, without having to `cd` into the zone file directory:

```
[donnie@localhost ~]$ sudo firewall-cmd --get-zones
[sudo] password for donnie:
block dmz drop external home internal public trusted work
[donnie@localhost ~]$
```

A quick way to see how each zone is configured is to use the `--list-all-zones` option:

```
[donnie@localhost ~]$ sudo firewall-cmd --list-all-zones
block
   target: %%REJECT%%
   icmp-block-inversion: no
   interfaces:
   sources:
   services:
   ports:
   protocols:
   masquerade: no
   forward-ports:
   source-ports:
   icmp-blocks:
   rich rules:
  ' ' '
  ' ' '
```

Of course, this is only a portion of the output, because the listing for all zones is more than we can display here. More likely, you'll just want to see information about one particular zone:

```
[donnie@localhost ~]$ sudo firewall-cmd --info-zone=internal
internal
   target: default
   icmp-block-inversion: no
   interfaces:
   sources:
   services: ssh mdns samba-client dhcpv6-client
   ports:
   protocols:
   masquerade: no
   forward-ports:
```

```
    source-ports:
    icmp-blocks:
    rich rules:

[donnie@localhost ~]$
```

So, the `internal` zone allows the `ssh`, `mdns`, `samba-client`, and `dhcpv6-client` services. This would be handy for setting up client machines on your internal LAN.

Any given server or client will have one or more installed network interface adapter. Each adapter in a machine can be assigned one, and only one, firewalld zone. To see the default zone:

```
[donnie@localhost ~]$ sudo firewall-cmd --get-default-zone
public
[donnie@localhost ~]$
```

That's great, except that it doesn't tell you anything about which network interface is associated with this zone. To see that information:

```
[donnie@localhost ~]$ sudo firewall-cmd --get-active-zones
public
   interfaces: enp0s3
[donnie@localhost ~]$
```

When you first install Red Hat or CentOS, the firewall will already be active with the public zone as the default. Now, let's say that you're setting up your server in the DMZ, and you want to make sure that its firewall is locked down for that. You can change the default zone to the `dmz` zone. Let's take a look at the `dmz.xml` file to see what that does for us:

```
<?xml version="1.0" encoding="utf-8"?>
<zone>
  <short>DMZ</short>
  <description>For computers in your demilitarized zone that are publicly-
accessible with limited access to your internal network. Only selected
incoming connections are accepted.</description>
  <service name="ssh"/>
</zone>
```

So, the only thing that the DMZ allows through is the Secure Shell. Okay, that's good enough for now, so let's set the `dmz` zone as the default:

```
[donnie@localhost ~]$ sudo firewall-cmd --set-default-zone=dmz
[sudo] password for donnie:
success
[donnie@localhost ~]$
```

We'll verify:

```
[donnie@localhost ~]$ sudo firewall-cmd --get-default-zone
dmz
[donnie@localhost ~]$
```

And we're all good. Except, that is, that an internet-facing server in the DMZ probably needs to do more than just allow SSH connections. This is where we'll use the firewalld services. But, before we look at that, let's consider one more important point.

You never want to modify the files in the /usr/lib/firewalld directory. Whenever you modify the firewalld configuration, you'll see the modified files show up in the /etc/firewalld directory. So far, all we've modified is the default zone. So, we'll see this in /etc/firewalld:

```
[donnie@localhost ~]$ sudo ls -l /etc/firewalld
total 12
-rw-------. 1 root root 2003 Oct 11 17:37 firewalld.conf
-rw-r--r--. 1 root root 2006 Aug 4 17:14 firewalld.conf.old
. . .
```

We can do a diff on those two files to see the difference between them:

```
[donnie@localhost ~]$ sudo diff /etc/firewalld/firewalld.conf
/etc/firewalld/firewalld.conf.old
6c6
< DefaultZone=dmz
---
> DefaultZone=public
[donnie@localhost ~]$
```

So, the newer of the two files shows that the dmz zone is now the default.

To get more information about firewalld zones, enter:

man firewalld.zones

firewalld services

Each service file contains a list of ports that need to be opened for a particular service. Optionally, the service files may contain one or more destination addresses, or call in any needed modules, such as for connection tracking. For some services, all you need to do is to open just one port. Other services, such as the Samba service, require that multiple ports be opened. Either way, it's sometimes handier to remember the service name, rather than the port numbers, that goes with each service.

The services files are in the `/usr/lib/firewalld/services` directory. You can look at the list of them with the `firewall-cmd` command, just as you could do with the list of zones:

```
[donnie@localhost ~]$ sudo firewall-cmd --get-services
[sudo] password for donnie:
RH-Satellite-6 amanda-client amanda-k5-client bacula bacula-client bitcoin
bitcoin-rpc bitcoin-testnet bitcoin-testnet-rpc ceph ceph-mon cfengine
condor-collector ctdb dhcp dhcpv6 dhcpv6-client dns docker-registry
dropbox-lansync elasticsearch freeipa-ldap freeipa-ldaps freeipa-
replication freeipa-trust ftp ganglia-client ganglia-master high-
availability http https imap imaps ipp ipp-client ipsec iscsi-target kadmin
kerberos kibana klogin kpasswd kshell ldap ldaps libvirt libvirt-tls
managesieve mdns mosh mountd ms-wbt mssql mysql nfs nrpe ntp openvpn ovirt-
imageio ovirt-storageconsole ovirt-vmconsole pmcd pmproxy pmwebapi
pmwebapis pop3 pop3s postgresql privoxy proxy-dhcp ptp pulseaudio
puppetmaster quassel radius rpc-bind rsh rsyncd samba samba-client sane sip
sips smtp smtp-submission smtps snmp snmptrap spideroak-lansync squid ssh
synergy syslog syslog-tls telnet tftp tftp-client tinc tor-socks
transmission-client vdsm vnc-server wbem-https xmpp-bosh xmpp-client xmpp-
local xmpp-server
[donnie@localhost ~]$
```

The `dropbox-lansync` service would be very handy for us Dropbox users. Let's see which ports this opens:

```
[donnie@localhost ~]$ sudo firewall-cmd --info-service=dropbox-lansync
[sudo] password for donnie:
dropbox-lansync
  ports: 17500/udp 17500/tcp
  protocols:
  source-ports:
  modules:
  destination:
[donnie@localhost ~]$
```

It looks like Dropbox uses ports 17500 UDP and TCP.

Now, let's say that we have our web server set up in the DMZ, with the dmz zone set as its default:

```
[donnie@localhost ~]$ sudo firewall-cmd --info-zone=dmz
dmz (active)
  target: default
  icmp-block-inversion: no
  interfaces: enp0s3
  sources:
  services: ssh
  ports:
  protocols:
  masquerade: no
  forward-ports:
  source-ports:
  icmp-blocks:
  rich rules:

[donnie@localhost ~]$
```

As we saw before, the Secure Shell port is the only one that's open. Let's fix that so that users can actually access our website:

```
[donnie@localhost ~]$ sudo firewall-cmd --add-service=http
success
[donnie@localhost ~]$
```

When we look at the info for the dmz zone again, we'll see:

```
[donnie@localhost ~]$ sudo firewall-cmd --info-zone=dmz
dmz (active)
  target: default
  icmp-block-inversion: no
  interfaces: enp0s3
  sources:
  services: ssh http
  ports:
  protocols:
  masquerade: no
  forward-ports:
  source-ports:
  icmp-blocks:
  rich rules:

[donnie@localhost ~]$
```

We see that the http service is now allowed through. But look what happens when we add the --permanent option to this info command:

```
[donnie@localhost ~]$ sudo firewall-cmd --permanent --info-zone=dmz
dmz
  target: default
  icmp-block-inversion: no
  interfaces:
  sources:
  services: ssh
  ports:
  protocols:
  masquerade: no
  forward-ports:
  source-ports:
  icmp-blocks:
  rich rules:
[donnie@localhost ~]$
```

Oops! The http service isn't here. What's going on?

For pretty much every command-line alteration of either zones or services, you need to add the --permanent option to make the change persistent across reboots. But, without that --permanent option, the change takes effect immediately. With the --permanent option, you'll have to reload the firewall configuration in order for the change to take effect. To demo, I'm going to reboot the virtual machine to get rid of the http service.

Okay, I've rebooted, and the http service is now gone:

```
[donnie@localhost ~]$ sudo firewall-cmd --info-zone=dmz
[sudo] password for donnie:
dmz (active)
  target: default
  icmp-block-inversion: no
  interfaces: enp0s3
  sources:
  services: ssh
  ports:
  protocols:
  masquerade: no
  forward-ports:
  source-ports:
  icmp-blocks:
  rich rules:

[donnie@localhost ~]$
```

This time, I'll add two services with just one command, and specify for the change to be permanent:

```
[donnie@localhost ~]$ sudo firewall-cmd --permanent --add-
service={http,https}
[sudo] password for donnie:
success
[donnie@localhost ~]$
```

You can add as many services as you need to with a single command, but you have to separate them with commas and enclose the whole list within a pair of curly brackets. Let's look at the results:

```
[donnie@localhost ~]$ sudo firewall-cmd --info-zone=dmz
dmz (active)
  target: default
  icmp-block-inversion: no
  interfaces: enp0s3
  sources:
  services: ssh
  ports:
  protocols:
  masquerade: no
  forward-ports:
  source-ports:
  icmp-blocks:
  rich rules:

[donnie@localhost ~]$
```

Since we decided to make this configuration permanent, it hasn't yet taken effect. But, if we add the `--permanent` option to this `--info-zone` command, we'll see that the configuration files have indeed been changed:

```
[donnie@localhost ~]$ sudo firewall-cmd --permanent --info-zone=dmz
dmz
  target: default
  icmp-block-inversion: no
  interfaces:
  sources:
  services: ssh http https
  ports:
  protocols:
  masquerade: no
  forward-ports:
  source-ports:
  icmp-blocks:
```

```
    rich rules:

[donnie@localhost ~]$
```

We now need to make that change take effect by reloading the configuration:

```
[donnie@localhost ~]$ sudo firewall-cmd --reload
success
[donnie@localhost ~]$
```

Run the `sudo firewall-cmd --info-zone=dmz` command again, and you'll see that the new configuration is now in effect.

To remove a service from a zone, just replace `--add-service` with `--remove-service`.

 Note that we never specified which zone we're working with in any of these service commands. That's because if we don't specify a zone, firewalld just assumes that we're working with the default zone. If you want to add a service to something other than the default zone, just add a `--zone=` option to your commands.

Adding ports to a firewalld zone

Having the service files is handy, except that not every service that you'll need to run has its own predefined service file. Let's say that you've installed Webmin on your server, which requires port `10000/tcp` to be open. A quick `grep` operation will show that port `10000` isn't in any of our predefined services:

```
donnie@localhost services]$ pwd
/usr/lib/firewalld/services
[donnie@localhost services]$ grep '10000' *
[donnie@localhost services]$
```

So, let's just add that port to our default zone, which is still the dmz zone:

```
donnie@localhost ~]$ sudo firewall-cmd --add-port=10000/tcp
[sudo] password for donnie:
success
[donnie@localhost ~]$
```

Again, this isn't permanent, because we didn't include the `--permanent` option. Let's do it again and then reload:

```
[donnie@localhost ~]$ sudo firewall-cmd --permanent --add-port=10000/tcp
success
[donnie@localhost ~]$ sudo firewall-cmd --reload
success
[donnie@localhost ~]$
```

You can also add multiple ports at once by enclosing the comma-separated list within a pair of curly brackets, just as we did with the services (yeah, I purposely left the `--permanent` out):

```
[donnie@localhost ~]$ sudo firewall-cmd --add-
port={636/tcp,637/tcp,638/udp}
success
[donnie@localhost ~]$
```

And of course, you can remove ports from a zone by substituting `--remove-port` for `--add-port`.

firewalld rich language rules

What we've looked at so far might be all you'll ever need for general use scenarios, but for more granular control, you'll want to know about **rich language rules**. (Yes, that really is what they're called.)

Compared to iptables rules, rich language rules are a bit less cryptic, and are closer to plain English. So, if you're new to the business of writing firewall rules, you might find rich language a bit easier to learn. On the other hand, if you're already used to writing iptables rules, you might find some elements of rich language a bit quirky. Let's look at one example:

```
sudo firewall-cmd --add-rich-rule='rule family="ipv4" source
address="200.192.0.0/24" service name="http" drop'
```

So, we're adding a rich rule. Note that the entire rule is surrounded by a pair of single quotes, and the assigned value for each parameter is surrounded by a pair of double quotes. With this rule, we're saying that we're working with IPv4, and that we want to silently block the `http` port from accepting packets from the `200.192.0.0/24` network. We didn't use the `--permanent` option, so this rule will disappear when we reboot the machine. Let's see what our zone looks like with this new rule:

```
[donnie@localhost ~]$ sudo firewall-cmd --info-zone=dmz
[sudo] password for donnie:
dmz (active)
  target: default
  icmp-block-inversion: no
  interfaces: enp0s3
  sources:
  services: ssh http https
  ports: 10000/tcp 636/tcp 637/tcp 638/udp
  protocols:
  masquerade: no
  forward-ports:
  source-ports:
  icmp-blocks:
  rich rules:
    rule family="ipv4" source address="200.192.0.0/24" service name="http"
drop
[donnie@localhost ~]$
```

The rich rule shows up at the bottom. After we've tested this rule to make sure that it does what we need it to do, we'll make it permanent:

```
sudo firewall-cmd --permanent --add-rich-rule='rule family="ipv4" source
address="200.192.0.0/24" service name="http" drop'

sudo firewall-cmd --reload
```

You could just as easily write a rule for IPv6 by replacing `family="ipv4"` with `family="ipv6"`, and supplying the appropriate IPv6 address range.

Some rules are generic, and apply to either IPv4 or IPv6. Let's say that we want to log messages about **Network Time Protocol** (**NTP**) packets, and you want to log no more than one message per minute. The command to create that rule would look like this:

```
sudo firewall-cmd --permanent --add-rich-rule='rule service name="ntp"
audit limit value="1/m" accept'
```

There is, of course, a lot more to firewalld rich language rules than we can present here. But, you at least now know the basics. For more information, consult the man page:

```
man firewalld.richlanguage
```

Hands-on lab for firewalld commands

With this lab, you'll get some practice with basic firewalld commands:

1. Log into your CentOS 7 virtual machine and run the following commands. Observe the output after each one:

```
sudo firewall-cmd --get-zones
sudo firewall-cmd --get-default-zone
sudo firewall-cmd --get-active-zones
```

2. Briefly view the man pages that deal with firewalld zones:

```
man firewalld.zones
man firewalld.zone
```

(Yes, there are two of them. One explains the zone configuration files, and the other explains the zones themselves.)

3. Look at the configuration information for all of the available zones:

```
sudo firewall-cmd --list-all-zones
```

4. Look at the list of predefined services. Then, look at information about the dropbox-lansync service:

```
sudo firewall-cmd --get-services
sudo firewall-cmd --info-service=dropbox-lansync
```

5. Set the default zone to dmz. Look at information about the zone, add the http and https services, and then look at the zone information again:

```
sudo firewall-cmd --set-default-zone=dmz
sudo firewall-cmd --permanent --add-service={http,https}
sudo firewall-cmd --info-zone=dmz
sudo firewall-cmd --permanent --info-zone=dmz
```

6. Reload the firewall configuration, and look at zone info again. Also, look at the list of services that are being allowed:

```
sudo firewall-cmd --reload
sudo firewall-cmd --info-zone=dmz
sudo firewall-cmd --list-services
```

7. Permanently open port `10000/tcp`, and view the results:

```
sudo firewall-cmd --permanent --add-port=10000/tcp
sudo firewall-cmd --list-ports
sudo firewall-cmd --reload
sudo firewall-cmd --list-ports
sudo firewall-cmd --info-zone=dmz
```

8. Remove the port that you just added:

```
sudo firewall-cmd --permanent --remove-port=10000/tcp
sudo firewall-cmd --reload
sudo firewall-cmd --list-ports
sudo firewall-cmd --info-zone=dmz
```

9. View the list of main pages for firewalld:

```
apropos firewall
```

10. End of lab.

nftables – a more universal type of firewall system

Let's now turn our attention to nftables, the new kid on the block. So, what does nftables bring to the table? (Yes, the pun was intended.):

- You can now forget about needing separate daemons and utilities for all of the different networking components. The functionality of iptables, ip6tables, ebtables, and arptables is now all combined in one neat package. The nft utility is now the only firewall utility that you'll need.
- With nftables, you can create multidimensional trees to display your rulesets. This makes troubleshooting vastly easier, because it's now easier to trace a packet all the way through all of the rules.
- With iptables, you have the filter, NAT, mangle, and security tables installed by default, whether or not you use each one. With nftables, you only create the tables that you intend to use, resulting in enhanced performance.
- Unlike iptables, you can specify multiple actions in one rule, instead of having to create multiple rules for each action.

- Unlike iptables, new rules get added atomically. (That's a fancy way of saying that there's no longer a need to reload the entire ruleset in order to just add one rule.)
- nftables has its own built-in scripting engine, allowing you to write scripts that are more efficient and more human-readable.
- If you already have lots of iptables scripts that you still need to use, you can install a set of utilities that will help you convert them to nftables format.

nftables tables and chains

If you're used to iptables, you might recognize some of the nftables terminology. The only problem is, some of the terms are used in different ways, with different meanings. Here's some of what I'm talking about:

- **Tables**: Tables in nftables refer to a particular protocol family. The table types are ip, ip6, inet, arp, bridge, and netdev.
- **Chains**: Chains in nftables roughly equate to tables in iptables. For example, in nftables you could have filter, route, or NAT chains.

Getting started with nftables

Let's start with a clean snapshot of our Ubuntu virtual machine, and install the nftables package.

 The command-line utility for nftables is `nft`. You can either do `nft` commands from the Bash shell, or you can do `sudo nft -i` to run nft in interactive mode. For our present demos, we'll just run the commands from the Bash shell.

Now, let's take a look at the list of installed tables:

```
sudo apt install nftables
sudo nft list tables
```

Hmmm... You didn't see any tables, did you? So, let's load some up.

If you look at the `nftables.conf` file in the `/etc` directory, you'll see the beginnings of a basic nft firewall configuration:

```
#!/usr/sbin/nft -f
flush ruleset
table inet filter {
        chain input {
                type filter hook input priority 0;

                # accept any localhost traffic
                iif lo accept

                # accept traffic originated from us
                ct state established,related accept

                # activate the following line to accept
                  common local services
                # tcp dport { 22, 80, 443 } ct state new accept

                # accept neighbour discovery otherwise
                  IPv6 connectivity breaks.
                ip6 nexthdr icmpv6 icmpv6 type { nd-neighbor-solicit,
                  nd-router-advert, nd-neighbor-advert } accept

                # count and drop any other traffic
                counter drop
        }
}
```

Here's the breakdown of what all this means:

- `#!/usr/sbin/nft -f`: Although you can create normal Bash shell scripts with nftables commands, it's better to use the built-in scripting engine that's included with nftables. That way, we can make our scripts more human-readable, and we don't have to type `nft` in front of everything we want to do.
- `flush ruleset`: We want to start with a clean slate, so we'll flush out any rules that may have already been loaded.
- `table inet filter`: This creates an inet family filter, which works for both IPv4 and IPv6. The name of this table is `filter`, but it could just as well have been something a bit more descriptive.
- `chain input`: Within the first pair of curly brackets, we have a chain with the name of `input`. (Again, the name could have been something more descriptive.)

- `type filter hook input priority 0;`: Within the next pair of curly brackets, we define our chain and then list the rules. This chain is defined as a `filter` type. `hook input` indicates that this chain is meant to process incoming packets. Because this chain has both a `hook` and a `priority`, it will accept packets directly from the network stack.
- Finally, we have the standard rules for a very basic host firewall, starting with the `iif` rule that allows the loopback interface to accept packets (**iif** stands for **input interface**.)
- Next is the standard connection tracking (`ct`) rule, which accepts traffic that's in response to a connection request from this host.
- Then, there's a commented-out rule to accept Secure Shell and both secure and nonsecure web traffic. The `ct state new` indicates that the firewall will allow other hosts to initiate connections to our server on these ports.
- The `ipv6` rule accepts neighbor discovery packets, allowing for IPv6 functionality.
- The `counter drop` rule at the end silently blocks all other traffic, and counts both the number of packets and the number of bytes that it blocks. (This is an example of how you can have one rule perform two different actions.)

If all you need on your Ubuntu server is a basic, no-frills firewall, your best bet is to just edit this `/etc/nftables.conf` file to suit your own needs. For starters, let's remove the comment symbol from in front of the `tcp dport` line, and get rid of ports `80` and `443`. The line should now look like:

```
tcp dport 22 ct state new accept
```

Note that when you're only opening one port, you don't need to enclose that port number within curly brackets. When opening multiple ports, just include the comma-separated list within curly brackets, with a blank space before the first element and after the last element.

Load the configuration file, and view the results:

```
sudo nft -f /etc/nftables.conf

donnie@ubuntu2:~$ sudo nft list table inet filter
table inet filter {
  chain input {
    type filter hook input priority 0; policy accept;
    iif lo accept
    ct state established,related accept
    tcp dport ssh ct state new accept
    ip6 nexthdr ipv6-icmp icmpv6 type { nd-router-advert, nd-neighbor-
```

```
solicit, nd-neighbor-advert} accept
   counter packets 67 bytes 10490 drop
 }
}
donnie@ubuntu2:~$
```

Now, let's say that we want to block certain IP addresses from reaching the Secure Shell port of this machine. We can edit the file, placing a drop rule above the rule that opens port 22. The relevant section of the file would look like this:

```
tcp dport 22 ip saddr { 192.168.0.7, 192.168.0.10 } drop
tcp dport 22 ct state new accept
```

After we reload the file, we'll be blocking SSH access from two different IPv4 addresses. Note that we've placed the drop rule ahead of the accept rule, because if the accept rule gets read first, the drop rule will never have any effect.

Another really cool thing to note is how we've mixed IPv4 (ip) rules with IPv6 (ip6) rules in the same configuration file. That's the beauty of using an inet-type table. For simplicity and flexibility, you'll want to use inet tables as much as possible, rather than separate ip and ip6 tables.

Most of the time, when all you need is just a simple host firewall, your best bet would be to just use this nftables.conf file as your starting point, and edit the file to suit your own needs. However, there's also a command-line component that you may at times find useful.

Using nft commands

There are two ways to use the nft utility. You can just do everything directly from the Bash shell, prefacing every action you want to perform with nft, followed by the nft subcommands. You can also use nft in interactive mode. For our present purposes, we'll just go with the Bash shell.

Let's first delete our previous configuration, and create an inet table, since we want something that works for both IPv4 and IPv6. We'll want to give it a somewhat descriptive name, so let's call it ubuntu_filter:

```
sudo nft delete table inet filter
sudo nft list tables
sudo nft add table inet ubuntu_filter
sudo nft list tables
```

Next, we'll add an `input` filter chain to the table that we just created. (Note that since we're doing this from the Bash shell, we need to escape the semi-colon with a backslash.)

```
sudo nft add chain inet ubuntu_filter input { type filter hook input
priority 0\; policy drop\; }
```

In this command, the first `input` after the `ubuntu_filter` is the name of the chain. (We could have given it a more descriptive name, but for now, `input` works.) Within the pair of curly brackets, we're setting the parameters for this chain.

Each nftables protocol family has its own set of hooks, which define how packets will be processed. For now, we're only concerned with the ip/ip6/inet families, which have these hooks:

- Prerouting
- Input
- Forward
- Output
- Postrouting

Of these, we're presently only concerned with the input and output hooks, which would apply to filter-type chains. By specifying a hook and a priority for our input chain, we're saying that we want this chain to be a base chain, which will accept packets directly from the network stack. You also see that certain parameters must be terminated by a semicolon, which in turn would need to be escaped with a backslash if you're running the commands from the Bash shell. Finally, we're specifying a default policy of `drop`. If we had not specified `drop` as the default policy, then the policy would have been `accept` by default.

Every `nft` command that you enter takes effect immediately. So, if you're doing this remotely, you'll drop your Secure Shell connection as soon as you create a filter chain with a default `drop` policy.

Some people like to create chains with a default `accept` policy, and then add a `drop` rule as the final rule. Other people like to create chains with a default `drop` policy, and then leave off the drop rule at the end. The advantage of using a default `accept` rule is that you would be able to perform these firewall commands remotely, without having to worry about locking yourself out.

Verify that the chain has been added, and you should see something like this:

```
donnie@ubuntu2:~$ sudo nft list table inet ubuntu_filter
[sudo] password for donnie:
table inet filter {
    chain input {
        type filter hook input priority 0; policy drop;
    }
}
donnie@ubuntu2:~$
```

That's great, but we still need some rules. Let's start with a connection tracking rule and a rule to open the Secure Shell port. We'll then verify that they got added:

```
sudo nft add rule inet ubuntu_filter input ct state established accept
sudo nft add rule inet ubuntu_filter input tcp dport 22 ct state new accept

donnie@ubuntu2:~$ sudo nft list table inet ubuntu_filter
table inet ubuntu_filter {
  chain input {
    type filter hook input priority 0; policy drop;
    ct state established accept
    tcp dport ssh ct state new accept
  }
}
donnie@ubuntu2:~
```

Okay, that looks good. You now have a basic, working firewall that allows Secure Shell connections. Well, except that just as we did in the ufw chapter, we forgot to create a rule to allow the loopback adapter to accept packets. Since we want this rule to be at the top of the rules list, we'll use insert instead of add:

```
sudo nft insert rule inet ubuntu_filter input iif lo accept

donnie@ubuntu2:~$ sudo nft list table inet ubuntu_filter
table inet ubuntu_filter {
    chain input {
        type filter hook input priority 0; policy drop;
        iif lo accept
        ct state established accept
        tcp dport ssh ct state new accept
    }
}
donnie@ubuntu2:~$
```

Now, we're all set. But what if we want to insert a rule in a specific location? For that, you'll need to use `list` with the `-a` option to see the `handles` rule:

```
donnie@ubuntu2:~$ sudo nft list table inet ubuntu_filter -a
table inet ubuntu_filter {
    chain input {
        type filter hook input priority 0; policy drop;
        iif lo accept # handle 4
        ct state established accept # handle 2
        tcp dport ssh ct state new accept # handle 3
    }
}
donnie@ubuntu2:~$
```

As you can see, there's no real rhyme or reason to the way the handles are numbered. Let's say that we want to insert the rule about blocking certain IP addresses from accessing the Secure Shell port. We see that the `ssh accept` rule is `handle 3`, so we'll need to insert our `drop` rule before it. Our command to do that would look like this:

```
sudo nft insert rule inet ubuntu_filter input position 3 tcp dport 22 ip
saddr { 192.168.0.7, 192.168.0.10 } drop

donnie@ubuntu2:~$ sudo nft list table inet ubuntu_filter -a
table inet ubuntu_filter {
    chain input {
        type filter hook input priority 0; policy drop;
        iif lo accept # handle 4
        ct state established accept # handle 2
        tcp dport ssh ip saddr { 192.168.0.10, 192.168.0.7} drop # handle 6
        tcp dport ssh ct state new accept # handle 3
    }
}
donnie@ubuntu2:~$
```

So, to place the rule before the rule with the `handle 3` label, we have to `insert` to `position 3`. The new rule that we just inserted has the label `handle 6`. To delete a rule, we'll specify the rule's handle number:

```
sudo nft delete rule inet ubuntu_filter input handle 6


donnie@ubuntu2:~$ sudo nft list table inet ubuntu_filter -a
table inet ubuntu_filter {
    chain input {
        type filter hook input priority 0; policy drop;
        iif lo accept # handle 4
        ct state established accept # handle 2
```

```
                    tcp dport ssh ct state new accept # handle 3
        }
}
donnie@ubuntu2:~$
```

As is the case with iptables, everything you do from the command line will disappear once you reboot the machine. To make it permanent, let's redirect the output of the `list` subcommand into a configuration file (of course, we'll want to give the file a unique name that's different from the name of our default file):

```
sudo sh -c "nft list table inet ubuntu_filter > new_nftables.conf"
```

Due to a quirk in the Bash shell, we can't just redirect output to a file in the /etc directory in the normal manner, even when we use `sudo`. That's why I had to add the `sh -c` command, with the `nft list` command surrounded by double quotes. Now, when we look at the file, we'll see that there are a couple of things that are missing:

```
table inet ubuntu_filter {
        chain input {
                type filter hook input priority 0; policy drop;
                iif lo accept
                ct state established accept
                tcp dport ssh ct state new accept
        }
}
```

You sharp-eyed folk will see that we're missing the `flush` rule, and the `shebang` line to specify the shell that we want to interpret this script. Let's add them in:

```
#!/usr/sbin/nft -f
flush ruleset

table inet ubuntu_filter {
        chain input {
                type filter hook input priority 0; policy drop;
                iif lo accept
                ct state established accept
                tcp dport ssh ct state new accept
        }
}
```

Much better. Let's test it by loading the new configuration and observing the `list` output:

```
sudo nft -f /etc/new_nftables.conf

donnie@ubuntu2:~$ sudo nft list table inet ubuntu_filter
table inet ubuntu_filter {
```

```
      chain input {
        type filter hook input priority 0; policy drop;
        iif lo accept
        ct state established accept
        tcp dport ssh ct state new accept
      }
    }
donnie@ubuntu2:~$
```

That's all there is to creating your own simple host firewall. Of course, running commands from the command line, rather than just creating a script file in your text editor, does make for a lot more typing. But, it does allow you to test your rules on the fly, as you create them. And, creating your configuration in this manner and then redirecting the list output to your new configuration file relieves you of the burden of having to keep track of all of those curly brackets.

It's also possible to take all of the nft commands that we just did, and place them into a regular, old-fashioned Bash shell script. Trust me, though, you really don't want to do that. Just use the nft-native scripting format as we've done here, and you'll have a script that performs better, and that is much more human-readable.

Hands-on lab for nftables on Ubuntu

For this lab, you need a clean snapshot of your Ubuntu virtual machine:

1. Restore your Ubuntu virtual machine to a clean snapshot to clear out any firewall configurations that you created previously. Verify with the commands:

    ```
    sudo ufw status
    sudo iptables -L
    ```

    You should see no rules listed for iptables, and the ufw status should be inactive.

2. Install the nftables package:

    ```
    sudo apt install nftables
    ```

3. List the tables, which should give you no output. Load the default configuration file, and list both the tables and the rules:

    ```
    sudo nft list tables
    sudo nft -f /etc/nftables.conf
    ```

```
sudo nft list tables
sudo nft list table inet filter
```

4. Make a backup copy of the nftables configuration file:

```
sudo cp /etc/nftables.conf /etc/nftables.conf.bak
```

5. Open the original /etc/nftables.conf file in your text editor. Just before the
   tcp dport . . . accept line, insert this line:

```
tcp dport ssh ip saddr { 192.168.0.7, 192.168.0.10 } drop
```

Save the file and exit the text editor.

6. Reload the configuration and view the results:

```
sudo nft list tables
sudo nft -f /etc/nftables.conf
sudo nft list tables
sudo nft list table inet filter
```

7. End of lab.

Summary

In this chapter, we've looked at four different frontends for the netfilter firewall. We first
looked at our trusty old friend, iptables. We saw that even though it's been around forever
and still works, it does have some shortcomings. We then saw how Ubuntu's
Uncomplicated Firewall can vastly simplify setting up an iptables-based firewall. For you
Red Hatters, we looked at firewalld, which is specific to Red Hat-type distros. Finally, we
wrapped things up by looking at the latest in Linux firewall technology, nftables.

In the space allotted, I've only been able to present the bare essentials that you need to set
up basic host protection. But, it is at least enough to get you started.

4
Encrypting and SSH Hardening

You may work for a super-secret government agency, or you may be just a regular Joe or Jane citizen. Either way, you will still have sensitive data that you need to protect from prying eyes. Business secrets, government secrets, personal secrets—it doesn't matter; it all needs protection. Locking down user's home directories with restrictive permissions settings, as we saw in Chapter 2, *Securing User Accounts,* is only part of the puzzle; we also need encryption.

The two general types of data encryption that we'll look at in this chapter are meant to protect *data at rest* and *data in transit.* We'll begin with using file, partition, and directory encryption to protect data at rest. We'll then cover **Secure Shell** (**SSH**) to protect data in transit.

In this chapter, we'll cover:

- **GNU Privacy Guard** (**GPG**)
- Encrypting partitions with **Linux Unified Key Setup** (**LUKS**)
- Encrypting directories with eCryptfs
- Using VeraCrypt for the cross-platform sharing of encrypted containers
- Ensuring that SSH protocol 1 is disabled
- Creating and managing keys for password-less logins
- Disabling root user login
- Disabling username/password logins
- Setting up a chroot environment for SFTP users

GNU Privacy Guard

We'll begin with **GNU Privacy Guard** (**GPG**). This is a free open source implementation of Phil Zimmermann's *Pretty Good Privacy*, which he created back in 1991. You can use either one of them to either encrypt or cryptographically sign files or messages. In this section, we'll focus strictly on GPG.

There are some advantages of using GPG:

- It uses strong, hard-to-crack encryption algorithms.
- It uses the private/public key scheme, which eliminates the need to transfer a password to a message or file recipient in a secure manner. Instead, just send along your public key, which is useless to anyone other than the intended recipient.
- You can use GPG to just encrypt your own files for your own use, the same as you'd use any other encryption utility.
- It can be used to encrypt email messages, allowing you to have true end-to-end encryption for sensitive emails.
- There are a few GUI-type frontends available to make it somewhat easier to use.

But, as you might know, there are also some disadvantages:

- Using public keys instead of passwords is great when you work directly only with people who you implicitly trust. But, for anything beyond that, such as distributing a public key to the general population so that everyone can verify your signed messages, you're dependent upon a web-of-trust model that can be very hard to set up.
- For the end-to-end encryption of email, the recipients of your email must also have GPG set up on their systems, and know how to use it. That might work in a corporate environment, but lots of luck getting your friends to set that up. (I've never once succeeded in getting someone else to set up email encryption.)
- If you use a standalone email client, such as Mozilla Thunderbird, you can install a plugin that will encrypt and decrypt messages automatically. But, every time a new Thunderbird update is released, the plugin breaks, and it always takes a while before a new working version gets released.

Even with its numerous weaknesses, GPG is still one of the best ways to share encrypted files and emails. GPG comes preinstalled on both Ubuntu Server and CentOS. So, you can use either of your virtual machines for these demos.

Creating your GPG keys

Getting started with GPG requires you to first generate your GPG keys. You'll do that with:

```
gpg --gen-key
```

 Note that, since you're setting this up for yourself, you don't need sudo privileges.

The output of this command is too long to show all at once, so I'll show relevant sections of it, and break down what it means.

The first thing that this command does is to create a populated .gnupg directory in your home directory:

```
gpg: directory `/home/donnie/.gnupg' created
gpg: new configuration file `/home/donnie/.gnupg/gpg.conf' created
gpg: WARNING: options in `/home/donnie/.gnupg/gpg.conf' are not yet active
during this run
gpg: keyring `/home/donnie/.gnupg/secring.gpg' created
gpg: keyring `/home/donnie/.gnupg/pubring.gpg' created
```

You'll then be asked to select which kinds of keys you want. We'll just go with the default RSA and RSA. (RSA keys are stronger and harder to crack than the older DSA keys. Elgamal keys are good, but they may not be supported by older versions of GPG.):

```
Please select what kind of key you want:
    (1) RSA and RSA (default)
    (2) DSA and Elgamal
    (3) DSA (sign only)
    (4) RSA (sign only)
Your selection?
```

For decent encryption, you'll want to go with a key of at least 2048 bits, because anything smaller is now considered vulnerable. Since 2048 just happens to be the default, we'll go with it:

```
RSA keys may be between 1024 and 4096 bits long.
What keysize do you want? (2048)
```

Next, select how long you want for the keys to remain valid before they automatically expire. For our purposes, we'll go with the default `key does not expire`.

```
Please specify how long the key should be valid.
         0 = key does not expire
      <n>  = key expires in n days
      <n>w = key expires in n weeks
      <n>m = key expires in n months
      <n>y = key expires in n years
Key is valid for? (0)
```

Provide your personal information:

```
GnuPG needs to construct a user ID to identify your key.

Real name: Donald A. Tevault
Email address: donniet@something.net
Comment: No comment
You selected this USER-ID:
    "Donald A. Tevault (No comment) <donniet@something.net>"

Change (N)ame, (C)omment, (E)mail or (O)kay/(Q)uit?
```

Create a passphrase for your private key:

```
You need a Passphrase to protect your secret key.

We need to generate a lot of random bytes. It is a good idea to perform
some other action (type on the keyboard, move the mouse, utilize the
disks) during the prime generation; this gives the random number
generator a better chance to gain enough entropy.
```

This could take a while, even when you're doing all of the recommended things to create entropy. Be patient; it will eventually finish. By running a `sudo yum upgrade` in another window, I created enough entropy so that the process didn't take too long:

```
gpg: /home/donnie/.gnupg/trustdb.gpg: trustdb created
gpg: key 19CAEC5B marked as ultimately trusted
public and secret key created and signed.

gpg: checking the trustdb
gpg: 3 marginal(s) needed, 1 complete(s) needed, PGP trust model
gpg: depth: 0  valid:   1  signed:   0  trust: 0-, 0q, 0n, 0m, 0f, 1u
pub   2048R/19CAEC5B 2017-10-26
      Key fingerprint = 8DE5 8894 2E37 08C4 5B26  9164 C77C 6944 19CA EC5B
uid                  Donald A. Tevault (No comment) <donniet@something.net>
sub   2048R/37582F29 2017-10-26
```

Verify that the keys did get created:

```
[donnie@localhost ~]$ gpg --list-keys
/home/donnie/.gnupg/pubring.gpg
-------------------------------
pub    2048R/19CAEC5B 2017-10-26
uid                   Donald A. Tevault (No comment) <donniet@something.net>
sub    2048R/37582F29 2017-10-26

[donnie@localhost ~]$
```

And, while you're at it, take a look at the files that you created:

```
[donnie@localhost ~]$ ls -l .gnupg
total 28
-rw-------. 1 donnie donnie 7680 Oct 26 13:22 gpg.conf
drwx------. 2 donnie donnie    6 Oct 26 13:40 private-keys-v1.d
-rw-------. 1 donnie donnie 1208 Oct 26 13:45 pubring.gpg
-rw-------. 1 donnie donnie 1208 Oct 26 13:45 pubring.gpg~
-rw-------. 1 donnie donnie  600 Oct 26 13:45 random_seed
-rw-------. 1 donnie donnie 2586 Oct 26 13:45 secring.gpg
srwxrwxr-x. 1 donnie donnie    0 Oct 26 13:40 S.gpg-agent
-rw-------. 1 donnie donnie 1280 Oct 26 13:45 trustdb.gpg
[donnie@localhost ~]$
```

These files are your public and private keyrings, your own `gpg.conf` file, a random seed file, and a trusted users database.

Symmetrically encrypting your own files

You may find GPG useful for encrypting your own files, even when you never plan to share them with anyone else. For this, you'll use symmetric encryption, which involves using your own private key for encryption. Before you try this, you'll need to generate your keys, as I outlined in the previous section.

 Symmetric key encryption is, well, just that, symmetric. It's symmetric in the sense that the same key that you would use to encrypt a file is the same key that you would use to decrypt the file. That's great for if you're just encrypting files for your own use. But, if you need to share an encrypted file with someone else, you'll need to figure out a secure way to give that person the password. I mean, it's not like you'd want to just send the password in a plain-text email.

Let's encrypt a super-secret file that we just can't allow to fall into the wrong hands:

```
[donnie@localhost ~]$ gpg -c secret_squirrel_stuff.txt
[donnie@localhost ~]$
```

Note that the -c option indicates that I chose to use symmetric encryption with a passphrase for the file. The passphrase that you enter will be for the file, not for your private key.

One slight flaw with this is that GPG makes an encrypted copy of the file, but it also leaves the original, unencrypted file intact:

```
[donnie@localhost ~]$ ls -l
total 1748
-rw-rw-r--. 1 donnie donnie        37 Oct 26 14:22 secret_squirrel_stuff.txt
-rw-rw-r--. 1 donnie donnie        94 Oct 26 14:22
secret_squirrel_stuff.txt.gpg
[donnie@localhost ~]$
```

Let's get rid of that unencrypted file with shred. We'll use the -u option to delete the file, and the -z option to overwrite the deleted file with zeros:

```
[donnie@localhost ~]$ shred -u -z secret_squirrel_stuff.txt
[donnie@localhost ~]$
```

It doesn't look like anything happened, because shred doesn't give you any output. But, an ls -l will prove that the file is gone. Now, if I were to look at the encrypted file with less secret_squirrel_stuff.txt.gpg, I would be able to see its contents, after being asked to enter my private key passphrase:

```
Shhh!!!!  This file is super-secret.
secret_squirrel_stuff.txt.gpg (END)
```

As long as my private key remains loaded into my keyring, I'll be able to view my encrypted file again without having to reenter the passphrase. Now, just to prove to you that the file really is encrypted, I'll create a shared directory, and move the file there for others to access:

```
sudo mkdir /shared
sudo chown donnie: /shared
sudo chmod 755 /shared
mv secret_squirrel_stuff.txt.gpg /shared
```

When I go into that directory to view the file with `less`, I can still see its contents, without having to reenter my passphrase. But now, let's see what happens when Maggie tries to view the file:

```
[maggie@localhost shared]$ less secret_squirrel_stuff.txt.gpg
"secret_squirrel_stuff.txt.gpg" may be a binary file.  See it anyway?
```

And when she hits the *Y* key to see it anyway:

```
<8C>^M^D^C^C^B<BD>2=<D3>u<93><CE><C9>MOOy<B6>^O<A2><AD>}Rg9<94><EB><C4>^W^E
<A6><8D><B9><B8><D3>(<98><C4>æF^_8Q2b
<B8>C<B5><DB>^]<F1><CD>#<90>H<EB><90><C5>^S%X   [<E9><EF><C7>
^@y+<FC><F2><BA><U+058C>H'+<D4>v<84>Y<98>G<D7>˸
secret_squirrel_stuff.txt.gpg (END)
```

Poor Maggie really wants to see my file, but all she can see is encrypted gibberish.

What I've just demonstrated is another advantage of GPG. After entering your private key passphrase once, you can view any of your encrypted files without having to manually decrypt them, and without having to reenter your passphrase. With other symmetric file encryption tools, such as Bcrypt, you wouldn't be able to view your files without manually decrypting them first.

But, let's now say that you no longer need to have this file encrypted, and you want to decrypt it in order to let other people see it. Just use `gpg` with the `-d` option:

```
[donnie@localhost shared]$ gpg -d secret_squirrel_stuff.txt.gpg
gpg: CAST5 encrypted data
gpg: encrypted with 1 passphrase
Shhh!!!!  This file is super-secret.
gpg: WARNING: message was not integrity protected
[donnie@localhost shared]$
```

The `WARNING` message about the message not being integrity protected means that I had encrypted the file, but I never signed the file. Without a digital signature, someone could alter the file without me knowing about it, and I wouldn't be able to prove that I am the originator of the file. (Have no fear, we'll talk about signing files in just a bit.)

Hands-on lab – combining gpg and tar for encrypted backups

For this lab, you'll combine `tar` and `gpg` to create an encrypted backup on a simulated backup device. You can perform this lab on either one of your virtual machines:

1. Start off by creating your GPG keys. You will do that with the following command:

   ```
   gpg --gen-key
   ```

2. Create some dummy files in your home directory, so that you'll have something to back up:

   ```
   touch {file1.txt, file2.txt, file3.txt, file4.txt}
   ```

3. Create a backup directory at the root level of the filesystem. (In real life, you would have the backup directory on a separate device, but for now, this works.) Change ownership of the directory to your own account, and set the permissions so that only you can access it:

   ```
   sudo mkdir /backup
   sudo chown your_username: /backup
   sudo chmod 700 /backup
   ```

4. Create an encrypted backup file of your own home directory. Compression is optional, but we'll go ahead and use `xz` for the best compression. (Note that you'll need to use `sudo` for this, because the `.viminfo` directory in your home directory is owned by the root user.):

   ```
   cd /home
   sudo tar cJvf - your_username/ | gpg -c >
   /backup/your_username_backup.tar.xz.gpg
   ```

5. Now, let's say that either your home directory got deleted, or that you accidentally deleted some important files from your own home directory. Extract and decrypt the original home directory within the `/backup` directory:

   ```
   cd /backup
   sudo gpg -d your_username.tar.xz.gpg | tar xvJ
   ls -la your_username/
   ```

Note that, by combining `tar` with `gpg`, the `-C` option of `tar` to automatically place your home directory back within the `/home` directory won't work. So, you'll either need to manually copy the extracted directory back to `/home`, or move the encrypted backup file to `/home` before you extract it. Also, be aware that when you extract an encrypted archive with `gpg`, the ownership of the files will change to that of whoever extracted the archive. So, this probably wouldn't be a good choice for backing up an entire `/home` directory with home directories for multiple users. Finally, since this creates one huge archive file, any type of corruption in the archive file could cause you to lose the entire backup.

6. End of Lab.

Using private and public keys for asymmetric encryption and signing

Symmetric encryption is great if you're just using GPG locally for your own stuff, but what if you want to share an encrypted file with someone, while ensuring that they can decrypt it? With symmetric encryption, you'd need to find a secure way to transmit the passphrase for the file to the file's recipient. In doing so, there will always be the risk that some third party could intercept the passphrase, and could then get into your stuff. Here's where asymmetric encryption comes to the rescue. To demonstrate, I'm going to create a file, encrypt it, and send it to my buddy Frank to decrypt.

 Asymmetric encryption, is, well, asymmetric. Being asymmetric means that you would use one key to encrypt a file, and another key to decrypt it. You would keep your private key to yourself and guard it with your life, but you would share the public key with the whole world. The beauty of this is that you can share encrypted files with another person, and only that person would be able to decrypt them. This is all done without having to share a password with the recipient.

To begin, both Frank and I have to create a key set, as we've already shown you. Next, each of us needs to extract our public keys, and send them to each other. We'll extract the key into an ASCII text file:

```
cd .gnupg
gpg --export -a -o donnie_public-key.txt

donnie@ubuntu:~/.gnupg$ ls -1
total 36
-rw-rw-r-- 1 donnie donnie 1706 Oct 27 18:14 donnie_public-key.txt
```

```
. . .

frank@ubuntu:~/.gnupg$ ls -l
total 36
-rw-rw-r-- 1 frank frank 1714 Oct 27 18:18 frank_public-key.txt
```

Normally, the participants in this would either send their keys to each other through an email attachment, or by placing the keys in a shared directory. In this case, Frank and I will receive each other's public key files, and place them into our respective .gnupg directories. Once that's done, we're ready to import each other's keys:

```
donnie@ubuntu:~/.gnupg$ gpg --import frank_public-key.txt
gpg: key 4CFC6990: public key "Frank Siamese (I am a cat.) <frank@any.net>"
imported
gpg: Total number processed: 1
gpg: imported: 1 (RSA: 1)
donnie@ubuntu:~/.gnupg$

frank@ubuntu:~/.gnupg$ gpg --import donnie_public-key.txt
gpg: key 9FD7014B: public key "Donald A. Tevault <donniet@something.net>"
imported
gpg: Total number processed: 1
gpg:                imported: 1   (RSA: 1)
frank@ubuntu:~/.gnupg$
```

Now for the good stuff. I've created a super-secret message for Frank, and will asymmetrically encrypt it (-e) and sign it (-s). (Signing the message is the verification that the message really is from me, rather than from an impostor.):

```
donnie@ubuntu:~$ gpg -s -e secret_stuff_for_frank.txt

You need a passphrase to unlock the secret key for
user: "Donald A. Tevault <donniet@something.net>"
2048-bit RSA key, ID 9FD7014B, created 2017-10-27

gpg: gpg-agent is not available in this session
You did not specify a user ID. (you may use "-r")

Current recipients:

Enter the user ID.  End with an empty line: frank
gpg: CD8104F7: There is no assurance this key belongs to the named user

pub  2048R/CD8104F7 2017-10-27 Frank Siamese (I am a cat.) <frank@any.net>
 Primary key fingerprint: 4806 7483 5442 D62B B9BD  95C1 9564 92D4 4CFC
6990
        Subkey fingerprint: 9DAB 7C3C 871D 6711 4632  A5E0 6DDD E3E5 CD81
```

```
04F7

It is NOT certain that the key belongs to the person named
in the user ID.  If you *really* know what you are doing,
you may answer the next question with yes.

Use this key anyway? (y/N) y

Current recipients:
2048R/CD8104F7 2017-10-27 "Frank Siamese (I am a cat.) <frank@any.net>"

Enter the user ID.  End with an empty line:
donnie@ubuntu:~$
```

So, the first thing I had to do was to enter the passphrase for my private key. Where it says to enter the user ID, I entered `frank`, since he's the intended recipient of my message. But, look at the line after that, where it says, `There is no assurance this key belongs to the named user`. That's because I still haven't *trusted* Frank's public key. We'll get to that in a bit. The last line of the output again says to enter a user ID, so that we can designate multiple recipients. But, Frank is the only one I care about right now, so I just hit the *Enter* key to break out of the routine. This results in a `.gpg` version of my message to Frank:

```
donnie@ubuntu:~$ ls -l
total 8
. . .
-rw-rw-r-- 1 donnie donnie 143 Oct 27 18:37 secret_stuff_for_frank.txt
-rw-rw-r-- 1 donnie donnie 790 Oct 27 18:39 secret_stuff_for_frank.txt.gpg
donnie@ubuntu:~$
```

My final step is to send Frank his encrypted message file, by whatever means available.

When Frank receives his message, he'll use the `-d` option to view it:

```
frank@ubuntu:~$ gpg -d secret_stuff_for_frank.txt.gpg

You need a passphrase to unlock the secret key for
user: "Frank Siamese (I am a cat.) <frank@any.net>"
2048-bit RSA key, ID CD8104F7, created 2017-10-27 (main key ID 4CFC6990)

gpg: gpg-agent is not available in this session
gpg: encrypted with 2048-bit RSA key, ID CD8104F7, created 2017-10-27
      "Frank Siamese (I am a cat.) <frank@any.net>"
This is TOP SECRET stuff that only Frank can see!!!!!
If anyone else see it, it's the end of the world as we know it.
(With apologies to REM.)
```

```
gpg: Signature made Fri 27 Oct 2017 06:39:15 PM EDT using RSA key ID
9FD7014B
gpg: Good signature from "Donald A. Tevault <donniet@something.net>"
gpg: WARNING: This key is not certified with a trusted signature!
gpg:            There is no indication that the signature belongs to the
owner.
Primary key fingerprint: DB0B 31B8 876D 9B2C 7F12  9FC3 886F 3357 9FD7 014B
frank@ubuntu:~$
```

Frank enters the passphrase for his private key, and he sees the message. At the bottom, he sees the warning about how my public key isn't trusted, and that there's no indication that the signature belongs to the owner. Well, since Frank knows me personally, and he knows for a fact that the public key really is mine, he can add my public key to the *trusted* list:

```
frank@ubuntu:~$ cd .gnupg
frank@ubuntu:~/.gnupg$ gpg --edit-key donnie
gpg (GnuPG) 1.4.20; Copyright (C) 2015 Free Software Foundation, Inc.
This is free software: you are free to change and redistribute it.
There is NO WARRANTY, to the extent permitted by law.


gpg: checking the trustdb
gpg: 3 marginal(s) needed, 1 complete(s) needed, PGP trust model
gpg: depth: 0  valid:   2  signed:   0  trust: 0-, 0q, 0n, 0m, 0f, 2u
pub  2048R/9FD7014B  created: 2017-10-27  expires: never       usage: SC
                     trust: ultimate       validity: ultimate
sub  2048R/9625E7E9  created: 2017-10-27  expires: never       usage: E
[ultimate] (1). Donald A. Tevault <donniet@something.net>

gpg>
```

The last line of this output is the command prompt for the gpg shell. Frank is concerned with trust, so he'll enter the command, trust:

```
gpg> trust
pub  2048R/9FD7014B  created: 2017-10-27  expires: never       usage: SC
                     trust: unknown        validity: unknown
sub  2048R/9625E7E9  created: 2017-10-27  expires: never       usage: E
[ unknown] (1). Donald A. Tevault <donniet@something.net>

Please decide how far you trust this user to correctly verify other users'
keys
(by looking at passports, checking fingerprints from different sources,
etc.)

  1 = I don't know or won't say
```

```
2 = I do NOT trust
3 = I trust marginally
4 = I trust fully
5 = I trust ultimately
m = back to the main menu

Your decision? 5
Do you really want to set this key to ultimate trust? (y/N) y
```

Frank has known me for quite a while, and he knows for a fact that I'm the one who sent the key. So, he chooses option 5 for ultimate trust. Once Frank logs out and logs back in, that trust will take effect:

```
frank@ubuntu:~$ gpg -d secret_stuff_for_frank.txt.gpg

You need a passphrase to unlock the secret key for
user: "Frank Siamese (I am a cat.) <frank@any.net>"
2048-bit RSA key, ID CD8104F7, created 2017-10-27 (main key ID 4CFC6990)

gpg: gpg-agent is not available in this session
gpg: encrypted with 2048-bit RSA key, ID CD8104F7, created 2017-10-27
        "Frank Siamese (I am a cat.) <frank@any.net>"
This is TOP SECRET stuff that only Frank can see!!!!!
If anyone else see it, it's the end of the world as we know it.
(With apologies to REM.)
gpg: Signature made Fri 27 Oct 2017 06:39:15 PM EDT using RSA key ID
9FD7014B
gpg: Good signature from "Donald A. Tevault <donniet@something.net>"
frank@ubuntu:~$
```

With no more warning messages, this looks much better. At my end, I'll do the same thing with Frank's public key.

What's so very cool about this is that even though the whole world may have my public key, it's useless to anyone who isn't a designated recipient of my message.

 On an Ubuntu machine, to get rid of the `gpg-agent is not available in this session` messages, and to be able to cache your passphrase in the keyring, install the `gnupg-agent` package:

```
sudo apt install gnupg-agent
```

Signing a file without encryption

If a file isn't secret, but you still need to ensure authenticity and integrity, you can just sign it without encrypting it:

```
donnie@ubuntu:~$ gpg -s not_secret_for_frank.txt

You need a passphrase to unlock the secret key for
user: "Donald A. Tevault <donniet@something.net>"
2048-bit RSA key, ID 9FD7014B, created 2017-10-27

gpg: gpg-agent is not available in this session
donnie@ubuntu:~$ ls -l
. . .
-rw-rw-r-- 1 donnie donnie  40 Oct 27 19:30 not_secret_for_frank.txt
-rw-rw-r-- 1 donnie donnie 381 Oct 27 19:31 not_secret_for_frank.txt.gpg
```

Just as before, I create a .gpg version of the file. When Frank receives the file, he may try to open it with less:

```
frank@ubuntu:~$ less not_secret_for_frank.txt.gpg
"not_secret_for_frank.txt.gpg" may be a binary file.  See it anyway?

<A3>^A^Av^A<89><FE><90>^M^C^@^B^A<88>o3W<9F><D7>^AK^A<AC>Fb^Xnot_secret_for
_frank.txtY<F3><C1><C0>This isn't secret, so I just signed it.
<89>^A^\^D^@^A^B^@^F^E^BY<F3><C1><C0>^@
^P<88>o3W<9F><D7>^AK6<AF>^G<FF>Bs<9A>^Lc^@<E9><ED><C2>-2<AE><A7><DF>ąB
<EC>/[:<D1>{<B2><FD>o8<C6><C9>x<FE>*4^D<CD>^G^O^F<F3>@v<87>_1<D0>^Bp<FE>q^N
3<B0><BE><85><D2>9]{<D6><EF><9A><D8>   `<C2><E4>^NC<9B>
"Ω^?M<89>s<9F>z^B"<DF>
s}`<A4>:<B4>&<F7><F4>\EjǑ!^Q
<9C>6^E|H<E2>ESC<D9>9<DC>p_ӟESCB<DE>^P<FF>i<CA>)^O
<A0>
<CB><C4>+<81><F5><A7>`5<90><BF>Y<DE><FF><<A0>z<BC><BD>5<C5><E8><FE>>
<B7><A2>^L^_^D<DD>Kk<E0><9A>8<C6>S^E<D0>fjz<B2>&G<A4><A8>^Lg$8Q>{<FF><FA>^M
_A
<A1><93><C3>4<DC><C4>x<86><D9>^]- <8A>
F0<87><8A><94>%A<96><DF><CD>C<80><C3>1
<D3>K<E5>^G<8E><90>d<8C><DA>Aṃb<86><89><DA>S<B6><91><D8><D2><E0><B3>K<FC><9
E>
<ED>^@*<EF>x<E7>jø<FD><D3><FA><9A>^]
not_secret_for_frank.txt.gpg (END)
```

There's a lot of gibberish there because of the signature, but if you look carefully, you'll see the plain, unencrypted message. Frank will use `gpg` with the `--verify` option to verify that the signature really does belong to me:

```
frank@ubuntu:~$ gpg --verify not_secret_for_frank.txt.gpg
gpg: Signature made Fri 27 Oct 2017 07:31:12 PM EDT using RSA key ID
9FD7014B
gpg: Good signature from "Donald A. Tevault <donniet@something.net>"
frank@ubuntu:~$
```

Encrypting partitions with Linux Unified Key Setup – LUKS

Being able to encrypt individual files can be handy, but it can be quite unwieldy for a large number of files. For that, we need something better, and we have three different methods:

- **Block encryption**: We can use this for either whole-disk encryption, or to encrypt individual partitions
- **File-level encryption**: We'd use this to encrypt individual directories, without having to encrypt the underlying partitions
- **Containerized Encryption**: Using third-party software that doesn't come with any Linux distribution, we can create encrypted, cross-platform containers that can be opened on either Linux, Mac, or Windows machines

The **Linux Unified Key Setup** (LUKS), falls into the first category. It's built into pretty much every Linux distribution, and directions for use are the same for each. For our demos, I'll use the CentOS virtual machine, since LUKS is now the default encryption mechanism for Red Hat Enterprise Linux 7 and CentOS 7.

Disk encryption during operating system installation

When you install Red Hat Enterprise Linux 7 or one of its offspring, you have the option of encrypting the drive. All you have to do is to click on a checkbox:

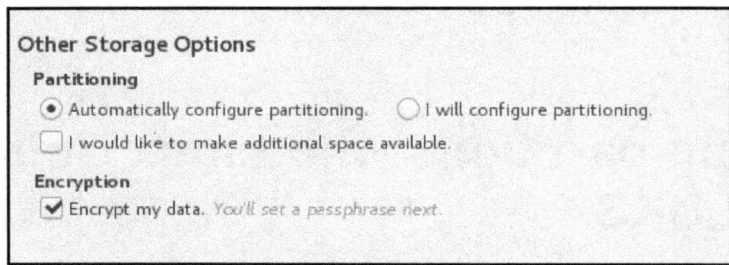

Other than that, I just let the installer create the default partitioning scheme, which means that the / filesystem and the `swap` partition will both be logical volumes. (I'll cover that in a moment.)

Before the installation can continue, I have to create a passphrase to mount the encrypted disk:

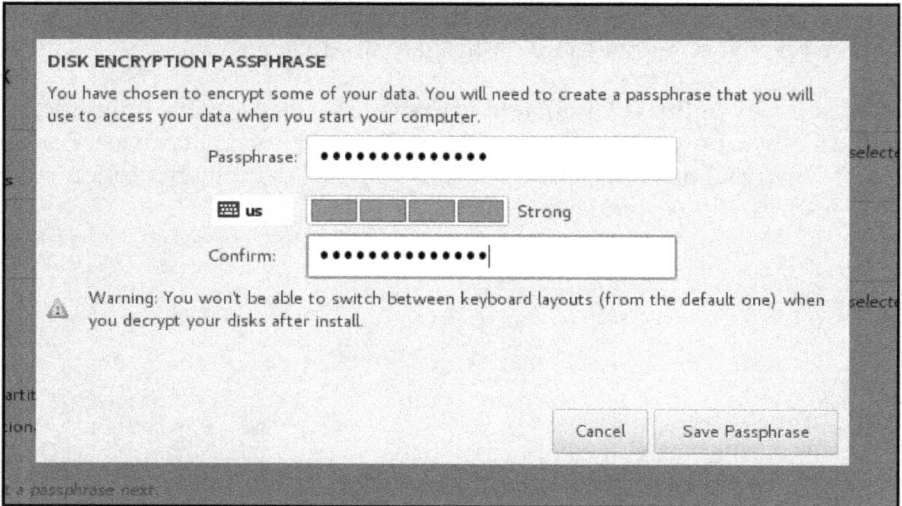

Now, whenever I reboot the system, I need to enter this passphrase:

```
Please enter passphrase for disk VBOX_HARDDISK (luks-2d7f02c7-864f-42ce-b362-50d
d830d9772)!:_
```

Once the machine is up and running, I can look at the list of logical volumes. I see both the /
logical volume and the `swap` logical volume:

```
[donnie@localhost etc]$ sudo lvdisplay
  --- Logical volume ---
  LV Path /dev/centos/swap
  LV Name swap
  VG Name centos
  LV UUID tsme2v-uy87-uech-vpNp-W4E7-fHLf-3bf817
  LV Write Access read/write
  LV Creation host, time localhost, 2017-10-28 13:00:11 -0400
  LV Status available
  # open 2
  LV Size 2.00 GiB
  Current LE 512
  Segments 1
  Allocation inherit
  Read ahead sectors auto
  - currently set to 8192
  Block device 253:2

  --- Logical volume ---
  LV Path /dev/centos/root
  LV Name root
  VG Name centos
  LV UUID MKXVO9-X8fo-w2FC-LnGO-GLnq-k2Xs-xI1gn0
  LV Write Access read/write
  LV Creation host, time localhost, 2017-10-28 13:00:12 -0400
  LV Status available
  # open 1
  LV Size 17.06 GiB
  Current LE 4368
  Segments 1
  Allocation inherit
  Read ahead sectors auto
  - currently set to 8192
  Block device 253:1

[donnie@localhost etc]$
```

And I can look at the list of physical volumes. (Actually, there's only one physical volume in the list, and it's listed as a `luks` physical volume.):

```
[donnie@localhost etc]$ sudo pvdisplay
  --- Physical volume ---
  PV Name               /dev/mapper/luks-2d7f02c7-864f-42ce-
b362-50dd830d9772
  VG Name               centos
  PV Size               <19.07 GiB / not usable 0
  Allocatable           yes
  PE Size               4.00 MiB
  Total PE              4881
  Free PE               1
  Allocated PE          4880
  PV UUID               V50E4d-jOCU-kVRn-67w9-5zwR-nbwg-4P725S

[donnie@localhost etc]$
```

This shows that the underlying physical volume is encrypted, which means that both the / and the `swap` logical volumes are also encrypted. That's a good thing, because leaving the swap space unencrypted—a common mistake when setting up disk encryption up manually—can lead to data leakage.

Adding an encrypted partition with LUKS

There may be times when you'll need to either add another encrypted drive to an existing machine, or encrypt a portable device, such as a USB memory stick. This procedure works for both scenarios.

To demonstrate, I'll shut down my CentOS VM and add another virtual drive:

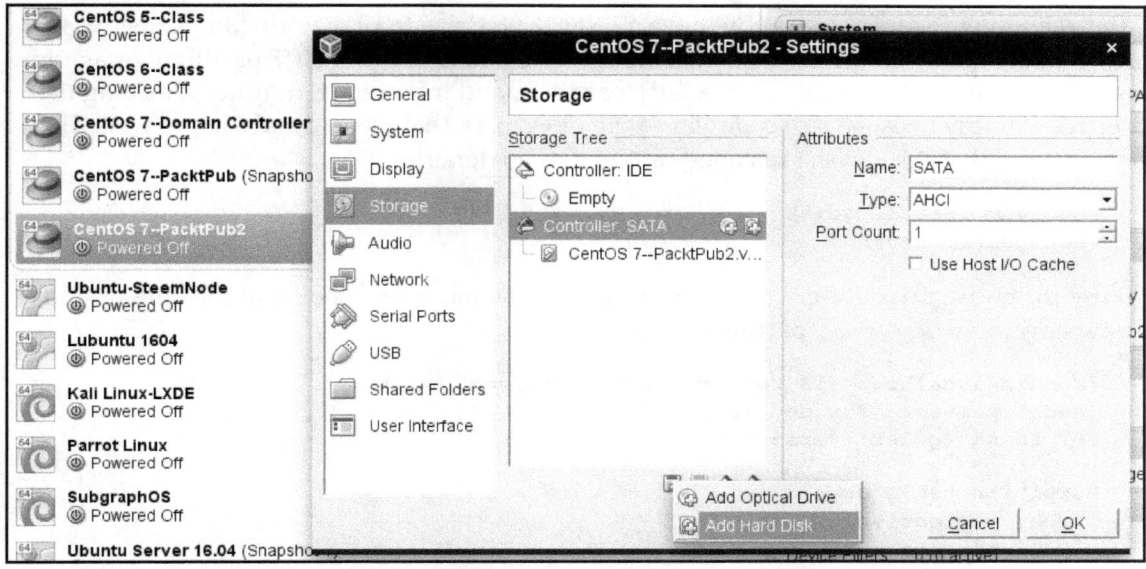

I'll bump the drive capacity up to 20 GB, which will give me plenty of room to play with:

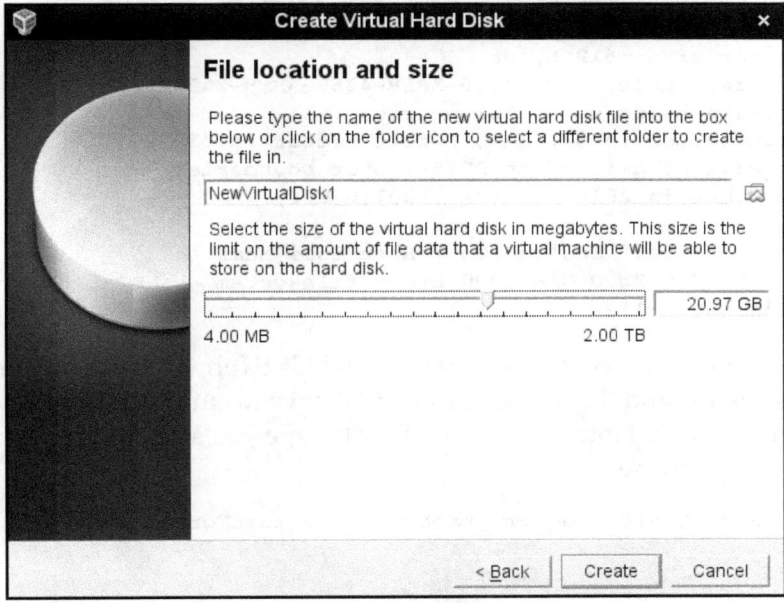

After rebooting the machine, I now have a /dev/sdb drive to play with. My next step is to create a partition. It doesn't matter whether I create a new-fangled GPT partition, or an old-fashioned MBR partition. I'll create a GPT partition, and my preferred utility for doing that is gdisk, simply because it's so similar to the old fdisk that I know and love so well. The only catch is that gdisk isn't installed on CentOS by default:

```
sudo yum install gdisk
sudo gdisk /dev/sdb
```

I'll use the entire drive for my partition, and leave the partition type set at the default 8300. I now have the /dev/sdb1 partition:

```
[donnie@localhost ~]$ sudo gdisk -l /dev/sdb
[sudo] password for donnie:
GPT fdisk (gdisk) version 0.8.6

Partition table scan:
  MBR: protective
  BSD: not present
  APM: not present
  GPT: present

Found valid GPT with protective MBR; using GPT.
Disk /dev/sdb: 43978112 sectors, 21.0 GiB
Logical sector size: 512 bytes
Disk identifier (GUID): DC057EC6-3BA8-4269-ABE9-2A28B4FDC84F
Partition table holds up to 128 entries
First usable sector is 34, last usable sector is 43978078
Partitions will be aligned on 2048-sector boundaries
Total free space is 2014 sectors (1007.0 KiB)

Number Start (sector) End (sector) Size Code Name
   1 2048 43978078 21.0 GiB 8300 Linux filesystem
[donnie@localhost ~]$
```

I'll next use cryptsetup to convert the partition to LUKS format. In this command, the -v signifies verbose mode, and the -y signifies that I'll have to enter my passphrase twice in order to properly verify it. Note that when it says to type yes all in uppercase, it really does mean to type it in uppercase:

```
[donnie@localhost ~]$ sudo cryptsetup -v -y luksFormat /dev/sdb1

WARNING!
========
This will overwrite data on /dev/sdb1 irrevocably.
```

```
Are you sure? (Type uppercase yes): YES
Enter passphrase:
Verify passphrase:
Command successful.
[donnie@localhost ~]$
```

Although I don't have to, I'd like to look at the information about my new encrypted partition:

```
[donnie@localhost ~]$ sudo cryptsetup luksDump /dev/sdb1
LUKS header information for /dev/sdb1

Version:         1
Cipher name:     aes
Cipher mode:     xts-plain64
Hash spec:       sha256
.  .  .
.  .  .
```

There's a lot more to the output than what I can show here, but you get the idea.

Next, I'll map the partition to a device name. You can name the device pretty much whatever you want, and I'll just name mine `secrets`. (I know, it's a corny name. You probably won't want to make it so obvious where you're storing your secrets.):

```
[donnie@localhost ~]$ sudo cryptsetup luksOpen /dev/sdb1 secrets
Enter passphrase for /dev/sdb1:
[donnie@localhost ~]$
```

When I look in the `/dev/mapper` directory, I see my new `secrets` device, listed as a symbolic link to the `dm-3` device:

```
[donnie@localhost mapper]$ pwd
/dev/mapper
[donnie@localhost mapper]$ ls -l se*
lrwxrwxrwx. 1 root root 7 Oct 28 17:39 secrets -> ../dm-3
[donnie@localhost mapper]$
```

I'll use `dmsetup` to look at the information about my new device:

```
[donnie@localhost mapper]$ sudo dmsetup info secrets
[sudo] password for donnie:
Name:            secrets
State:           ACTIVE
Read Ahead:      8192
Tables present:  LIVE
Open count:      0
```

```
Event number:        0
Major, minor:        253, 3
Number of targets: 1
UUID: CRYPT-LUKS1-6cbdce1748d441a18f8e793c0fa7c389-secrets

[donnie@localhost mapper]$
```

The next step is to format the partition in the usual manner. I could use any filesystem that's supported by Red Hat and CentOS. But, since everything else on my system is already formatted with XFS, that's what I'll go with here, as well:

```
[donnie@localhost ~]$ sudo mkfs.xfs /dev/mapper/secrets
meta-data=/dev/mapper/secrets    isize=512      agcount=4, agsize=1374123
blks
         =                       sectsz=512     attr=2, projid32bit=1
         =                       crc=1          finobt=0, sparse=0
data     =                       bsize=4096     blocks=5496491, imaxpct=25
         =                       sunit=0        swidth=0 blks
naming   =version 2              bsize=4096     ascii-ci=0 ftype=1
log      =internal log           bsize=4096     blocks=2683, version=2
         =                       sectsz=512     sunit=0 blks, lazy-count=1
realtime =none                   extsz=4096     blocks=0, rtextents=0
[donnie@localhost ~]$
```

My final step is to create a mount point and to mount the encrypted partition:

```
[donnie@localhost ~]$ sudo mkdir /secrets
[sudo] password for donnie:
[donnie@localhost ~]$ sudo mount /dev/mapper/secrets /secrets
[donnie@localhost ~]$
```

The mount command will verify that the partition is mounted properly:

```
[donnie@localhost ~]$ mount | grep 'secrets'
/dev/mapper/secrets on /secrets type xfs
(rw,relatime,seclabel,attr2,inode64,noquota)
[donnie@localhost ~]$
```

Configuring the LUKS partition to mount automatically

The only missing piece of the puzzle is to configure the system to automatically mount the LUKS partition upon boot-up. To do that, I'll configure two different files:

- /etc/crypttab
- /etc/fstab

Had I not chosen to encrypt the disk when I installed the operating system, I wouldn't have a crypttab file, and I would have to create it myself. But, since I did choose to encrypt the drive, I already have one with information about that drive:

```
luks-2d7f02c7-864f-42ce-b362-50dd830d9772 UUID=2d7f02c7-864f-42ce-
b362-50dd830d9772 none
```

The first two fields describe the name and location of the encrypted partition. The third field is for the encryption passphrase. If it's set to none, as it is here, then the passphrase will have to be manually entered upon boot-up.

In the fstab file, we have the entry that actually mounts the partition:

```
/dev/mapper/centos-root /                       xfs       defaults,x-
systemd.device-timeout=0 0 0
UUID=9f9fbf9c-d046-44fc-a73e-ca854d0ca718 /boot                      xfs
defaults        0 0
/dev/mapper/centos-swap swap                    swap      defaults,x-
systemd.device-timeout=0 0 0
```

Well, there are actually two entries in this case, because I have two logical volumes, / and swap, on top of my encrypted physical volume. The UUID line is the /boot partition, which is the only part of the drive that isn't encrypted. Now, let's add our new encrypted partition so that it will mount automatically, as well.

This is where it would be extremely helpful to remotely log into your virtual machine from your desktop host machine. By using a GUI-type Terminal, whether it be the Terminal from a Linux or MacOS machine, or Cygwin from a Windows machine, you'll have the ability to perform copy-and-paste operations, which you won't have if you work directly from the virtual machine terminal. (Trust me, you don't want to be typing in those long UUIDs.)

The first step is to obtain the UUID of the encrypted partition:

```
[donnie@localhost etc]$ sudo cryptsetup luksUUID /dev/sdb1
[sudo] password for donnie:
6cbdce17-48d4-41a1-8f8e-793c0fa7c389
[donnie@localhost etc]$
```

I'll copy that UUID, and paste it into the /etc/crypttab file. (Note that you'll paste it in twice. The first time, you'll prepend it with luks-, and the second time you'll append it with UUID=.):

```
luks-2d7f02c7-864f-42ce-b362-50dd830d9772 UUID=2d7f02c7-864f-42ce-
b362-50dd830d9772 none
luks-6cbdce17-48d4-41a1-8f8e-793c0fa7c389
UUID=6cbdce17-48d4-41a1-8f8e-793c0fa7c389 none
```

Finally, I'll edit the /etc/fstab file, adding the last line in the file for my new encrypted partition. (Note that I again used luks-, followed by the UUID number.):

```
/dev/mapper/centos-root / xfs defaults,x-systemd.device-timeout=0 0 0
UUID=9f9fbf9c-d046-44fc-a73e-ca854d0ca718 /boot xfs defaults 0 0
/dev/mapper/centos-swap swap swap defaults,x-systemd.device-timeout=0 0 0
/dev/mapper/luks-6cbdce17-48d4-41a1-8f8e-793c0fa7c389 /secrets xfs defaults
0 0
```

When editing the fstab file for adding normal, unencrypted partitions, I always like to do a sudo mount -a to check the fstab file for typos. That won't work with LUKS partitions though, because mount won't recognize the partition until the system reads in the crypttab file, and that won't happen until I reboot the machine. So, just be extra careful with editing fstab when adding LUKS partitions.

Now for the moment of truth. I'll reboot the machine to see if everything works.

Okay, the machine has rebooted, and mount shows that my endeavors have been successful:

```
[donnie@localhost ~]$ mount | grep 'secrets'
/dev/mapper/luks-6cbdce17-48d4-41a1-8f8e-793c0fa7c389 on /secrets type xfs
(rw,relatime,seclabel,attr2,inode64,noquota)
[donnie@localhost ~]$
```

Encrypting directories with eCryptfs

Encrypting entire partitions is cool, but you might, at times, just need to encrypt an individual directory. For that, we can use eCryptfs. We'll need to use our Ubuntu machines for this, because Red Hat and CentOS no longer include eCryptfs in version 7 of their products. (It was in Red Hat 6 and CentOS 6, but it's no longer even available for installation in version 7.)

Home directory and disk encryption during Ubuntu installation

When you install Ubuntu Server, you have two chances to implement encryption. You'll first be given the chance to encrypt your home directory:

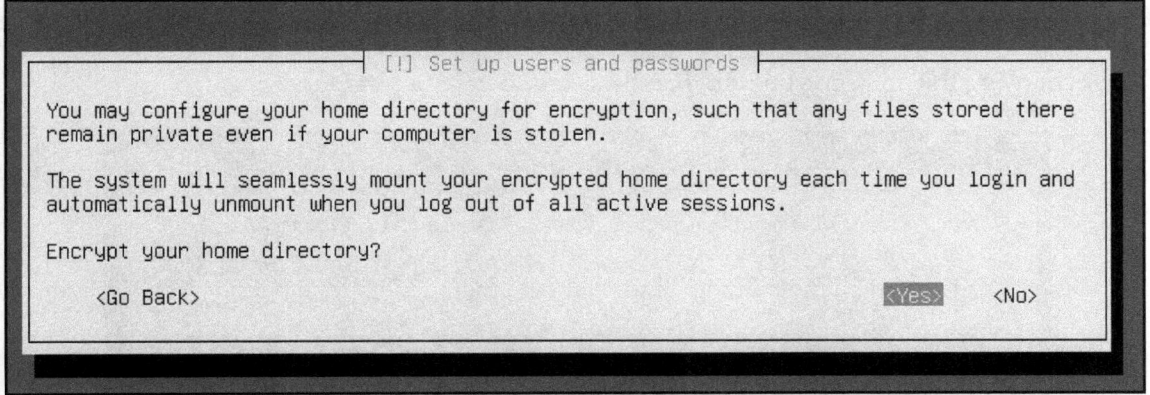

Later, on the **Partition disks** screen, you'll be given the chance to set up encrypted logical volumes for whole disk encryption:

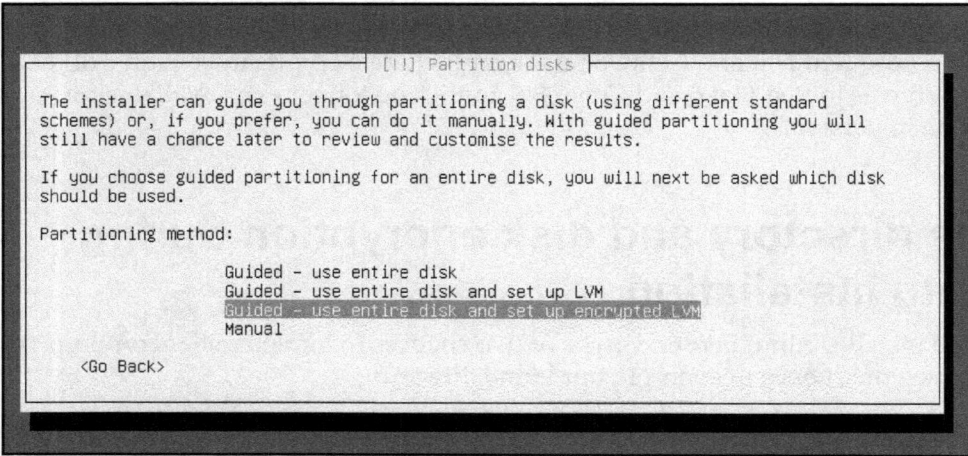

After choosing this option, you will then be asked to enter a passphrase:

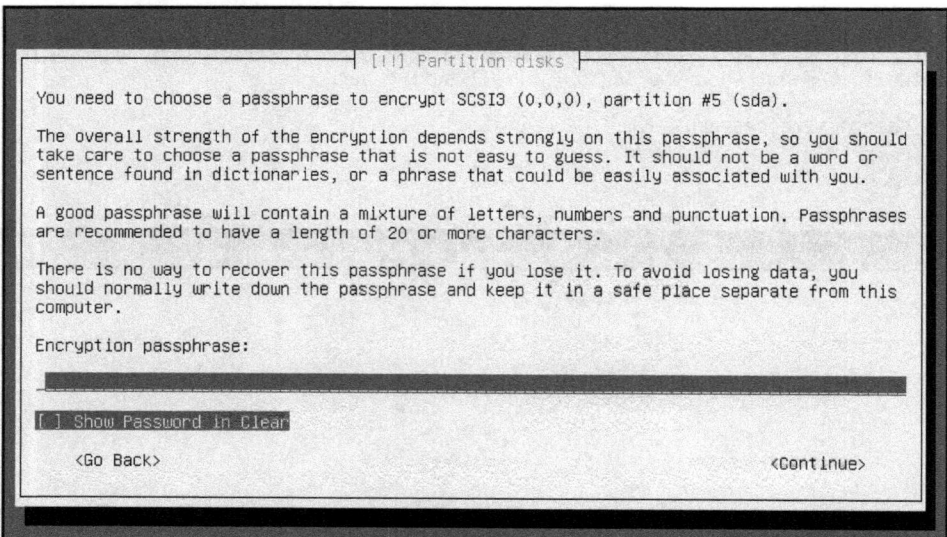

The disk encryption uses LUKS, just the same as we saw on the CentOS machine. To prove this, all we have to do is look for a populated `crypttab` file in the `/etc` directory:

```
donnie@ubuntu3:~$ cd /etc
donnie@ubuntu3:/etc$ cat crypttab
sda5_crypt UUID=56190c2b-e46b-40a9-af3c-4cb26c4fe998 none luks,discard
cryptswap1 UUID=60661042-0dbd-4c2a-9cf9-7f02a73864ae /dev/urandom
swap,offset=1024,cipher=aes-xts-plain64
donnie@ubuntu3:/etc$
```

 Unlike Red Hat and CentOS, an Ubuntu machine will always have the `/etc/crypttab` file, even if there are no LUKS partitions. Without LUKS partitions, the file will be empty.

The home directory encryption uses eCryptfs, as evidenced by the `.ecryptfs` directory in the `/home` directory:

```
donnie@ubuntu3:/home$ ls -la
total 16
drwxr-xr-x 4 root root 4096 Oct 29 15:06 .
drwxr-xr-x 23 root root 4096 Oct 29 15:23 ..
drwx------ 3 donnie donnie 4096 Oct 29 15:29 donnie
drwxr-xr-x 3 root root 4096 Oct 29 15:06 .ecryptfs
donnie@ubuntu3:/home$
```

So, what we have here is encryption on top of encryption, for double protection. Is that really necessary? Probably not, but choosing to encrypt my home directory ensured that the access permissions for it got set to the more restrictive 700 setting, rather than the default 755 setting. Be aware though, that any user accounts you create now will have wide open permissions settings on their home directories. Unless, that is, we create user accounts with the encryption option.

Encrypting a home directory for a new user account

In Chapter 2, *Securing User Accounts*, I showed you how Ubuntu allows you to encrypt a user's home directory as you create his or her user account. To review, let's see the command for creating Goldie's account:

```
sudo adduser --encrypt-home goldie
```

When Goldie logs in, the first thing she'll want to do is to unwrap her mount passphrase, write it down, and store it in a secure place. (She'll need this if she ever needs to recover a corrupted directory.):

```
ecryptfs-unwrap-passphrase .ecryptfs/wrapped-passphrase
```

When you use adduser --encrypt-home, home directories for new users will automatically be set to a restrictive permissions value that will keep everyone out except for the owner of the directory. This happens even when you leave the adduser.conf file set with its default settings.

Creating a private directory within an existing home directory

Let's say that you have users who, for whatever strange reason, don't want to encrypt their entire home directories, and want to keep the 755 permissions settings on their home directories so that other people can access their files. But, they also want a private directory that nobody but them can access.

Instead of encrypting an entire home directory, any user can create an encrypted private directory within his or her own home directory. The first step, if it hasn't already been done, is for someone with admin privileges to install the ecryptfs-utils package:

```
sudo apt install ecryptfs-utils
```

To create this private directory, we'll use the interactive ecryptfs-setup-private utility. If you have admin privileges, you can do this for other users. Users without admin privileges can do it for themselves. For our demo, let's say that Charlie, my big Siamese/Gray tabby guy, needs his own encrypted private space. (Who knew that cats had secrets, right?):

```
charlie@ubuntu2:~$ ecryptfs-setup-private
Enter your login passphrase [charlie]:
Enter your mount passphrase [leave blank to generate one]:
Enter your mount passphrase (again):

************************************************************************
YOU SHOULD RECORD YOUR MOUNT PASSPHRASE AND STORE IT IN A SAFE LOCATION.
  ecryptfs-unwrap-passphrase ~/.ecryptfs/wrapped-passphrase
THIS WILL BE REQUIRED IF YOU NEED TO RECOVER YOUR DATA AT A LATER TIME.
************************************************************************
```

```
Done configuring.

Testing mount/write/umount/read...
Inserted auth tok with sig [e339e1ebf3d58c36] into the user session keyring
Inserted auth tok with sig [7a40a176ac647bf0] into the user session keyring
Inserted auth tok with sig [e339e1ebf3d58c36] into the user session keyring
Inserted auth tok with sig [7a40a176ac647bf0] into the user session keyring
Testing succeeded.

Logout, and log back in to begin using your encrypted directory.

charlie@ubuntu2:~$
```

For the `login` passphrase, Charlie enters his normal password or passphrase for logging into his user account. He could have let the system generate its own `mount` passphrase, but he decided to enter his own. Since he did enter his own mount passphrase, he didn't need to do the `ecryptfs-unwrap-passphrase` command to find out what the passphrase is. But, just to show how that command works, let's say that Charlie entered `TurkeyLips` as his mount passphrase:

```
charlie@ubuntu2:~$ ecryptfs-unwrap-passphrase .ecryptfs/wrapped-passphrase
Passphrase:
TurkeyLips
charlie@ubuntu2:~$
```

Yes, it's a horribly weak passphrase, but for our demo purposes, it works.

After Charlie logs out and logs back in, he can start using his new private directory. Also, you can see that he has three new hidden directories within his home directory. All three of these new directories are only accessible by Charlie, even though his top-level home directory is still wide open to everybody:

```
charlie@ubuntu2:~$ ls -la
total 40
drwxr-xr-x 6 charlie charlie 4096 Oct 30 17:00 .
drwxr-xr-x 4 root root 4096 Oct 30 16:38 ..
-rw------- 1 charlie charlie 270 Oct 30 17:00 .bash_history
-rw-r--r-- 1 charlie charlie 220 Aug 31 2015 .bash_logout
-rw-r--r-- 1 charlie charlie 3771 Aug 31 2015 .bashrc
drwx------ 2 charlie charlie 4096 Oct 30 16:39 .cache
drwx------ 2 charlie charlie 4096 Oct 30 16:57 .ecryptfs
drwx------ 2 charlie charlie 4096 Oct 30 16:57 Private
drwx------ 2 charlie charlie 4096 Oct 30 16:57 .Private
-rw-r--r-- 1 charlie charlie 655 May 16 08:49 .profile
charlie@ubuntu2:~$
```

If you do a `grep 'ecryptfs' *` command in the `/etc/pam.d` directory, you'll see that PAM is configured to automatically mount users' encrypted directories whenever they log into the system:

```
donnie@ubuntu2:/etc/pam.d$ grep 'ecryptfs' *
common-auth:auth    optional    pam_ecryptfs.so unwrap
common-password:password    optional    pam_ecryptfs.so
common-session:session    optional    pam_ecryptfs.so unwrap
common-session-noninteractive:session    optional    pam_ecryptfs.so unwrap
donnie@ubuntu2:/etc/pam.d$
```

Encrypting other directories with eCryptfs

Encrypting other directories is a simple matter of mounting them with the `ecryptfs` filesystem. For our example, let's create a `secrets` directory in the top level of our filesystem, and encrypt it. Note how you list the directory name twice, because you also need to specify a mount point. (Essentially, you're using the directory that you're mounting as its own mount point.)

```
sudo mkdir /secrets
sudo mount -t ecryptfs /secrets /secrets
```

The output from this command is a bit lengthy, so let's break it down.

First, you'll enter your desired passphrase, and choose the encryption algorithm and the key length:

```
donnie@ubuntu2:~$ sudo mount -t ecryptfs /secrets /secrets
[sudo] password for donnie:
Passphrase:
Select cipher:
 1) aes: blocksize = 16; min keysize = 16; max keysize = 32
 2) blowfish: blocksize = 8; min keysize = 16; max keysize = 56
 3) des3_ede: blocksize = 8; min keysize = 24; max keysize = 24
 4) twofish: blocksize = 16; min keysize = 16; max keysize = 32
 5) cast6: blocksize = 16; min keysize = 16; max keysize = 32
 6) cast5: blocksize = 8; min keysize = 5; max keysize = 16
Selection [aes]:
Select key bytes:
 1) 16
 2) 32
 3) 24
Selection [16]:
```

We'll go with the default of `aes`, and 16 bytes for the key.

I'm going to go with the default of no for `plaintext passthrough`, and with yes for filename encryption:

```
Enable plaintext passthrough (y/n) [n]:
Enable filename encryption (y/n) [n]: y
```

I'll go with the default `Filename Encryption Key`, and verify the mounting options:

```
Filename Encryption Key (FNEK) Signature [e339e1ebf3d58c36]:
Attempting to mount with the following options:
  ecryptfs_unlink_sigs
  ecryptfs_fnek_sig=e339e1ebf3d58c36
  ecryptfs_key_bytes=16
  ecryptfs_cipher=aes
  ecryptfs_sig=e339e1ebf3d58c36
```

This warning only comes up when you mount the directory for the first time. For the final two questions, I'll type `yes` in order to prevent that warning from coming up again:

```
WARNING: Based on the contents of [/root/.ecryptfs/sig-cache.txt],
it looks like you have never mounted with this key
before. This could mean that you have typed your
passphrase wrong.

Would you like to proceed with the mount (yes/no)? : yes
Would you like to append sig [e339e1ebf3d58c36] to
[/root/.ecryptfs/sig-cache.txt]
in order to avoid this warning in the future (yes/no)? : yes
Successfully appended new sig to user sig cache file
Mounted eCryptfs
donnie@ubuntu2:~$
```

Just for fun, I'll create a file within my new encrypted `secrets` directory, and then unmount the directory:

```
cd /secrets
sudo vim secret_stuff.txt
cd
sudo umount /secrets
ls -l /secrets

donnie@ubuntu2:/secrets$ ls -l
total 12
-rw-r--r-- 1 root root 12288 Oct 31 18:24
ECRYPTFS_FNEK_ENCRYPTED.FXbXCS5fwxKABUQtEPlumGPaN-RGvqd13yybkpTr1eCVWVHdr-
```

```
lrmi1X9Vu-mLM-A-VeqIdN6KNZGcs-
donnie@ubuntu2:/secrets$
```

By choosing to encrypt filenames, nobody can even tell what files you have when the directory is unmounted. When I'm ready to access my encrypted files again, I'll just remount the directory the same as I did before.

Encrypting the swap partition with eCryptfs

If you're just encrypting individual directories with eCryptfs instead of using LUKS whole-disk encryption, you'll need to encrypt your swap partition in order to prevent accidental data leakage. Fixing that problem requires just one simple command:

```
donnie@ubuntu:~$ sudo ecryptfs-setup-swap
[sudo] password for donnie:

WARNING:
An encrypted swap is required to help ensure that encrypted files are not
leaked to disk in an unencrypted format.

HOWEVER, THE SWAP ENCRYPTION CONFIGURATION PRODUCED BY THIS PROGRAM WILL
BREAK HIBERNATE/RESUME ON THIS SYSTEM!

NOTE: Your suspend/resume capabilities will not be affected.

Do you want to proceed with encrypting your swap? [y/N]: y

INFO: Setting up swap: [/dev/sda5]
WARNING: Commented out your unencrypted swap from /etc/fstab
swapon: stat of /dev/mapper/cryptswap1 failed: No such file or directory
donnie@ubuntu:~$
```

Don't mind the warning about the missing /dev/mapper/cryptswap1 file. It will get created the next time you reboot the machine.

Using VeraCrypt for cross-platform sharing of encrypted containers

Once upon a time, there was TrueCrypt, a cross-platform program that allowed the sharing of encrypted containers across different operating systems. But the project was always shrouded in mystery, because its developers would never reveal their identities. And then, right out of the blue, the developers released a cryptic message about how TrueCrypt was no longer secure, and shut down the project.

VeraCrypt is the successor to TrueCrypt, and it allows the sharing of encrypted containers across Linux, Windows, MacOS, and FreeBSD machines. Although LUKS and eCryptfs are good, VeraCrypt does offer more flexibility in certain ways:

- As mentioned, VeraCrypt offers cross-platform sharing, whereas LUKS and eCryptfs don't
- VeraCrypt allows you to encrypt either whole partitions or whole storage devices, or to create virtual encrypted disks
- Not only can you create encrypted volumes with VeraCrypt, you can also hide them, giving you plausible deniability
- VeraCrypt comes in both command-line and GUI variants, so it's appropriate for either server use or for the casual desktop user
- Like LUKS and eCryptfs, VeraCrypt is free open source software, which means that it's free to use, and that the source code can be audited for either bugs or backdoors

Getting and installing VeraCrypt

The Linux version of VeraCrypt comes as a set of universal installer scripts that should work on any Linux distribution. Once you extract the `.tar.bz2` archive file, you'll see two scripts for GUI installation, and two for console-mode installation. One of each of those is for 32-bit Linux, and one of each is for 64-bit Linux:

```
donnie@linux-0ro8:~/Downloads> ls -l vera*
-r-xr-xr-x 1 donnie users  2976573 Jul  9 05:10 veracrypt-1.21-setup-
console-x64
-r-xr-xr-x 1 donnie users  2967950 Jul  9 05:14 veracrypt-1.21-setup-
console-x86
-r-xr-xr-x 1 donnie users  4383555 Jul  9 05:08 veracrypt-1.21-setup-gui-
x64
-r-xr-xr-x 1 donnie users  4243305 Jul  9 05:13 veracrypt-1.21-setup-gui-
```

```
x86
-rw-r--r-- 1 donnie users 14614830 Oct 31 23:49 veracrypt-1.21-
setup.tar.bz2
donnie@linux-0ro8:~/Downloads>
```

For the server demo, I used `scp` to transfer the 64-bit console-mode installer to one of my Ubuntu virtual machines. The executable permission is already set, so all you have to do to install is:

```
donnie@ubuntu:~$ ./veracrypt-1.21-setup-console-x64
```

You'll need sudo privileges, but the installer will prompt you for your sudo password. After reading and agreeing to a rather lengthy license agreement, the installation only takes a few seconds.

Creating and mounting a VeraCrypt volume in console mode

I haven't been able to find any documentation for the console-mode variant of VeraCrypt, but you can see a list of the available commands just by typing `veracrypt`. For this demo, I'm creating a 2 GB encrypted volume in my own home directory. But you can just as easily do it elsewhere, such as on a USB memory stick.

To create a new encrypted volume, type:

```
veracrypt -c
```

This will take you into an easy-to-use, interactive utility. For the most part, you'll be fine just accepting the default options:

```
donnie@ubuntu:~$ veracrypt -c
Volume type:
 1) Normal
 2) Hidden
Select [1]:

Enter volume path: /home/donnie/good_stuff

Enter volume size (sizeK/size[M]/sizeG): 2G

Encryption Algorithm:
 1) AES
 2) Serpent
 3) Twofish
```

```
 4) Camellia
 5) Kuznyechik
 6) AES(Twofish)
 7) AES(Twofish(Serpent))
 8) Serpent(AES)
 9) Serpent(Twofish(AES))
 10) Twofish(Serpent)
Select [1]:

Hash algorithm:
 1) SHA-512
 2) Whirlpool
 3) SHA-256
 4) Streebog
Select [1]:
 . . .
 . . .
```

For the filesystem, the default option of FAT will give you the best cross-platform compatibility between Linux, MacOS, and Windows:

```
Filesystem:
 1) None
 2) FAT
 3) Linux Ext2
 4) Linux Ext3
 5) Linux Ext4
 6) NTFS
 7) exFAT
Select [2]:
```

You'll then select your password and a PIM, which stands for Personal Iterations Multiplier. (For the PIM, I entered 8891. High PIM values give better security, but they will also cause the volume to take longer to mount.) Then, type at least 320 random characters in order to generate the encryption key. (This is where it would be handy to have my cats walking across my keyboard.):

```
Enter password:
Re-enter password:

Enter PIM: 8891

Enter keyfile path [none]:

Please type at least 320 randomly chosen characters and then press Enter:
```

After you hit *Enter*, be patient, because the final generation of your encrypted volume will take a few moments. Here, you see that my 2 GB `good_stuff` container has been successfully created:

```
donnie@ubuntu:~$ ls -l good_stuff
-rw------- 1 donnie donnie 2147483648 Nov  1 17:02 good_stuff
donnie@ubuntu:~$
```

To use this container, I have to mount it. I'll begin by creating a mount point directory; the same as I would for mounting normal partitions:

```
donnie@ubuntu:~$ mkdir good_stuff_dir
donnie@ubuntu:~$
```

Use the `veracrypt` utility to mount your container on this mount point:

```
donnie@ubuntu:~$ veracrypt good_stuff good_stuff_dir
Enter password for /home/donnie/good_stuff:
Enter PIM for /home/donnie/good_stuff: 8891
Enter keyfile [none]:
Protect hidden volume (if any)? (y=Yes/n=No) [No]:
Enter your user password or administrator password:
donnie@ubuntu:~$
```

To see what VeraCrypt volumes you have mounted, use `veracrypt -l`:

```
donnie@ubuntu:~$ veracrypt -l
1: /home/donnie/secret_stuff /dev/mapper/veracrypt1
/home/donnie/secret_stuff_dir
2: /home/donnie/good_stuff /dev/mapper/veracrypt2
/home/donnie/good_stuff_dir
donnie@ubuntu:~$
```

And, that's all there is to it.

Using VeraCrypt in GUI mode

Desktop users of any of the supported operating systems can install the GUI variant of VeraCrypt. Be aware though, that you can't install both the console-mode variant and the GUI variant on the same machine, because one will overwrite the other. Here, you see the GUI version running on my CentOS 7 virtual machine:

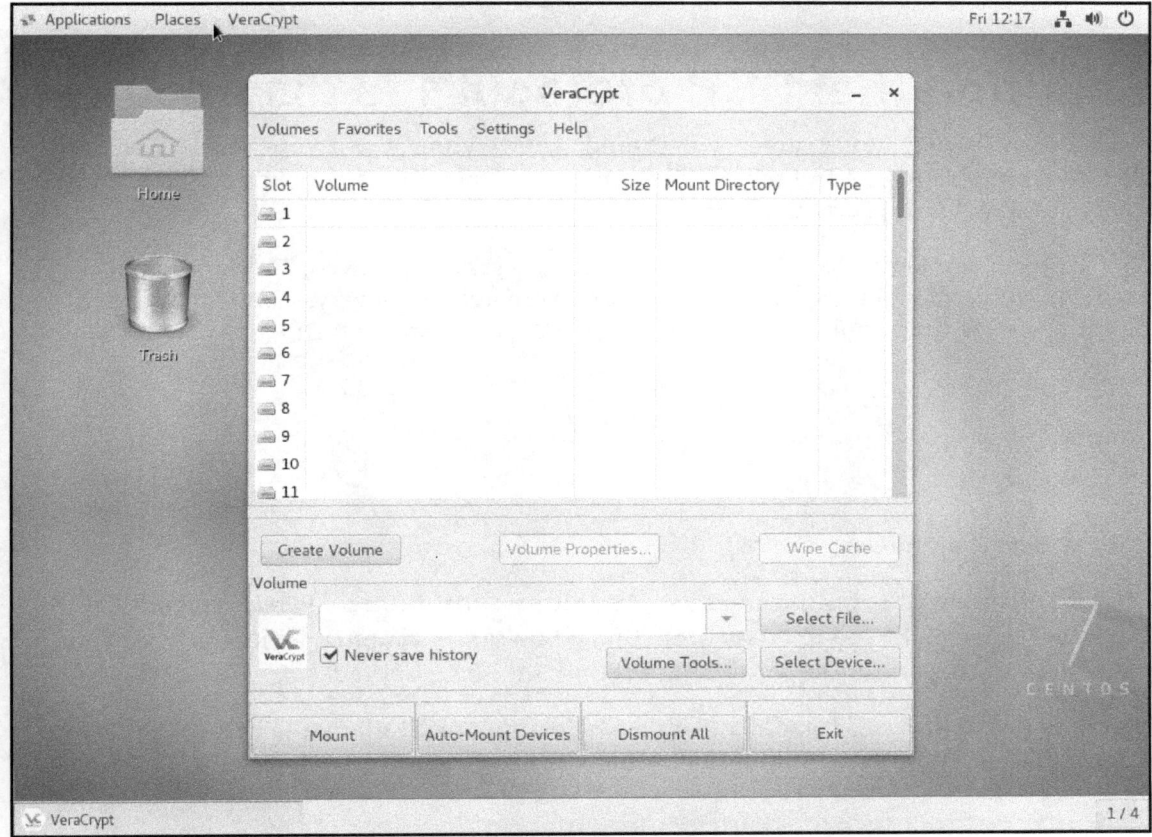

Since the main focus of this book is sever security, I won't go into the details of the GUI version here. But, it's fairly self-explanatory, and you can view the full VeraCrypt documentation on their website.

 You can get VeraCrypt from here: `https://www.veracrypt.fr/en/Home.html`

For the rest of this chapter, we'll turn our attention to the subject of protecting data in transit, by locking down Secure Shell.

Ensuring that SSH protocol 1 is disabled

By this stage in your Linux career, you should already know how to use Secure Shell, or SSH, to do remote logins and remote file transfers. What you may not know is that a default configuration of SSH is actually quite insecure.

SSH protocol version 1, the original SSH protocol, is severely flawed, and should never be used. It's still in most Linux distributions, but fortunately, it's always disabled by default. But, if you ever open your `/etc/ssh/sshd_config` file and see this:

```
Protocol 1
```

Or this:

```
Protocol 1, 2
```

Then you have a problem.

The Ubuntu main page for the `sshd_config` file says that protocol version 1 is still available for use with `legacy devices`. But, if you're still running devices that are that old, you need to start seriously thinking about doing some upgrades.

As Linux distributions get updated, you'll see SSH protocol 1 gradually being completely removed, as has happened with Red Hat and CentOS 7.4.

Creating and managing keys for password-less logins

The Secure Shell Suite, or SSH, is a great set of tools that provides secure, encrypted communications with remote servers. You can use the SSH component to remotely log into the command-line of a remote machine, and you can use either `scp` or `sftp` to securely transfer files. The default way to use any of these SSH components is to use the username and password of a person's normal Linux user account. So, logging into a remote machine from the terminal of my OpenSUSE workstation would look something like:

```
donnie@linux-0ro8:~> ssh donnie@192.168.0.8
donnie@192.168.0.8's password:
```

While it's true that the username and password go across the network in an encrypted format, making it hard for malicious actors to intercept, it's still not the most secure way of doing business. The problem is that attackers have access to automated tools that can perform brute-force password attacks against an SSH server. Botnets, such as the Hail Mary Cloud, perform continuous scans across the internet to find internet-facing servers with SSH enabled. If a botnet finds that the servers allow SSH access via username and password, it will then launch a brute-force password attack. Sadly, such attacks have been successful quite a few times, especially when the server operators allow the root user to log in via SSH.

This older article gives more details about the Hail Mary Cloud botnet: `http://futurismic.com/2009/11/16/the-hail-mary-cloud-slow-but-steady-brute-force-password-guessing-botnet/`

In the next section, we'll look at two ways to help prevent these types of attacks:

- Enable SSH logins through an exchange of public keys
- Disable the root user login through SSH

Creating a user's SSH key set

Each user has the ability to create his or her own set of private and public keys. It doesn't matter whether the user's client machine is running Linux, MacOS, or Cygwin on Windows. In all three cases, the procedure is exactly the same. To demo, I'll create keys on my OpenSUSE workstation and transfer the public key to one of my virtual machines. It doesn't matter which virtual machine I use, but since I haven't shown much love to the CentOS machine lately, I'll use it.

I'll begin by creating the keys on my OpenSUSE workstation:

```
donnie@linux-0ro8:~> ssh-keygen
Generating public/private rsa key pair.
Enter file in which to save the key (/home/donnie/.ssh/id_rsa):
Enter passphrase (empty for no passphrase):
Enter same passphrase again:
Your identification has been saved in /home/donnie/.ssh/id_rsa.
Your public key has been saved in /home/donnie/.ssh/id_rsa.pub.
The key fingerprint is:
SHA256:oqDpCvAptbE8srN6Z4FNXxgkhPhjh1sEKazfMpxhVI8 donnie@linux-0ro8
The key's randomart image is:
+---[RSA 2048]----+
|...*+..          |
|o.+ .+.          |
|.+ oE .o         |
|. B + . .        |
|.=+% ...S        |
|.*O*+...         |
|* Bo..           |
|++..o            |
|B= o             |
+----[SHA256]-----+
donnie@linux-0ro8:~>
```

There are several different types of keys that you can create, but the default 2048-bit RSA keys are considered as plenty strong enough for the foreseeable future. The private and public SSH keys work the same as we saw with GPG. You'll keep your private keys to yourself, but you can share the public key with the world, if you so desire. In this case though, I'm only going to share my public key with just one server.

When prompted for the location and name of the keys, I'll just hit *Enter* to accept the defaults. You could just leave the private key with a blank passphrase, but that's not a recommended practice.

 Note that if you choose an alternative name for your key files, you'll need to type in the entire path to make things work properly. For example, in my case, I would specify the path for `donnie_rsa` keys as:

```
/home/donnie/.ssh/donnie_rsa
```

In the `.ssh` directory in my home directory, I can see the keys that I created:

```
donnie@linux-0ro8:~/.ssh> ls -l
total 12
-rw-------  1 donnie users 1766 Nov  2 17:52 id_rsa
-rw-r--r--  1 donnie users  399 Nov  2 17:52 id_rsa.pub
-rw-r--r--  1 donnie users 2612 Oct 31 18:40 known_hosts
donnie@linux-0ro8:~/.ssh>
```

The `id_rsa` key is the private key, with read and write permissions only for me. The `id_rsa.pub` public key has to be world-readable.

Transferring the public key to the remote server

Transferring my public key to a remote server allows the server to readily identify both me and my client machine. Before I can transfer the public key to the remote server, I need to add the private key to my session keyring. This requires two commands. (One command is to invoke the `ssh-agent`, and the other command actually adds the private key to the keyring.):

```
donnie@linux-0ro8:~> exec /usr/bin/ssh-agent $SHELL
donnie@linux-0ro8:~> ssh-add
Enter passphrase for /home/donnie/.ssh/id_rsa:
Identity added: /home/donnie/.ssh/id_rsa (/home/donnie/.ssh/id_rsa)
donnie@linux-0ro8:~>
```

Finally, I can transfer my public key to my CentOS server, which is at address `192.168.0.101`:

```
donnie@linux-0ro8:~> ssh-copy-id donnie@192.168.0.101
/usr/bin/ssh-copy-id: INFO: attempting to log in with the new key(s), to
filter out any that are already installed
/usr/bin/ssh-copy-id: INFO: 1 key(s) remain to be installed -- if you are
prompted now it is to install the new keys
```

```
donnie@192.168.0.101's password:

Number of key(s) added: 1

Now try logging into the machine, with:   "ssh 'donnie@192.168.0.101'"
and check to make sure that only the key(s) you wanted were added.

donnie@linux-0ro8:~>
```

The next time that I log in, I'll use the key exchange, and I won't have to enter a password:

```
donnie@linux-0ro8:~> ssh donnie@192.168.0.101
Last login: Wed Nov  1 20:11:20 2017
[donnie@localhost ~]$
```

So, now you're wondering, *"How is that secure if I can log in without entering my password?"* The answer is that once you close the client machine's terminal window that you used for logging in, the private key will be removed from your session keyring. When you open a new terminal and try to log in to the remote server, you'll see this:

```
donnie@linux-0ro8:~> ssh donnie@192.168.0.101
Enter passphrase for key '/home/donnie/.ssh/id_rsa':
```

Now, every time I log into this server, I'll need to enter the passphrase for my private key. (That is, unless I add it back to the session keyring with the two commands that I showed you in the preceding section.)

Disabling root user login

A few years ago, there was a somewhat celebrated case where malicious actors had managed to plant malware on quite a few Linux servers somewhere in southeast Asia. There were three reasons that the bad guys found this so easy to do:

- The internet-facing servers involved were set up to use username/password authentication for SSH
- The root user was allowed to log in through SSH
- User passwords, including the root user's password, were incredibly weak

All this meant that it was easy for Hail Mary to brute-force its way in.

Different distributions have different default settings for root user login. In the `/etc/ssh/sshd_config` file of your CentOS machine, you'll see this line:

```
#PermitRootLogin yes
```

Unlike what you have in most configuration files, the commented-out lines in `sshd_config` define the default settings for the Secure Shell daemon. So, this line indicates that the root user is indeed allowed to log in through SSH. To change that, I'll remove the comment symbol and change the setting to `no`:

```
PermitRootLogin no
```

To make the new setting take effect, I'll restart the SSH daemon, which is named `sshd` on CentOS, and is named `ssh` on Ubuntu:

```
sudo systemctl restart sshd
```

On the Ubuntu machine, the default setting looks a bit different:

```
PermitRootLogin prohibit-password
```

This means that the root user is allowed to log in, but only via a public key exchange. That's probably secure enough, if you really need to allow the root user to log in. But in most cases, you'll want to force admin users to log in with their normal user accounts, and to use `sudo` for their admin needs. So, in most cases, you can still change this setting to `no`.

 Be aware that if you deploy an instance of Ubuntu Server on a cloud service, such as Azure, Rackspace, or Vultr, the service owners will have you log into the virtual machine with the root user account. The first thing you'll want to do is to create your own normal user account, log back in with that account, disable the root user account, and disable the root user login in `sshd_config`.

Disabling username/password logins

This is something that you'll only want to do after you've set up the key exchange with your clients. Otherwise, clients will be locked out of doing remote logins.

For both Ubuntu and CentOS machines, look for this line in the `sshd_config` file:

```
#PasswordAuthentication yes
```

Remove the comment symbol, change the parameter value to no, and restart the SSH daemon. The line should now look like this:

```
PasswordAuthentication no
```

Now, when the botnets scan your system, they'll see that doing a brute-force password attack would be useless. They'll then just go away and leave you alone.

Setting up a chroot environment for SFTP users

Secure File Transfer Protocol (**SFTP**) is a great tool for performing secure file transfers. There is a command-line client, but users will most likely use a graphical client, such as Filezilla. A common use-case for SFTP is to allow website owners to upload web content files to the proper content directories on a web server. With a default SSH setup, anyone who has a user account on a Linux machine can log in through either SSH or SFTP, and can navigate through the server's entire filesystem. What we really want for SFTP users is to prevent them from logging into a command-prompt via SSH, and to confine them to their own designated directories.

Creating a group and configuring the sshd_config file

With the exception of the slight difference in user-creation commands, this procedure works the same for either CentOS or Ubuntu. So, you can use either one of your virtual machines to follow along. We'll begin by creating an sftpusers group.

```
sudo groupadd sftpusers
```

Create the user accounts, and add them to the sftpusers group. We'll do both operations in one step. On your CentOS machine, the command for creating Max's account would be:

```
sudo useradd -G sftpusers max
```

On your Ubuntu machine, it would be:

```
sudo useradd -m -d /home/max -s /bin/bash -G sftpusers max
```

Open the `/etc/ssh/sshd_config` file in your favorite text editor. Find the line that says:

```
Subsystem sftp /usr/lib/openssh/sftp-server
```

Change it to:

```
Subsystem sftp internal-sftp
```

This setting allows you to disable normal SSH login for certain users.

At the bottom of the `sshd_config` file, add a `Match Group` stanza:

```
Match Group sftpusers
        ChrootDirectory /home
        AllowTCPForwarding no
        AllowAgentForwarding no
        X11Forwarding no
        ForceCommand internal-sftp
```

An important consideration here is that the `ChrootDirectory` has to be owned by the root user, and it can't be writable by anyone other than the root user. When Max logs in, he'll be in the `/home` directory, and will then have to `cd` into his own directory. This also means that you want for all users' home directories to have the restrictive `700` permissions settings, in order to keep everyone out of everyone else's stuff.

Save the file and restart the SSH daemon. Then, try to log on as Max through normal SSH, just to see what happens:

```
donnie@linux-0ro8:~> ssh max@192.168.0.8
max@192.168.0.8's password:
This service allows sftp connections only.
Connection to 192.168.0.8 closed.
donnie@linux-0ro8:~>
```

Okay, so he can't do that. Let's now have him try to log in through SFTP, and verify that he is in the `/home` directory:

```
donnie@linux-0ro8:~> sftp max@192.168.0.8
max@192.168.0.8's password:
Connected to 192.168.0.8.
drwx------    7 1000     1000         4096 Nov  4 22:53 donnie
drwx------    5 1001     1001         4096 Oct 27 23:34 frank
drwx------    3 1003     1004         4096 Nov  4 22:43 katelyn
drwx------    2 1002     1003         4096 Nov  4 22:37 max
sftp>
```

Now, let's see him try to `cd` out of the `/home` directory:

```
sftp> cd /etc
Couldn't stat remote file: No such file or directory
sftp>
```

So, our chroot jail does indeed work.

Hands-on lab – setting up a chroot directory for sftpusers group

For this lab, you can use either the CentOS virtual machine or the Ubuntu virtual machine. You'll add a group, then configure the `sshd_config` file to allow group members to only be able to log in via SFTP, and to confine them to their own directories. For the simulated client machine, you can use the terminal of your MacOS or Linux desktop machine, or Cygwin from your Windows machine:

1. Create the `sftpusers` group:

   ```
   sudo groupadd sftpusers
   ```

2. Create a user account for Max, and add him to the `sftpusers` group. On CentOS, do:

   ```
   sudo useradd –G sftpusers max
   ```

   On Ubuntu, do:

   ```
   sudo useradd –m –d /home/max –s /bin/bash –G sftpusers max
   ```

3. For Ubuntu, ensure that the users' home directories are all set with read, write, and execute permissions for only the directory's user. If that's not the case, do:

   ```
   sudo chmod 700 /home/*
   ```

4. Open the `/etc/ssh/sshd_config` file in your preferred text editor. Find the line that says:

   ```
   Subsystem sftp /usr/lib/openssh/sftp-server
   ```

   Change it to:

   ```
   Subsystem sftp internal-sftp
   ```

5. At the end of the `sshd_config` file, add the following stanza:

```
Match Group sftpusers
        ChrootDirectory /home
        AllowTCPForwarding no
        AllowAgentForwarding no
        X11Forwarding no
        ForceCommand internal-sftp
```

6. Restart the SSH daemon. On CentOS, do:

`sudo systemctl sshd restart`

On Ubuntu, do:

`sudo systemctl ssh restart`

7. Have Max try to log in through normal SSH, to see what happens:

`ssh max@IP_Address_of_your_vm`

8. Now, have Max log in through SFTP. Once he's in, have him try to `cd` out of the `/home` directory:

`sftp max@IP_Address_of_your_vm`

9. End of Lab.

Summary

In this chapter, we've seen how to work with various encryption technologies that can help us safeguard our secrets. We started with GNU Privacy Guard for encrypting individual files. We then moved on to the disk, partition, and directory encryption utilities. LUKS and eCryptfs are specific to Linux, but we also looked at VeraCrypt, which can be used on any of the major operating systems.

In the next chapter, we'll take an in-depth look at the subject of discretionary access control. I'll see you there.

5
Mastering Discretionary Access Control

Discretionary Access Control, DAC, really just means that each user has the ability to control who can get into his or her stuff. If I wanted to open my home directory so that every other user on the system can get into it, I could do that. Having done so, I could then control who can access each specific file. In the next chapter, we'll use our DAC skills to manage shared directories, where members of a group might need different levels of access to the files within.

By this point in your Linux career, you likely know the basics of controlling access by setting file and directory permissions. In this chapter, we'll do a review of the basics, and then we'll look at some more advanced concepts. Topics that we'll cover include:

- Using `chown` to change the ownership of files and directories
- Using `chmod` to set permissions on files and directories
- What SUID and SGID settings can do for us on regular files
- The security implications of having the SUID and SGID permissions set on files that don't need them
- How to use extended file attributes to protect sensitive files

Using chown to change ownership of files and directories

Controlling access to files and directories really just boils down to ensuring that the proper users own files and directories, and that each file and directory has permissions set in such a way that only authorized users can access them. The chown utility covers the first part of this equation.

One unique thing about chown is that you must have sudo privileges to use it, even if you're working with your own files in your own directory. You can use it to change the user of a file or directory, the group that's associated with a file or directory, or both at the same time.

First, let's say that you own the perm_demo.txt file and you want to change both the user and group association to that of another user. In this case, I'll change the file ownership from me to Maggie:

```
[donnie@localhost ~]$ ls -l perm_demo.txt
-rw-rw-r--. 1 donnie donnie 0 Nov  5 20:02 perm_demo.txt

[donnie@localhost ~]$ sudo chown maggie:maggie perm_demo.txt

[donnie@localhost ~]$ ls -l perm_demo.txt
-rw-rw-r--. 1 maggie maggie 0 Nov  5 20:02 perm_demo.txt
[donnie@localhost ~]$
```

The first maggie in maggie:maggie is the user to whom you want to grant ownership. The second maggie, after the colon, represents the group with which you want the file to be associated. Since I was changing both the user and group to maggie, I could have left off the second maggie, with the first maggie followed by a colon, and I would have achieved the same result:

```
sudo chown maggie: perm_demo.txt
```

To just change the group association without changing the user, just list the group name, preceded by a colon:

```
[donnie@localhost ~]$ sudo chown :accounting perm_demo.txt

[donnie@localhost ~]$ ls -l perm_demo.txt
-rw-rw-r--. 1 maggie accounting 0 Nov  5 20:02 perm_demo.txt
[donnie@localhost ~]$
```

Finally, to just change the user without changing the group, list the username without the trailing colon:

```
[donnie@localhost ~]$ sudo chown donnie perm_demo.txt

[donnie@localhost ~]$ ls -l perm_demo.txt
-rw-rw-r--. 1 donnie accounting 0 Nov  5 20:02 perm_demo.txt
[donnie@localhost ~]$
```

These commands work the same way on a directory as they do on a file. But, if you want to also change the ownership and/or the group association of the contents of a directory, while also making the change on the directory itself, use the -R option, which stands for *recursive*. In this case, I just want to change the group for the perm_demo_dir directory to accounting:

```
[donnie@localhost ~]$ ls -ld perm_demo_dir
drwxrwxr-x. 2 donnie donnie 74 Nov  5 20:17 perm_demo_dir

[donnie@localhost ~]$ ls -l perm_demo_dir
total 0
-rw-rw-r--. 1 donnie donnie 0 Nov  5 20:17 file1.txt
-rw-rw-r--. 1 donnie donnie 0 Nov  5 20:17 file2.txt
-rw-rw-r--. 1 donnie donnie 0 Nov  5 20:17 file3.txt
-rw-rw-r--. 1 donnie donnie 0 Nov  5 20:17 file4.txt

[donnie@localhost ~]$ sudo chown -R :accounting perm_demo_dir

[donnie@localhost ~]$ ls -ld perm_demo_dir
drwxrwxr-x. 2 donnie accounting 74 Nov  5 20:17 perm_demo_dir

[donnie@localhost ~]$ ls -l perm_demo_dir
total 0
-rw-rw-r--. 1 donnie accounting 0 Nov  5 20:17 file1.txt
-rw-rw-r--. 1 donnie accounting 0 Nov  5 20:17 file2.txt
-rw-rw-r--. 1 donnie accounting 0 Nov  5 20:17 file3.txt
-rw-rw-r--. 1 donnie accounting 0 Nov  5 20:17 file4.txt
[donnie@localhost ~]$
```

And, that's all there is to chown.

Using chmod to set permissions values on files and directories

On Unix and Linux systems, you would use the chmod utility to set permissions values on files and directories. You can set permissions for the user of the file or directory, the group that's associated with the file or directory, and others. The three basic permissions are:

- r: This indicates a read permission.
- w: This is for a write permission.
- x: This is the executable permission. You can apply it to any type of program file, or to directories. If you apply an executable permission to a directory, authorized people will be able to cd into it.

Do an ls -l on a file, and you'll see something like this:

```
-rw-rw-r--. 1 donnie donnie    804692 Oct 28 18:44 yum_list.txt
```

The first character of this line indicates the type of file. In this case, we see a dash, which indicates a regular file. (A regular file is pretty much every type of file that a normal user would be able to access in his or her daily routine.) The next three characters, rw-, indicate that the file has read and write permissions for the user, which is the person who owns the file. We then see rw- permissions for the group, and r-- permissions for others. A program file would also have the executable permissions set:

```
-rwxr-xr-x. 1 root root     62288 Nov 20  2015 xargs
```

Here, we see that the xargs program file has executable permissions set for everybody.

There are two ways that you can use chmod to change permissions settings:

- The symbolic method
- The numerical method

Setting permissions with the symbolic method

Whenever you create a file as a normal user, by default, it will have read and write permissions for the user and the group, and read permissions for others. If you create a program file, you have to add the executable permissions yourself. With the symbolic method, you could use one of the following commands to do so:

```
chmod u+x donnie_script.sh
chmod g+x donnie_script.sh
chmod o+x donnie_script.sh
chmod u+x,g+x donnie_script.sh
chmod a+x donnie_script.sh
```

The first three commands add the executable permission for the user, the group, and others. The fourth command adds executable permissions for both the user and the group, and the last command adds executable permissions for everybody (a for all). You could also remove the executable permissions by replacing the + with a –. And, you can also add or remove the read or write permissions, as appropriate.

While this method can be handy at times, it also has a bit of a flaw. That is, it can only add permissions to what's already there, or remove permissions from what's already there. If you need to ensure that all of the permissions for a particular file get set to a certain value, the symbolic method can get a bit unwieldy. And for shell scripting, forget about it. In a shell script, you'd need to add all kinds of extra code just to determine which permissions are already set. The numerical method can vastly simplify things for us.

Setting permissions with the numerical method

With the numerical method, you'll use an octal value to represent the permissions settings on a file or directory. To the r, w, and x permissions, you assign the numerical values 4, 2, and 1, respectively. Do this for the user, group, and others positions, and add them all up to get the permissions value for the file or directory:

User	Group	Others
rwx	rwx	rwx
421	421	421
7	7	7

So, if you have all the permissions set for everybody, the file or directory will have a value of 777. If I were to create a shell script file, by default, it would have the standard 664 permissions, meaning read and write for the user and group, and read-only for others:

```
-rw-rw-r--. 1 donnie donnie 0 Nov  6 19:18 donnie_script.sh
```

 If you create a file with root privileges, either with sudo or from the root user command prompt, you'll see that the default permissions setting is the more restrictive 644.

Let's say that I want to make this script executable, but I want to be the only person in the whole world who can do anything with it. I could do:

```
[donnie@localhost ~]$ chmod 700 donnie_script.sh

[donnie@localhost ~]$ ls -l donnie_script.sh
-rwx------. 1 donnie donnie 0 Nov  6 19:18 donnie_script.sh
[donnie@localhost ~]$
```

With this one simple command, I've removed all permissions from the group and from others, and set the executable permission for myself. This is the sort of thing that makes the numerical method so handy for writing shell scripts.

Once you've been working with the numerical method for a while, looking at a file and figuring out its numerical permissions value will become second nature. In the meantime, you can use stat with the -c %a option to show you the values. For example:

```
[donnie@localhost ~]$ stat -c %a yum_list.txt
664
[donnie@localhost ~]$


[donnie@localhost ~]$ stat -c %a donnie_script.sh
700
[donnie@localhost ~]$

[donnie@localhost ~]$ stat -c %a /etc/fstab
644
[donnie@localhost ~]$
```

Using SUID and SGID on regular files

When a regular file has its SUID permission set, whoever accesses the file will have the same privileges as the user of the file. When the SGID permission is set on a regular file, whoever accesses the file will have the same privileges as the group that's associated with the file. This is especially useful on program files.

To demo this, let's say that Maggie, a regular, unprivileged user, wants to change her own password. Since it's her own password, she would just use the one-word command, passwd, without using sudo:

```
[maggie@localhost ~]$ passwd
Changing password for user maggie.
Changing password for maggie.
(current) UNIX password:
New password:
Retype new password:
passwd: all authentication tokens updated successfully.
[maggie@localhost ~]$
```

To change a password, a person has to make changes to the /etc/shadow file. On my CentOS machine, the shadow file permissions look like this:

```
[donnie@localhost etc]$ ls -l shadow
----------. 1 root root 840 Nov  6 19:37 shadow
[donnie@localhost etc]$
```

On the Ubuntu machine, they look like this:

```
donnie@ubuntu:/etc$ ls -l shadow
-rw-r----- 1 root shadow 1316 Nov  4 18:38 shadow
donnie@ubuntu:/etc$
```

Either way, the permissions settings don't allow Maggie to modify the shadow file. Yet, by changing her password, she is able to modify the shadow file. So, what's going on? To answer this, let's go into the /usr/bin directory and look at the permissions settings for the passwd executable file:

```
[donnie@localhost etc]$ cd /usr/bin

[donnie@localhost bin]$ ls -l passwd
-rwsr-xr-x. 1 root root 27832 Jun 10 2014 passwd
[donnie@localhost bin]$
```

For the user permissions, you see `rws` instead of `rwx`. The `s` indicates that this file has the SUID permission set. Since the file belongs to the root user, anyone who accesses this file has the same privileges as the root user. The fact that we see a lower-case `s` means that the file also has the executable permission set for the root user. Since the root user is allowed to modify the shadow file, whoever uses this `passwd` utility to change his or her own password can also modify the shadow file.

A file with the SGID permission set has an `s` in the executable position for the group:

```
[donnie@localhost bin]$ ls -l write
-rwxr-sr-x. 1 root tty 19536 Aug  4 07:18 write
[donnie@localhost bin]$
```

The `write` utility, which is associated with the `tty` group, allows users to send messages to other users via their command-line consoles. Having `tty` group privileges allows users to do this.

The security implications of the SUID and SGID permissions

As useful as it may be to have SUID or SGID permissions on your executable files, we should consider it as just a necessary evil. While having SUID or SGID set on certain operating system files is essential to the proper operation of your Linux system, it becomes a security risk when users set SUID or SGID on other files. The problem is that, if intruders find an executable file that belongs to the root user and has the SUID bit set, they can use that to exploit the system. Before they leave, they might leave behind their own root-owned file with SUID set, which will allow them to easily gain entry into the system the next time. If the intruder's SUID file isn't found, the intruder will still have access, even if the original problem is fixed.

The numerical value for SUID is 4000, and for SGID it's 2000. To set SUID on a file, you'd just add 4000 to whichever permissions value that you would set otherwise. For example, if you have a file with a permissions value of 755, you'd set SUID by changing the permissions value to 4755. (This would give you read/write/execute for the user, read/execute for the group, and read/execute for others, with the SUID bit added on.)

Finding spurious SUID or SGID files

One quick security trick is to run a `find` command to take inventory of the SUID and SGID files on your system. You could save the output to a text file, so that you can verify whether anything got added the next time you run the command. Your command would look something like this:

```
sudo find / -type f \( -perm -4000 -o -perm 2000 \) > suid_sgid_files.txt
```

Here's the breakdown:

- `/`: We're searching through the entire filesystem. Since some directories are only accessible to someone with root privileges, we need to use `sudo`.
- `-type f`: This means that we're searching for regular files, which would include executable program files and shell scripts.
- `-perm 4000`: We're searching for files with the `4000`, or SUID, permission bit set.
- `-o`: The or operator.
- `-perm 2000`: We're searching for files with the `2000`, or SGID, permission bit set.
- `>`: And, of course, we're redirecting the output into the `suid_sgid_files.txt` text file with the > operator.

Note that the two `-perm` items need to be combined into a term that's enclosed in a pair of parentheses. In order to prevent the Bash shell from interpreting the parenthesis characters incorrectly, we need to escape each one with a backslash. We also need to place a blank space between the first parenthesis character and the first `-perm`, and another between the `2000` and the last backslash. Also, the and operator between the `-type f` and the `-perm` term is understood to be there, even without inserting `-a`. The text file that you create should look something like this:

```
/usr/bin/chfn
/usr/bin/chsh
/usr/bin/chage
/usr/bin/gpasswd
/usr/bin/newgrp
/usr/bin/mount
/usr/bin/su
/usr/bin/umount
/usr/bin/sudo
/usr/bin/pkexec
/usr/bin/crontab
/usr/bin/passwd
/usr/sbin/pam_timestamp_check
/usr/sbin/unix_chkpwd
```

```
/usr/sbin/usernetctl
/usr/lib/polkit-1/polkit-agent-helper-1
/usr/lib64/dbus-1/dbus-daemon-launch-helper
```

Optionally, if you want to see details about which files are SUID and which are SGID, you can add in the -ls option:

```
sudo find / -type f \( -perm -4000 -o -perm 2000 \) -ls >
suid_sgid_files.txt
```

Now, let's say that Maggie, for whatever reason, decides to set the SUID bit on a shell script file in her home directory:

```
[maggie@localhost ~]$ chmod 4755 bad_script.sh

[maggie@localhost ~]$ ls -l
total 0
-rwsr-xr-x. 1 maggie maggie 0 Nov  7 13:06 bad_script.sh
[maggie@localhost ~]$
```

Run the find command again, saving the output to a different text file. Then, do a diff operation on the two files to see what changed:

```
[donnie@localhost ~]$ diff suid_sgid_files.txt suid_sgid_files2.txt
17a18
> /home/maggie/bad_script.sh
[donnie@localhost ~]$
```

The only difference is the addition of Maggie's shell script file.

Hands-on lab – searching for SUID and SGID files

You can do this lab on either of your virtual machines. You'll save the output of the find command to a text file:

1. Search through the entire filesystem for all files that have either SUID or SGID set, saving the output to a text file:

   ```
   sudo find / -type f \( -perm -4000 -o -perm 2000 \) -ls >
   suid_sgid_files.txt
   ```

2. Log into any other user account that you have on the system, and create a dummy shell script file. Then, set the SUID permission on that file, and log back out into your own user account:

```
su - desired_user_account
touch some_shell_script.sh
chmod 4755 some_shell_script.sh
ls -l some_shell_script.sh
exit
```

3. Run the find command again, saving the output to a different text file:

```
sudo find / -type f \( -perm -4000 -o -perm 2000 \) -ls >
suid_sgid_files_2.txt
```

4. View the difference between the two files:

```
diff suid_sgid_files.txt suid_sgid_files_2.txt
```

5. End of lab.

Preventing SUID and SGID usage on a partition

As we said before, you don't want users to assign SUID and SGID to files that they create, because of the security risk that it presents. You can prevent SUID and SGID usage on a partition by mounting it with the nosuid option. So, the /etc/fstab file entry for the luks partition that I created in the previous chapter would look like this:

```
/dev/mapper/luks-6cbdce17-48d4-41a1-8f8e-793c0fa7c389 /secrets          xfs
nosuid  0 0
```

Different Linux distributions have different ways of setting up default partition schemes during an operating system installation. Mostly, the default way of doing business is to have all directories, except for the /boot directory, under the / partition. If you were to set up a custom partition scheme instead, you could have the /home directory on its own partition, where you could set the nosuid option. Keep in mind, you don't want to set nosuid for the / partition, or else you'll have an operating system that doesn't function properly.

Using extended file attributes to protect sensitive files

Extended file attributes are another tool for helping you to protect sensitive files. They won't keep intruders from accessing your files, but they can help you prevent sensitive files from being altered or deleted. There are quite a few extended attributes, but we only need to look at the ones that deal with file security.

First, let's do an `lsattr` command to see which extended attributes you already have set. On the CentOS machine, your output would look something like this:

```
[donnie@localhost ~]$ lsattr
---------------- ./yum_list.txt
---------------- ./perm_demo.txt
---------------- ./perm_demo_dir
---------------- ./donnie_script.sh
---------------- ./suid_sgid_files.txt
---------------- ./suid_sgid_files2.txt
[donnie@localhost ~]$
```

So, as yet, I don't have any extended attributes set on any of my files.

On the Ubuntu machine, the output would look more like this:

```
donnie@ubuntu:~$ lsattr
-------------e-- ./file2.txt
-------------e-- ./secret_stuff_dir
-------------e-- ./secret_stuff_for_frank.txt.gpg
-------------e-- ./good_stuff
-------------e-- ./secret_stuff
-------------e-- ./not_secret_for_frank.txt.gpg
-------------e-- ./file4.txt
-------------e-- ./good_stuff_dir
donnie@ubuntu:~$
```

We won't worry about that `e` attribute, because that only means that the partition is formatted with the ext4 filesystem. CentOS doesn't have that attribute set, because its partition is formatted with the XFS filesystem.

The two attributes that we'll look at are:

- `a`: You can append text to the end of a file that has this attribute, but you can't overwrite it. Only someone with proper sudo privileges can set or delete this attribute.

- i: This makes a file immutable, and only someone with proper sudo privileges can set or delete it. Files with this attribute can't be deleted or changed in any way. It's also not possible to create hard links to files that have this attribute.

To set or delete attributes, you'll use the chattr command. You can set more than one attribute on a file, but only when it makes sense. For example, you wouldn't set both the a and the i attributes on the same file, because the i will override the a.

Let's start by creating the perm_demo.txt file with this text:

```
This is Donnie's sensitive file that he doesn't want to have overwritten.
```

Setting the a attribute

I'll now set the a attribute:

```
[donnie@localhost ~]$ sudo chattr +a perm_demo.txt
[sudo] password for donnie:
[donnie@localhost ~]$
```

You'll use a + to add an attribute, and a – to delete it. Also, it doesn't matter that the file does belong to me, and is in my own home directory. I still need sudo privileges to add or delete this attribute.

Now, let's see what happens when I try to overwrite this file:

```
[donnie@localhost ~]$ echo "I want to overwrite this file." > perm_demo.txt
-bash: perm_demo.txt: Operation not permitted

[donnie@localhost ~]$ sudo echo "I want to overwrite this file." >
perm_demo.txt
-bash: perm_demo.txt: Operation not permitted
[donnie@localhost ~]$
```

With or without sudo privileges, I can't overwrite it. So, how about if I try to append something to it?

```
[donnie@localhost ~]$ echo "I want to append this to the end of the file."
>> perm_demo.txt
[donnie@localhost ~]$
```

There's no error message this time. Let's see what's now in the file:

```
This is Donnie's sensitive file that he doesn't want to have overwritten.
I want to append this to the end of the file.
```

In addition to not being able to overwrite the file, I'm also unable to delete it:

```
[donnie@localhost ~]$ rm perm_demo.txt
rm: cannot remove 'perm_demo.txt': Operation not permitted

[donnie@localhost ~]$ sudo rm perm_demo.txt
[sudo] password for donnie:
rm: cannot remove 'perm_demo.txt': Operation not permitted
[donnie@localhost ~]$
```

So, the a works. But, I've decided that I no longer want this attribute set, so I'll remove it:

```
[donnie@localhost ~]$ sudo chattr -a perm_demo.txt
[donnie@localhost ~]$ lsattr perm_demo.txt
---------------- perm_demo.txt
[donnie@localhost ~]$
```

Setting the i attribute

When a file has the i attribute set, the only thing you can do with it is view its contents. You can't change it, move it, delete it, rename it, or create hard links to it. Let's test this with the perm_demo.txt file:

```
[donnie@localhost ~]$ sudo chattr +i perm_demo.txt
[donnie@localhost ~]$ lsattr perm_demo.txt
----i----------- perm_demo.txt
[donnie@localhost ~]$
```

Now, for the fun part:

```
[donnie@localhost ~]$ sudo echo "I want to overwrite this file." >
perm_demo.txt
-bash: perm_demo.txt: Permission denied
[donnie@localhost ~]$ echo "I want to append this to the end of the file."
>> perm_demo.txt
-bash: perm_demo.txt: Permission denied
[donnie@localhost ~]$ sudo echo "I want to append this to the end of the
file." >> perm_demo.txt
-bash: perm_demo.txt: Permission denied
[donnie@localhost ~]$ rm -f perm_demo.txt
rm: cannot remove 'perm_demo.txt': Operation not permitted
```

```
[donnie@localhost ~]$ sudo rm -f perm_demo.txt
rm: cannot remove 'perm_demo.txt': Operation not permitted
[donnie@localhost ~]$ sudo rm -f perm_demo.txt
```

There are a few more commands that I could try, but you get the idea. To remove the i attribute, I'll do:

```
[donnie@localhost ~]$ sudo chattr -i perm_demo.txt
[donnie@localhost ~]$ lsattr perm_demo.txt
----------------- perm_demo.txt
[donnie@localhost ~]$
```

Hands-on lab – setting security-related extended file attributes

For this lab, you'll create a perm_demo.txt file with the text of your own choosing. You'll set the i and a attributes, and view the results:

1. Using your preferred text editor, create the perm_demo.txt file with a line of text.
2. View the extended attributes of the file:

   ```
   lsattr perm_demo.txt
   ```

3. Add the a attribute:

   ```
   sudo chattr +a perm_demo.txt
   lsattr perm_demo.txt
   ```

4. Try to overwrite and delete the file:

   ```
   echo "I want to overwrite this file." > perm_demo.txt
   sudo echo "I want to overwrite this file." > perm_demo.txt
   rm perm_demo.txt
   sudo rm perm_demo.txt
   ```

5. Now, append something to the file:

   ```
   echo "I want to append this line to the end of the file." >>
   perm_demo.txt
   ```

6. Remove the `a` attribute, and add the `i` attribute:

```
sudo chattr -a perm_demo.txt
lsattr perm_demo.txt
sudo chattr +i perm_demo.txt
lsattr perm_demo.txt
```

7. Repeat Step 4.

8. Additionally, try to change the filename and to create a hard link to the file:

```
mv perm_demo.txt some_file.txt
sudo mv perm_demo.txt some_file.txt
ln ~/perm_demo.txt ~/some_file.txt
sudo ln ~/perm_demo.txt ~/some_file.txt
```

9. Now, try to create a symbolic link to the file:

```
ln -s ~/perm_demo.txt ~/some_file.txt
```

Note that the `i` attribute won't let you create hard links to a file, but it will let you create symbolic links.

10. End of lab.

Summary

In this chapter, we reviewed the basics of setting ownership and permissions for files and directories. We then covered what SUID and SGID can do for us when used properly, and the risk of setting them on our own executable files. Finally, we completed this roundup by looking at the two extended file attributes that deal with file security.

In the next chapter, we'll extend what we've learned here to more advanced file and directory access techniques. I'll see you there.

6
Access Control Lists and Shared Directory Management

In the previous chapter, we reviewed the basics of Discretionary Access Control. In this chapter, we'll take our discussion of DAC a step further. We'll look at some more advanced techniques that you can use to make DAC do exactly what you want it to do.

Topics in this chapter include:

- Creating an **access control list** (**ACL**) for either a user or a group
- Creating an inherited ACL for a directory
- Removing a specific permission by using an ACL mask
- Using the `tar --acls` option to prevent loss of ACLs during a backup
- Creating a user group and adding members to it
- Creating a shared directory for a group, and setting the proper permissions on it
- Setting the SGID bit and the sticky bit on the shared directory
- Using ACLs to allow only certain members of the group to access a file in the shared directory

Creating an access control list for either a user or a group

The normal Linux file and directory permissions settings are okay, but they're not very granular. With an ACL, we can allow only a certain person to access a file or directory, or we can allow multiple people to access a file or directory with different permissions for each person. If we have a file or a directory that's wide open for everyone, we can use an ACL to allow different levels of access for either a group or an individual. Towards the end of the chapter, we'll put what we've learned all together in order to manage a shared directory for a group.

You would use get facl to view an access control list for a file or directory. (Note that you can't use it to view all files in a directory at once.) To begin, let's use getfacl to see if we have any access control lists already set on the acl_demo.txt file:

```
[donnie@localhost ~]$ touch acl_demo.txt

[donnie@localhost ~]$ getfacl acl_demo.txt
# file: acl_demo.txt
# owner: donnie
# group: donnie
user::rw-
group::rw-
other::r--

[donnie@localhost ~]$
```

All we see here are just the normal permissions settings, so there's no ACL.

The first step for setting an ACL is to remove all permissions from everyone except for the user of the file. That's because the default permissions settings allow members of the group to have read/write access, and others to have read access. So, setting an ACL without removing those permissions would be rather senseless:

```
[donnie@localhost ~]$ chmod 600 acl_demo.txt

[donnie@localhost ~]$ ls -l acl_demo.txt
-rw-------. 1 donnie donnie 0 Nov  9 14:37 acl_demo.txt
[donnie@localhost ~]$
```

When using `setfacl` to set an ACL, you can allow a user or a group to have any combination of read, write, or execute privileges. In our case, let's say that I want to let Maggie read the file, and to prevent her from having write or execute privileges:

```
[donnie@localhost ~]$ setfacl -m u:maggie:r acl_demo.txt

[donnie@localhost ~]$ getfacl acl_demo.txt
# file: acl_demo.txt
# owner: donnie
# group: donnie
user::rw-
user:maggie:r--
group::---
mask::r--
other::---

[donnie@localhost ~]$ ls -l acl_demo.txt
-rw-r-----+ 1 donnie donnie 0 Nov  9 14:37 acl_demo.txt
[donnie@localhost ~]$
```

The `-m` option of `setfacl` means that we're about to modify the ACL. (Well, to create one in this case, but that's okay.) The `u:` means that we're setting an ACL for a user. We then list the user's name, followed by another colon, and the list of permissions that we want to grant to this user. In this case, we're only allowing Maggie read access. We complete the command by listing the file to which we want to apply this ACL. The `getfacl` output shows that Maggie does indeed have read access. Finally, we see in the `ls -l` output that the group is listed as having read access, even though we've set the `600` permissions setting on this file. But, there's also a + sign, which tells us that the file has an ACL. When we set an ACL, the permissions for the ACL show up as group permissions in `ls -l`.

To take this a step further, let's say that I want Frank to have read/write access to this file:

```
[donnie@localhost ~]$ setfacl -m u:frank:rw acl_demo.txt

[donnie@localhost ~]$ getfacl acl_demo.txt
# file: acl_demo.txt
# owner: donnie
# group: donnie
user::rw-
user:maggie:r--
user:frank:rw-
group::---
mask::rw-
other::---

[donnie@localhost ~]$ ls -l acl_demo.txt
```

```
-rw-rw----+ 1 donnie donnie 0 Nov  9 14:37 acl_demo.txt
[donnie@localhost ~]$
```

So, we can have two or more different ACLs assigned to the same file. In the `ls -l` output, we see that we have `rw` permissions set for the group, which is really just a summary of permissions that we've set in the two ACLs.

We can set an ACL for group access by replacing the `u:` with a `g::`

```
[donnie@localhost ~]$ getfacl new_file.txt
# file: new_file.txt
# owner: donnie
# group: donnie
user::rw-
group::rw-
other::r--

[donnie@localhost ~]$ chmod 600 new_file.txt

[donnie@localhost ~]$ setfacl -m g:accounting:r new_file.txt

[donnie@localhost ~]$ getfacl new_file.txt
# file: new_file.txt
# owner: donnie
# group: donnie
user::rw-
group::---
group:accounting:r--
mask::r--
other::---

[donnie@localhost ~]$ ls -l new_file.txt
-rw-r-----+ 1 donnie donnie 0 Nov  9 15:06 new_file.txt
[donnie@localhost ~]$
```

Members of the `accounting` group now have read access to this file.

Creating an inherited access control list for a directory

There may be times when you'll want all files that get created in a shared directory to have the same access control list. We can do that by applying an inherited ACL to the directory. Although, understand that, even though this sounds like a cool idea, creating files in the normal way will cause files to have the read/write permissions set for the group, and the read permission set for others. So, if you're setting this up for a directory where users just create files normally, the best that you can hope to do is to create an ACL that adds either the write or execute permissions for someone. Either that, or ensure that users set the 600 permissions settings on all files that they create, assuming that users really do need to restrict access to their files.

On the other hand, if you're creating a shell script that creates files in a specific directory, you can include chmod commands to ensure that the files get created with the restrictive permissions that are necessary to make your ACL work as intended.

To demo, let's create the new_perm_dir directory, and set the inherited ACL on it. I want to have read/write access for files that my shell script creates in this directory, and for Frank to have only read access. I don't want anyone else to be able to read any of these files:

```
[donnie@localhost ~]$ setfacl -m d:u:frank:r new_perm_dir

[donnie@localhost ~]$ ls -ld new_perm_dir
drwxrwxr-x+ 2 donnie donnie 26 Nov 12 13:16 new_perm_dir
[donnie@localhost ~]$ getfacl new_perm_dir
# file: new_perm_dir
# owner: donnie
# group: donnie
user::rwx
group::rwx
other::r-x
default:user::rwx
default:user:frank:r--
default:group::rwx
default:mask::rwx
default:other::r-x

[donnie@localhost ~]$
```

All I had to do to make this an inherited ACL was to add the `d:` before the `u:frank`. I left the default permissions settings on the directory, which allows everyone read access to the directory. Next, I'll create the `donnie_script.sh` shell script that will create a file within that directory, and that will set read/write permissions for only the user of the new files:

```
#!/bin/bash
cd new_perm_dir
touch new_file.txt
chmod 600 new_file.txt
exit
```

After making the script executable, I'll run it and view the results:

```
[donnie@localhost ~]$ ./donnie_script.sh

[donnie@localhost ~]$ cd new_perm_dir

[donnie@localhost new_perm_dir]$ ls -l
total 0
-rw-------+ 1 donnie donnie 0 Nov 12 13:16 new_file.txt
[donnie@localhost new_perm_dir]$ getfacl new_file.txt
# file: new_file.txt
# owner: donnie
# group: donnie
user::rw-
user:frank:r-- #effective:---
group::rwx #effective:---
mask::---
other::---

[donnie@localhost new_perm_dir]$
```

So, `new_file.txt` got created with the correct permissions settings, and with an ACL that allows Frank to read it. (I know that this is a really simplified example, but you get the idea.)

Removing a specific permission by using an ACL mask

You can remove an ACL from a file or directory with the `-x` option. Let's go back to the `acl_demo.txt` file that I created earlier, and remove the ACL for Maggie:

```
[donnie@localhost ~]$ setfacl -x u:maggie acl_demo.txt
```

```
[donnie@localhost ~]$ getfacl acl_demo.txt
# file: acl_demo.txt
# owner: donnie
# group: donnie
user::rw-
user:frank:rw-
group::---
mask::rw-
other::---

[donnie@localhost ~]$
```

So, Maggie's ACL is gone. But, the -x option removes the entire ACL, even if that's not what you really want. If you have an ACL with multiple permissions set, you might just want to remove one permission, while leaving the others. Here, we see that Frank still has his ACL that grants him read/write access. Let's now say that we want to remove the write permission, while still allowing him the read permission. For that, we'll need to apply a mask:

```
[donnie@localhost ~]$ setfacl -m m::r acl_demo.txt

[donnie@localhost ~]$ ls -l acl_demo.txt

-rw-r-----+ 1 donnie donnie 0 Nov  9 14:37 acl_demo.txt
[donnie@localhost ~]$ getfacl acl_demo.txt
# file: acl_demo.txt
# owner: donnie
# group: donnie
user::rw-
user:frank:rw-              #effective:r--
group::---
mask::r--
other::---

[donnie@localhost ~]$
```

The m::r sets a read-only mask on the ACL. Running getfacl shows that Frank still has a read/write ACL, but the comment to the side shows his effective permissions to be read-only. So, Frank's write permission for the file is now gone. And, if we had ACLs set for other users, this mask would affect them the same way.

Using the tar --acls option to prevent the loss of ACLs during a backup

If you ever need to use `tar` to create a backup of either a file or a directory that has ACLs assigned to it, you'll need to include the `--acls` option switch. Otherwise, the ACLs will be lost. To show this, I'll create a backup of the `perm_demo_dir` directory without the `--acls` option. First, note that I do have ACLs on files in this directory, as indicated by the + sign on the last two files:

```
[donnie@localhost ~]$ cd perm_demo_dir
[donnie@localhost perm_demo_dir]$ ls -l
total 0
-rw-rw-r--. 1 donnie accounting 0 Nov  5 20:17 file1.txt
-rw-rw-r--. 1 donnie accounting 0 Nov  5 20:17 file2.txt
-rw-rw-r--. 1 donnie accounting 0 Nov  5 20:17 file3.txt
-rw-rw-r--. 1 donnie accounting 0 Nov  5 20:17 file4.txt
-rw-rw----+ 1 donnie donnie     0 Nov  9 15:19 frank_file.txt
-rw-rw----+ 1 donnie donnie     0 Nov 12 12:29 new_file.txt
[donnie@localhost perm_demo_dir]$
```

Now, I'll do the backup without the `--acls`:

```
[donnie@localhost perm_demo_dir]$ cd
[donnie@localhost ~]$ tar cJvf perm_demo_dir_backup.tar.xz perm_demo_dir/
perm_demo_dir/
perm_demo_dir/file1.txt
perm_demo_dir/file2.txt
perm_demo_dir/file3.txt
perm_demo_dir/file4.txt
perm_demo_dir/frank_file.txt
perm_demo_dir/new_file.txt
[donnie@localhost ~]$
```

It looks good, right? Ah, but looks can be deceiving. Watch what happens when I delete the directory, and then restore it from the backup:

```
[donnie@localhost ~]$ rm -rf perm_demo_dir/

[donnie@localhost ~]$ tar xJvf perm_demo_dir_backup.tar.xz
perm_demo_dir/
perm_demo_dir/file1.txt
perm_demo_dir/file2.txt
perm_demo_dir/file3.txt
perm_demo_dir/file4.txt
perm_demo_dir/frank_file.txt
```

```
perm_demo_dir/new_file.txt
[donnie@localhost ~]$ ls -l
total 812
. . .
drwxrwxr-x+ 2 donnie donnie 26 Nov 12 13:16 new_perm_dir
drwxrwx---. 2 donnie donnie 116 Nov 12 12:29 perm_demo_dir
-rw-rw-r--. 1 donnie donnie 284 Nov 13 13:45 perm_demo_dir_backup.tar.xz
. . .
[donnie@localhost ~]$ cd perm_demo_dir/

[donnie@localhost perm_demo_dir]$ ls -l
total 0
-rw-rw-r--. 1 donnie donnie 0 Nov 5 20:17 file1.txt
-rw-rw-r--. 1 donnie donnie 0 Nov 5 20:17 file2.txt
-rw-rw-r--. 1 donnie donnie 0 Nov 5 20:17 file3.txt
-rw-rw-r--. 1 donnie donnie 0 Nov 5 20:17 file4.txt
-rw-rw----. 1 donnie donnie 0 Nov 9 15:19 frank_file.txt
-rw-rw----. 1 donnie donnie 0 Nov 12 12:29 new_file.txt
[donnie@localhost perm_demo_dir]$
```

I don't even have to use `getfacl` to see that the ACLs are gone from the `perm_demo_dir` directory and all of its files, because the + signs are now gone from them. Now, let's see what happens when I include the `--acls` option. First, I'll show you that an ACL is set for this directory and its only file:

```
[donnie@localhost ~]$ ls -ld new_perm_dir
drwxrwxr-x+ 2 donnie donnie 26 Nov 13 14:01 new_perm_dir

[donnie@localhost ~]$ ls -l new_perm_dir
total 0
-rw-------+ 1 donnie donnie 0 Nov 13 14:01 new_file.txt
[donnie@localhost ~]$
```

Now, I'll use tar with `--acls`:

```
[donnie@localhost ~]$ tar cJvf new_perm_dir_backup.tar.xz new_perm_dir/ --acls
new_perm_dir/
new_perm_dir/new_file.txt
[donnie@localhost ~]$
```

I'll now delete the `new_perm_dir` directory, and restore it from backup. Again, I'll use the `--acls` option:

```
[donnie@localhost ~]$ rm -rf new_perm_dir/

[donnie@localhost ~]$ tar xJvf new_perm_dir_backup.tar.xz --acls
```

```
new_perm_dir/
new_perm_dir/new_file.txt

[donnie@localhost ~]$ ls -ld new_perm_dir
drwxrwxr-x+ 2 donnie donnie 26 Nov 13 14:01 new_perm_dir

[donnie@localhost ~]$ ls -l new_perm_dir
total 0
-rw-------+ 1 donnie donnie 0 Nov 13 14:01 new_file.txt
[donnie@localhost ~]$
```

The presence of the + signs indicates that the ACLs did survive the backup and restore procedure. The one slightly tricky part about this is that you must use --acls for both the backup and the restoration. If you omit the option either time, you will lose your ACLs.

Creating a user group and adding members to it

So far, I've been doing all of the demos inside my own home directory, just for the sake of showing the basic concepts. But, the eventual goal is to show you how to use this knowledge to do something more practical, such as controlling file access in a shared group directory. The first step is to create a user group and to add members to it.

Let's say that we want to create a marketing group for members of—you guessed it—the marketing department:

```
[donnie@localhost ~]$ sudo groupadd marketing
[sudo] password for donnie:
[donnie@localhost ~]$
```

Let's now add some members. You can do that in three different ways:

- Add members as we create their user accounts
- Use usermod to add members that already have user accounts
- Edit the /etc/group file

Adding members as we create their user accounts

First, we can add members to the group as we create their user accounts, using the −G option of `useradd`. On Red Hat or CentOS, the command would look like this:

```
[donnie@localhost ~]$ sudo useradd -G marketing cleopatra
[sudo] password for donnie:

[donnie@localhost ~]$ groups cleopatra
cleopatra : cleopatra marketing
[donnie@localhost ~]$
```

On Debian/Ubuntu, the command would look like this:

```
donnie@ubuntu3:~$ sudo useradd -m -d /home/cleopatra -s /bin/bash -G
marketing cleopatra

donnie@ubuntu3:~$ groups cleopatra
cleopatra : cleopatra marketing
donnie@ubuntu3:~$
```

And, of course, I'll need to assign Cleopatra a password in the normal manner:

```
[donnie@localhost ~]$ sudo passwd cleopatra
```

Using usermod to add an existing user to a group

The good news is that this works the same on either Red Hat or CentOS or Debian/Ubuntu:

```
[donnie@localhost ~]$ sudo usermod -a -G marketing maggie
[sudo] password for donnie:

[donnie@localhost ~]$ groups maggie
maggie : maggie marketing
[donnie@localhost ~]$
```

In this case, the −a wasn't necessary, because Maggie wasn't a member of any other secondary group. But, if she had already belonged to another group, the −a would have been necessary to keep from overwriting any existing group information, thus removing her from the previous groups.

This method is especially handy for use on Ubuntu systems, where it was necessary to use `adduser` in order to create encrypted home directories. (As we saw in a previous chapter, `adduser` doesn't give you the chance to add a user to a group as you create the account.)

Adding users to a group by editing the /etc/group file

This final method is a good way to cheat, to speed up the process of adding multiple existing users to a group. First, just open the /etc/group file in your favorite text editor, and look for the line that defines the group to which you want to add members:

```
. . .
marketing:x:1005:cleopatra,maggie
. . .
```

So, I've already added Cleopatra and Maggie to this group. Let's edit this to add a couple more members:

```
. . .
marketing:x:1005:cleopatra,maggie,vicky,charlie
. . .
```

When you're done, save the file and exit the editor.

A `groups` command for each of them will show that our wee bit of cheating works just fine:

```
[donnie@localhost etc]$ sudo vim group

[donnie@localhost etc]$ groups vicky
vicky : vicky marketing

[donnie@localhost etc]$ groups charlie
charlie : charlie marketing
[donnie@localhost etc]$
```

This method is extremely handy for whenever you need to add lots of members to a group at the same time.

Creating a shared directory

The next act in our scenario involves creating a shared directory that all the members of our marketing department can use. Now, this is another one of those areas that engenders a bit of controversy. Some people like to put shared directories in the root level of the filesystem, while others like to put shared directories in the /home directory. And, some people even have other preferences. But really, it's a matter of personal preference and/or company policy. Other than that, it really doesn't much matter where you put them. For our purposes, to make things simple, I'll just create the directory in the root level of the filesystem:

```
[donnie@localhost ~]$ cd /

[donnie@localhost /]$ sudo mkdir marketing
[sudo] password for donnie:

[donnie@localhost /]$ ls -ld marketing
drwxr-xr-x. 2 root root 6 Nov 13 15:32 marketing
[donnie@localhost /]$
```

The new directory belongs to the root user. It has a permissions setting of 755, which permits read and execute access to everybody, and write access only to the root user. What we really want is to allow only members of the marketing department to access this directory. We'll first change ownership and group association, and then we'll set the proper permissions:

```
[donnie@localhost /]$ sudo chown nobody:marketing marketing

[donnie@localhost /]$ sudo chmod 770 marketing

[donnie@localhost /]$ ls -ld marketing
drwxrwx---. 2 nobody marketing 6 Nov 13 15:32 marketing
[donnie@localhost /]$
```

In this case, we don't have any one particular user that we want to own the directory, and we don't really want for the root user to own it. So, assigning ownership to the nobody pseudo user account gives us a way to deal with that. I then assigned the 770 permissions value to the directory, which allows read/write/execute access to all marketing group members, while keeping everyone else out. Now, let's let one of our group members log in to see if she can create a file in this directory:

```
[donnie@localhost /]$ su - vicky
Password:
```

```
[vicky@localhost ~]$ cd /marketing

[vicky@localhost marketing]$ touch vicky_file.txt

[vicky@localhost marketing]$ ls -l
total 0
-rw-rw-r--. 1 vicky vicky 0 Nov 13 15:41 vicky_file.txt
[vicky@localhost marketing]$
```

Okay, it works, except for one minor problem. The file belongs to Vicky, as it should. But, it's also associated with Vicky's personal group. For the best access control of these shared files, we need them to be associated with the marketing group.

Setting the SGID bit and the sticky bit on the shared directory

I've told you before that it's a bit of a security risk to set either the SUID or SGID permissions on files, especially on executable files. But, it is both completely safe and very useful to set SGID on a shared directory.

SGID behavior on a directory is completely different from SGID behavior on a file. On a directory, SGID will cause any files that anybody creates to be associated with the same group with which the directory is associated. So, bearing in mind that the SGID permission value is 2000, let's set SGID on our marketing directory:

```
[donnie@localhost /]$ sudo chmod 2770 marketing
[sudo] password for donnie:

[donnie@localhost /]$ ls -ld marketing
drwxrws---. 2 nobody marketing 28 Nov 13 15:41 marketing
[donnie@localhost /]$
```

The s in the executable position for the group indicates that the command was successful. Let's now let Vicky log back in to create another file:

```
[donnie@localhost /]$ su - vicky
Password:
Last login: Mon Nov 13 15:41:19 EST 2017 on pts/0

[vicky@localhost ~]$ cd /marketing

[vicky@localhost marketing]$ touch vicky_file_2.txt
```

```
[vicky@localhost marketing]$ ls -l
total 0
-rw-rw-r--. 1 vicky marketing 0 Nov 13 15:57 vicky_file_2.txt
-rw-rw-r--. 1 vicky vicky     0 Nov 13 15:41 vicky_file.txt
[vicky@localhost marketing]$
```

Vicky's second file is associated with the marketing group, which is just what we want. Just for fun, let's let Charlie do the same:

```
[donnie@localhost /]$ su - charlie
Password:

[charlie@localhost ~]$ cd /marketing

[charlie@localhost marketing]$ touch charlie_file.txt

[charlie@localhost marketing]$ ls -l
total 0
-rw-rw-r--. 1 charlie marketing 0 Nov 13 15:59 charlie_file.txt
-rw-rw-r--. 1 vicky   marketing 0 Nov 13 15:57 vicky_file_2.txt
-rw-rw-r--. 1 vicky   vicky     0 Nov 13 15:41 vicky_file.txt
[charlie@localhost marketing]$
```

Again, Charlie's file is associated with the marketing group. But, for some strange reason that nobody understands, Charlie really doesn't like Vicky, and decides to delete her files, just out of pure spite:

```
[charlie@localhost marketing]$ rm vicky*
rm: remove write-protected regular empty file 'vicky_file.txt'? y

[charlie@localhost marketing]$ ls -l
total 0
-rw-rw-r--. 1 charlie marketing 0 Nov 13 15:59 charlie_file.txt
[charlie@localhost marketing]$
```

The system complains that Vicky's original file is write-protected, since it's still associated with her personal group. But, the system does still allow Charlie to delete it, even without sudo privileges. And, since Charlie has write access to the second file, due to its association with the marketing group, the system allows him to delete it without question.

Okay. So, Vicky complains about this, and tries to get Charlie fired. But, our intrepid administrator has a better idea. He'll just set the sticky bit in order to keep this from happening again. Since the SGID bit has a value of 2000, and the sticky bit has a value of 1000, we can just add the two together to get a value of 3000:

```
[donnie@localhost /]$ sudo chmod 3770 marketing
[sudo] password for donnie:

[donnie@localhost /]$ ls -ld marketing
drwxrws--T. 2 nobody marketing 30 Nov 13 16:03 marketing
[donnie@localhost /]$
```

The T in the executable position for others indicates that the sticky bit has been set. Since the T is uppercase, we know that the executable permission for others has not been set. Having the sticky bit set will prevent group members from deleting anybody else's files. Let's let Vicky show us what happens when she tries to retaliate against Charlie:

```
[donnie@localhost /]$ su - vicky
Password:
Last login: Mon Nov 13 15:57:41 EST 2017 on pts/0

[vicky@localhost ~]$ cd /marketing

[vicky@localhost marketing]$ ls -l
total 0
-rw-rw-r--. 1 charlie marketing 0 Nov 13 15:59 charlie_file.txt

[vicky@localhost marketing]$ rm charlie_file.txt
rm: cannot remove 'charlie_file.txt': Operation not permitted

[vicky@localhost marketing]$ rm -f charlie_file.txt
rm: cannot remove 'charlie_file.txt': Operation not permitted

[vicky@localhost marketing]$ ls -l
total 0
-rw-rw-r--. 1 charlie marketing 0 Nov 13 15:59 charlie_file.txt
[vicky@localhost marketing]$
```

Even with the -f option, Vicky still can't delete Charlie's file. Vicky doesn't have sudo privileges on this system, so it would be useless for her to try that.

Using ACLs to access files in the shared directory

As things currently stand, all members of the marketing group have read/write access to all other group members' files. Restricting access to a file to only specific group members is the same two-step process that we've already covered.

Setting the permissions and creating the ACL

First, Vicky sets the normal permissions to allow only her to access her file. Then, she'll set the ACL:

```
[vicky@localhost marketing]$ echo "This file is only for my good friend,
Cleopatra." > vicky_file.txt

[vicky@localhost marketing]$ chmod 600 vicky_file.txt

[vicky@localhost marketing]$ setfacl -m u:cleopatra:r vicky_file.txt

[vicky@localhost marketing]$ ls -l
total 4
-rw-rw-r--. 1 charlie marketing 0 Nov 13 15:59 charlie_file.txt
-rw-r-----+ 1 vicky marketing 49 Nov 13 16:24 vicky_file.txt

[vicky@localhost marketing]$ getfacl vicky_file.txt
# file: vicky_file.txt
# owner: vicky
# group: marketing
user::rw-
user:cleopatra:r--
group::---
mask::r--
other::---

[vicky@localhost marketing]$
```

There's nothing here that you haven't already seen. Vicky just removed all permissions from the group and from others, and set an ACL that only allows Cleopatra to read the file. Let's see if Cleopatra actually can read it:

```
[donnie@localhost /]$ su - cleopatra
Password:
```

```
[cleopatra@localhost ~]$ cd /marketing

[cleopatra@localhost marketing]$ ls -l
total 4
-rw-rw-r--. 1 charlie marketing 0 Nov 13 15:59 charlie_file.txt
-rw-r-----+ 1 vicky marketing 49 Nov 13 16:24 vicky_file.txt

[cleopatra@localhost marketing]$ cat vicky_file.txt
This file is only for my good friend, Cleopatra.
[cleopatra@localhost marketing]$
```

So far, so good. But, can Cleopatra write to it?

```
[cleopatra@localhost marketing]$ echo "You are my friend too, Vicky." >>
vicky_file.txt
-bash: vicky_file.txt: Permission denied
[cleopatra@localhost marketing]$
```

Okay, Cleopatra can't do that, since Vicky only allowed her the read privilege in the ACL.

Charlie tries to access Vicky's file with an ACL set for Cleopatra

Now, though, what about that sneaky Charlie, who wants to go snooping in other users' files?

```
[donnie@localhost /]$ su - charlie
Password:
Last login: Mon Nov 13 15:58:56 EST 2017 on pts/0

[charlie@localhost ~]$ cd /marketing

[charlie@localhost marketing]$ cat vicky_file.txt
cat: vicky_file.txt: Permission denied
[charlie@localhost marketing]$
```

So, yes, it's really true that only Cleopatra can access Vicky's file, and even then only for reading.

Hands-on lab – creating a shared group directory

For this lab, you'll just put together everything that you've learned in this chapter to create a shared directory for a group. You can do this on either of your virtual machines:

1. On either virtual machine, create the `sales` group:

   ```
   sudo groupadd sales
   ```

2. Create the users Mimi, Mr. Gray, and Mommy, adding them to the sales group as you create the accounts.

   On the CentOS VM, do:

   ```
   sudo useradd -G sales mimi
   sudo useradd -G sales mrgray
   sudo useradd -G sales mommy
   ```

   On the Ubuntu VM, do:

   ```
   sudo useradd -m -d /home/mimi -s /bin/bash -G sales mimi
   sudo useradd -m -d /home/mrgray -s /bin/bash -G sales mrgray
   sudo useradd -m -d /home/mommy -s /bin/bash -G sales mommy
   ```

3. Assign each user a password.
4. Create the `sales` directory in the root level of the filesystem. Set proper ownership and permissions, including the SGID and sticky bits:

   ```
   sudo mkdir /sales
   sudo chown nobody:sales /sales
   sudo chmod 3770 /sales
   ls -ld /sales
   ```

5. Log in as Mimi, and have her create a file:

   ```
   su - mimi
   cd /sales
   echo "This file belongs to Mimi." > mimi_file.txt
   ls -l
   ```

6. Have Mimi set an ACL on her file, allowing only Mr. Gray to read it. Then, have Mimi log back out:

   ```
   chmod 600 mimi_file.txt
   setfacl -m u:mrgray:r mimi_file.txt
   getfacl mimi_file.txt
   ```

```
ls -l
exit
```

7. Have Mr. Gray log in to see what he can do with Mimi's file. Then, have Mr. Gray create his own file and log back out:

```
su - mrgray
cd /sales
cat mimi_file.txt
echo "I want to add something to this file." >>
mimi_file.txt

echo "Mr. Gray will now create his own file." >
mr_gray_file.txt

ls -l
exit
```

8. Mommy will now log in and try to wreak havoc by snooping in other users' files, and by trying to delete them:

```
su - mommy
cat mimi_file.txt
cat mr_gray_file.txt
rm -f mimi_file.txt
rm -f mr_gray_file.txt
exit
```

9. End of Lab.

Summary

In this chapter, we saw how to take Discretionary Access Control to the proverbial next level. We first saw how to create and manage access control lists to provide more fine-grained access control over files and directories. We then saw how to create a user group for a specific purpose, and how to add members to it. Then, we saw how we can use the SGID bit, the sticky bit, and access control lists to manage a shared group directory.

But, sometimes, Discretionary Access Control might not be enough to do the job. For those times, we also have mandatory access control, which we'll cover in the next chapter. I'll see you there.

7
Implementing Mandatory Access Control with SELinux and AppArmor

As we saw in the previous chapters, Discretionary Access Control allows users to control who can access their own files and directories. But, what if your company needs to have more administrative control over who accesses what? For this, we need some sort of Mandatory Access Control or MAC.

The best way I know to explain the difference between DAC and MAC is to hearken back to my Navy days. I was riding submarines at the time, and I had to have a Top Secret clearance to do my job. With DAC, I had the physical ability to take one of my Top Secret books to the mess decks, and hand it to a cook who didn't have that level of clearance. With MAC, there were rules that prevented me from doing so. On operating systems, things work pretty much the same way.

There are several different MAC systems that are available for Linux. The two that we'll cover in this chapter are SELinux and AppArmor.

In this chapter, we'll cover the following topics:

- What SELinux is and how it can benefit a system's administrator
- How to set security contexts for files and directories
- How to use setroubleshoot to troubleshoot SELinux problems
- Looking at SELinux policies and how to create custom policies
- What AppArmor is and how it can benefit a systems administrator
- Looking at AppArmor policies

- Working with AppArmor command-line utilities
- Troubleshooting AppArmor problems

How SELinux can benefit a systems administrator

SELinux is a free open source software project that was developed by the U.S. National Security Agency. While it can theoretically be installed on any Linux distro, the Red Hat-type distros are the only ones that come with it already set up and enabled. It uses code in Linux kernel modules, along with filesystem-extended attributes, to help ensure that only authorized users and processes can access either sensitive files or system resources. There are three ways in which SELinux can be used:

- It can help prevent intruders from exploiting a system
- It can be used to ensure that only users with the proper security clearance can access files that are labeled with a security classification
- In addition to MAC, SELinux can also be used as a type of role-based access control

In this chapter, I'll only be covering the first of these three uses because that is the most common way in which SELinux is used. There's also the fact that covering all three of these uses would require writing a whole book, which I don't have space to do here.

 If you go through this introduction to SELinux and find that you still need more SELinux information, you'll find whole books and courses on just this subject at the Packt Publishing website.

So how can SELinux benefit the busy systems administrator? Well, you might remember when a few years ago, news about the *Shellshock* bug hit the world's headlines. Essentially, Shellshock was a bug in the Bash shell that allowed intruders to break into a system and to exploit it by gaining root privileges. For systems that were running SELinux, it was still possible for the bad guys to break in, but SELinux would have prevented them from successfully running their exploits.

SELinux is also yet another mechanism that can help protect data in users' home directories. If you have a machine that's set up as a Network File System server, a Samba server, or a web server, SELinux will prevent those daemons from accessing users' home directories, unless you explicitly configure SELinux to allow that behavior.

On web servers, you can use SELinux to prevent the execution of malicious CGI scripts or PHP scripts. If you don't need for your server to run CGI or PHP scripts, you can disable them in SELinux.

With older versions of Docker and without Mandatory Access Control, it was trivially easy for a normal user to break out of a Docker container and gain root-level access to the host machine. Although Docker security has since improved, SELinux is still a useful tool for hardening servers that run Docker containers.

So now, you're likely thinking that everyone would use such a great tool, right? Sadly, that's not the case. In its beginning, SELinux got a reputation for being difficult to work with, and many administrators would just disable it. In fact, a lot of tutorials you see on the web or on YouTube have *disable SELinux* as the first step. In this section, I'd like to show you that things have improved and that SELinux no longer deserves its bad reputation.

Setting security contexts for files and directories

Think of SELinux as a glorified labeling system. It adds labels, known as *security contexts*, to files and directories through extended file attributes. It also adds the same type of labels, known as domains, to system processes. To see these contexts and domains on your CentOS machines, use the `-Z` option with either `ls` or `ps`. For example, files and directories in my own home directory would look as follows:

```
[donnie@localhost ~]$ ls -Z
drwxrwxr-x. donnie donnie unconfined_u:object_r:user_home_t:s0 acl_demo_dir
-rw-rw-r--. donnie donnie unconfined_u:object_r:user_home_t:s0 yum_list.txt
[donnie@localhost ~]$
```

Processes on my system would look something like this:

```
[donnie@localhost ~]$ ps -Z
LABEL                             PID TTY          TIME CMD
unconfined_u:unconfined_r:unconfined_t:s0-s0:c0.c1023 1322 pts/0 00:00:00
bash
unconfined_u:unconfined_r:unconfined_t:s0-s0:c0.c1023 3978 pts/0 00:00:00
ps
[donnie@localhost ~]$
```

Now, let's break this down. In the outputs of both the `ls -Z` and `ps -Z` commands, we have the following parts:

- **The SELinux user**: In both cases, the SELinux user is the generic `unconfined_u`
- **The SELinux role**: In the `ls -Z` example, we see that the role is `object_r`, and in the `ps -Z` example it's `unconfined_r`
- **The type**: It's `user_home_t` in the `ls -Z` output, and `unconfined_t` in the `ps -Z` output
- **The sensitivity**: In the `ps -Z` output it's `s0`. In the `ps -Z` output it's `s0-s0`
- **The category**: We don't see a category in the `ls -Z` output, but we do see `c0.c1023` in the `ps -Z` output

Out of all of the preceding security context and security domain components, the only one that interests us now is the type. For the purposes of this chapter, we're only interested in covering what a normal Linux administrator would need to know to keep intruders from exploiting the system, and the type is the only one of these components that we need to use for that. All of the other components come into play when we set up advanced, security classification-based access control and role-based access control.

Okay, here's the somewhat over-simplified explanation of how this helps a Linux administrator maintain security. What we want is for system processes to only access objects that we allow them to access. (System processes include things like the web server daemon, the FTP daemon, the Samba daemon, and the Secure Shell daemon. Objects include things such as files, directories, and network ports.) To achieve this, we'll assign a *type* to all of our processes and all of our objects. We'll then create *policies* that define which process types can access which object types.

Fortunately, whenever you install any Red Hat-type distro, pretty much all of the hard work has already been done for you. Red Hat-type distros all come with SELinux already enabled and set up with the targeted policy. Think of this targeted policy as a somewhat relaxed policy, which allows a casual desktop user to sit down at the computer and actually conduct business without having to tweak any SELinux settings. But, if you're a server administrator, you may find yourself having to tweak this policy in order to allow server daemons to do what you need them to do.

 The targeted policy, which comes installed by default, is what a normal Linux administrator will use in his or her day-to-day duties. If you look in the repositories of your CentOS virtual machine, you'll see that there are also several others, which we won't cover in this book.

Installing the SELinux tools

For some bizarre reason that I'll never understand, the tools that you need to administer SELinux don't get installed by default, even though SELinux itself does. So, the first thing you'll need to do on your CentOS virtual machine is to install them:

```
sudo yum install setools policycoreutils policycoreutils-python
```

In a later portion of this chapter, we'll be looking at how to use setroubleshoot to help diagnose SELinux problems. In order to have some cool error messages to look at when we get there, go ahead and install setroubleshoot now, and activate it by restarting the auditd daemon. (There's no setroubleshoot daemon because setroubleshoot is meant to be controlled by the auditd daemon.) We have the following code:

```
sudo yum install setroubleshoot
sudo service auditd restart
```

One of the little systemd quirks that we have to deal with is that you can't stop or restart the auditd daemon with the normal systemctl command, as you're supposed to do when working with systemd daemons. However, the old-fashioned service command works. (And no, I don't know why that is.)

 Depending on the type of installation that you chose when installing CentOS, you might or might not already have setroubleshoot installed. To be sure, go ahead and run the command to install it. It won't hurt anything if setroubleshoot is already there.

You now have what you need to get started.

Creating web content files with SELinux enabled

Now, let's look at what can happen if you have web content files that are set with the wrong SELinux type. First, we'll install, enable, and start the Apache web server on our CentOS virtual machines. (Note that including the --now option allows us to enable and start a daemon all in one single step.) We have the following code:

```
sudo yum install httpd
sudo systemctl enable --now httpd
```

If you haven't done so already, you'll want to configure the firewall to allow access to the web server:

```
[donnie@localhost ~]$ sudo firewall-cmd --permanent --add-service=http
success
[donnie@localhost ~]$ sudo firewall-cmd --reload
success
[donnie@localhost ~]$
```

When we look at the SELinux information for the Apache processes, we'll see this:

```
[donnie@localhost ~]$ ps ax -Z | grep httpd
system_u:system_r:httpd_t:s0     3689 ?        Ss      0:00 /usr/sbin/httpd
-DFOREGROUND
system_u:system_r:httpd_t:s0     3690 ?        S       0:00 /usr/sbin/httpd
-DFOREGROUND
system_u:system_r:httpd_t:s0     3691 ?        S       0:00 /usr/sbin/httpd
-DFOREGROUND
system_u:system_r:httpd_t:s0     3692 ?        S       0:00 /usr/sbin/httpd
-DFOREGROUND
system_u:system_r:httpd_t:s0     3693 ?        S       0:00 /usr/sbin/httpd
-DFOREGROUND
system_u:system_r:httpd_t:s0     3694 ?        S       0:00 /usr/sbin/httpd
-DFOREGROUND
unconfined_u:unconfined_r:unconfined_t:s0-s0:c0.c1023 3705 pts/0 R+    0:00
grep --color=auto httpd
[donnie@localhost ~]$
```

As I said before, we're not interested in the user or the role. However, we are interested in the type, which in this case is httpd_t.

On Red Hat-type systems, we would normally place web content files in the /var/www/html directory. Let's look at the SELinux context for that html directory:

```
[donnie@localhost www]$ pwd
/var/www
[donnie@localhost www]$ ls -Zd html/
drwxr-xr-x. root root system_u:object_r:httpd_sys_content_t:s0 html/
[donnie@localhost www]$
```

The type is `httpd_sys_content`, so it stands to reason that the `httpd` daemon should be able to access this directory. It's currently empty, so let's `cd` into it and create a simple index file:

```
[donnie@localhost www]$ cd html
[donnie@localhost html]$ pwd
/var/www/html
[donnie@localhost html]$ sudo vim index.html
```

I'll put this into the file, as follows:

```
<html>
<head>
<title>
Test of SELinux
</title>
</head>
<body>
Let's see if this SELinux stuff really works!
</body>
</html>
```

Okay, as I said, it's simple, as my HTML hand-coding skills aren't what they used to be. But still, it serves our present purposes.

Looking at the SELinux context, we see that the file has the same type as the `html` directory:

```
[donnie@localhost html]$ ls -Z
-rw-r--r--. root root unconfined_u:object_r:httpd_sys_content_t:s0
index.html
[donnie@localhost html]$
```

I can now navigate to this page from the web browser of my trusty OpenSUSE workstation:

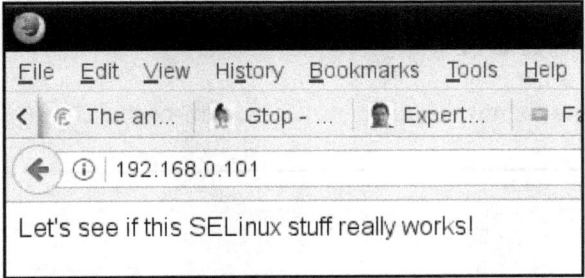

Now though, let's see what happens if I decide to create content files in my own home directory and then move them to the `html` directory. First, let's see what the SELinux context is for my new file:

```
[donnie@localhost ~]$ pwd
/home/donnie
[donnie@localhost ~]$ ls -Z index.html
-rw-rw-r--. donnie donnie unconfined_u:object_r:user_home_t:s0 index.html
[donnie@localhost ~]$
```

The context type is now `user_home_t`, which is a sure-fire indicator that I created this in my home directory. I'll now move the file to the `html` directory, overwriting the old file:

```
[donnie@localhost ~]$ sudo mv index.html /var/www/html/
[sudo] password for donnie:

[donnie@localhost ~]$ cd /var/www/html

[donnie@localhost html]$ ls -Z
-rw-rw-r--. donnie donnie unconfined_u:object_r:user_home_t:s0 index.html
[donnie@localhost html]$
```

Even though I moved the file over to the `/var/www/html` directory, the SELinux type is still associated with users' home directories. Now, I'll go to the browser of my host machine to refresh the page:

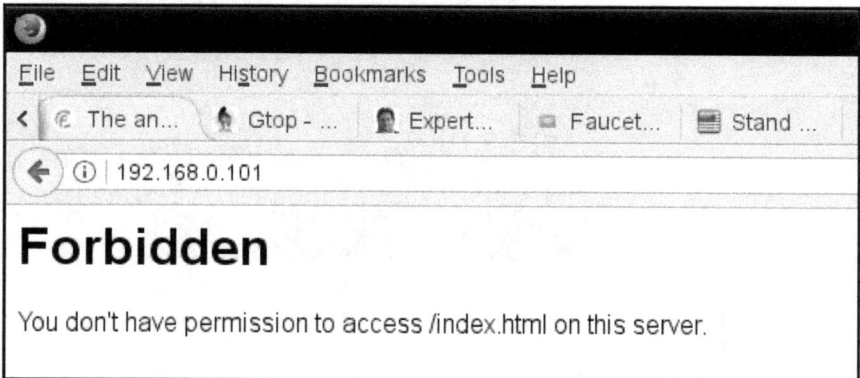

So, I have a slight bit of a problem. The type that's assigned to my file doesn't match with the type of the httpd daemon processes, so SELinux doesn't allow the `httpd` processes to access the file.

> Had I copied the file to the `html` directory instead of moving it, the SELinux context would have changed to match that of the destination directory.

Fixing an incorrect SELinux context

Okay, so I have this web content file that nobody can access, and I really don't feel up to creating a new one. So, what do I do? Actually, we have three different utilities for fixing this:

- `chcon`
- `restorecon`
- `semanage`

Using chcon

There are two ways to use `chcon` to fix an incorrect SELinux type on a file or directory. The first is to just manually specify the proper type:

```
[donnie@localhost html]$ sudo chcon -t httpd_sys_content_t index.html
[sudo] password for donnie:

[donnie@localhost html]$ ls -Z
-rw-rw-r--. donnie donnie unconfined_u:object_r:httpd_sys_content_t:s0
index.html
[donnie@localhost html]$
```

We can use `chcon` to change any part of the context, but as I keep saying, we're only interested in the type, which gets changed with the -t option. You can see in the `ls -Z` output that the command was successful.

The other way to use chcon is to reference a file that has the proper context. For demo purposes, I changed the index.html file back to the home directory type and have created a new file within the /var/www/html directory:

```
[donnie@localhost html]$ ls -Z
-rw-rw-r--. donnie donnie unconfined_u:object_r:user_home_t:s0 index.html
-rw-r--r--. root    root   unconfined_u:object_r:httpd_sys_content_t:s0
some_file.html
[donnie@localhost html]$
```

As you can see, any files that I create within this directory will automatically have the proper SELinux context settings. Now, let's use that new file as a reference in order to set the proper context on the index.html file:

```
[donnie@localhost html]$ sudo chcon --reference some_file.html index.html
[sudo] password for donnie:

[donnie@localhost html]$ ls -Z
-rw-rw-r--. donnie donnie unconfined_u:object_r:httpd_sys_content_t:s0
index.html
-rw-r--r--. root    root   unconfined_u:object_r:httpd_sys_content_t:s0
some_file.html
[donnie@localhost html]$
```

So, I used the --reference option and specified the file that I wanted to use as a reference. The file that I wanted to change is listed at the end of the command.

Now, that's all good, but I want to find an easier way that doesn't require quite as much typing. After all, I am an old man, and I don't want to overexert myself. So, let's take a look at the restorecon utility.

Using restorecon

Using restorecon is easy. Just type restorecon, followed by the name of the file that you need to change. Once again, I've changed the context of the index.html file back to the home directory type. This time though, I'm using restorecon to set the correct type:

```
[donnie@localhost html]$ ls -Z
-rw-rw-r--. donnie donnie unconfined_u:object_r:user_home_t:s0 index.html

[donnie@localhost html]$ sudo restorecon index.html

[donnie@localhost html]$ ls -Z
-rw-rw-r--. donnie donnie unconfined_u:object_r:httpd_sys_content_t:s0
```

```
index.html
[donnie@localhost html]$
```

And, that's all there is to it.

You can also use `chcon` and `restorecon` to change the context of an entire directory and its contents. For either one, just use the `-R` option. For example:

```
sudo chcon -R -t httpd_sys_content_t /var/www/html/
sudo restorecon -R /var/www/html/
```

(Remember: `-R` stands for recursive.)

There's still one last thing to take care of, even though it isn't really affecting our ability to access this file. That is, I need to change ownership of the file to the Apache user:

```
[donnie@localhost html]$ sudo chown apache: index.html
[sudo] password for donnie:

[donnie@localhost html]$ ls -l
total 4
-rw-rw-r--. 1 apache apache 125 Nov 22 16:14 index.html
[donnie@localhost html]$
```

Using semanage

In the scenario I've just presented, either `chcon` or `restorecon` will suit your needs just fine. The active SELinux policy mandates what the security contexts in certain directories are supposed to look like. As long as you're using `chcon` or `restorecon` within directories that are defined in the active SELinux policy, you're good. But let's say that you've created a directory elsewhere that you want to use for serving out web content files. You would need to set the `httpd_sys_content_t` type on that directory and all of the files within it. However, if you use `chcon` or `restorecon` for that, the change won't survive a system reboot. To make the change permanent, you'll need to use `semanage`.

For some strange reason, let's say that I want to serve web content out of a directory that I've created in the `/home` directory:

```
[donnie@localhost home]$ pwd
/home

[donnie@localhost home]$ sudo mkdir webdir
```

```
[sudo] password for donnie:

[donnie@localhost home]$ ls -Zd webdir
drwxr-xr-x. root root unconfined_u:object_r:home_root_t:s0 webdir
[donnie@localhost home]$
```

Because I had to use my powers of sudo to create the directory here, it's associated with the root user's `home_root_t` type, instead of the normal `user_home_dir_t` type. Any files that I create within this directory will have the same type:

```
[donnie@localhost webdir]$ ls -Z
-rw-r--r--. root root unconfined_u:object_r:home_root_t:s0 index.html
[donnie@localhost webdir]$
```

The next step is to use `semanage` to add a permanent mapping of this directory and the `httpd_sys_content_t` type to the active policy's context list:

```
[donnie@localhost home]$ sudo semanage fcontext -a -t httpd_sys_content_t
"/home/webdir(/.*)?"

[donnie@localhost home]$ ls -Zd /home/webdir
drwxr-xr-x. root root unconfined_u:object_r:httpd_sys_content_t:s0
/home/web_dir
[donnie@localhost home]$
```

Okay, here's the breakdown of the `semanage` command:

- `fcontext`: Because `semanage` has many purposes, we have to specify that we want to work with a file context.
- `-a`: This specifies that we're adding a new record to the context list for the active SELinux policy.
- `-t`: This specifies the type that we want to map to the new directory. In this case, we're creating a new mapping with the `httpd_sys_content` type.
- `/home/webdir(/.*)?`: This bit of gibberish is what's known as a *regular expression*. I can't go into the nitty-gritty details of regular expressions here, so suffice it to say that *regular expressions* is a language that we use to match text patterns. (And yes, I did mean to say *is* instead of *are*, since regular expressions is the name of the overall language.) In this case, I had to use this particular regular expression in order to make this `semanage` command recursive because `semanage` doesn't have a `-R` option switch. With this regular expression, I'm saying that I want for anything that gets created in this directory to have the same SELinux type as the directory itself.

The final step is to do a `restorecon -R` on this directory to ensure that the proper labels have been set:

```
[donnie@localhost home]$ sudo restorecon -R webdir

[donnie@localhost home]$ ls -Zd /home/webdir
drwxr-xr-x. root root unconfined_u:object_r:httpd_sys_content_t:s0
/home/webdir
[donnie@localhost home]$
```

Yeah, I know. You're looking at this and saying, "*But, this 'ls -Zd' output looks the same as it did after you did the semanage command.*" And, you're right. After running the `semanage` command, the type seems to be set correctly. But the `semanage-fcontext` man page says to run `restorecon` anyway, so I did.

> For more information on how to use `semanage` to manage security contexts, see the man page by entering `man semanage-fcontext`.

Hands-on lab – SELinux type enforcement

In this lab, you'll install the Apache web server and the appropriate SELinux tools. You'll then view the effects of having the wrong SELinux type assigned to a web content file.

1. Install Apache, along with all the required SELinux tools:

   ```
   sudo yum install httpd setroubleshoot setools
   policycoreutils policycoreutils-python
   ```

2. Activate setroubleshoot by restarting the `auditd` service:

   ```
   sudo service auditd restart
   ```

3. Enable and start the Apache service and open port 80 on the firewall:

   ```
   sudo systemctl enable --now httpd
   sudo firewall-cmd --permanent --add-service=http
   sudo firewall-cmd --reload
   ```

4. In the `/var/www/html` directory, create an `index.html` file with the following contents:

```html
<html>
  <head>
    <title>SELinux Test Page</title>
  </head>
  <body>
    This is a test of SELinux.
  </body>
</html>
```

5. View the SELinux information about the `index.html` file:

```
ls -Z index.html
```

6. In your host machine's web browser, navigate to the IP address of the CentOS virtual machine. You should be able to view the page.

7. Induce an SELinux violation by changing the type of the `index.html` file to something that's incorrect:

```
sudo chcon -t tmp_t index.html
ls -Z index.html
```

8. Go back to your host machine's web browser, and reload the document. You should now see a **Forbidden** message.

9. Use `restorecon` to change the file back to its correct type:

```
sudo restorecon index.html
```

10. Reload the page in your host machine's web browser. You should now be able to view the page.

Troubleshooting with setroubleshoot

So, you're now scratching your head and saying, *"When I can't access something that I should be able to, how do I know that it's an SELinux problem?"* Ah, I'm glad you asked.

Viewing setroubleshoot messages

Whenever something happens that violates an SELinux rule, it gets logged in the /var/log/audit/audit.log file. Tools are available that can let you directly read that log, but to diagnose SELinux problems, it's way better to use setroubleshoot. The beauty of setroubleshoot is that it takes the cryptic, hard-to-interpret SELinux messages from the audit.log file and translates them into plain, natural language. The messages that it sends to the /var/log/messages file even contain suggestions about how to fix the problem. To show how this works, let's go back to our problem where a file in the /var/www/html directory had been assigned the wrong SELinux type. Of course, we knew right away what the problem was because there was only one file in that directory and a simple ls -Z showed the problem with it. However, let's ignore that for the moment and say that we didn't know what the problem was. By opening the /var/log/messages file in less and searching for sealert, we'll find this message:

```
Nov 26 21:30:21 localhost python: SELinux is preventing httpd from open
access on the file /var/www/html/index.html.#012#012*****  Plugin
restorecon (92.2 confidence) suggests   *************************#012#012If
you want to fix the label. #012/var/www/html/index.html default label
should be httpd_sys_content_t.#012Then you can run restorecon.#012Do#012#
/sbin/restorecon -v /var/www/html/index.html#012#012*****  Plugin
catchall_boolean (7.83 confidence) suggests   *****************#012#012If
you want to allow httpd to read user content#012Then you must tell SELinux
about this by enabling the 'httpd_read_user_content'
boolean.#012#012Do#012setsebool -P httpd_read_user_content 1#012#012*****
Plugin catchall (1.41 confidence) suggests
*************************#012#012If you believe that httpd should be
allowed open access on the index.html file by default.#012Then you should
report this as a bug.#012You can generate a local policy module to allow
this access.#012Do#012allow this access for now by executing:#012# ausearch
-c 'httpd' --raw | audit2allow -M my-httpd#012# semodule -i my-httpd.pp#012
```

The first line of this message tells us what the problem is. It's saying that SELinux is preventing us from accessing the /var/www/html/index.html file because it's set with the wrong type. It then gives us several suggestions on how to fix the problem, with the first one being to run the restorecon command, as I've already shown you how to do.

A good rule-of-thumb to remember when reading these setroubleshoot messages is that the first suggestion in the message is normally the one that will fix the problem.

Using the graphical setroubleshoot utility

So far, I've only talked about using setroubleshoot on text-mode servers. After all, it's very common to see Linux servers running in text-mode, so all of us Linux folk have to be text-mode warriors. But on desktop systems or on servers that have a desktop interface installed, there is a graphical utility that will automatically alert you when setroubleshoot detects a problem:

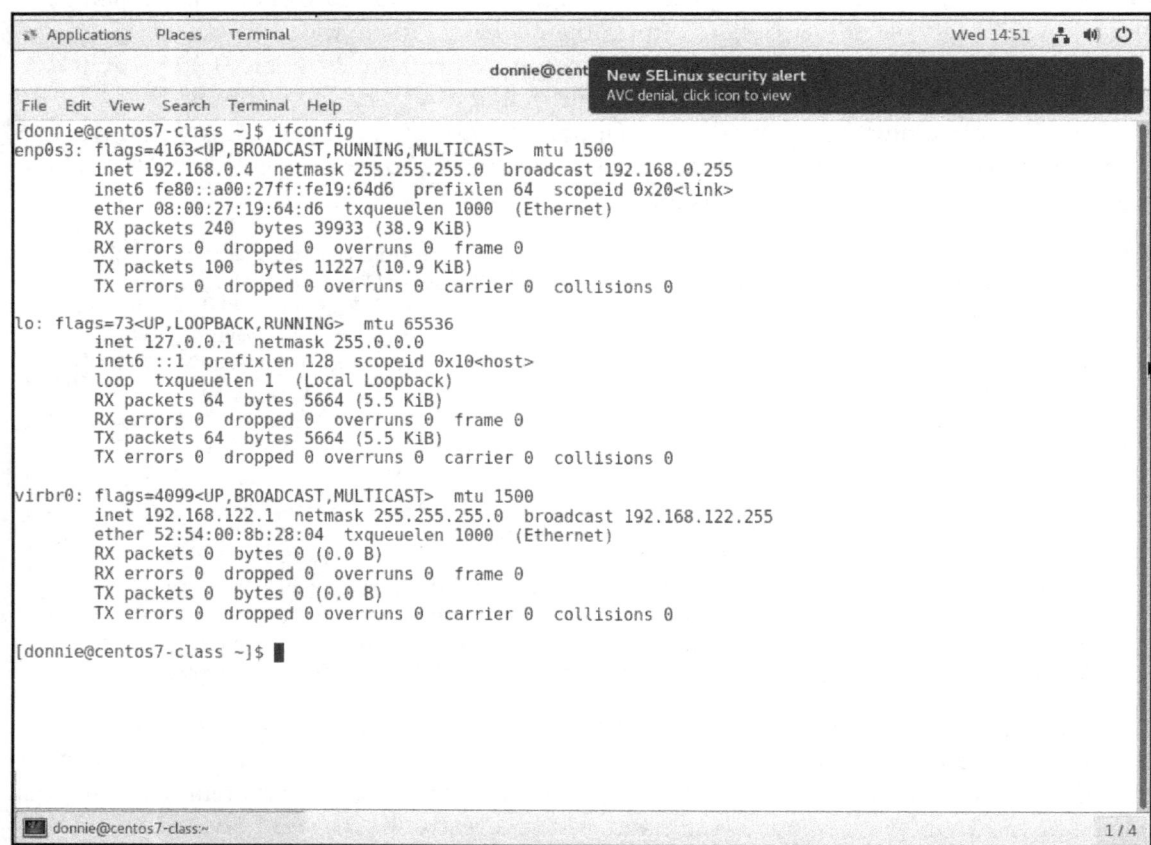

Click on that alert icon, and you'll see this:

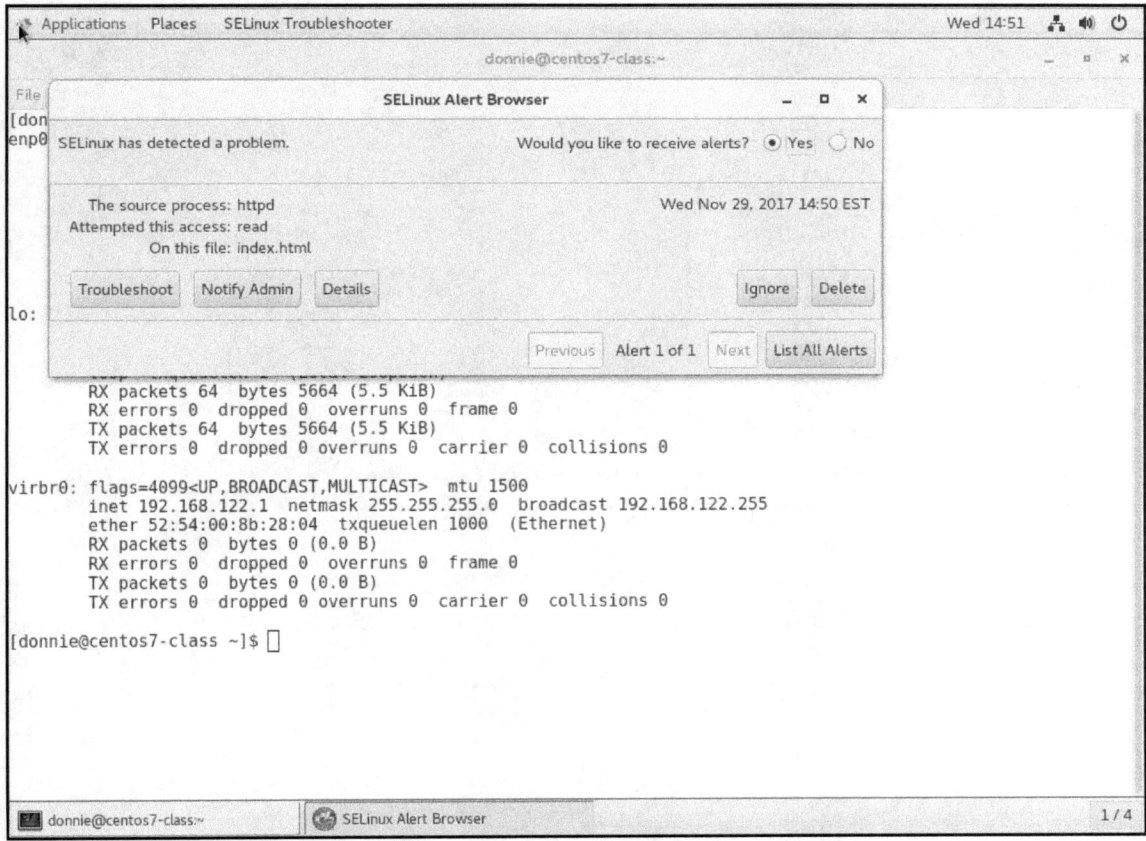

Click the **Troubleshoot** button, and you'll see your list of suggestions for how to fix the problem:

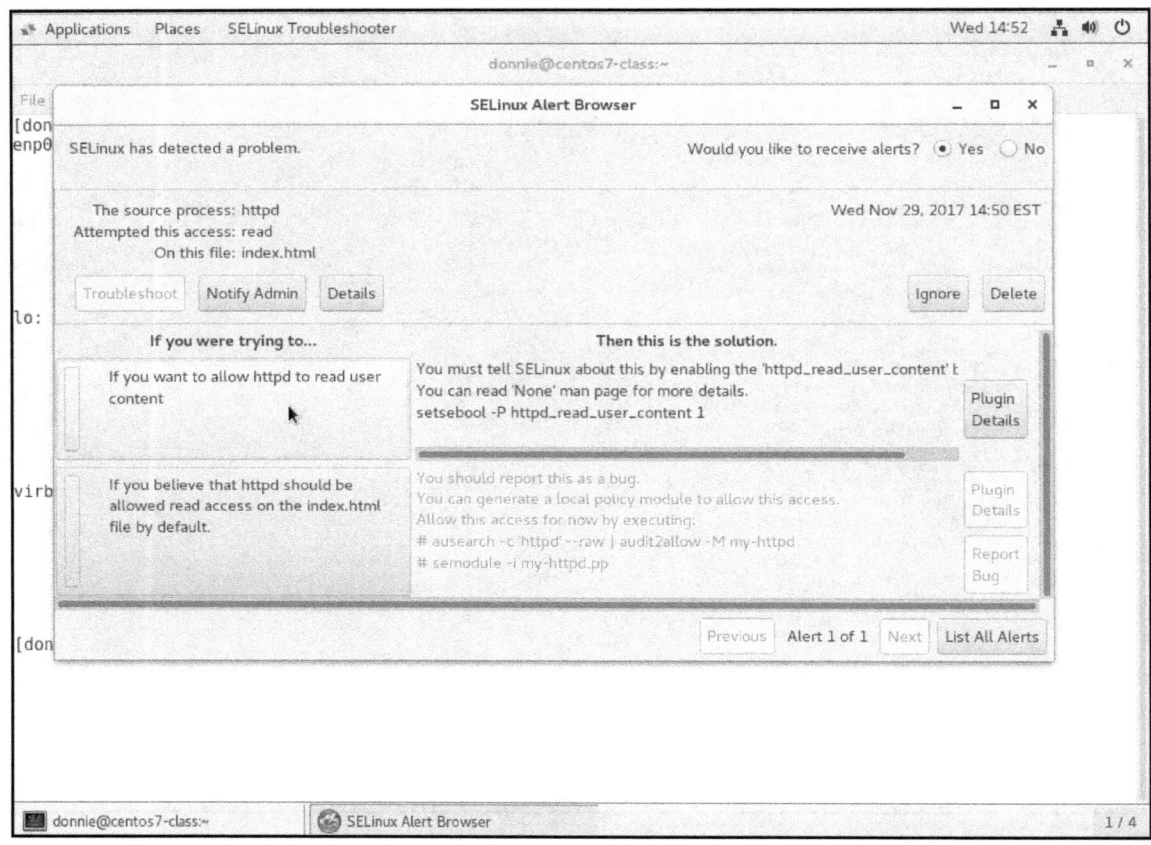

As it is often the case with GUI thingies, this is mostly self-explanatory, so you shouldn't have any problem with figuring it out.

Troubleshooting in permissive mode

If you're dealing with a simple problem like the one I've just shown you, then you can probably assume that you're safe in doing what the first suggestion in the setroubleshoot message tells you to do. But there will be times when things get a bit more complex, where you might have more than one problem. For times like these, you need to use *permissive mode*.

When you first install your Red Hat or CentOS system, SELinux is in *enforcing mode*, which is the default. This means that SELinux will actually stop actions that are in violation of the active SELinux policy. This also means that if you have multiple SELinux problems when you try to perform a certain action, SELinux will stop the action from taking place after the first violation occurs. When it happens, SELinux won't even see the remaining problems, and they won't show up in the `messages` log file. If you try to troubleshoot these types of problems while in enforcing mode, you'll be like the proverbial dog who chases its own tail. You'll go round and round and will accomplish nothing.

In permissive mode, SELinux allows actions that violate policy to occur, but it will log them. By switching to permissive mode and doing something to induce the problem that you were seeing, the prohibited actions will take place, but setroubleshoot will log all of them in the `messages` file. This way, you'll get a better view of what you need to do to get things working properly.

First, let's use `getenforce` to verify what our current mode is:

```
[donnie@localhost ~]$ sudo getenforce
Enforcing
[donnie@localhost ~]$
```

Now, let's temporarily place the system into permissive mode:

```
[donnie@localhost ~]$ sudo setenforce 0

[donnie@localhost ~]$ sudo getenforce
Permissive
[donnie@localhost ~]$
```

When I say *temporarily*, I mean that this will only last until you do a system reboot. After a reboot, you'll be back in enforcing mode. Also, note that a 0 after the `setenforce` denotes that I'm setting permissive mode. To get back to enforcing mode after you're done with troubleshooting, replace the 0 with a 1:

```
[donnie@localhost ~]$ sudo setenforce 1

[donnie@localhost ~]$ sudo getenforce
Enforcing
[donnie@localhost ~]$
```

We're now back in enforcing mode.

At times, you may need to make permissive mode persist after a system reboot. An example of this would be if you ever have to deal with a system that has had SELinux disabled for a long period of time. In a case like that, you wouldn't want to just put SELinux into enforcing mode and reboot. If you try that, it will take forever for the system to properly create the file and directory labels that make SELinux work, and the system might lock up before it's done. By placing the system into permissive mode first, you'll avoid having the system lock up, although it will still take a long time for the relabeling process to complete.

To make permissive mode persistent across system reboots, you'll edit the `selinux` file in the `/etc/sysconfig` directory. Here's what it looks like by default:

```
# This file controls the state of SELinux on the system.
# SELINUX= can take one of these three values:
#     enforcing - SELinux security policy is enforced.
#     permissive - SELinux prints warnings instead of enforcing.
#     disabled - No SELinux policy is loaded.
SELINUX=enforcing
# SELINUXTYPE= can take one of three two values:
#     targeted - Targeted processes are protected,
#     minimum - Modification of targeted policy. Only selected processes
are protected.
#     mls - Multi Level Security protection.
SELINUXTYPE=targeted
```

The two important things you see here are that SELinux is in enforcing mode, and that it's using the targeted policy. To switch to permissive mode, just change the `SELINUX=` line, and save the file:

```
# This file controls the state of SELinux on the system.
# SELINUX= can take one of these three values:
#     enforcing - SELinux security policy is enforced.
#     permissive - SELinux prints warnings instead of enforcing.
#     disabled - No SELinux policy is loaded.
SELINUX=permissive
# SELINUXTYPE= can take one of three two values:
#     targeted - Targeted processes are protected,
#     minimum - Modification of targeted policy. Only selected processes
are protected.
#     mls - Multi Level Security protection.
SELINUXTYPE=targeted
```

The `sestatus` utility shows us lots of cool information about what's going on with SELinux:

```
[donnie@localhost ~]$ sudo sestatus
SELinux status:                 enabled
```

```
SELinuxfs mount:                    /sys/fs/selinux
SELinux root directory:             /etc/selinux
Loaded policy name:                 targeted
Current mode:                       enforcing
Mode from config file:              permissive
Policy MLS status:                  enabled
Policy deny_unknown status:         allowed
Max kernel policy version:          28
[donnie@localhost ~]$
```

The two items that interest us here are current mode and mode from a configuration file. By changing the configuration file to permissive, we haven't changed the current running mode. So, we're still in enforcing mode. The switch to permissive won't happen until I either reboot this machine or until I manually switch by issuing a `sudo setenforce 0` command. And of course, you don't want to stay in permissive mode forever. As soon as you no longer need permissive mode, change the configuration file back to enforcing and do a `sudo setenforce 1` to change the running mode.

Working with SELinux policies

So far, all we've looked at is what happens when we have an incorrect SELinux type set on a file and what to do to set the correct type. Another problem we may have would come about if we need to allow an action that is prohibited by the active SELinux policy.

Viewing the Booleans

Booleans are part of what makes up an SELinux policy, and each Boolean represents a binary choice. In SELinux policies, a Boolean either allows something or it prohibits something. To see all of the Booleans on your system, run the `getsebool -a` command. (It's a long list, so I'll only show partial output here.):

```
[donnie@localhost ~]$ getsebool -a
abrt_anon_write --> off
abrt_handle_event --> off
abrt_upload_watch_anon_write --> on
antivirus_can_scan_system --> off
antivirus_use_jit --> off
auditadm_exec_content --> on
. . .

. . .
xserver_object_manager --> off
zabbix_can_network --> off
```

```
zarafa_setrlimit --> off
zebra_write_config --> off
zoneminder_anon_write --> off
zoneminder_run_sudo --> off
[donnie@localhost ~]$
```

To view more than one Boolean, the -a switch is mandatory. If you just happen to know the name of the Boolean that you want to see, leave the -a out and list the Boolean. In keeping with the Apache web server theme that we've had going, let's see whether we're allowing Apache to access files in users' home directories:

```
[donnie@localhost html]$ getsebool httpd_enable_homedirs
httpd_enable_homedirs --> off
[donnie@localhost html]$
```

The fact that this Boolean is off means that the Apache server daemon isn't allowed to access any content within the users' home directories. This is an important protection, and you really don't want to change it. Instead, just put web content files elsewhere so that you don't have to change this Boolean.

Most likely, you'll rarely want to look at the entire list, and you likely won't know the name of the specific Boolean that you want to see. Rather, you'll probably want to filter the output through grep in order to look at just certain things. For example, to see all of the Booleans that affect a web server, follow this:

```
[donnie@localhost html]$ getsebool -a | grep 'http'
httpd_anon_write --> off
httpd_builtin_scripting --> on
httpd_can_check_spam --> off
httpd_can_connect_ftp --> off
httpd_can_connect_ldap --> off
httpd_can_connect_mythtv --> off
httpd_can_connect_zabbix --> off
httpd_can_network_connect --> off
 .  .  .

 .  .  .
httpd_use_nfs --> off
httpd_use_openstack --> off
httpd_use_sasl --> off
httpd_verify_dns --> off
named_tcp_bind_http_port --> off
prosody_bind_http_port --> off
[donnie@localhost html]$
```

It's also a rather long list, but scroll down a ways, and you'll find the Boolean that you seek.

Configuring the Booleans

Realistically, you'll likely never have reason to allow users to serve web content out of their home directories. It's much more probable that you'll set up something like a Samba server, which would allow users on Windows machines to use their graphical **Windows Explorer** to access their home directories on Linux servers. But if you set up a Samba server and don't do anything with SELinux, users will be complaining about how they don't see any of their files in their home directories of the Samba server. Because you're the proactive type and you want to avoid the pain of listening to complaining users, you'll surely just go ahead and configure SELinux to allow the Samba daemon to access users' home directories. You might not know the exact name of the Boolean, but you can find it easily enough, as follows:

```
[donnie@localhost html]$ getsebool -a | grep 'home'
git_cgi_enable_homedirs --> off
git_system_enable_homedirs --> off
httpd_enable_homedirs --> off
mock_enable_homedirs --> off
mpd_enable_homedirs --> off
openvpn_enable_homedirs --> on
samba_create_home_dirs --> off
samba_enable_home_dirs --> off
sanlock_enable_home_dirs --> off
spamd_enable_home_dirs --> on
ssh_chroot_rw_homedirs --> off
tftp_home_dir --> off
use_ecryptfs_home_dirs --> off
use_fusefs_home_dirs --> off
use_nfs_home_dirs --> off
use_samba_home_dirs --> off
xdm_write_home --> off
[donnie@localhost html]$
```

Okay, you knew that the Boolean name probably had the word home in it, so you filtered for that word. About half-way down the list, you see samba_enable_home_dirs --> off. You'll need to change this to on to let users access their home directories from their Windows machines:

```
[donnie@localhost html]$ sudo setsebool samba_enable_home_dirs on

[sudo] password for donnie:
[donnie@localhost html]$ getsebool samba_enable_home_dirs
samba_enable_home_dirs --> on
[donnie@localhost html]$
```

Users can now access their home directories as they should be able to, but only until you do a system reboot. Without the -P option, any changes you make with setsebool will only be temporary. So, let's make the change permanent with -P:

```
[donnie@localhost html]$ sudo setsebool -P samba_enable_home_dirs on

[donnie@localhost html]$ getsebool samba_enable_home_dirs
samba_enable_home_dirs --> on
[donnie@localhost html]$
```

Congratulations, you've just made your first change to SELinux policy.

Protecting your web server

Look at the output of the getsebool -a | grep 'http' command again, and you'll see that most of the httpd-related Booleans are turned off by default, with only a few turned on. There are two of them that you'll commonly need to turn on when setting up a web server.

If you ever need to set up a website with some sort of PHP-based content management system, such as Joomla or Wordpress, you may have to turn on the httpd_unified Boolean. With this Boolean turned off, the Apache web server won't be able to interact properly with all of the components of the PHP engine:

```
[donnie@localhost ~]$ getsebool httpd_unified
httpd_unified --> off

[donnie@localhost ~]$ sudo setsebool -P httpd_unified on
[sudo] password for donnie:

[donnie@localhost ~]$ getsebool httpd_unified
httpd_unified --> on
[donnie@localhost ~]$
```

The other Boolean that you'll commonly need to turn on is the httpd_can_sendmail Boolean. If you ever need for a website to send mail out through a form or if you need to set up a mail server with a web-based frontend, you'll definitely need to set this to on:

```
[donnie@localhost ~]$ getsebool httpd_can_sendmail
httpd_can_sendmail --> off

[donnie@localhost ~]$ sudo setsebool -P httpd_can_sendmail on

[donnie@localhost ~]$ getsebool httpd_can_sendmail
httpd_can_sendmail --> on
```

```
[donnie@localhost ~]$
```

On the other hand, there are some Booleans that are turned on by default, and you might want to consider whether you really need them turned on. For example, allowing CGI scripts to run on a web server does represent a potential security risk. If an intruder were to somehow upload a malicious CGI script to the server and run it, much damage could occur as a result. Yet, for some bizarre reason, the default SELinux policy allows CGI scripts to run. If you're absolutely certain that nobody who hosts websites on your server will ever need to run CGI scripts, you might want to consider turning this Boolean off:

```
[donnie@localhost ~]$ getsebool httpd_enable_cgi
httpd_enable_cgi --> on

[donnie@localhost ~]$ sudo setsebool -P httpd_enable_cgi off

[donnie@localhost ~]$ getsebool httpd_enable_cgi
httpd_enable_cgi --> off
[donnie@localhost ~]$
```

Protecting network ports

Each network daemon that's running on your system has a specific network port or set of network ports assigned to it, on which it will listen. The /etc/services file contains the list of common daemons and their associated network ports, but it doesn't prevent someone from configuring a daemon to listen on some non-standard port. So, without some mechanism to prevent it, some sneaky intruder could potentially plant some sort of malware that would cause a daemon to listen on a non-standard port, possibly listening for commands from its master.

SELinux protects against this sort of malicious activity by only allowing daemons to listen on certain ports. Use semanage to look at the list of allowed ports:

```
[donnie@localhost ~]$ sudo semanage port -l
[sudo] password for donnie:
SELinux Port Type              Proto     Port Number

afs3_callback_port_t           tcp       7001
afs3_callback_port_t           udp       7001
afs_bos_port_t                 udp       7007
afs_fs_port_t                  tcp       2040
afs_fs_port_t                  udp       7000, 7005
afs_ka_port_t                  udp       7004
afs_pt_port_t                  tcp       7002
afs_pt_port_t                  udp       7002
```

```
afs_vl_port_t                    udp        7003
. . .
. . .
zebra_port_t                     tcp        2606, 2608-2609, 2600-2604
zebra_port_t                     udp        2606, 2608-2609, 2600-2604
zented_port_t                    tcp        1229
zented_port_t                    udp        1229
zookeeper_client_port_t          tcp        2181
zookeeper_election_port_t        tcp        3888
zookeeper_leader_port_t          tcp        2888
zope_port_t                      tcp        8021
[donnie@localhost ~]$
```

This is yet another of those very long lists, so I'm only showing partial output. However, let's narrow things down a bit. Let's say that I only want to look at the list of ports on which the Apache web server can listen. For this, I'll use my good friend, `grep`:

```
[donnie@localhost ~]$ sudo semanage port -l | grep 'http'
[sudo] password for donnie:
http_cache_port_t                tcp        8080, 8118, 8123, 10001-10010
http_cache_port_t                udp        3130
http_port_t                      tcp        80, 81, 443, 488, 8008, 8009, 8443,
9000
pegasus_http_port_t              tcp        5988
pegasus_https_port_t             tcp        5989
[donnie@localhost ~]$
```

Several `http` items come up, but I'm only interested in the `http_port_t` item because it's the one that affects normal web server operation. We see here that SELinux will allow Apache to listen on ports 80, 81, 443, 488, 8008, 8009, 8443, and 9000. As the Apache server is the most likely daemon for which you'd ever have a legitimate reason for adding a non-standard port, let's demo with it.

First, let's go into the `/etc/httpd/conf/httpd.conf` file and look at the ports on which Apache is currently listening. Search for `Listen`, and you'll see the following line:

```
Listen 80
```

I don't have the SSL module installed on this machine, but if I did, I would have an `ssl.conf` file in the `/etc/httpd/conf.d` directory with the following line:

```
Listen 443
```

So for normal, non-encrypted website connections, the default configuration only has Apache listening on port 80. For secure, encrypted website connections, Apache listens on port 443. Now, let's go into the `httpd.conf` file and change `Listen 80` to a port number that SELinux doesn't allow. For example, port 82:

```
Listen 82
```

After saving the file, I'll restart Apache to read in the new configuration:

```
[donnie@localhost ~]$ sudo systemctl restart httpd
Job for httpd.service failed because the control process exited with error
code. See "systemctl status httpd.service" and "journalctl -xe" for
details.
[donnie@localhost ~]$
```

Yes, I have a problem. I'll look in the `/var/log/messages` file to see if setroubleshoot gives me a clue:

```
Nov 29 16:39:21 localhost python: SELinux is preventing /usr/sbin/httpd
from name_bind access on the tcp_socket port 82.#012#012***** Plugin
bind_ports (99.5 confidence) suggests ************************#012#012If
you want to allow /usr/sbin/httpd to bind to network port 82#012Then you
need to modify the port type.#012Do#012# semanage port -a -t PORT_TYPE -p
tcp 82#012 where PORT_TYPE is one of the following: http_cache_port_t,
http_port_t, jboss_management_port_t, jboss_messaging_port_t, ntop_port_t,
puppet_port_t.#012#012***** Plugin catchall (1.49 confidence) suggests
*************************#012#012If you believe that httpd should be
allowed name_bind access on the port 82 tcp_socket by default.#012Then you
should report this as a bug.#012You can generate a local policy module to
allow this access.#012Do#012allow this access for now by executing:#012#
ausearch -c 'httpd' --raw | audit2allow -M my-httpd#012# semodule -i my-
httpd.pp#012
```

The problem that SELinux is preventing `httpd` from binding to port 82 is defined in the first line of the message. The first suggestion we see for fixing this is to use `semanage` to add the port to the list of allowed ports. So, let's do that and look at the list of Apache ports:

```
[donnie@localhost ~]$ sudo semanage port -a 82 -t http_port_t -p tcp

[donnie@localhost ~]$ sudo semanage port -l | grep 'http_port_t'
http_port_t                    tcp      82, 80, 81, 443, 488, 8008, 8009,
8443, 9000
pegasus_http_port_t            tcp      5988
[donnie@localhost ~]$
```

It's not clear in the setroubleshoot message, but you need to specify the port number that you want to add after the `port -a`. The `-t http_port_t` specifies the type for which you want to add the port, and the `-p tcp` specifies that you want to use the TCP protocol.

Now, for the moment of truth. Will the Apache daemon start this time? Let's see:

```
[donnie@localhost ~]$ sudo systemctl restart httpd
[sudo] password for donnie:
[donnie@localhost ~]$ sudo systemctl status httpd
● httpd.service - The Apache HTTP Server
   Loaded: loaded (/usr/lib/systemd/system/httpd.service; enabled; vendor
preset: disabled)
   Active: active (running) since Wed 2017-11-29 20:09:51 EST; 7s ago
     Docs: man:httpd(8)
. . .
. . .
```

It works, and we have achieved coolness. But now, I've decided that I no longer need this oddball port. Deleting it is just as easy as adding it:

```
[donnie@localhost ~]$ sudo semanage port -d 82 -t http_port_t -p tcp

[donnie@localhost ~]$ sudo semanage port -l | grep 'http_port_t'
http_port_t                    tcp      80, 81, 443, 488, 8008, 8009, 8443,
9000
pegasus_http_port_t            tcp      5988
[donnie@localhost ~]$
```

All I had to do was to replace the `port -a` with `port -d`. And of course, I still need to go into the `/etc/httpd/conf/httpd.conf` file to change `Listen 82` back to `Listen 80`.

Creating custom policy modules

Sometimes, you'll run into a problem that you can't fix by either changing the type or by setting a Boolean. In times like these, you'll need to create a custom policy module, and you'll use the `audit2allow` utility to do that.

Here's a screenshot of a problem I had several years ago, when I was helping a client set up a Postfix mail server on CentOS 7:

```
SELinux is preventing /usr/libexec/dovecot/dict from read access on the file .

*****   Plugin catchall (100. confidence) suggests   ***************************

If you believe that dict should be allowed read access on the  file by default.
Then you should report this as a bug.
You can generate a local policy module to allow this access.
Do
allow this access for now by executing:
# grep dict /var/log/audit/audit.log | audit2allow -M mypol
# semodule -i mypol.pp
```

So, for some strange reason that I never understood, SELinux wouldn't allow Dovecot, the Mail Delivery Agent component of the mail server, to read its own dict file. There's no Boolean to change and there wasn't a type problem, so setroubleshoot suggested that I create a custom policy module. It's easy enough to do, but you do need to be aware that this won't work with sudo on your normal user account. This is one of those rare times when you'll just have to go to the root user command prompt, and you'll also need to be in the root user's home directory:

sudo su -

Before you do it, be sure to put SELinux into the permissive mode and then do something to induce the SELinux error. This way, you'll be sure that one problem isn't masking others.

When you run the command to create the new policy module, be sure to replace mypol with a custom policy name of your own choosing. In my case, I named the module dovecot_dict, and the command looked like this:

grep dict /var/log/audit/audit.log | audit2allow -M dovecot_dict

What I'm doing here is using grep to search through the audit.log file for SELinux messages that contain the word dict. I then piped the output of that into audit2allow and used the -M option to create a custom module with the name, dovecot_dict.

After I created the new policy module, I inserted it into the SELinux policy like so:

semodule -i dovecot_dict.pp

There was a also a second problem that required another custom module, but I just repeated this procedure to produce another module of a different name. After I got all that done, I reloaded the SELinux policy, in order to get my new modules to take effect:

```
semodule -R
```

With `semodule`, the `-R` switch stands for reload, rather than recursive, as it does with most Linux commands.

With all that done, I put SELinux back into enforcing mode and exited back to my own user account. And, I tested the setup to make sure that I had fixed the problem.

Of course, you also want to bear in mind that you don't want to just modify SELinux policy or contexts every time you see an `sealert` message in the log files. For example, consider this snippet from the `messages` file of my Oracle Linux 7 machine, which I set up mainly to run Docker and Docker containers:

```
Jun  8 19:32:17 docker-1 setroubleshoot: SELinux is preventing
/usr/bin/docker from getattr access on the file /etc/exports. For complete
SELinux messages. run sealert -l b267929a-d3ad-45d5-806e-907449fc2739
Jun  8 19:32:17 docker-1 python: SELinux is preventing /usr/bin/docker from
getattr access on the file /etc/exports.#012#012***** Plugin catchall
(100. confidence) suggests   ************************#012#012If you
believe that docker should be allowed getattr access on the exports file by
default.#012Then you should report this as a bug.#012You can generate a
local policy module to allow this access.#012Do#012allow this access for
now by executing:#012# grep docker /var/log/audit/audit.log | audit2allow -
M mypol#012# semodule -i mypol.pp#012
Jun  8 19:32:17 docker-1 setroubleshoot: SELinux is preventing
/usr/bin/docker from getattr access on the file /etc/shadow.rpmnew. For
complete SELinux messages. run sealert -l bc566655-1fbc-4141-af48-
ccd6c76a3d3b
Jun  8 19:32:17 docker-1 python: SELinux is preventing /usr/bin/docker from
getattr access on the file /etc/shadow.rpmnew.#012#012***** Plugin
catchall (100. confidence) suggests   ************************#012#012If
you believe that docker should be allowed getattr access on the
shadow.rpmnew file by default.#012Then you should report this as a
bug.#012You can generate a local policy module to allow this
access.#012Do#012allow this access for now by executing:#012# grep docker
/var/log/audit/audit.log | audit2allow -M mypol#012# semodule -i
mypol.pp#012
```

These messages were caused by an early version of Docker trying to access resources on the host machine. As you can see, Docker is trying to access some rather sensitive files, and SELinux is preventing Docker from doing so. With early versions of Docker and without some sort of Mandatory Access Control, it would have been a trivial matter for a normal, unprivileged user to escape from the Docker container and have root user privileges on the host system. Naturally, when you see these sorts of messages, you don't want to automatically tell SELinux to allow the prohibited actions. It just may be that SELinux is preventing something truly bad from taking place.

Be sure to get your copy of *The SELinux Coloring Book* at: `https://opensource.com/business/13/11/selinux-policy-guide`.

Hands-on lab – SELinux Booleans and ports

In this lab, you'll view the effects of having Apache try to listen on an unauthorized port:

1. View the ports that SELinux allows the Apache web server daemon to use:

   ```
   sudo semanage port -l | grep 'http'
   ```

2. Open the `/etc/httpd/conf/httpd.conf` file in your favorite text editor. Find the line that says `Listen 80` and change it to `Listen 82`. Restart Apache by entering the following:

   ```
   sudo systemctl restart httpd
   ```

3. View the error message you receive by entering:

   ```
   sudo tail -20 /var/log/messages
   ```

4. Add port `82` to the list of authorized ports and restart Apache:

   ```
   sudo semanage port -a 82 -t http_port_t -p tcp
   sudo semanage port -l
   sudo systemctl restart httpd
   ```

5. Delete the port that you just added:

   ```
   sudo semanage -d 82 -t http_port_t -p tcp
   ```

6. Go back into the `/etc/httpd/conf/httpd.conf` file, and change `Listen 82` back to `Listen 80`. Restart the Apache daemon to return to normal operation.

How AppArmor can benefit a systems administrator

AppArmor is the Mandatory Access Control system that comes installed with the SUSE and the Ubuntu families of Linux. Although it's designed to do pretty much the same job as SELinux, its mode of operation is substantially different:

- SELinux labels all system processes and all objects such as files, directories, or network ports. For files and directories, SELinux stores the labels in their respective inodes as extended attributes. (An inode is the basic filesystem component that contains all information about a file, except for the file name.)
- AppArmor uses pathname enforcement, which means that you specify the path to the executable file that you want for AppArmor to control. This way, there's no need to insert labels into the extended attributes of files or directories.
- With SELinux, you have system-wide protection out of the box.
- With AppArmor, you have a profile for each individual application.
- With either SELinux or AppArmor, you might occasionally find yourself having to create custom policy modules from scratch, especially if you're dealing with either third-party applications or home-grown software. With AppArmor, this is easier, because the syntax for writing AppArmor profiles is much easier than the syntax for writing SELinux policies. And, AppArmor comes with utilities that can help you automate the process.
- Just as SELinux can, AppArmor can help prevent malicious actors from ruining your day and can help protect user data.

So, you see that there are advantages and disadvantages to both SELinux and AppArmor, and a lot of Linux administrators have strong feelings about which one they prefer. (To avoid being subjected to a flame-war, I'll refrain from stating my own preference.) Also, note that even though we're working with an Ubuntu virtual machine, the information I present here, other than the Ubuntu-specific package installation commands, also works with the SUSE Linux distos.

Looking at AppArmor profiles

In the /etc/apparmor.d directory, you'll see the AppArmor profiles for your system. (The SELinux folk say policies, but the AppArmor folk say profiles.):

```
donnie@ubuntu3:/etc/apparmor.d$ ls -l
total 72
drwxr-xr-x 5 root root  4096 Oct 29 15:21 abstractions
drwxr-xr-x 2 root root  4096 Nov 15 09:34 cache
drwxr-xr-x 2 root root  4096 Oct 29 14:43 disable
drwxr-xr-x 2 root root  4096 Apr  5  2016 force-complain
drwxr-xr-x 2 root root  4096 Oct 29 15:21 local
drwxr-xr-x 2 root root  4096 Oct 29 15:02 lxc
-rw-r--r-- 1 root root   198 Jun 14 16:15 lxc-containers
-rw-r--r-- 1 root root  3310 Apr 12  2016 sbin.dhclient
drwxr-xr-x 5 root root  4096 Oct 29 15:21 tunables
-rw-r--r-- 1 root root   125 Jun 14 16:15 usr.bin.lxc-start
-rw-r--r-- 1 root root   281 May 23  2017 usr.lib.lxd.lxd-bridge-proxy
-rw-r--r-- 1 root root 17667 Oct 18 05:04 usr.lib.snapd.snap-confine.real
-rw-r--r-- 1 root root  1527 Jan  5  2016 usr.sbin.rsyslogd
-rw-r--r-- 1 root root  1469 Sep  8 15:27 usr.sbin.tcpdump
donnie@ubuntu3:/etc/apparmor.d$
```

The sbin.dhclient file and the usr.* files are all AppArmor profiles. You'll find a few other profiles in the lxc and lxc-containers subdirectories. Still, though, there's not a whole lot there in the way of application profiles.

For some reason, a default installation of OpenSUSE comes with more installed profiles than does Ubuntu Server. To install more profiles on Ubuntu, use the following:

```
sudo apt install apparmor-profiles apparmor-profiles-
extra
```

In the abstractions subdirectory, you'll find files that aren't complete profiles, but that can be included in complete profiles. Any one of these abstraction files can be included in any number of profiles. This way, you don't have to write the same code over and over every time you create a profile. Just include an abstraction file instead.

 If you're familiar with programming concepts, just think of abstraction files as include files by another name.

Here's a partial listing of the abstraction files:

```
donnie@ubuntu3:/etc/apparmor.d/abstractions$ ls -l
total 320
-rw-r--r-- 1 root root  695 Mar 15  2017 apache2-common
drwxr-xr-x 2 root root 4096 Oct 29 15:21 apparmor_api
-rw-r--r-- 1 root root  308 Mar 15  2017 aspell
-rw-r--r-- 1 root root 1582 Mar 15  2017 audio
-rw-r--r-- 1 root root 1544 Mar 15  2017 authentication
-rw-r--r-- 1 root root 6099 Mar 15  2017 base
-rw-r--r-- 1 root root 1512 Mar 15  2017 bash
-rw-r--r-- 1 root root  798 Mar 15  2017 consoles
-rw-r--r-- 1 root root  714 Mar 15  2017 cups-client
-rw-r--r-- 1 root root  593 Mar 15  2017 dbus
. . .
. . .
-rw-r--r-- 1 root root  705 Mar 15  2017 web-data
-rw-r--r-- 1 root root  739 Mar 15  2017 winbind
-rw-r--r-- 1 root root  585 Mar 15  2017 wutmp
-rw-r--r-- 1 root root 1819 Mar 15  2017 X
-rw-r--r-- 1 root root  883 Mar 15  2017 xad
-rw-r--r-- 1 root root  673 Mar 15  2017 xdg-desktop
donnie@ubuntu3:/etc/apparmor.d/abstractions$
```

To get a feel for how AppArmor rules work, let's peek inside the web-data abstraction file:

```
/srv/www/htdocs/ r,
/srv/www/htdocs/** r,
# virtual hosting
/srv/www/vhosts/ r,
/srv/www/vhosts/** r,
# mod_userdir
@{HOME}/public_html/ r,
@{HOME}/public_html/** r,

/srv/www/rails/*/public/ r,
/srv/www/rails/*/public/** r,

/var/www/html/ r,
/var/www/html/** r,
```

This file is nothing but a list of directories from which the Apache daemon is allowed to read files. Let's break it down:

- Note that each rule ends with `r,`. This denotes that we want for Apache to have read access on each listed directory. Also note that each rule has to end with a comma.
- `/srv/www/htdocs/ r,` means that the listed directory itself has read access for Apache.
- `/srv/www.htdocs/* * r,` the `*` `*` wildcards make this rule recursive. In other words, Apache can read all files in all subdirectories of this specified directory.
- `# mod_userdir` if installed, this Apache module allows Apache to read web content files from a subdirectory that's within a user's home directory. The next two lines go along with that.
- `@{HOME}/public_html/ r,` and `@{HOME}/public_html/ r,` the `@{HOME}` variable allows this rule to work with any user's home directory. (You'll see this variable defined in the `/etc/apparmor.d/tunables/home` file.)
- Note that there's no specific rule that prohibits Apache from reading from other locations. It's just understood that anything that's not listed here is off-limits to the Apache web server daemon.

The `tunables` subdirectory contains files that have predefined variables. You can also use this directory to either define new variables or make profile tweaks:

```
donnie@ubuntu3:/etc/apparmor.d/tunables$ ls -l
total 56
-rw-r--r-- 1 root root  624 Mar 15  2017 alias
-rw-r--r-- 1 root root  376 Mar 15  2017 apparmorfs
-rw-r--r-- 1 root root  804 Mar 15  2017 dovecot
-rw-r--r-- 1 root root  694 Mar 15  2017 global
-rw-r--r-- 1 root root  983 Mar 15  2017 home
drwxr-xr-x 2 root root 4096 Oct 29 15:21 home.d
-rw-r--r-- 1 root root  792 Mar 15  2017 kernelvars
-rw-r--r-- 1 root root  631 Mar 15  2017 multiarch
drwxr-xr-x 2 root root 4096 Mar 15  2017 multiarch.d
-rw-r--r-- 1 root root  440 Mar 15  2017 proc
-rw-r--r-- 1 root root  430 Mar 15  2017 securityfs
-rw-r--r-- 1 root root  368 Mar 15  2017 sys
-rw-r--r-- 1 root root  868 Mar 15  2017 xdg-user-dirs
drwxr-xr-x 2 root root 4096 Oct 29 15:02 xdg-user-dirs.d
donnie@ubuntu3:/etc/apparmor.d/tunables$
```

Space doesn't permit me to show you the details of how to write your own profiles from scratch, and thanks to the suite of utilities that we'll look at in the next section, you might never need to do that. Still, just to give you a better understanding about how AppArmor does what it does, here's a chart of some example rules that you might find in any given profile:

`/var/run/some_program.pid rw,`	**The process will have read and write privileges for this process ID file.**
`/etc/ld.so.cache r,`	The process will have read privileges for this file.
`/tmp/some_program.* l,`	The process will be able to create and delete links with the `some_program` name.
`/bin/mount ux`	The process has executable privileges for the `mount` utility, which will then run unconstrained. (Unconstrained means, without an AppArmor profile.)

Working with AppArmor command-line utilities

Whether or not you have all the AppArmor utilities you need will depend on which Linux distro you have. On my OpenSUSE Leap workstation, the utilities were there out of the box. On my Ubuntu Server virtual machine, I had to install them myself:

```
sudo apt install apparmor-utils
```

First, let's look at the status of AppArmor on the Ubuntu machine:

```
donnie@ubuntu5:~$ sudo aa-status
[sudo] password for donnie:

apparmor module is loaded.
13 profiles are loaded.
13 profiles are in enforce mode.
   /sbin/dhclient
   /usr/bin/lxc-start
   /usr/lib/NetworkManager/nm-dhcp-client.action
   /usr/lib/NetworkManager/nm-dhcp-helper
   /usr/lib/connman/scripts/dhclient-script
   /usr/lib/snapd/snap-confine
   /usr/lib/snapd/snap-confine//mount-namespace-capture-helper
```

```
/usr/sbin/mysqld
/usr/sbin/tcpdump
lxc-container-default
lxc-container-default-cgns
lxc-container-default-with-mounting
lxc-container-default-with-nesting
0 profiles are in complain mode.
1 processes have profiles defined.
1 processes are in enforce mode.
   /usr/sbin/mysqld (679)
0 processes are in complain mode.
0 processes are unconfined but have a profile defined.
donnie@ubuntu5:~$
```

The first thing to note here is that AppArmor has an enforce mode and a complain mode. The enforce mode does the same job as its enforcing mode counterpart in SELinux. It prevents system processes from doing things that the active policy doesn't allow, and it logs any violations. The complain mode is the same as the permissive mode in SELinux. It allows processes to perform actions that are prohibited by the active policy, but it records those actions in either the `/var/log/audit/audit.log` file, or the system log file, depending on whether you have `auditd` installed. (Unlike the Red Hat-type distros, `auditd` doesn't come installed by default on Ubuntu.) You would use the complain mode to either help with troubleshooting or to test new profiles.

Most of the enforce mode profiles we see here have to do with either network management or with `lxc` container management. Two exceptions we see are the two profiles for `snapd`, which is the daemon that makes the snap packaging technology work. The third exception is for the `mysqld` profile.

 Snap packages are universal binary files that are designed to work on multiple distros. Snap technology is currently available for Ubuntu and Fedora.

Curiously, when you install a daemon package on Ubuntu, you'll sometimes get a predefined profile for that daemon and sometimes you won't. Even when a profile does come with the package that you've installed, it's sometimes already in the enforce mode and sometimes it isn't. For example, if you're setting up a **Domain Name Service** (**DNS**) server and you install the `bind9` package for it, you'll get an AppArmor profile that's already in enforce mode. If you're setting up a database server and install the `mysql-server` package, you'll also get a working profile that's already in the enforce mode.

But, if you're setting up a database server and you prefer to install the `mariadb-server` instead of `mysql-server`, you'll get an AppArmor profile that's completely disabled and that can't be enabled. When you look in the `usr.sbin.mysqld` profile file that gets installed with the `mariadb-server` package, you'll see this:

```
# This file is intensionally empty to disable apparmor by default for newer
# versions of MariaDB, while providing seamless upgrade from older versions
# and from mysql, where apparmor is used.
#
# By default, we do not want to have any apparmor profile for the MariaDB
# server. It does not provide much useful functionality/security, and
causes
# several problems for users who often are not even aware that apparmor
# exists and runs on their system.
#
# Users can modify and maintain their own profile, and in this case it will
# be used.
#
# When upgrading from previous version, users who modified the profile
# will be promptet to keep or discard it, while for default installs
# we will automatically disable the profile.
```

Okay, so apparently, AppArmor isn't good for *everything*. (And, whoever wrote this needs to take spelling lessons.)

And then, there's Samba, which is a special case in more ways than one. When you install the `samba` package to set up a Samba server, you don't get any AppArmor profiles at all. For Samba and several other different applications as well, you'll need to install the AppArmor profiles separately:

```
sudo apt install apparmor-profiles apparmor-profiles-extras
```

When you install these two profile packages, the profiles will all be in the complain mode. That's okay, because we have a handy utility to put them into enforce mode. Since Samba has two different daemons that we need to protect, there are two different profiles that we'll need to place into enforce mode:

```
donnie@ubuntu5:/etc/apparmor.d$ ls *mbd
usr.sbin.nmbd  usr.sbin.smbd
donnie@ubuntu5:/etc/apparmor.d$
```

We'll use `aa-enforce` to activate enforce mode for both of these profiles:

```
donnie@ubuntu5:/etc/apparmor.d$ sudo aa-enforce /usr/sbin/nmbd
usr.sbin.nmbd
Setting /usr/sbin/nmbd to enforce mode.
```

```
Setting /etc/apparmor.d/usr.sbin.nmbd to enforce mode.

donnie@ubuntu5:/etc/apparmor.d$ sudo aa-enforce /usr/sbin/smbd
usr.sbin.smbd
Setting /usr/sbin/smbd to enforce mode.
Setting /etc/apparmor.d/usr.sbin.smbd to enforce mode.
donnie@ubuntu5:/etc/apparmor.d$
```

To use `aa-enforce`, you first need to specify the path to the executable file of the process that you want to protect. (Fortunately, you normally won't even have to look that up, since the path name is normally part of the profile filename.) The last part of the command is the name of the profile. Note that you'll need to restart the Samba daemon to get this AppArmor protection to take effect.

Placing a profile into other modes is just as easy. All you have to do is to replace the `aa-enforce` utility with the utility for the mode that you need to use. Here's a chart of the utilities for the other modes:

`aa-audit`	**Audit mode is the same as enforce mode, except that allowed actions get logged, as well as the actions that have been blocked. (Enforce mode only logs actions that have been blocked.)**
`aa-disable`	This completely disables a profile.
`aa-complain`	This places a profile into complain mode.

Troubleshooting AppArmor problems

So, I've been here racking my brain for the past several days, trying to come up with a good troubleshooting scenario. It turns out that I didn't need to. The Ubuntu folk have handed me a good scenario on a silver platter, in the form of a buggy Samba profile.

As you've just seen, I used `aa-enforce` to put the two Samba-related profiles into enforce mode. But, watch what happens now when I try to restart Samba in order to get the profiles to take effect:

```
donnie@ubuntu3:/etc/apparmor.d$ sudo systemctl restart smbd
Job for smbd.service failed because the control process exited with error
code. See "systemctl status smbd.service" and "journalctl -xe" for details.
donnie@ubuntu3:/etc/apparmor.d$
```

Okay, that's not good. Looking at the status for the smbd service, I see this:

```
donnie@ubuntu3:/etc/apparmor.d$ sudo systemctl status smbd
● smbd.service - LSB: start Samba SMB/CIFS daemon (smbd)
   Loaded: loaded (/etc/init.d/smbd; bad; vendor preset: enabled)
   Active: failed (Result: exit-code) since Tue 2017-12-05 14:56:35 EST;
13s ago
     Docs: man:systemd-sysv-generator(8)
  Process: 31160 ExecStop=/etc/init.d/smbd stop (code=exited,
status=0/SUCCESS)
  Process: 31171 ExecStart=/etc/init.d/smbd start (code=exited,
status=1/FAILURE)

Dec 05 14:56:35 ubuntu3 systemd[1]: Starting LSB: start Samba SMB/CIFS
daemon (smbd)...
Dec 05 14:56:35 ubuntu3 smbd[31171]:  * Starting SMB/CIFS daemon smbd
Dec 05 14:56:35 ubuntu3 smbd[31171]:    ...fail!
Dec 05 14:56:35 ubuntu3 systemd[1]: smbd.service: Control process exited,
code=exited status=1
Dec 05 14:56:35 ubuntu3 systemd[1]: Failed to start LSB: start Samba
SMB/CIFS daemon (smbd).
Dec 05 14:56:35 ubuntu3 systemd[1]: smbd.service: Unit entered failed
state.
Dec 05 14:56:35 ubuntu3 systemd[1]: smbd.service: Failed with result 'exit-
code'.
donnie@ubuntu3:/etc/apparmor.d$
```

The important things to see here are all of the places where some form of the word fail shows up.

The original error message said to use journalctl -xe to view the log message. But, journalctl has this bad habit of truncating lines of output at the right edge of the screen. So instead, I'll just use either less or tail to look in the regular /var/log/syslog log file:

```
Dec  5 20:09:10 ubuntu3 smbd[14599]:  * Starting SMB/CIFS daemon smbd
Dec  5 20:09:10 ubuntu3 kernel: [174226.392671] audit: type=1400
audit(1512522550.765:510): apparmor="DENIED" operation="mknod"
profile="/usr/sbin/smbd" name="/run/samba/msg.
lock/14612" pid=14612 comm="smbd" requested_mask="c" denied_mask="c"
fsuid=0 ouid=0
Dec  5 20:09:10 ubuntu3 smbd[14599]:    ...fail!
Dec  5 20:09:10 ubuntu3 systemd[1]: smbd.service: Control process exited,
code=exited status=1
Dec  5 20:09:10 ubuntu3 systemd[1]: Failed to start LSB: start Samba
SMB/CIFS daemon (smbd).
Dec  5 20:09:10 ubuntu3 systemd[1]: smbd.service: Unit entered failed
state.
```

```
Dec  5 20:09:10 ubuntu3 systemd[1]: smbd.service: Failed with result 'exit-
code'.
```

So, we see `apparmor=DENIED`. Obviously, Samba is trying to do something that the profile doesn't allow. Samba needs to write temporary files to the `/run/samba/msg.lock` directory, but it isn't allowed to. I'm guessing that the profile is missing a rule that allows that to happen.

But, even if this log file entry were to give me no clue at all, I could just cheat, using a troubleshooting technique that has served me well for many years. That is, I could just copy and paste the error message from the log file into my favorite search engine. Pretty much every time I've ever done that, I've found that other people before me have already had the same problem:

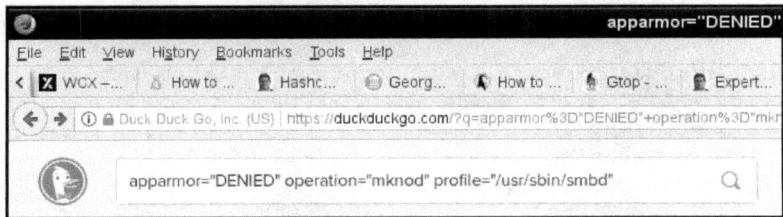

Okay, I didn't paste in the entire error message, but I did paste in enough for DuckDuckGo to work with. And, lo and behold, it worked:

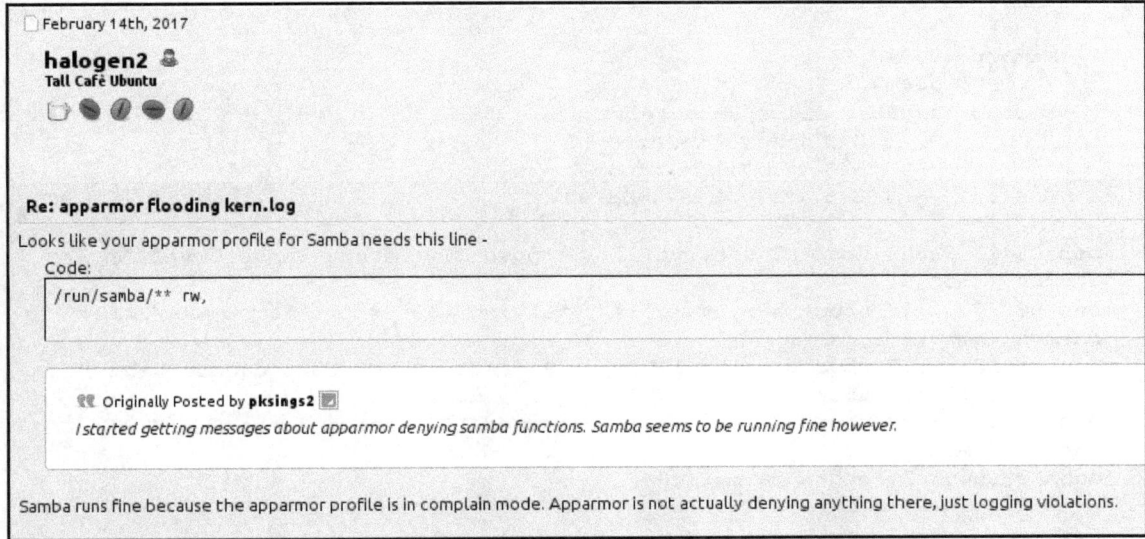

Hmmm, it looks like my profile file might be missing an important line. So, I'll open the `usr.sbin.smbd` file and place this line at the end of the rule set:

```
/run/samba/** rw,
```

This line will allow read and write access to everything in the `/run/samba` directory. After making the edit, I'll need to reload this profile because it's already been loaded with `aa-enforce`. For this, I'll use the `apparmor_parser` utility:

```
donnie@ubuntu3:/etc/apparmor.d$ sudo apparmor_parser -r usr.sbin.smbd
donnie@ubuntu3:/etc/apparmor.d$
```

All you need to do is use the `-r` option for reloading and list the name of the profile file. Now, let's try to restart Samba:

```
donnie@ubuntu3:/etc/apparmor.d$ sudo systemctl restart smbd

donnie@ubuntu3:/etc/apparmor.d$ sudo systemctl status smbd
● smbd.service - LSB: start Samba SMB/CIFS daemon (smbd)
   Loaded: loaded (/etc/init.d/smbd; bad; vendor preset: enabled)
   Active: active (running) since Wed 2017-12-06 13:31:32 EST; 3min 6s ago
     Docs: man:systemd-sysv-generator(8)
  Process: 17317 ExecStop=/etc/init.d/smbd stop (code=exited,
status=0/SUCCESS)
  Process: 16474 ExecReload=/etc/init.d/smbd reload (code=exited,
status=0/SUCCESS)
  Process: 17326 ExecStart=/etc/init.d/smbd start (code=exited,
status=0/SUCCESS)
    Tasks: 3
   Memory: 9.3M
      CPU: 594ms
   CGroup: /system.slice/smbd.service
           ├─17342 /usr/sbin/smbd -D
           ├─17343 /usr/sbin/smbd -D
           └─17345 /usr/sbin/smbd -D

Dec 06 13:31:28 ubuntu3 systemd[1]: Stopped LSB: start Samba SMB/CIFS
daemon (smbd).
Dec 06 13:31:28 ubuntu3 systemd[1]: Starting LSB: start Samba SMB/CIFS
daemon (smbd)...
Dec 06 13:31:32 ubuntu3 smbd[17326]:  * Starting SMB/CIFS daemon smbd
Dec 06 13:31:32 ubuntu3 smbd[17326]:    ...done.
Dec 06 13:31:32 ubuntu3 systemd[1]: Started LSB: start Samba SMB/CIFS
daemon (smbd).
donnie@ubuntu3:/etc/apparmor.d$
```

And, it works. The two Samba profiles are in enforce mode, and Samba finally starts up just fine.

The odd part about this is that I had this same problem with both Ubuntu 16.04 and Ubuntu 17.10. So, the bug has been there for a long time, and it would seem that the Ubuntu folk either don't know about it or don't care to fix it. In a way, I hope that it never does get fixed because getting it fixed would ruin a perfectly good training demo for me.

Summary

In this chapter, we looked at the basic principles of Mandatory Access Control and compared two different Mandatory Access Control systems. We saw what SELinux and AppArmor are and how they can help safeguard your systems from malicious actors. We then looked at the basics of how to use them and the basics of how to troubleshoot them. We also saw that even though they're both meant to do the same job, they work in vastly different ways.

Whether you're working with AppArmor or with SELinux, you'll always want to thoroughly test a new system in either complain or permissive mode before you put it into production. Make sure that what you want to protect gets protected, while at the same time, what you want to allow gets allowed. After you place the machine into production, don't just assume that you can automatically change a policy setting every time you see a policy violation occur. It could be that nothing is wrong with your Mandatory Access Control setup and that MAC is just doing its job in protecting you from the bad guys.

There's a lot more to both of these topics than we can cover here. Hopefully, though, I've given you enough to whet your appetite and enough to help you out in your day-to-day duties.

In the next chapter, we'll look at scanning, auditing, and hardening. I'll see you there.

8
Scanning, Auditing, and Hardening

A common misconception is that Linux users never need to worry about malware. Yes, it's true that Linux is much more resistant to viruses than Windows is. But, viruses are only one type of malware, and other types of malware can be planted on Linux machines. And, if you're running a server that will share files with Windows users, you'll want to make sure that you don't share any virus-infected files with them.

While Linux system log files are nice, they don't always give a good picture of who does what or who accesses what. It could be that either intruders or insiders are trying to access data that they're not authorized to access. What we really want is a good auditing system to alert us when people do things that they're not supposed to do.

And then, there's the issue of regulatory compliance. Your organization may have to deal with one or more regulatory bodies that dictate how you harden your servers against attacks. If you're not in compliance, you could be fined or put out of business.

Fortunately, we have ways to deal with all of these issues, and they aren't all that complicated.

In this chapter, we'll cover the following topics:

- Installing and updating ClamAV and maldet
- Scanning with ClamAV and maldet
- SELinux considerations
- Scanning for rootkits with Rootkit Hunter
- Controlling the auditd daemon
- Creating audit rules

- Using the `ausearch` and `aureport` utilities to search the audit logs for problems
- `oscap`, the command-line utility in order to manage and apply OpenSCAP policies
- OpenSCAP Workbench, the GUI utility to manage and apply OpenSCAP policies
- OpenSCAP policy files and the compliance standards that each of them is designed to meet
- Applying a policy during operating system installation

Installing and updating ClamAV and maldet

Although we don't have to worry much about viruses infecting our Linux machines, we do need to worry about sharing infected files with Windows users. ClamAV is a **Free Open Source Software** (**FOSS**) antivirus solution that can either run as a standalone program or can be integrated with a mail server daemon, such as Postfix. It's a traditional antivirus scanner that works pretty much the same as the antivirus program on your typical Windows workstation. The included `freshclam` utility allows you to update virus signatures.

Linux Malware Detect, which you'll often see abbreviated as either **LMD** or **maldet**, is another FOSS antivirus program that can work alongside ClamAV. (To save typing, I'll just refer to it as LMD from now on.) As far as I know, it's not available in the repositories of any Linux distro, but it's still simple enough to install and configure. One of its features is that it automatically generates malware detection signatures when it sees malware on the network's edge intrusion detection systems. End users can also submit their own malware samples. When you install it, you'll get a systemd service that's already enabled and a cron job that will periodically update both the malware signatures and the program itself. It works with the Linux kernel's inotify capability to automatically monitor directories for files that have changed. The procedure to install it is pretty much the same for any systemd-based Linux distro.

 You can get all the nitty-gritty details about Linux Malware Detect at: `https://www.rfxn.com/projects/linux-malware-detect/`.

The reason that we're installing ClamAV and LMD together is that, as the LMD folk freely admit, the ClamAV scan engine gives a much better performance when scanning large file sets. Also, by having them both together, ClamAV can use the LMD malware signatures as well as its own malware signatures.

Installing ClamAV and maldet

We'll begin by installing ClamAV. (It's in the normal repository for Ubuntu, but not for CentOS. For CentOS, you'll need to install the EPEL repository, as I showed you how to do in Chapter 1, *Running Linux in a Virtual Environment*.) We'll also install Wget, which we'll use to download LMD.

The following command will help you install ClamAV and Wget on Ubuntu:

```
donnie@ubuntu3:~$ sudo apt install clamav wget
```

The following command will help you install ClamAV and Wget on CentOS:

```
[donnie@localhost ~]$ sudo yum install clamav clamav-update wget
```

For Ubuntu, the `clamav` package contains everything you need. For CentOS, you'll need to also install `clamav-update` in order to obtain virus updates.

The rest of the steps will be the same for either virtual machine.

Next, you'll download and install LMD. Here, you'll want to do something that I rarely tell people to do. That is, you'll want to log in to the root user shell. The reason is that although the LMD installer works fine with sudo, you'll end up with the program files being owned by the user who performed the installation, instead of by the root user. Performing the installation from the root user's shell saves us the trouble of tracking down those files and changing ownership. So, download the file as follows:

```
sudo su -
wget http://www.rfxn.com/downloads/maldetect-current.tar.gz
```

You'll now have the file in the root user's home directory. Now, extract the archive, enter the resultant directory, and run the installer. Once the installer finishes, copy the README file to your own home directory so that you can have it for ready reference. (This README file is the documentation for LMD.) Then, exit from the root user's shell back to your own shell:

```
tar xzvf maldetect-current.tar.gz
cd maldetect-1.6.2/

root@ubuntu3:~/maldetect-1.6.2# ./install.sh
Created symlink from /etc/systemd/system/multi-
user.target.wants/maldet.service to /usr/lib/systemd/system/maldet.service.
update-rc.d: error: initscript does not exist: /etc/init.d/maldet
Linux Malware Detect v1.6
            (C) 2002-2017, R-fx Networks <proj@r-fx.org>
```

```
            (C) 2017, Ryan MacDonald <ryan@r-fx.org>
This program may be freely redistributed under the terms of the GNU GPL

installation completed to /usr/local/maldetect
config file: /usr/local/maldetect/conf.maldet
exec file: /usr/local/maldetect/maldet
exec link: /usr/local/sbin/maldet
exec link: /usr/local/sbin/lmd
cron.daily: /etc/cron.daily/maldet
maldet(22138): {sigup} performing signature update check...
maldet(22138): {sigup} local signature set is version 2017070716978
maldet(22138): {sigup} new signature set (201708255569) available
maldet(22138): {sigup} downloading
https://cdn.rfxn.com/downloads/maldet-sigpack.tgz
maldet(22138): {sigup} downloading
https://cdn.rfxn.com/downloads/maldet-cleanv2.tgz
maldet(22138): {sigup} verified md5sum of maldet-sigpack.tgz
maldet(22138): {sigup} unpacked and installed maldet-sigpack.tgz
maldet(22138): {sigup} verified md5sum of maldet-clean.tgz
maldet(22138): {sigup} unpacked and installed maldet-clean.tgz
maldet(22138): {sigup} signature set update completed
maldet(22138): {sigup} 15218 signatures (12485 MD5 | 1954 HEX | 779 YARA |
0 USER)

root@ubuntu3:~/maldetect-1.6.2# cp README /home/donnie

root@ubuntu3:~/maldetect-1.6.2# exit
logout
donnie@ubuntu3:~$
```

As you can see, the installer automatically creates the symbolic link that enables the maldet service, and it also automatically downloads and installs the newest malware signatures.

Configuring maldet

If you try to start the maldet service at this point, it will fail. To make it work, you need to configure the directories that you want it to automatically monitor and scan. To do this, you'll add the directories to the /usr/local/maldetect/monitor_paths file. For now, I just want to monitor the /home and /root directories, so my monitor_paths file looks like this:

```
/home
/root
```

After you save the file, you'll be able to start the maldet daemon:

```
sudo systemctl start maldet
```

You can add more directories to the `monitor_paths` file at any time, but remember to restart the maldet daemon any time that you do, in order to read in the new additions.

The configuration file for LMD is `/usr/local/maldetect/conf.maldet`. It's very well-documented with well-written comments for every configuration item, so you shouldn't have any trouble figuring it out. For now, we're only going to make a few configuration changes.

At the top of the file, enable email alerts and set your username as the email address. The two lines should now look something like this:

```
email_alert="1"
email_addr="donnie"
```

LMD isn't already configured to move suspicious files to the quarantine folder, and we want to make it do that. Open the `conf.maldet` file in your text editor and look for the line that says:

```
quarantine_hits="0"
```

Change the previous line to the following line:

```
quarantine_hits="1"
```

You'll see a few other quarantine actions that you can configure, but for now, this is all we need. After you save the file, restart maldet:

```
sudo systemctl restart maldet
```

The new changes will now be in effect.

Updating ClamAV and maldet

The good news for busy admins is that you don't have to do anything to keep either of these programs updated. Both of them run with a cron job that gets created automatically and that does the updates for us. To prove that ClamAV is getting updated, we can look in the system log file:

```
Dec 8 20:02:09 localhost freshclam[22326]: ClamAV update process started at
Fri Dec 8 20:02:09 2017
Dec 8 20:02:29 localhost freshclam[22326]: Can't query
```

```
current.cvd.clamav.net
Dec 8 20:02:29 localhost freshclam[22326]: Invalid DNS reply. Falling back
to HTTP mode.
Dec 8 20:02:29 localhost freshclam[22326]: Reading CVD header (main.cvd):
Dec 8 20:02:35 localhost freshclam[22326]: OK
Dec 8 20:02:47 localhost freshclam[22326]: Downloading main-58.cdiff [100%]
Dec 8 20:03:19 localhost freshclam[22326]: main.cld updated (version: 58,
sigs: 4566249, f-level: 60, builder: sigmgr)
. . .
. . .
Dec 8 20:04:45 localhost freshclam[22326]: Downloading daily.cvd [100%]
Dec 8 20:04:53 localhost freshclam[22326]: daily.cvd updated (version:
24111, sigs: 1799769, f-level: 63, builder: neo)
Dec 8 20:04:53 localhost freshclam[22326]: Reading CVD header
(bytecode.cvd):
Dec 8 20:04:54 localhost freshclam[22326]: OK
Dec 8 20:04:54 localhost freshclam[22326]: Downloading bytecode-279.cdiff
[100%]
Dec 8 20:04:55 localhost freshclam[22326]: Downloading bytecode-280.cdiff
[100%]
Dec 8 20:04:55 localhost freshclam[22326]: Downloading bytecode-281.cdiff
[100%]
Dec 8 20:04:56 localhost freshclam[22326]: Downloading bytecode-282.cdiff
[100%]
. . .
. . .
```

You'll see these same entries in either the Ubuntu logs or the CentOS logs. However, there is a difference between how the updates get run automatically.

In the `/etc/clamav/freshclam.conf` file of your Ubuntu machine, you'll see the following lines at the end:

```
# Check for new database 24 times a day
Checks 24
DatabaseMirror db.local.clamav.net
DatabaseMirror database.clamav.net
```

So essentially, this means that on Ubuntu, ClamAV will be checking for updates every hour.

On your CentOS machine, you'll see a `clamav-update` cron job in the `/etc/cron.d` directory that looks like this:

```
## Adjust this line...
MAILTO=root

## It is ok to execute it as root; freshclam drops privileges and becomes
```

```
## user 'clamupdate' as soon as possible
0  */3 * * * root /usr/share/clamav/freshclam-sleep
```

The */3 in the second column from the left indicates that ClamAV will check for updates every 3 hours. You can change that if you like, but you'll also need to change the setting in the /etc/sysconfig/freshclam file. Let's say that you want for CentOS to also check for ClamAV updates every hour. In the cron job file, change the */3 to *. (You don't need to do */1 because the asterisk by itself in that position already indicates that the job will run every hour.) Then, in the /etc/sysconfig/freshclam file, look for this line:

```
# FRESHCLAM_MOD=
```

Uncomment that line and add the number of minutes that you want between updates. To set it to 1 hour, in order to match the cron job, it will look like this:

```
FRESHCLAM_MOD=60
```

To prove that maldet is getting updated, you can look in its own log files in the /usr/local/maldetect/logs/ directory. In the event_log file, you'll see the following code:

```
Dec 06 22:06:14 localhost maldet(3728): {sigup} performing signature update
check...
Dec 06 22:06:14 localhost maldet(3728): {sigup} local signature set is
version 2017070716978
Dec 06 22:07:13 localhost maldet(3728): {sigup} downloaded
https://cdn.rfxn.com/downloads/maldet.sigs.ver
Dec 06 22:07:13 localhost maldet(3728): {sigup} new signature set
(201708255569) available
Dec 06 22:07:13 localhost maldet(3728): {sigup} downloading
https://cdn.rfxn.com/downloads/maldet-sigpack.tgz
. . .

. . .
Dec 06 22:07:43 localhost maldet(3728): {sigup} unpacked and installed
maldet-clean.tgz
Dec 06 22:07:43 localhost maldet(3728): {sigup} signature set update
completed
Dec 06 22:07:43 localhost maldet(3728): {sigup} 15218 signatures (12485 MD5
| 1954 HEX | 779 YARA | 0 USER)
Dec 06 22:14:55 localhost maldet(4070): {scan} signatures loaded: 15218
(12485 MD5 | 1954 HEX | 779 YARA | 0 USER)
```

In the `/usr/local/maldetect/conf.maldet` file, you'll see these two lines, but with some comments in between them:

```
autoupdate_signatures="1"

autoupdate_version="1"
```

Not only will LMD automatically update its malware signatures, it will also ensure that you have the latest version of LMD itself.

Scanning with ClamAV and maldet

LMD's maldet daemon constantly monitors the directories that you specify in the `/usr/local/maldetect/monitor_paths` file. When it finds a file that it suspects might be malware, it automatically takes whatever action that you specified in the `conf.maldet` file. To see how this works, I'll create a simulated malware file in my home directory. Fortunately, that's easier than it sounds, because we have a website that will help us out.

 **EICAR**, which used to be known by its full name of **European Institute for Computer Antivirus Research**, provides a virus signature that you can include in a plain text file. You can get it at: `http://www.eicar.org/86-0-Intended-use.html`.

To create the simulated virus file, go to the page that I've listed in the preceding link.

Scroll down toward the bottom of the page until you see this line of text within a text box:

```
X5O!P%@AP[4\PZX54(P^)7CC)7}$EICAR-STANDARD-ANTIVIRUS-TEST-FILE!$H+H*
```

Copy that line of text and insert it into a text file that you'll save to your home directory of either virtual machine. (You can name it anything you want, but I'll just name mine `testing.txt`.) Wait just a few moments, and you should see the file disappear. Then, look in the `/usr/local/maldetect/logs/event_log` file to verify that the LMD moved the file to quarantine:

```
Dec 09 19:03:43 localhost maldet(7192): {quar} malware quarantined from
'/home/donnie/testing.txt' to
'/usr/local/maldetect/quarantine/testing.txt.89513558'
```

There's still a bit more to LMD than what I can show you here. However, you can read all about it in the README file that comes with it.

SELinux considerations

It used to be that doing an antivirus scan on a Red Hat-type system would trigger an SELinux alert. But, in the course of proofing this chapter, the scans all worked as they should, and SELinux never bothered me even once. So, it would appear that that problem is now fixed.

If you ever do generate any SELinux alerts with your virus scans, all you need to do to fix it is to change one Boolean:

```
[donnie@localhost ~]$ getsebool -a | grep 'virus'
antivirus_can_scan_system --> off
antivirus_use_jit --> off
[donnie@localhost ~]$
```

What interests us here is the `antivirus_can_scan_system` Boolean, which is off by default. To turn it on to enable virus scans, just follow this:

```
[donnie@localhost ~]$ sudo setsebool -P antivirus_can_scan_system on
[sudo] password for donnie:

[donnie@localhost ~]$ getsebool antivirus_can_scan_system
antivirus_can_scan_system --> on
[donnie@localhost ~]$
```

That should fix any SELinux-related scan problems that you may have. But, as things stand now, you probably won't need to worry about it.

Scanning for rootkits with Rootkit Hunter

Rootkits are exceedingly nasty pieces of malware that can definitely ruin your day. They can listen for commands from their masters, steal sensitive data and send it to their masters, or provide an easy-access back door for their masters. They're designed to be stealthy, with the ability to hide themselves from plain view. Sometimes, they'll replace utilities such as `ls` or `ps` with their own trojaned versions that will show all files or processes on the system except for the ones that are associated with the rootkit. Rootkits can infect any operating system, even our beloved Linux.

In order to plant a rootkit, an attacker has to have already gained administrative privileges on a system. This is one of the many reasons why I always cringe when I see people doing all of their work from the root user's shell and why I'm a firm advocate of using sudo whenever possible. I mean, really, why should we make it easy for the bad guys?

 Several years ago, back in the dark days of Windows XP, Sony Music got into a bit of trouble when someone discovered that they had planted a rootkit on their music CDs. They didn't mean to do anything malicious, but only wanted to stop people from using their computers to make illegal copies. Of course, most people ran Windows XP with an administrator account, which made it really easy for the rootkit to infect their computers. Windows users still mostly run with administrator accounts, but they at least now have User Access Control to help mitigate these types of problems.

There are a couple of different programs that scan for rootkits, and both are used pretty much the same way. The one that we'll look at now is named, Rootkit Hunter.

Installing and updating Rootkit Hunter

For Ubuntu, Rootkit Hunter is in the normal repository. For CentOS, you'll need to install the EPEL repository, as I showed you how to do in Chapter 1, *Running Linux in a Virtual Environment*. For both Linux distros, the package name is rkhunter.

For Ubuntu:

```
sudo apt install rkhunter
```

For CentOS:

```
sudo yum install rkhunter
```

After it's installed, you can look at its options with:

```
man rkhunter
```

Easy, right?

The next thing you'll need to do is to update the rootkit signatures, using the --update option:

```
[donnie@localhost ~]$ sudo rkhunter --update
[ Rootkit Hunter version 1.4.4 ]

Checking rkhunter data files...
  Checking file mirrors.dat [ Updated ]
  Checking file programs_bad.dat [ Updated ]
  Checking file backdoorports.dat [ No update ]
  Checking file suspscan.dat [ Updated ]
```

```
    Checking file i18n/cn [ No update ]
    Checking file i18n/de [ Updated ]
    Checking file i18n/en [ Updated ]
    Checking file i18n/tr [ Updated ]
    Checking file i18n/tr.utf8 [ Updated ]
    Checking file i18n/zh [ Updated ]
    Checking file i18n/zh.utf8 [ Updated ]
    Checking file i18n/ja [ Updated ]
[donnie@localhost ~]$
```

Now, we're ready to scan.

Scanning for rootkits

To run your scan, use the -c option. (That's -c for check.) Be patient, because it will take a while:

```
sudo rkhunter -c
```

When you run the scan in this manner, Rootkit Hunter will periodically stop and ask you to hit the *Enter* key to continue. When the scan completes, you'll find an rkhunter.log file in the /var/log directory.

To have Rootkit Hunter automatically run as a cron job, you'll want to use the --cronjob option, which will cause the program to run all the way through without prompting you to keep hitting the *Enter* key. You might also want to use the --rwo option, which will cause the program to only report warnings, instead of also reporting on everything that's good. From the command line, the command would look like this:

```
sudo rkhunter -c --cronjob --rwo
```

To create a cron job that will automatically run Rootkit Hunter on a nightly basis, open the crontab editor for the root user:

```
sudo crontab -e -u root
```

Let's say that you want to run Rootkit Hunter every night at 20 minutes past 10. Enter this into the crontab editor:

```
20 22 * * * /usr/bin/rkhunter -c --cronjob --rwo
```

Since cron only works with 24 hour clock time, you'll have to express 10:00 P.M. as 22. (Just add 12 to the normal P.M. clock times that you're used to using.) The three asterisks mean, respectively, that the job will run every day of the month, every month, and every day of the week. You'll need to list the entire path for the command, or else cron won't be able to find it.

You'll find more options that might interest you in the `rkhunter` man page, but this should be enough to get you going with it.

Controlling the auditd daemon

So, you have a directory full of super-secret files that only a very few people need to see, and you want to know when unauthorized people try to see them. Or, maybe you want to see when a certain file gets changed. Or, maybe you want to see when people log into the system and what they're doing once they do log in. For all this and more, you have the auditd system. It's a really cool system, and I think that you'll like it.

> One of the beauties of auditd is that it works at the Linux kernel level, rather than at the user-mode level. This makes it much harder for attackers to subvert.

On Red Hat-type systems, auditd comes installed and enabled by default. So, you'll find it already there on your CentOS machine. On Ubuntu, it isn't already installed, so you'll have to do it yourself:

```
sudo apt install auditd
```

On Ubuntu, you can control the auditd daemon with the normal `systemctl` commands. So, if you need to restart auditd to read in a new configuration, you can do that with the following:

```
sudo systemctl restart auditd
```

On CentOS 7, for some reason that I don't understand, the normal `systemctl` commands don't work with auditd. (For all other daemons, they do.) So, on your CentOS 7 machine, you'll restart the auditd daemon with the old-fashioned `service` command, like so:

```
sudo service auditd restart
```

Other than this minor difference, everything I tell you about auditd from here on will apply to both Ubuntu and CentOS.

Creating audit rules

Okay, let's start with something simple and work our way up to something awesome. First, let's check to see whether any audit rules are in effect:

```
[donnie@localhost ~]$ sudo auditctl -l
[sudo] password for donnie:
No rules
[donnie@localhost ~]$
```

As you can see, the `auditctl` command is what we use to manage audit rules. The `-l` option lists the rules.

Auditing a file for changes

Now, let's say that we want to see when someone changes the `/etc/passwd` file. (The command that we'll use will look a bit daunting, but I promise that it will make sense once we break it down.) Look at the following code:

```
[donnie@localhost ~]$ sudo auditctl -w /etc/passwd -p wa -k passwd_changes
[sudo] password for donnie:

[donnie@localhost ~]$ sudo auditctl -l
-w /etc/passwd -p wa -k passwd_changes
[donnie@localhost ~]$
```

Here's the breakdown:

- `-w`: This stands for where, and it points to the object that we want to monitor. In this case, it's `/etc/passwd`.
- `-p`: This indicates the object's permissions that we want to monitor. In this case, we're monitoring to see when anyone either tries to (w)rite to the file, or tries to make (a)ttribute changes. (The other two permissions that we can audit are (r)ead and e(x)ecute.)
- `-k`: The `k` stands for key, which is just auditd's way of assigning a name to a rule. So, `passwd_changes` is the key, or the name, of the rule that we're creating.

The `auditctl -l` command shows us that the rule is indeed there.

Now, the slight problem with this is that the rule is only temporary and will disappear when we reboot the machine. To make it permanent, we need to create a custom rules file in the `/etc/audit/rules.d/` directory. Then, when you restart the auditd daemon, the custom rules will get inserted into the `/etc/audit/audit.rules` file. Because the `/etc/audit/` directory can only be accessed by someone with root privileges, I'll just open the file by listing the entire path to the file, rather than trying to enter the directory:

```
sudo less /etc/audit/audit.rules
```

There's not a whole lot in this default file:

```
## This file is automatically generated from /etc/audit/rules.d
-D
-b 8192
-f 1
```

Here's the breakdown for this file:

- `-D`: This will cause all rules and watches that are currently in effect to be deleted, so that we can start from a clean slate. So, if I were to restart the auditd daemon right now, it would read this `audit.rules` file, which would delete the rule that I just now created.
- `-b 8192`: This sets the number of outstanding audit buffers that we can have going at one time. If all of the buffers get full, the system can't generate any more audit messages.
- `-f 1`: This sets the failure mode for critical errors, and the value can be either 0, 1, or 2. A `-f 0` would set the mode to silent, meaning that auditd wouldn't do anything about critical errors. A `-f 1`, as we see here, tells auditd to only report the critical errors, and a `-f 2` would cause the Linux kernel to go into panic mode. According to the `auditctl` man page, anyone in a high-security environment would likely want to change this to `-f 2`. For our purposes though, `-f1` works.

You could use your text editor to create a new rules file in the `/etc/audit/rules.d/` directory. Or, you could just redirect the `auditctl -l` output into a new file, like this:

```
[donnie@localhost ~]$ sudo sh -c "auditctl -l >
/etc/audit/rules.d/custom.rules"
[donnie@localhost ~]$ sudo service auditd restart
```

Since the Bash shell doesn't allow me to directly redirect information into a file in the `/etc` directory, even with sudo, I have to use the `sudo sh -c` command in order to execute the `auditctl` command. After restarting the auditd daemon, our `audit.rules` file now looks like this:

```
## This file is automatically generated from /etc/audit/rules.d
-D
-b 8192
-f 1

-w /etc/passwd -p wa -k passwd_changes
```

Now, the rule will take effect every time the machine gets rebooted, and every time that you manually restart the auditd daemon.

Auditing a directory

Vicky and Cleopatra, my solid gray kitty and my gray-and-white tabby kitty, have some supersensitive secrets that they need to safeguard. So, I created the `secretcats` group and added them to it. I then created the `secretcats` shared directory and set the access controls on it as I showed you how to do in Chapter 6, *Access Control Lists and Shared Directory Management*:

```
[donnie@localhost ~]$ sudo groupadd secretcats
[sudo] password for donnie:

[donnie@localhost ~]$ sudo usermod -a -G secretcats vicky
[donnie@localhost ~]$ sudo usermod -a -G secretcats cleopatra

[donnie@localhost ~]$ sudo mkdir /secretcats
[donnie@localhost ~]$ sudo chown nobody:secretcats /secretcats/
[donnie@localhost ~]$ sudo chmod 3770 /secretcats/

[donnie@localhost ~]$ ls -ld /secretcats/
drwxrws--T. 2 nobody secretcats 6 Dec 11 14:47 /secretcats/
[donnie@localhost ~]$
```

Vicky and Cleopatra want to be absolutely sure that nobody gets into their stuff, so they requested that I set up an auditing rule for their directory:

```
[donnie@localhost ~]$ sudo auditctl -w /secretcats/ -k secretcats_watch
[sudo] password for donnie:

[donnie@localhost ~]$ sudo auditctl -l
```

```
-w /etc/passwd -p wa -k passwd_changes
-w /secretcats -p rwxa -k secretcats_watch
[donnie@localhost ~]$
```

As before, the -w denotes what we want to monitor, and the -k denotes the name of the audit rule. This time, I left out the -p option because I want to monitor for every type of access. In other words, I want to monitor for any read, write, attribute change, or execute actions. (Because this is a directory, the execute action happens when somebody tries to cd into the directory.) You can see in the auditctl -l output that by leaving out the -p, we will now monitor for everything. However, let's say that I only want to monitor for when someone tries to cd into this directory. Instead, I could have made the rule look like this:

```
sudo auditctl -w /secretcats/ -p x -k secretcats_watch
```

Easy enough so far, right? Let's now look at something a bit more complex.

Auditing system calls

Creating rules to monitor when someone performs a certain action isn't hard, but the command syntax is a bit trickier than what we've seen so far. With this rule, we're going to be alerted every time that Charlie either tries to open a file or tries to create a file:

```
[donnie@localhost ~]$ sudo auditctl -a always,exit -F arch=b64 -S openat -F
auid=1006
[sudo] password for donnie:

[donnie@localhost ~]$ sudo auditctl -l
-w /etc/passwd -p wa -k passwd_changes
-w /secretcats -p rwxa -k secretcats_watch
-a always,exit -F arch=b64 -S openat -F auid=1006
[donnie@localhost ~]$
```

Here's the breakdown:

- -a always,exit: Here, we have the action and the list. The exit part means that this rule will be added to the system call exit list. Whenever the operating system exits from a system call, the exit list will be used to determine if an audit event needs to be generated. The always part is the action, which means that an audit record for this rule will always be created on exit from the specified system call. Note that the action and list parameters have to be separated by a comma.

- `-F arch=b64`: The `-F` option is used to build a rule field, and we see two rule fields in this command. This first rule field specifies the machine's CPU architecture. The `b64` means that the computer is running with an x86_64 CPU. (Whether it's Intel or AMD doesn't matter.) Considering that 32-bit machines are dying off and that Sun SPARC and PowerPC machines aren't all that common, `b64` is what you'll now mostly see.
- `-S openat`: The `-S` option specifies the system call that we want to monitor. `openat` is the system call that either opens or creates a file.
- `-F auid=1006`: This second audit field specifies the user ID number of the user that we want to monitor. (Charlie's user ID number is `1006`.)

A complete explanation about system calls, or syscalls, is a bit too esoteric for our present purpose. For now, suffice it to say that a syscall happens whenever a user issues a command that requests that the Linux kernel provide a service. If you're so inclined, you can read more about syscalls at: `https://blog.packagecloud.io/eng/2016/04/05/the-definitive-guide-to-linux-system-calls/`.

What I've presented here are just a few of the many things that you can do with auditing rules. To see more examples, check out the `auditctl` man page:

man auditctl

So, now you're wondering, *"Now that I have these rules, how do I know when someone tries to violate them?"* As always, I'm glad that you asked.

Using ausearch and aureport

The auditd daemon logs events to the `/var/log/audit/audit.log` file. Although you could directly read the file with something like `less`, you really don't want to. The `ausearch` and `aureport` utilities will help you translate the file into a language that makes some sort of sense.

Searching for file change alerts

Let's start by looking at the rule that we created that will alert us whenever a change is made to the /etc/passwd file:

```
sudo auditctl -w /etc/passwd -p wa -k passwd_changes
```

Now, let's make a change to the file and look for the alert message. Rather than add another user, since I'm running out of cats whose names I can use, I'll just use the chfn utility to add contact information to the comment field for Cleopatra's entry:

```
[donnie@localhost etc]$ sudo chfn cleopatra
Changing finger information for cleopatra.
Name []: Cleopatra Tabby Cat
Office []: Donnie's back yard
Office Phone []: 555-5555
Home Phone []: 555-5556

Finger information changed.
[donnie@localhost etc]
```

I'll now use ausearch to look for any audit messages that this event may have generated:

```
[donnie@localhost ~]$ sudo ausearch -i -k passwd_changes
----
type=CONFIG_CHANGE msg=audit(12/11/2017 13:06:20.665:11393) : auid=donnie
ses=842 subj=unconfined_u:unconfined_r:unconfined_t:s0-s0:c0.c1023
op=add_rule key=passwd_changes li
st=exit res=yes
----
type=CONFIG_CHANGE msg=audit(12/11/2017 13:49:15.262:11511) : auid=donnie
ses=842 op=updated_rules path=/etc/passwd key=passwd_changes list=exit
res=yes
[donnie@localhost ~]$
```

Here's the breakdown:

- -i: This takes any numeric data and, whenever possible, converts it into text. In this case, it takes user ID numbers and converts them to the actual username, which shows up here as auid=donnie. If I were to leave the -i out, the user information would instead show up as auid=1000, which is my user ID number.
- -k passwd_changes: This specifies the key, or the name, of the audit rule for which we want to see audit messages.

You can see that there are two parts to this output. The first part just shows when I created the audit rule, so we're not interested in that. In the second part, you can see when I triggered the rule, but it doesn't show how I triggered it. So, let's use `aureport` to see if it will give us a bit more of a clue:

```
[donnie@localhost ~]$ sudo aureport -i -k | grep 'passwd_changes'
1. 12/11/2017 13:06:20 passwd_changes yes ? donnie 11393
2. 12/11/2017 13:49:15 passwd_changes yes ? donnie 11511
3. 12/11/2017 13:49:15 passwd_changes yes /usr/bin/chfn donnie 11512
4. 12/11/2017 14:54:11 passwd_changes yes /usr/sbin/usermod donnie 11728
5. 12/11/2017 14:54:25 passwd_changes yes /usr/sbin/usermod donnie 11736
[donnie@localhost ~]$
```

What's curious is that with `ausearch`, you have to specify the name, or key, of the audit rule that interests you after the `-k` option. With `aureport`, the `-k` option means that you want to look at all log entries that have to do with all audit rule keys. To see log entries for a specific key, just pipe the output into grep. The `-i` option does the same thing that it does for `ausearch`.

As you can see, `aureport` parses the cryptic language of the `audit.log` file into plain language that's easier to understand. I wasn't sure about what I had done to generate events 1 and 2, so I looked in the `/var/log/secure` file to see if I could find out. I saw these two entries for those times:

```
Dec 11 13:06:20 localhost sudo: donnie : TTY=pts/1 ; PWD=/home/donnie ;
USER=root ; COMMAND=/sbin/auditctl -w /etc/passwd -p wa -k passwd_changes
. . .
. . .
Dec 11 13:49:24 localhost sudo: donnie : TTY=pts/1 ; PWD=/home/donnie ;
USER=root ; COMMAND=/sbin/ausearch -i -k passwd_changes
```

So, event 1 was from when I initially created the audit rule, and event 2 happened when I did an `ausearch` operation.

I must confess that the events in lines 4 and 5 are a bit of a mystery. Both were created when I invoked the `usermod` command, and both of them correlate to the secure log entries where I added Vicky and Cleopatra to the `secretcats` group:

```
Dec 11 14:54:11 localhost sudo:  donnie : TTY=pts/1 ; PWD=/home/donnie ;
USER=root ; COMMAND=/sbin/usermod -a -G secretcats vicky
Dec 11 14:54:11 localhost usermod[14865]: add 'vicky' to group 'secretcats'
Dec 11 14:54:11 localhost usermod[14865]: add 'vicky' to shadow group
'secretcats'
Dec 11 14:54:25 localhost sudo:  donnie : TTY=pts/1 ; PWD=/home/donnie ;
USER=root ; COMMAND=/sbin/usermod -a -G secretcats cleopatra
```

```
Dec 11 14:54:25 localhost usermod[14871]: add 'cleopatra' to group
'secretcats'
Dec 11 14:54:25 localhost usermod[14871]: add 'cleopatra' to shadow group
'secretcats'
```

The strange part about this is that adding a user to a secondary group doesn't modify the passwd file. So, I really don't know why the rule got triggered to create the events in lines 4 and 5.

This leaves us with the event in line 3, which is where I used chfn to actually modify the passwd file. Here's the secure log entry for that:

```
Dec 11 13:48:49 localhost sudo:   donnie : TTY=pts/1 ; PWD=/etc ; USER=root
; COMMAND=/bin/chfn cleopatra
```

So, out of all of these events, the one in line 3 is the only one where the /etc/passwd file actually got modified.

> The /var/log/secure file that I keep mentioning here is on Red Hat-type operating systems, such as CentOS. On your Ubuntu machine, you'll see the /var/log/auth.log file, instead.

Searching for directory access rule violations

In our next scenario, we created a shared directory for Vicky and Cleopatra and created an audit rule for it that looks like this:

```
sudo auditctl -w /secretcats/ -k secretcats_watch
```

So, all accesses or attempted accesses to this directory should trigger an alert. First, let's have Vicky enter the /secretcats directory and run an ls -l command:

```
[vicky@localhost ~]$ cd /secretcats
[vicky@localhost secretcats]$ ls -l
total 4
-rw-rw-r--. 1 cleopatra secretcats 31 Dec 12 11:49 cleopatrafile.txt
[vicky@localhost secretcats]$
```

We see that Cleopatra has already been there and has created a file. (We'll get back to that in a moment.) When an event triggers an auditd rule, it often creates multiple records in the /var/log/audit/audit.log file. If you study through each record for an event, you'll see that each one covers a different aspect of that event. When I do an ausearch command, I see a total of five records just from that one ls -l operation. For the sake of saving space, I'll just put the first one and the last one here:

```
sudo ausearch -i -k secretcats_watch | less

type=PROCTITLE msg=audit(12/12/2017 12:15:35.447:14077) : proctitle=ls --
color=auto -l
type=PATH msg=audit(12/12/2017 12:15:35.447:14077) : item=0 name=.
inode=33583041 dev=fd:01 mode=dir,sgid,sticky,770 ouid=nobody
ogid=secretcats rdev=00:00 obj=unconfined_u:object_r:default_t:s0
objtype=NORMAL
type=CWD msg=audit(12/12/2017 12:15:35.447:14077) : cwd=/secretcats
type=SYSCALL msg=audit(12/12/2017 12:15:35.447:14077) : arch=x86_64
syscall=openat success=yes exit=3 a0=0xffffffffffffff9c a1=0x2300330
a2=O_RDONLY|O_NONBLOCK|O_DIRECTORY|O_CLOEXEC a3=0x0 items=1 ppid=10805
pid=10952 auid=vicky uid=vicky gid=vicky euid=vicky suid=vicky fsuid=vicky
egid=vicky sgid=vicky fsgid=vicky tty=pts0 ses=1789 comm=ls exe=/usr/bin/ls
subj=unconfined_u:unconfined_r:unconfined_t:s0-s0:c0.c1023
key=secretcats_watch
. . .
. . .
type=PROCTITLE msg=audit(12/12/2017 12:15:35.447:14081) : proctitle=ls --
color=auto -l
type=PATH msg=audit(12/12/2017 12:15:35.447:14081) : item=0
name=cleopatrafile.txt inode=33583071 dev=fd:01 mode=file,664
ouid=cleopatra ogid=secretcats rdev=00:00
obj=unconfined_u:object_r:default_t:s0 objtype=NORMAL
type=CWD msg=audit(12/12/2017 12:15:35.447:14081) : cwd=/secretcats
type=SYSCALL msg=audit(12/12/2017 12:15:35.447:14081) : arch=x86_64
syscall=getxattr success=no exit=ENODATA(No data available)
a0=0x7fff7c266e60 a1=0x7f0a61cb9db0 a2=0x0 a3=0x0 items=1 ppid=10805
pid=10952 auid=vicky uid=vicky gid=vicky euid=vicky suid=vicky fsuid=vicky
egid=vicky sgid=vicky fsgid=vicky tty=pts0 ses=1789 comm=ls exe=/usr/bin/ls
subj=unconfined_u:unconfined_r:unconfined_t:s0-s0:c0.c1023
key=secretcats_watch
```

In both records, you see the action that was taken (ls -l), and information about the person—or, cat, in this case—that took the action. Since this is a CentOS machine, you also see SELinux context information. In the second record, you also see the name of the file that Vicky saw when she did the ls command.

Next, let's say that that sneaky Charlie guy logs in and tries to get into the
/secretcats directory:

```
[charlie@localhost ~]$ cd /secretcats
-bash: cd: /secretcats: Permission denied
[charlie@localhost ~]$ ls -l /secretcats
ls: cannot open directory /secretcats: Permission denied
[charlie@localhost ~]$
```

Charlie isn't a member of the secretcats group and doesn't have permission to go into the
secretcats directory. So, he should trigger an alert message. Well, he actually triggered
one that consists of four records, and I'll again just list the first and the last:

```
sudo ausearch -i -k secretcats_watch | less
```

```
type=PROCTITLE msg=audit(12/12/2017 12:32:04.341:14152) : proctitle=ls --
color=auto -l /secretcats
type=PATH msg=audit(12/12/2017 12:32:04.341:14152) : item=0
name=/secretcats inode=33583041 dev=fd:01 mode=dir,sgid,sticky,770
ouid=nobody ogid=secretcats rdev=00:00
obj=unconfined_u:object_r:default_t:s0 objtype=NORMAL
type=CWD msg=audit(12/12/2017 12:32:04.341:14152) :  cwd=/home/charlie
type=SYSCALL msg=audit(12/12/2017 12:32:04.341:14152) : arch=x86_64
syscall=lgetxattr success=yes exit=35 a0=0x7ffd8d18f7dd a1=0x7f2496858f8a
a2=0x12bca30 a3=0xff items=1 ppid=11637 pid=11663 auid=charlie uid=charlie
gid=charlie euid=charlie suid=charlie fsuid=charlie egid=charlie
sgid=charlie fsgid=charlie tty=pts0 ses=1794 comm=ls exe=/usr/bin/ls
subj=unconfined_u:unconfined_r:unconfined_t:s0-s0:c0.c1023
key=secretcats_watch
    .   .   .
    .   .   .
type=PROCTITLE msg=audit(12/12/2017 12:32:04.341:14155) : proctitle=ls --
color=auto -l /secretcats
type=PATH msg=audit(12/12/2017 12:32:04.341:14155) : item=0
name=/secretcats inode=33583041 dev=fd:01 mode=dir,sgid,sticky,770
ouid=nobody ogid=secretcats rdev=00:00
obj=unconfined_u:object_r:default_t:s0 objtype=NORMAL
type=CWD msg=audit(12/12/2017 12:32:04.341:14155) :  cwd=/home/charlie
type=SYSCALL msg=audit(12/12/2017 12:32:04.341:14155) : arch=x86_64
syscall=openat success=no exit=EACCES(Permission denied)
a0=0xffffffffffffff9c a1=0x12be300
a2=O_RDONLY|O_NONBLOCK|O_DIRECTORY|O_CLOEXEC a3=0x0 items=1 ppid=11637
pid=11663 auid=charlie uid=charlie gid=charlie euid=charlie suid=charlie
fsuid=charlie egid=charlie sgid=charlie fsgid=charlie tty=pts0 ses=1794
comm=ls exe=/usr/bin/ls subj=unconfined_u:unconfined_r:unconfined_t:s0-
s0:c0.c1023 key=secretcats_watch
```

There are two things to note here. First, just attempting to `cd` into the directory doesn't trigger an alert. However, using `ls` to try to read the contents of the directory does. Secondly, note the `Permission denied` message that shows up in the second record.

The last set of alerts that we'll look at got created when Cleopatra created her `cleopatrafile.txt` file. This event triggered an alert that consists of 30 records. Here are two of them:

```
.  .  .
.  .  .
type=PROCTITLE msg=audit(12/12/2017 11:49:37.536:13856) : proctitle=vim
cleopatrafile.txt
type=PATH msg=audit(12/12/2017 11:49:37.536:13856) : item=0 name=.
inode=33583041 dev=fd:01 mode=dir,sgid,sticky,770 ouid=nobody
ogid=secretcats rdev=00:00 obj=unconfined_u:o
bject_r:default_t:s0 objtype=NORMAL
type=CWD msg=audit(12/12/2017 11:49:37.536:13856) :  cwd=/secretcats
type=SYSCALL msg=audit(12/12/2017 11:49:37.536:13856) : arch=x86_64
syscall=open success=yes exit=4 a0=0x5ab983 a1=O_RDONLY a2=0x0 a3=0x63
items=1 ppid=9572 pid=9593 auid=cle
opatra uid=cleopatra gid=cleopatra euid=cleopatra suid=cleopatra
fsuid=cleopatra egid=cleopatra sgid=cleopatra fsgid=cleopatra tty=pts0
ses=1779 comm=vim exe=/usr/bin/vim sub
j=unconfined_u:unconfined_r:unconfined_t:s0-s0:c0.c1023
key=secretcats_watch
----
type=PROCTITLE msg=audit(12/12/2017 11:49:56.001:13858) : proctitle=vim
cleopatrafile.txt
type=PATH msg=audit(12/12/2017 11:49:56.001:13858) : item=1
name=/secretcats/.cleopatrafile.txt.swp inode=33583065 dev=fd:01
mode=file,600 ouid=cleopatra ogid=secretcats rdev
=00:00 obj=unconfined_u:object_r:default_t:s0 objtype=DELETE
type=PATH msg=audit(12/12/2017 11:49:56.001:13858) : item=0
name=/secretcats/ inode=33583041 dev=fd:01 mode=dir,sgid,sticky,770
ouid=nobody ogid=secretcats rdev=00:00 obj=unc
onfined_u:object_r:default_t:s0 objtype=PARENT
type=CWD msg=audit(12/12/2017 11:49:56.001:13858) :  cwd=/secretcats
type=SYSCALL msg=audit(12/12/2017 11:49:56.001:13858) : arch=x86_64
syscall=unlink success=yes exit=0 a0=0x15ee7a0 a1=0x1 a2=0x1
a3=0x7ffc2c82e6b0 items=2 ppid=9572 pid=9593
auid=cleopatra uid=cleopatra gid=cleopatra euid=cleopatra suid=cleopatra
fsuid=cleopatra egid=cleopatra sgid=cleopatra fsgid=cleopatra tty=pts0
ses=1779 comm=vim exe=/usr/bin
/vim subj=unconfined_u:unconfined_r:unconfined_t:s0-s0:c0.c1023
key=secretcats_watch
.  .  .
.  .  .
```

You can tell that the first of these two messages happened when Cleopatra saved the file and exited vim because the second message shows `objtype=DELETE`, where her temporary vim swap file got deleted.

Okay, this is all good, but what if this is too much information? What if you just want a quick and sparse list of all of the security events that got triggered by this rule? For that, we'll use `aureport`. We'll use it just like we did before.

First, let's pipe the `aureport` output into `less` instead of into `grep` so that we can see the column headers:

```
[donnie@localhost ~]$ sudo aureport -i -k | less

Key Report
===============================================
# date time key success exe auid event
===============================================
1. 12/11/2017 13:06:20 passwd_changes yes ? donnie 11393
2. 12/11/2017 13:49:15 passwd_changes yes ? donnie 11511
3. 12/11/2017 13:49:15 passwd_changes yes /usr/bin/chfn donnie 11512
4. 12/11/2017 14:54:11 passwd_changes yes /usr/sbin/usermod donnie 11728
5. 12/11/2017 14:54:25 passwd_changes yes /usr/sbin/usermod donnie 11736
 . . .
 . . .
```

The status in the `success` column will be either `yes` or `no`, depending on if the user was able to successfully perform an action that violated a rule. Or, it could be a question mark if the event isn't the result of the rule getting triggered.

For Charlie, we see a `yes` event in line 48, with the events in lines 49 through 51 all having a `no` status. We also see that all of these entries were triggered by Charlie's use of the `ls` command:

```
sudo aureport -i -k | grep 'secretcats_watch'

[donnie@localhost ~]$ sudo aureport -i -k | grep 'secretcats_watch'
6. 12/11/2017 15:01:25 secretcats_watch yes ? donnie 11772
8. 12/12/2017 11:49:29 secretcats_watch yes /usr/bin/ls cleopatra 13828
9. 12/12/2017 11:49:37 secretcats_watch yes /usr/bin/vim cleopatra 13830
10. 12/12/2017 11:49:37 secretcats_watch yes /usr/bin/vim cleopatra 13829
 . . .
 . . .

48. 12/12/2017 12:32:04 secretcats_watch yes /usr/bin/ls charlie 14152
49. 12/12/2017 12:32:04 secretcats_watch no /usr/bin/ls charlie 14153
50. 12/12/2017 12:32:04 secretcats_watch no /usr/bin/ls charlie 14154
51. 12/12/2017 12:32:04 secretcats_watch no /usr/bin/ls charlie 14155
```

```
[donnie@localhost ~]$
```

You'd be tempted to think that the `yes` event in line 48 indicates that Charlie was successful in reading the contents of the `secretcats` directory. To analyze further, look at the event numbers at the end of each line and correlate them to the output of our previous `ausearch` command. You'll see that event numbers 14152 through 14155 belong to records that all have the same timestamp. We can see that in the first line of each record:

```
[donnie@localhost ~]$ sudo ausearch -i -k secretcats_watch | less

type=PROCTITLE msg=audit(12/12/2017 12:32:04.341:14152) : proctitle=ls --
color=auto -l /secretcats

type=PROCTITLE msg=audit(12/12/2017 12:32:04.341:14153) : proctitle=ls --
color=auto -l /secretcats

type=PROCTITLE msg=audit(12/12/2017 12:32:04.341:14154) : proctitle=ls --
color=auto -l /secretcats

type=PROCTITLE msg=audit(12/12/2017 12:32:04.341:14155) : proctitle=ls --
color=auto -l /secretcats
```

As we noted before, the last record of this series shows `Permission denied` for Charlie and that's what really counts.

Space doesn't permit me to give a full explanation of each individual item in an audit log record. But, you can read about it here in the official Red Hat documentation: https://access.redhat.com/documentation/en-us/red_hat_enterprise_linux/7/html/security_guide/sec-understanding_audit_log_files.

Searching for system call rule violations

The third rule that we created was to monitor that sneaky Charlie. This rule will alert us whenever Charlie tries to open or create a file. (As we noted before, `1006` is Charlie's user ID number.):

```
sudo auditctl -a always,exit -F arch=b64 -S openat -F auid=1006
```

Even though Charlie hasn't done that much on this system, this rule gives us a lot more log entries than what we bargained for. We'll look at just a couple of entries:

```
time->Tue Dec 12 11:49:29 2017
type=PROCTITLE msg=audit(1513097369.952:13828):
proctitle=6C73002D2D636F6C6F723D6175746F
type=PATH msg=audit(1513097369.952:13828): item=0 name="." inode=33583041
dev=fd:01 mode=043770 ouid=99 ogid=1009 rdev=00:00
obj=unconfined_u:object_r:default_t:s0 objtype=NO
RMAL
type=CWD msg=audit(1513097369.952:13828):  cwd="/secretcats"
type=SYSCALL msg=audit(1513097369.952:13828): arch=c000003e syscall=257
success=yes exit=3 a0=ffffffffffffff9c a1=10d1560 a2=90800 a3=0 items=1
ppid=9572 pid=9592 auid=1004 u
id=1004 gid=1006 euid=1004 suid=1004 fsuid=1004 egid=1006 sgid=1006
fsgid=1006 tty=pts0 ses=1779 comm="ls" exe="/usr/bin/ls"
subj=unconfined_u:unconfined_r:unconfined_t:s0-s0
:c0.c1023 key="secretcats_watch"
```

This record was generated when Charlie tried to access the /secretcats/ directory. So, we can expect to see this one. But, what we didn't expect to see was the exceedingly long list of records of files that Charlie indirectly accessed when he logged in to the system through Secure Shell. Here are just a couple:

```
time->Tue Dec 12 11:50:28 2017
type=PROCTITLE msg=audit(1513097428.662:13898):
proctitle=737368643A20636861726C6965407074732F30
type=PATH msg=audit(1513097428.662:13898): item=0 name="/proc/9726/fd"
inode=1308504 dev=00:03 mode=040500 ouid=0 ogid=0 rdev=00:00
obj=unconfined_u:unconfined_r:unconfined_t
:s0-s0:c0.c1023 objtype=NORMAL
type=CWD msg=audit(1513097428.662:13898):  cwd="/home/charlie"
type=SYSCALL msg=audit(1513097428.662:13898): arch=c000003e syscall=257
success=yes exit=3 a0=ffffffffffffff9c a1=7ffc7ca1d840 a2=90800 a3=0
items=1 ppid=9725 pid=9726 auid=1
006 uid=1006 gid=1008 euid=1006 suid=1006 fsuid=1006 egid=1008 sgid=1008
fsgid=1008 tty=pts0 ses=1781 comm="sshd" exe="/usr/sbin/sshd"
subj=unconfined_u:unconfined_r:unconfin
ed_t:s0-s0:c0.c1023 key=(null)
----
time->Tue Dec 12 11:50:28 2017
type=PROCTITLE msg=audit(1513097428.713:13900):
proctitle=737368643A20636861726C6965407074732F30
type=PATH msg=audit(1513097428.713:13900): item=0 name="/etc/profile.d/"
inode=33593031 dev=fd:01 mode=040755 ouid=0 ogid=0 rdev=00:00
obj=system_u:object_r:bin_t:s0 objtype=
NORMAL
```

```
type=CWD msg=audit(1513097428.713:13900):  cwd="/home/charlie"
type=SYSCALL msg=audit(1513097428.713:13900): arch=c000003e syscall=257
success=yes exit=3 a0=ffffffffffffff9c a1=1b27930 a2=90800 a3=0 items=1
ppid=9725 pid=9726 auid=1006 u
id=1006 gid=1008 euid=1006 suid=1006 fsuid=1006 egid=1008 sgid=1008
fsgid=1008 tty=pts0 ses=1781 comm="bash" exe="/usr/bin/bash"
subj=unconfined_u:unconfined_r:unconfined_t:s
0-s0:c0.c1023 key=(null)
```

In the first record, we see that Charlie accessed the `/usr/sbin/sshd` file. In the second, we see that he accessed the `/usr/bin/bash` file. It's not that Charlie chose to access those files. The operating system accessed those files for him in the course of just a normal login event. So as you can see, when you create audit rules, you have to be careful of what you wish because there's a definite danger that the wish might be granted. If you really need to monitor someone, you'll want to create a rule that won't give you quite this much information.

While we're at it, we might as well see what the `aureport` output for this looks like:

```
[donnie@localhost ~]$ sudo aureport -s -i | grep 'openat'
[sudo] password for donnie:
1068. 12/12/2017 11:49:29 openat 9592 ls cleopatra 13828
1099. 12/12/2017 11:50:28 openat 9665 sshd charlie 13887
1100. 12/12/2017 11:50:28 openat 9665 sshd charlie 13889
1101. 12/12/2017 11:50:28 openat 9665 sshd charlie 13890
1102. 12/12/2017 11:50:28 openat 9726 sshd charlie 13898
1103. 12/12/2017 11:50:28 openat 9726 bash charlie 13900
1104. 12/12/2017 11:50:28 openat 9736 grep charlie 13901
1105. 12/12/2017 11:50:28 openat 9742 grep charlie 13902
1108. 12/12/2017 11:50:51 openat 9766 ls charlie 13906
1110. 12/12/2017 12:15:35 openat 10952 ls vicky 14077
1115. 12/12/2017 12:30:54 openat 11632 sshd charlie 14129
1116. 12/12/2017 12:30:54 openat 11632 sshd charlie 14131
1117. 12/12/2017 12:30:54 openat 11632 sshd charlie 14132
1118. 12/12/2017 12:30:54 openat 11637 sshd charlie 14140
1119. 12/12/2017 12:30:54 openat 11637 bash charlie 14142
1120. 12/12/2017 12:30:54 openat 11647 grep charlie 14143
1121. 12/12/2017 12:30:54 openat 11653 grep charlie 14144
1125. 12/12/2017 12:32:04 openat 11663 ls charlie 14155
[donnie@localhost ~]$
```

In addition to what Charlie did, we also see what Vicky and Cleopatra did. That's because the rule that we set for the `/secretcats/` directory generated `openat` events when Vicky and Cleopatra accessed, viewed, or created files in that directory.

Generating authentication reports

You can generate user authentication reports without having to define any audit rules. Just use `aureport` with the `-au` option switch. (Remember au, the first two letters of authentication.):

```
[donnie@localhost ~]$ sudo aureport -au
[sudo] password for donnie:

Authentication Report
============================================
# date time acct host term exe success event
============================================
1. 10/28/2017 13:38:52 donnie localhost.localdomain tty1 /usr/bin/login yes
94
2. 10/28/2017 13:39:03 donnie localhost.localdomain /dev/tty1 /usr/bin/sudo
yes 102
3. 10/28/2017 14:04:51 donnie localhost.localdomain /dev/tty1 /usr/bin/sudo
yes 147
. . .
. . .
239. 12/12/2017 11:50:20 charlie 192.168.0.222 ssh /usr/sbin/sshd no 13880
244. 12/12/2017 12:10:06 cleopatra 192.168.0.222 ssh /usr/sbin/sshd no
13992
247. 12/12/2017 12:14:28 vicky 192.168.0.222 ssh /usr/sbin/sshd no 14049
250. 12/12/2017 12:30:49 charlie 192.168.0.222 ssh /usr/sbin/sshd no 14122
265. 12/12/2017 19:06:20 charlie 192.168.0.222 ssh /usr/sbin/sshd no 725
269. 12/12/2017 19:23:45 donnie ? /dev/pts/0 /usr/bin/sudo no 779
[donnie@localhost ~]$
```

For login events, this tells us whether the user logged in at the local terminal or remotely through Secure Shell. To see the details of any event, use `ausearch` with the `-a` option, followed by the event number that you see at the end of a line. (Strangely, the `-a` option stands for an event.) Let's look at event number 14122 for Charlie:

```
[donnie@localhost ~]$ sudo ausearch -a 14122
----
time->Tue Dec 12 12:30:49 2017
type=USER_AUTH msg=audit(1513099849.322:14122): pid=11632 uid=0
auid=4294967295 ses=4294967295 subj=system_u:system_r:sshd_t:s0-s0:c0.c1023
msg='op=pubkey acct="charlie" exe="/usr/sbin/sshd" hostname=?
addr=192.168.0.222 terminal=ssh res=failed'
```

The problem with this is that it really doesn't make any sense. I'm the one who did the logins for Charlie, and I know for a fact that Charlie never had any failed logins. In fact, we can correlate this with the matching entry from the /var/log/secure file:

```
Dec 12 12:30:53 localhost sshd[11632]: Accepted password for charlie from
192.168.0.222 port 34980 ssh2
Dec 12 12:30:54 localhost sshd[11632]: pam_unix(sshd:session): session
opened for user charlie by (uid=0)
```

The time stamps for these two entries are a few seconds later than the timestamp for the `ausearch` output, but that's okay. There's nothing in this log file to suggest that Charlie ever had a failed login, and these two entries clearly show that Charlie's login really was successful. The lesson here is that when you see something strange in either the `ausearch` or `aureport` output, be sure to correlate it with the matching entry in the proper authentication log file to get a better idea of what's going on. (By *authentication log file*, I mean `/var/log/secure` for Red Hat-type systems and `/var/log/auth.log` for Ubuntu systems. The names may vary for other Linux distros.)

Using predefined rules sets

In the `/usr/share/doc/audit-version_number/` directory of your CentOS machine, you'll see some premade rule sets for different scenarios. Once you install auditd on Ubuntu, you'll have audit rules for it too, but the location is different for Ubuntu 16.04 and Ubuntu 17.10. On Ubuntu 16.04, the rules are in the `/usr/share/doc/auditd/examples/` directory. On Ubuntu 17.10, they're in the `/usr/share/doc/auditd/examples/rules/` directory. In any case, some of the rule sets are common among all three of these distros. Let's look on the CentOS machine to see what we have there:

```
[donnie@localhost rules]$ pwd
/usr/share/doc/audit-2.7.6/rules
[donnie@localhost rules]$ ls -l
total 96
-rw-r--r--. 1 root root  163 Aug  4 17:29 10-base-config.rules
-rw-r--r--. 1 root root  284 Apr 19  2017 10-no-audit.rules
-rw-r--r--. 1 root root   93 Apr 19  2017 11-loginuid.rules
-rw-r--r--. 1 root root  329 Apr 19  2017 12-cont-fail.rules
-rw-r--r--. 1 root root  323 Apr 19  2017 12-ignore-error.rules
-rw-r--r--. 1 root root  516 Apr 19  2017 20-dont-audit.rules
-rw-r--r--. 1 root root  273 Apr 19  2017 21-no32bit.rules
-rw-r--r--. 1 root root  252 Apr 19  2017 22-ignore-chrony.rules
-rw-r--r--. 1 root root 4915 Apr 19  2017 30-nispom.rules
-rw-r--r--. 1 root root 5952 Apr 19  2017 30-pci-dss-v31.rules
-rw-r--r--. 1 root root 6663 Apr 19  2017 30-stig.rules
-rw-r--r--. 1 root root 1498 Apr 19  2017 31-privileged.rules
-rw-r--r--. 1 root root  218 Apr 19  2017 32-power-abuse.rules
-rw-r--r--. 1 root root  156 Apr 19  2017 40-local.rules
```

```
-rw-r--r--. 1 root root  439 Apr 19 2017 41-containers.rules
-rw-r--r--. 1 root root  672 Apr 19 2017 42-injection.rules
-rw-r--r--. 1 root root  424 Apr 19 2017 43-module-load.rules
-rw-r--r--. 1 root root  326 Apr 19 2017 70-einval.rules
-rw-r--r--. 1 root root  151 Apr 19 2017 71-networking.rules
-rw-r--r--. 1 root root   86 Apr 19 2017 99-finalize.rules
-rw-r--r--. 1 root root 1202 Apr 19 2017 README-rules
[donnie@localhost rules]$
```

The three files I want to focus on are the `nispom`, `pci-dss`, and `stig` files. Each of these three rule sets is designed to meet the auditing standards of a particular certifying agency. In order, these rules sets are:

- `nispom`: The National Industrial Security Program—you'll see this rule set used at either the U.S. Department of Defense or its contractors
- `pci-dss`: Payment Card Industry Data Security Standard—if you work in the banking or financial industries, or even if you're just running an online business that accepts credit cards, you'll likely become very familiar with this
- `stig`: Security Technical Implementation Guides—if you work for the U.S. Government or possibly other governments, you'll be dealing with this one

To use one of these rules sets, copy the appropriate files over to the `/etc/audit/rules.d/` directory:

```
[donnie@localhost rules]$ sudo cp 30-pci-dss-v31.rules /etc/audit/rules.d
[donnie@localhost rules]$
```

Then, restart the auditd daemon to read in the new rules.

For Red Hat or CentOS:

```
sudo service auditd restart
```

For Ubuntu:

```
sudo systemctl restart auditd
```

Of course, there's always the chance that a particular rule in one of these sets might not work for you or that you might need to enable a rule that's currently disabled. If so, just open the rules file in your text editor, and comment out what doesn't work or uncomment what you need to enable.

Even though auditd is very cool, bear in mind that it only alerts you about potential security breaches. It doesn't do anything to harden the system against them.

That pretty much wraps it up for our discussion of the auditd system. Give it a go and see what you think.

Applying OpenSCAP policies with oscap

SCAP, the **Security Content Automation Protocol** (**SCAP**), was created by the U.S. National Institute of Standards and Technology. It consists of hardening guides, hardening templates, and baseline configuration guides for setting up secure systems. OpenSCAP is a set of free open source software tools that can be used to implement SCAP. It consists of the following:

- Security profiles that you can apply to a system. There are different profiles for meeting the requirements of several different certifying agencies.
- Security guides to help with the initial setup of your system.
- The `oscap` command-line utility to apply security templates.
- On Red Hat-type systems that have a desktop interface, you have SCAP Workbench, a GUI-type utility.

You can install OpenSCAP on either the Red Hat or the Ubuntu distros, but it's much better implemented on the Red Hat distros. For one thing, the Red Hat world has the very cool SCAP Workbench, but the Ubuntu world doesn't. When you install a Red Hat-type operating system, you can choose to apply a SCAP profile during installation. You can't do that with Ubuntu. Finally, the Red Hat distros come with a fairly complete set of ready-to-use profiles. Curiously, Ubuntu only comes with profiles for older versions of Fedora and Red Hat, which aren't usable on an Ubuntu system. If you want usable profiles for Ubuntu, you'll have to download them from the OpenSCAP website and manually install them yourself. (We'll cover that in the last section of the chapter.) Having said this, let's see how to install OpenSCAP and how to use the command-line utility that's common to both of our distros. Since CentOS has the more complete implementation, I'll use it for the demos.

Installing OpenSCAP

On your CentOS machine, assuming that you didn't install OpenSCAP during operating system installation, follow this:

```
sudo yum install openscap-scanner scap-security-guide
```

On the Ubuntu machine, do this:

```
sudo apt install python-openscap
```

Viewing the profile files

On the CentOS machine, you'll see the profile files in the
/usr/share/xml/scap/ssg/content/ directory. On the Ubuntu machine, you'll see
what few profiles there are in the /usr/share/openscap/ directory. The profile files are
in the .xml format, and each one contains one or more profiles that you can apply to the
system:

```
[donnie@localhost content]$ pwd
/usr/share/xml/scap/ssg/content
[donnie@localhost content]$ ls -l
total 50596
-rw-r--r--. 1 root root   6734643 Oct 19 19:40 ssg-centos6-ds.xml
-rw-r--r--. 1 root root   1596043 Oct 19 19:40 ssg-centos6-xccdf.xml
-rw-r--r--. 1 root root  11839886 Oct 19 19:41 ssg-centos7-ds.xml
-rw-r--r--. 1 root root   2636971 Oct 19 19:40 ssg-centos7-xccdf.xml
-rw-r--r--. 1 root root       642 Oct 19 19:40 ssg-firefox-cpe-
dictionary.xml
 .  .  .
 .  .  .
-rw-r--r--. 1 root root  11961196 Oct 19 19:41 ssg-rhel7-ds.xml
-rw-r--r--. 1 root root    851069 Oct 19 19:40 ssg-rhel7-ocil.xml
-rw-r--r--. 1 root root   2096046 Oct 19 19:40 ssg-rhel7-oval.xml
-rw-r--r--. 1 root root   2863621 Oct 19 19:40 ssg-rhel7-xccdf.xml
[donnie@localhost content]$
```

The command-line utility for working with OpenSCAP is oscap. We can use this with the
info switch to view information about any of the profile files. Let's look at the ssg-
centos7-xccdf.xml file:

```
[donnie@localhost content]$ sudo oscap info ssg-centos7-xccdf.xml
Document type: XCCDF Checklist
Checklist version: 1.1
Imported: 2017-10-19T19:40:43
Status: draft
Generated: 2017-10-19
Resolved: true
Profiles:
    standard
    pci-dss
    C2S
```

```
      rht-ccp
      common
      stig-rhel7-disa
      stig-rhevh-upstream
      ospp-rhel7
      cjis-rhel7-server
      docker-host
      nist-800-171-cui
  Referenced check files:
      ssg-rhel7-oval.xml
          system: http://oval.mitre.org/XMLSchema/oval-definitions-5
      ssg-rhel7-ocil.xml
          system: http://scap.nist.gov/schema/ocil/2
      https://www.redhat.com/security/data/oval/com.redhat.rhsa-RHEL7.xml.bz2
          system: http://oval.mitre.org/XMLSchema/oval-definitions-5
  [donnie@localhost content]$
```

We can see that this file contains 11 different profiles that we can apply to the system. Among them, you see profiles for `stig` and `pci-dss`, just as we had for the auditing rules. And, if you're running Docker containers, the `docker-host` profile would be extremely handy.

Scanning the system

Now, let's say that we need to ensure that our systems are compliant with Payment Card Industry standards. We'll first scan the CentOS machine to see what needs remediation. (Note that the following command is very long and wraps around on the printed page.)

```
sudo oscap xccdf eval --profile pci-dss --results scan-xccdf-results.xml
/usr/share/xml/scap/ssg/content/ssg-centos7-xccdf.xml
```

As we always like to do, let's break this down:

- `xccdf eval`: The Extensible Configuration Checklist Description is one of the languages with which we can write security profile rules. We're going to use a profile that was written in this language to perform an evaluation of the system.
- `--profile pci-dss`: Here, I specified that I want to use the Payment Card Industry Data Security Standard profile to evaluate the system.
- `--results scan-xccdf-results.xml`: I'm going to save the scan results to this `.xml` format file. When the scan has finished, I'll create a report from this file.
- `/usr/share/xml/scap/ssg/content/ssg-centos7-xccdf.xml`: This is the file that contains the `pci-dss` profile.

As the scan progresses, the output will get sent to the screen as well as to the designated output file. It's a long list of items, so I'll only show you a few of them:

```
Ensure Red Hat GPG Key Installed
ensure_redhat_gpgkey_installed
pass

Ensure gpgcheck Enabled In Main Yum Configuration
ensure_gpgcheck_globally_activated
pass

Ensure gpgcheck Enabled For All Yum Package Repositories
ensure_gpgcheck_never_disabled
pass

Ensure Software Patches Installed
security_patches_up_to_date
notchecked

 . . .
 . . .


Install AIDE
package_aide_installed
fail

Build and Test AIDE Database
aide_build_database
fail
. . .
. . .
```

So, we have GPG encryption installed, which is good. But, it's a bad thing that we don't have the AIDE intrusion detection system installed.

Now that I've run the scan and created an output file with the results, I can build my report:

```
sudo oscap xccdf generate report scan-xccdf-results.xml > scan-xccdf-results.html
```

This extracts the information from the .xml format file, which isn't meant for humans to read, and transfers it to a .html file that you can open in your web browser. (For the record, the report says that there are total 20 problems that need to be fixed.)

Remediating the system

So, we have 20 problems that we need to fix before our system can be considered as compliant with Payment Card Industry standards. Let's see how many of them that oscap can fix for us:

```
sudo oscap xccdf eval --remediate --profile pci-dss --results scan-xccdf-
remediate-results.xml /usr/share/xml/scap/ssg/content/ssg-centos7-xccdf.xml
```

This is the same command that I used to perform the initial scan, except that I added the --remediate option, and I'm saving the results to a different file. You'll want to have a bit of patience when you run this command, because fixing some problems involves downloading and installing software packages. In fact, even as I type this, oscap is busy downloading and installing the missing AIDE intrusion detection system package.

Okay, the remediation is still running, but I can still show you some of the things that got fixed:

```
Disable Prelinking
disable_prelink
error

Install AIDE
package_aide_installed
fixed

Build and Test AIDE Database
aide_build_database
fixed

Configure Periodic Execution of AIDE
aide_periodic_cron_checking
fixed

Verify and Correct File Permissions with RPM
rpm_verify_permissions
error

Prevent Log In to Accounts With Empty Password
no_empty_passwords
fixed
. . .
. . .
```

There are a couple of errors because of things that `oscap` couldn't fix, but that's normal. At least you know about them so that you can try to fix them yourself.

And, check this out. Do you remember how in Chapter 2, *Securing User Accounts*, I made you jump through hoops to ensure that users had strong passwords that expire on a regular basis? Well, by applying this OpenSCAP profile, you get all that fixed for you automatically:

```
Set Password Maximum Age
accounts_maximum_age_login_defs
fixed

Set Account Expiration Following Inactivity
account_disable_post_pw_expiration
fixed

Set Password Strength Minimum Digit Characters
accounts_password_pam_dcredit
fixed

Set Password Minimum Length
accounts_password_pam_minlen
fixed

Set Password Strength Minimum Uppercase Characters
accounts_password_pam_ucredit
fixed

Set Password Strength Minimum Lowercase Characters
accounts_password_pam_lcredit
fixed

Set Deny For Failed Password Attempts
accounts_passwords_pam_faillock_deny
fixed

Set Lockout Time For Failed Password Attempts
accounts_passwords_pam_faillock_unlock_time
fixed

Limit Password Reuse
accounts_password_pam_unix_remember
fixed
```

So yeah, OpenSCAP is pretty cool, and even the command-line tools aren't hard to use.

Using SCAP Workbench

For Red Hat and CentOS machines with a desktop environment installed, we have SCAP Workbench. However, if the last time you ever worked with SCAP Workbench was on Red Hat/CentOS 7.0 or Red Hat/CentOS 7.1, you were likely quite disappointed. Indeed, the early versions of the Workbench were so bad that they weren't even usable. Thankfully, things greatly improved with the introduction of Red Hat 7.2 and CentOS 7.2. Now, the Workbench is quite the nice little tool.

To get it on your CentOS machine, just use the following code:

```
sudo yum install scap-workbench
```

Yeah, the package name is just `scap-workbench` instead of `openscap-workbench`. I don't know why, but I do know that you'll never find it if you're searching for `openscap` packages.

Once you get it installed, you'll see its menu item under the **System Tools** menu.

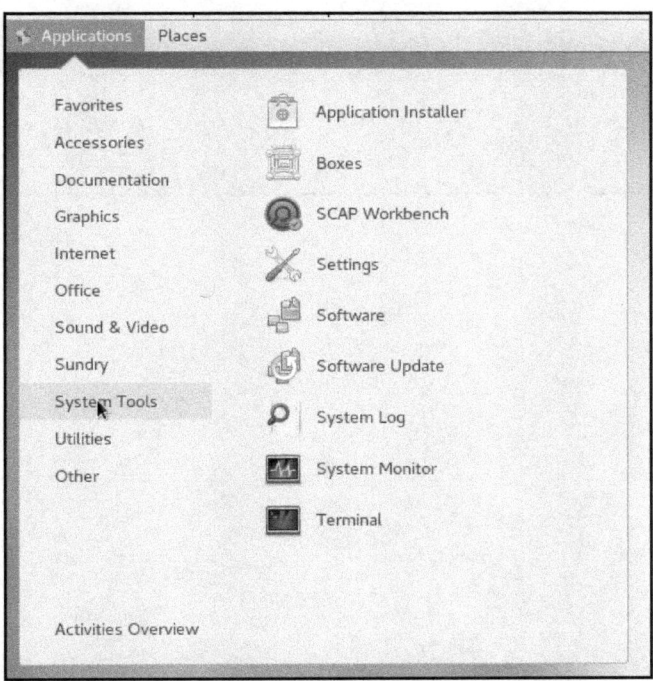

When you first open the program, you would think that the system would ask you for a root or sudo password. But, it doesn't. We'll see in a moment if that affects us.

The thing you'll see on the opening screen is a drop-down list for you to select the type of content that you want to load. I'll select **CentOS7** and then click on the **Load content** button:

Next, you'll see in the top panel where you can select the desired profile. You can also choose to customize the profile, and whether you want to run the scan on the local machine or on a remote machine. In the bottom pane, you'll see a list of rules for that profile. You can expand each rule item to get a description of that rule:

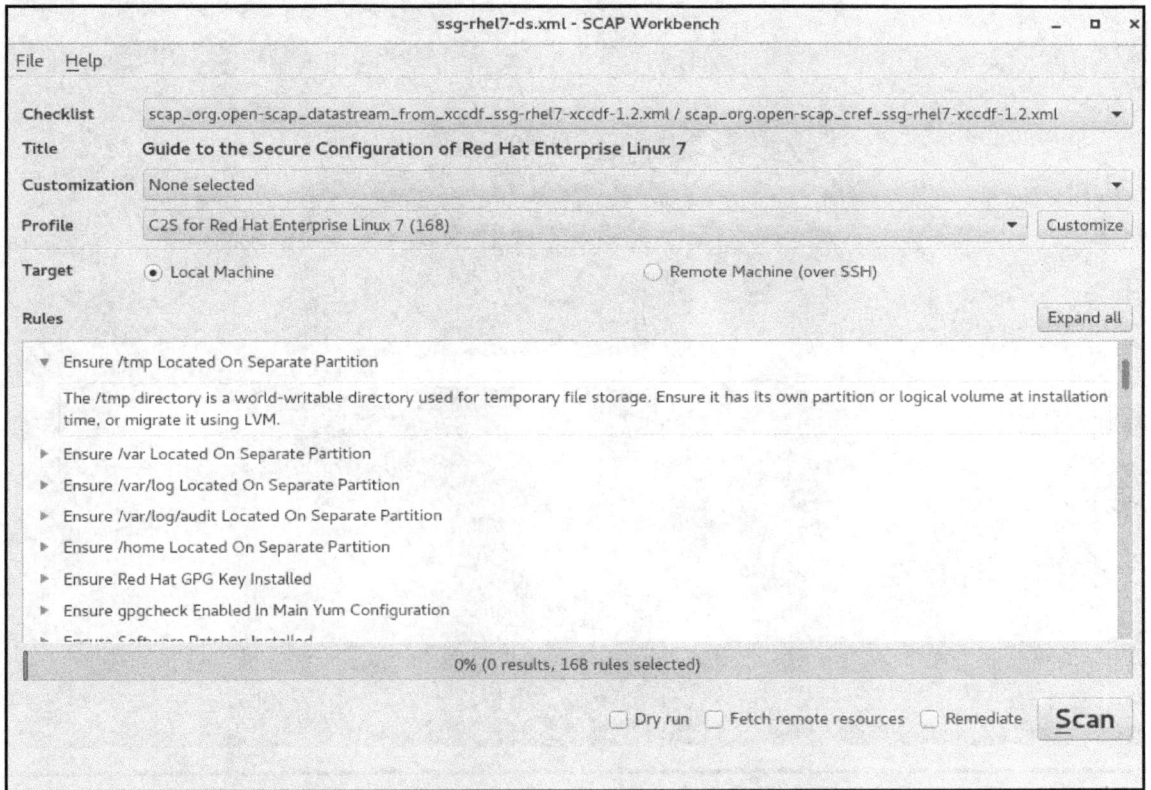

Now, let's click that **Scan** button to see what happens:

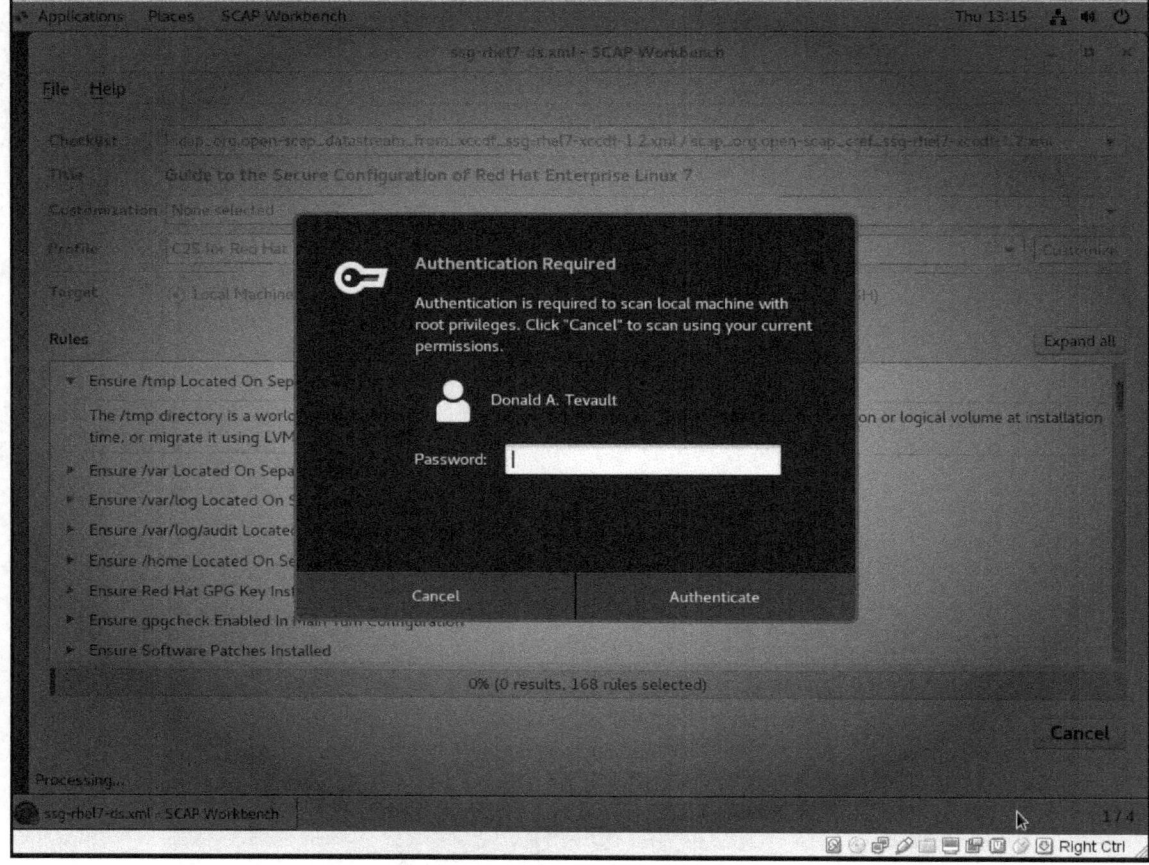

Cool. As I had hoped, it prompts you for your sudo password. Beyond that, I'll leave it to you to play with it. It's just another one of those GUI-thingies, so the rest of it should be fairly easy to figure out.

More about OpenSCAP profiles

So now you're saying, "*Okay, this is all good, but how do I find out what's in these profiles and which one I need?*" Well, there are several ways.

The first way, which I've just shown you, is to install the SCAP Workbench on a machine with a desktop interface and read through the descriptions of all the rules for each profile.

The second way, which might be a bit easier, is to go to the OpenSCAP website and look through the documentation that they have there.

 You'll find information about the available OpenSCAP profiles at `https:/` `/www.open-scap.org/security-policies/choosing-policy/`.

As far as knowing which profile to choose, there are a few things to consider:

- If you work in the financial sector or in a business that does online financial transactions, then go with the `pci-dss` profile.
- If you work for a government agency, especially if it's the U.S. government, then go with either the `stig` profile or the `nispom` profile, as dictated by the particular agency.
- If neither of these two considerations applies to your situation, then you'll just want to do some research and planning, in order to figure out what really needs to be locked down. Look through the rules in each profile and read through the documentation at the OpenSCAP website to help decide what you need.

The next thing on your mind is, *"What about Ubuntu? We've already seen that the profiles that come with Ubuntu are useless because they're for RHEL and Fedora."* That's true, but you'll find profiles for various different distros, including for the Long Term Support versions of Ubuntu, at the OpenSCAP website:

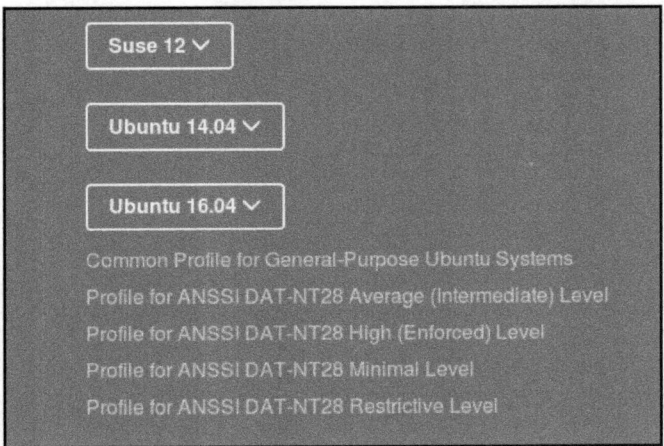

Applying an OpenSCAP profile during system installation

One of the things that I love about the Red Hat folk is that they totally get this whole security thing. Yeah, we can lock down other distros and make them more secure, as we've already seen. But, with Red Hat distros, it's a bit easier. For a lot of things, the maintainers of the Red Hat-type distros have set secure default options that aren't securely set on other distros. (For example, Red Hat distros are the only ones that come with users' home directories locked down by default.) For other things, the Red Hat-type distros come with tools and installation options that help make life easier for a busy, security-conscious administrator.

When you install a Red Hat 7-type distro, you'll be given the chance to apply an OpenSCAP profile during the operating system installation. Here on this CentOS 7 installer screen, you see the option to choose a security profile at the lower right-hand corner of the screen:

All you have to do is to click on that and then choose your profile:

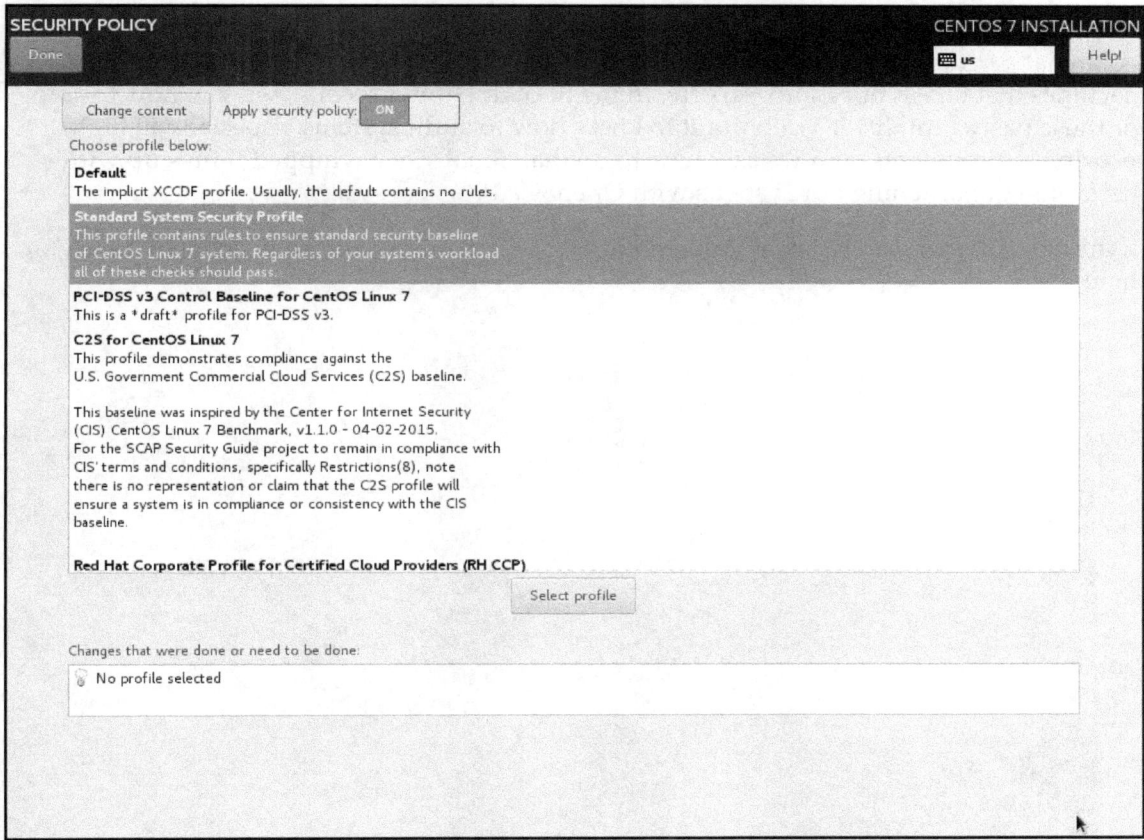

Okay, that pretty much wraps it up for our discussion of OpenSCAP. The only thing left to add is that, as great as OpenSCAP is, it won't do everything. For example, some security standards require that you have certain directories, such as /home/ or /var/, on their own separate partitions. An OpenSCAP scan will alert you if that's not the case, but it can't change your existing partitioning scheme. So for things like that, you'll need to get a checklist from the governing body that dictates your security requirements and do a bit of advanced work before you even touch OpenSCAP.

Summary

We covered a lot of ground in this chapter, and we saw some really cool stuff. We began by looking at a couple of antivirus scanners so that we can prevent infecting any Windows machines that access our Linux servers. In the Rootkit Hunter section, we saw how to scan for those nasty rootkits. It's important to know how to audit systems, especially in high-security environments, and we saw how to do that. Finally, we wrapped things up with a discussion of hardening our systems with OpenSCAP.

In the next chapter, we'll look at vulnerability scanning and intrusion detection. I'll see you there.

9
Vulnerability Scanning and Intrusion Detection

There are lots of threats out there, and some of them might even penetrate into your network. You'll want to know when that happens, so you'll want to have a good **Network Intrusion Detection System** (**NIDS**) in place. We'll look at Snort, which is probably the most famous one. I'll then show you a way to cheat so that you can have a Snort system up and running in no time at all.

We've already seen how to scan a machine for viruses and rootkits by installing scanning tools onto the machines that we want to scan. However, there are a lot more vulnerabilities for which we can scan, and I'll show you some cool tools that you can use for that.

The following topics are covered in this chapter:

- An introduction to Snort and Security Onion
- Scanning and hardening with Lynis
- Finding vulnerabilities with OpenVAS
- Web server scanning with Nikto

Looking at Snort and Security Onion

Snort is a NIDS, which is offered as a free open source software product. The program itself is free of charge, but you'll need to pay if you want to have a complete, up-to-date set of threat detection rules. Snort started out as a one-man project, but it's now owned by Cisco. Understand though, this isn't something that you install on the machine that you want to protect. Rather, you'll have at least one dedicated Snort machine someplace on the network, just monitoring all network traffic, watching for anomalies. When it sees traffic that shouldn't be there—something that indicates the presence of a bot, for example—it can either just send an alert message to an administrator or it can even block the anomalous traffic, depending on how the rules are configured. For a small network, you can have just one Snort machine that acts as both a control console and a sensor. For large networks, you could have one Snort machine set up as a control console and have it receive reports from other Snort machines that are set up as sensors.

Snort isn't too hard to deal with, but setting up a complete Snort solution from scratch can be a bit tedious. After we look at the basics of Snort usage, I'll show you how to vastly simplify things by setting up a prebuilt Snort appliance.

Space doesn't permit me to present a comprehensive tutorial about Snort. Instead, I'll present a high-level overview and then present you with other resources for learning Snort in detail.

Obtaining and installing Snort

Snort isn't in the official repository of any Linux distro, so you'll need to get it from the Snort website. On their downloads page, you'll see installer files in the .rpm format for Fedora and CentOS and a .exe installer file for Windows. However, you won't see any .deb installer files for Ubuntu. That's okay because they also provide source code files that you can compile on a variety of different Linux distros. To make things simple, let's just talk about installing Snort on CentOS 7 with the prebuilt .rpm packages.

You can get Snort and Snort training from the official Snort website: https://www.snort.org.

On the Snort home page, just scroll down a bit, and you'll see the guide on how to download and install Snort. Click on the **Centos** tab and follow the steps. The commands in **Step 1** will download and install Snort all in one smooth operation, as shown in the following screenshot:

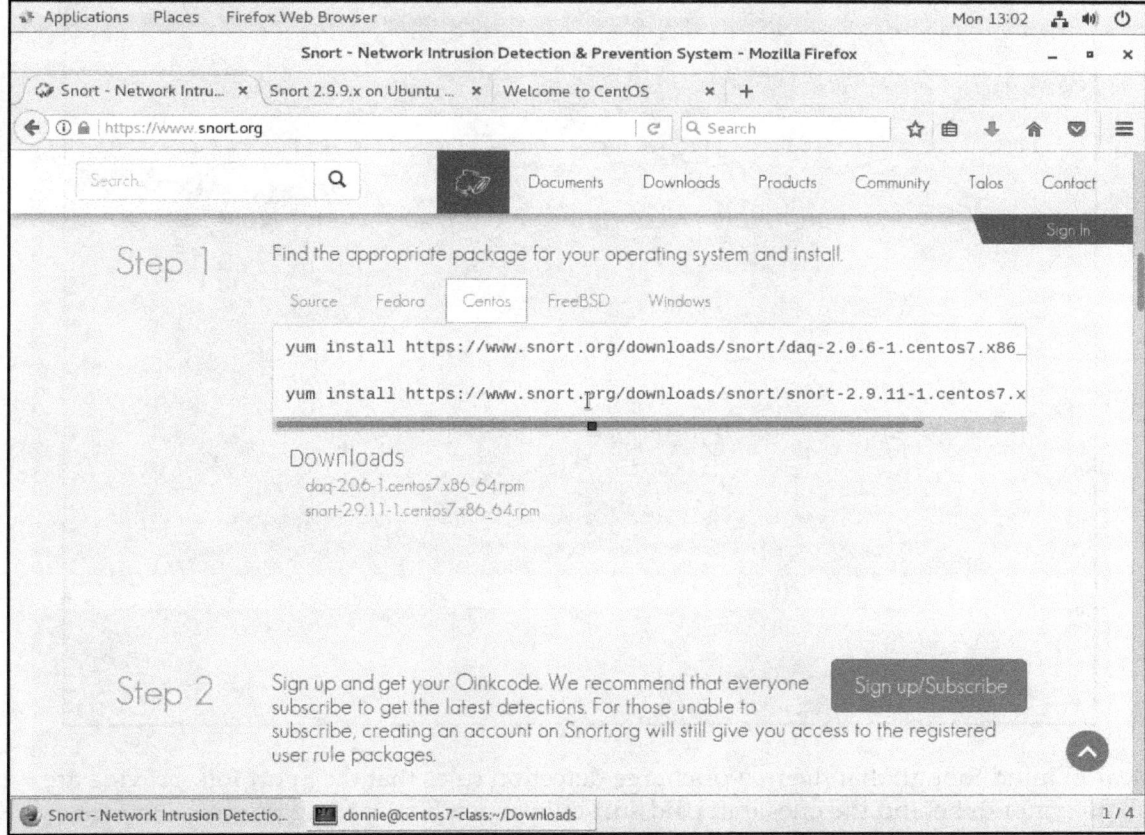

Step 2 and **Step 3** involve signing up for your Oinkcode so that you can download the official Snort detection rules and then installing **PulledPork** so that you can keep the rules updated automatically, as shown in the following screenshot:

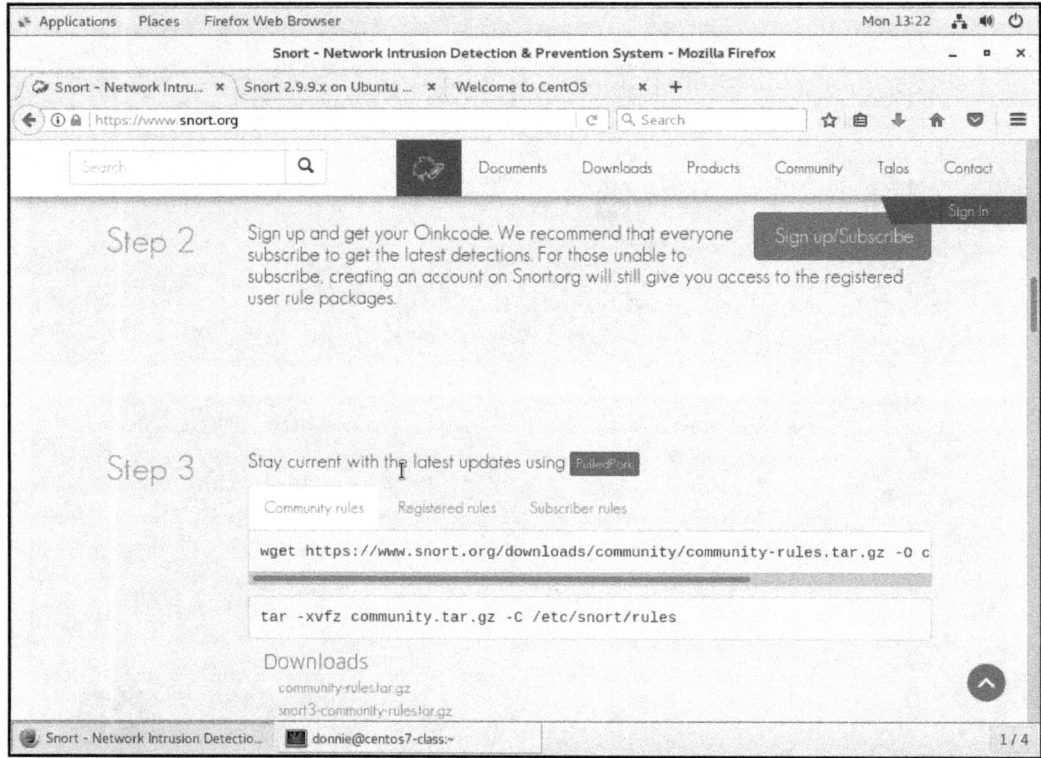

Bear in mind though that the free-of-charge detection rules that the Snort folk provide are about a month behind the ones that paid subscribers get. For learning purposes though, they're all that you need. Also, if you choose to not get the Oinkcode, you can just use the **Community rules**, which are a subset of the official Snort rules.

Step 4 is just to read the documentation:

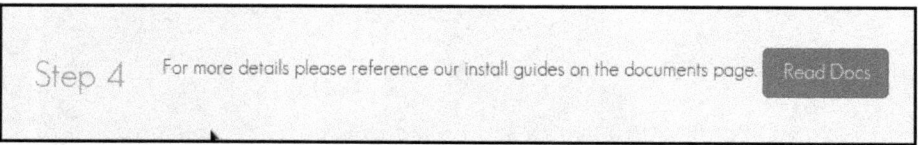

And, that's it. You now have a working copy of Snort. The only catch is all you have so far is just the command-line interface, which might not be what you want.

Graphical interfaces for Snort

Plain, unadorned Snort will do what you need it to do, and it will save its findings to its own set of log files. However, reading through log files to discern network traffic trends can get a bit tedious, so you'll want some tools to help you out. The best tools are the graphical ones, which can give you a good visualization of what's going on with your network.

One example is the **Basic Analysis and Security Engine** (**BASE**), as shown in the following screenshot:

There are several more, but I'll show them to you when we get to the *Security Onion* section.

 You can find out more about BASE from the author's *Professionally Evil* website: `https://professionallyevil.com/`

Getting Snort in prebuilt appliances

Snort itself isn't too terribly difficult to set up. However, if you're doing everything manually, it can be a bit tedious by the time you've set up the control console, the sensors, and your choice of graphical frontends. So—and, imagine me peering at you over my dark glasses as I say this—what if I told you that you can get your Snort setup as part of a ready-to-go appliance? What if I told you that setting up such an appliance is an absolute breeze? I imagine that you'd probably say, *So, show me already!*

 If you feel bad about cheating by making Snort deployment so easy, there's really no need to. An official Snort representative once told me that most people deploy Snort in this manner.

Since Snort is a **Free Open Source Software** (**FOSS**) project, it's perfectly legal for people to build it into their own FOSS applications. Also, if you think back to our discussion of firewalls in Chapter 3, *Securing Your Server with a Firewall*, I completely glossed over any discussion of creating the **Network Address Translation** (**NAT**) rules that you would need for setting up an edge or gateway type of firewall. That's because there are several Linux distros that have been created specifically for this purpose. What if I told you, that some of them also include a full implementation of Snort?

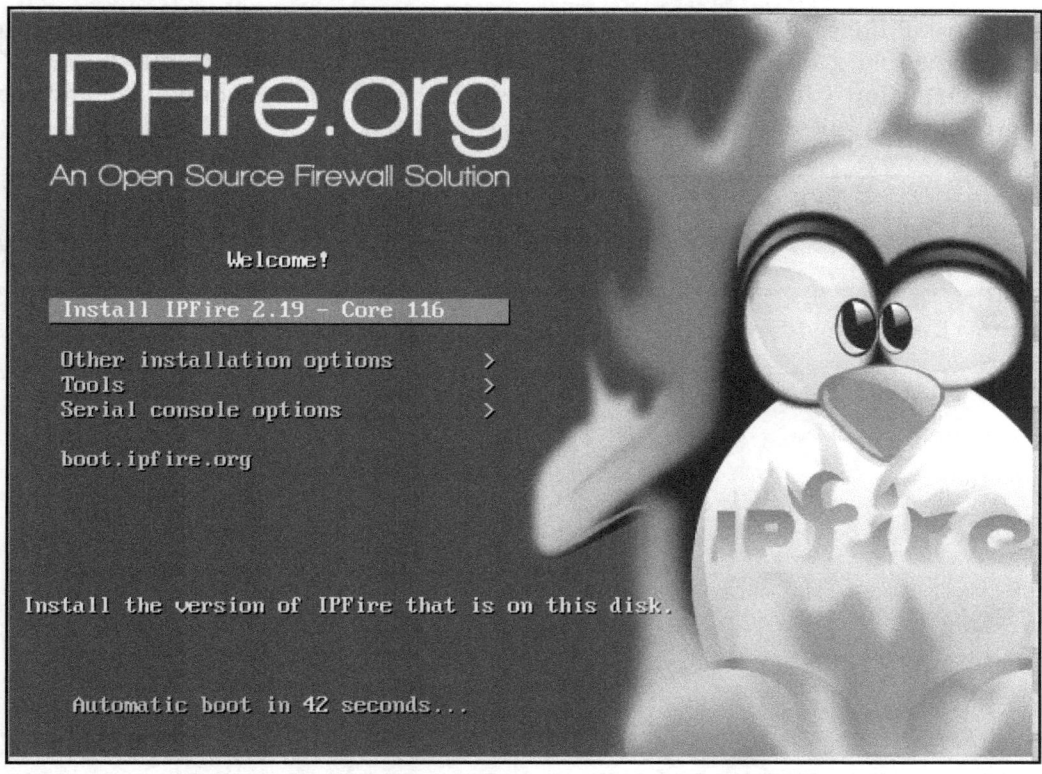

IPFire is completely free of charge, and it only takes a few minutes to set up. You install it on a machine with at least two network interface adapters and configure it to match your network configuration. It's a proxy-type of a firewall, which means that in addition to doing normal firewall-type packet inspection, it also includes caching, content-filtering, and NAT capabilities. You can set up IPFire in a number of different configurations:

- On a computer with two network interface adapters, you can have one connected to the internet, and the other connected to the internal LAN.
- With three network adapters, you can have one connection to the internet, one to the internal LAN, and one to the **Demilitarized Zone** (**DMZ**), where you have your internet-facing servers.
- With a fourth network adapter, you can have all the above, plus protection for a wireless network.

After you install IPFire, you'll need to use the web browser of your normal workstation to navigate to the IPFire dashboard. Under the **Services** menu, you'll see an entry for **Intrusion Detection**. Click on that to get to this screen, where you can download and enable the Snort detection rules:

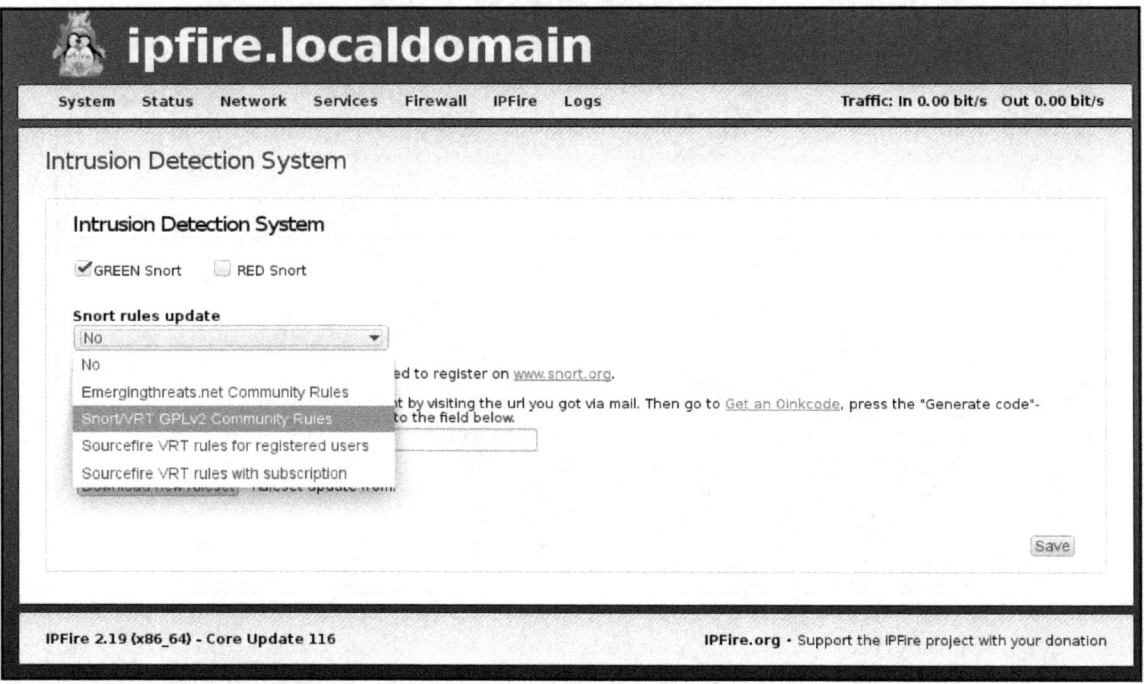

There's really only one slight bit of manual tweaking that you might need to do from the command line. That is, you might want to go into the rules directory and make sure that the rules that you want to enable are enabled. On my demo machine, I installed the community rules and the emerging threat rules:

```
[root@ipfire rules]# ls -l
total 19336
-rw-r--r-- 1 nobody nobody    1656 Dec 19 06:01 BSD-License.txt
-rw-r--r-- 1 nobody nobody    2638 Dec 19 06:01 classification.config
-rw-r--r-- 1 nobody nobody 1478085 Dec 19 06:01 community.rules
-rw-r--r-- 1 nobody nobody   15700 Dec 19 06:01 compromised-ips.txt
-rw-r--r-- 1 nobody nobody  378690 Dec 19 06:01 emerging-activex.rules
-rw-r--r-- 1 nobody nobody   79832 Dec 19 06:01 emerging-
attack_response.rules
-rw-r--r-- 1 nobody nobody   82862 Dec 19 06:01 emerging-
botcc.portgrouped.rules
```

```
-rw-r--r-- 1 nobody nobody   249176 Dec 19 06:01 emerging-botcc.rules
-rw-r--r-- 1 nobody nobody    34658 Dec 19 06:01 emerging-chat.rules
. . .
. . .
-rw-r--r-- 1 nobody nobody     1375 Dec 19 06:01 reference.config
-rw-r--r-- 1 nobody nobody  3691529 Dec 19 06:01 sid-msg.map
-rw-r--r-- 1 nobody nobody        0 Dec 19 06:01 snort-2.9.0-enhanced-
open.txt
-rw-r--r-- 1 nobody nobody    53709 Dec 19 06:01 unicode.map
-rw-r--r-- 1 nobody nobody    21078 Dec 19 04:46 VRT-License.txt
[root@ipfire rules]#
```

 When you first install IPFire, the only user account that it sets up is for the root user. However, the tools are there to create a normal user account and give it sudo privileges. I haven't yet done that on this machine because I wanted to show you the default configuration. But, I definitely would do it on a production machine. I would then disable the root account.

When you open one of these rules files, you'll see that a lot of them are disabled and relatively few are enabled. The disabled rules have a # sign in front of them, as do these two rules from the community.rules file:

```
#alert tcp $HOME_NET 2589 -> $EXTERNAL_NET any (msg:"MALWARE-BACKDOOR -
Dagger_1.4.0"; flow:to_client,established; content:"2|00 00 00 06 00 00
00|Drives|24 00|"; depth:16; metadata:ruleset community; classtype:misc-
activity; sid:105; rev:14;)
#alert tcp $EXTERNAL_NET any -> $HOME_NET 7597 (msg:"MALWARE-BACKDOOR QAZ
Worm Client Login access"; flow:to_server,established;
content:"qazwsx.hsq"; metadata:ruleset community; reference:mcafee,98775;
classtype:misc-activity; sid:108; rev:11;)
```

You've probably also noted that each rule begins with the keyword, alert. You can use grep to do a quick check to see which rules in a file are enabled:

```
[root@ipfire rules]# grep ^alert community.rules | less
[root@ipfire rules]#
```

The ^ character means that I'm searching through the community.rules file for every line that begins with the word alert, without the preceding # sign. Piping the output into less is optional, but it can help you better see all of the output data. You can also search through all the files at once using a wildcard:

```
[root@ipfire rules]# grep ^alert *.rules | less
[root@ipfire rules]#
```

You'll want to look through the rules to see which you need and which you don't need. Enable the desired rule by removing the # sign from in front of it and disable an undesired rule by placing a # sign in front of it.

Unfortunately, IPFire doesn't include a graphical frontend for visualizing Snort data, but it does come with an IDS log viewer:

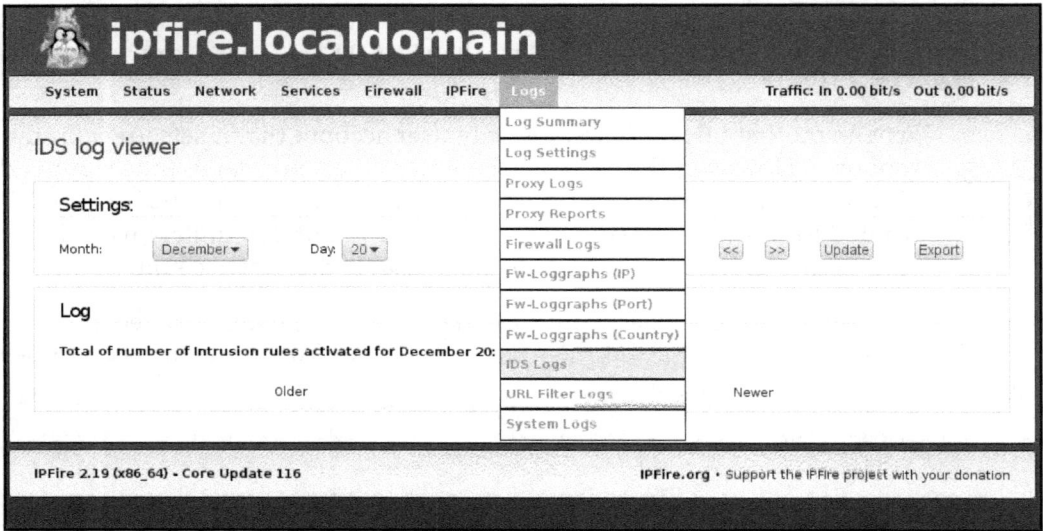

IPFire also has a lot of other cool features that I haven't yet mentioned. These include built-in **Virtual Private Network** (**VPN**) capabilities, a built-in DHCP server, a built-in dynamic DNS server, and Quality of Service controls. The best part is that it's totally free of charge unless you want to buy a subscription to always get the most up-to-date Snort rules.

 You can download IPFire from their website: `https://www.ipfire.org/`.

Using Security Onion

Okay, so maybe the firewall appliance with the built-in Snort isn't what you need right now. Maybe what you need instead is a full-blown NIDS. But, you're a busy person who needs something quick and easy, and your boss has put you on a rather strict budget. So, what do you do?

Security Onion is a free-of-charge specialty Linux distro that's built on top of the Xubuntu **Long-term Support** (**LTS**) distro. It includes a full implementation of Snort, complete with just about every graphical goody you can imagine to help you visualize what's happening on your network. If you can install a Linux distro and do some point-and-click configuration after the installation, then you can install Security Onion.

Note that the Xubuntu LTS version on which Security Onion is based is always at least one version behind the current LTS version of Xubuntu. At the time of writing, the current Xubuntu LTS version is version 16.04, whereas Security Onion is still based on Xubuntu 14.04. But, that may change by the time you read this book.

Also, if you want to try out Security Onion, you can set it up in a VirtualBox virtual machine. When you create the virtual machine, set it up with two network adapters, both in *Bridged* mode. For best performance, allocate at least 3 GB of memory.

Once you've finished installing the operating system, the configuration is just a simple matter of double-clicking the **Setup** icon and then following through with the dialog boxes:

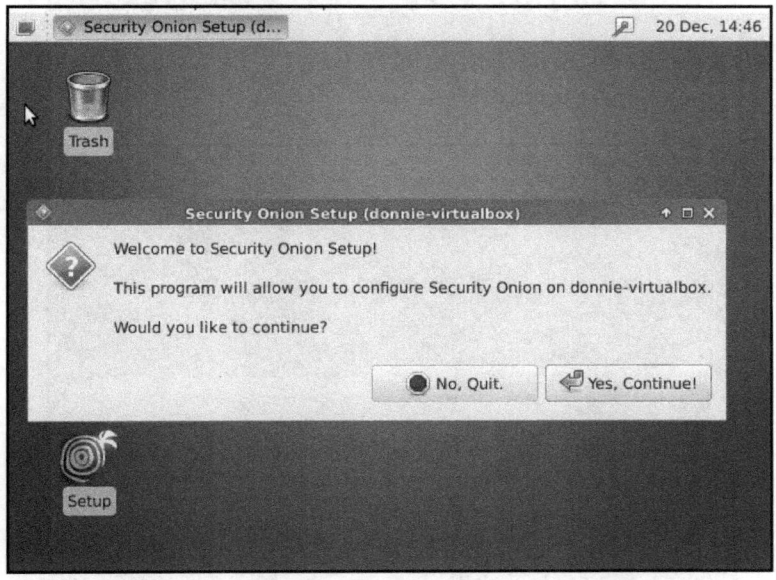

For setting up a machine with sensor capabilities, you'll need a machine with two interface cards. One interface, which will have an IP address assigned to it, will be the management interface:

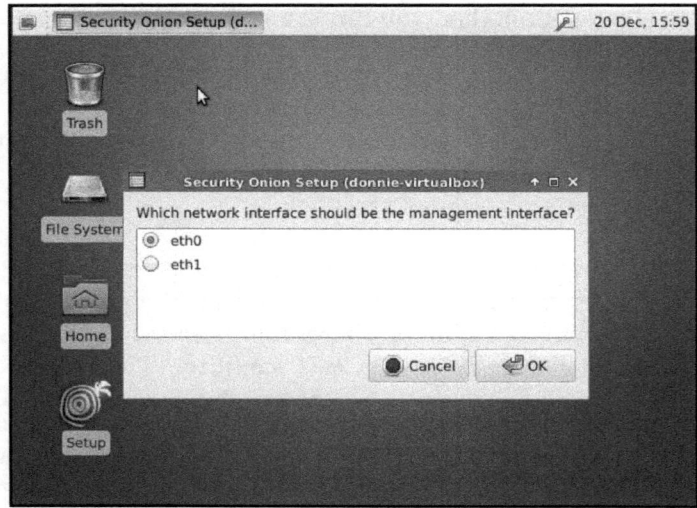

You can set the management interface to automatically get an IP address via DHCP, but it's much better to assign a static IP address:

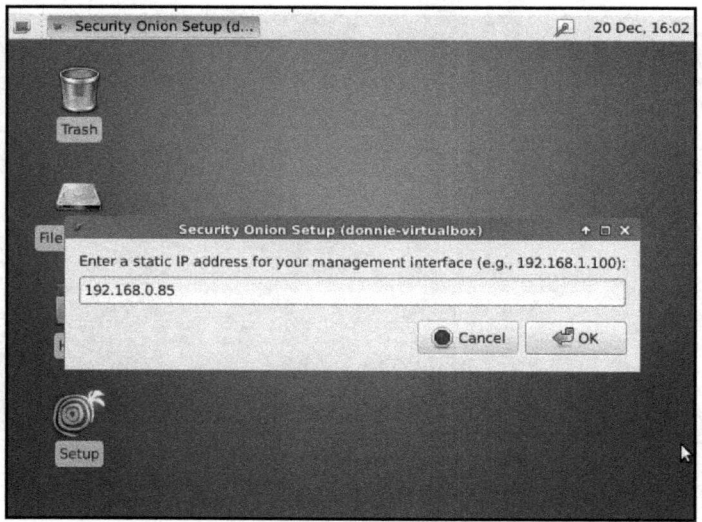

You'll use the other network adapter as the sniffing interface. You won't assign an IP address to it because you want that interface to be invisible to the bad guys:

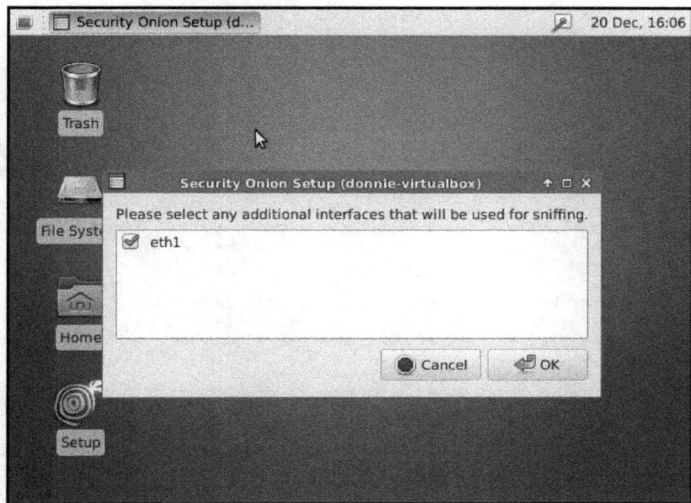

After you confirm the network configuration that you've selected, you'll reboot the machine:

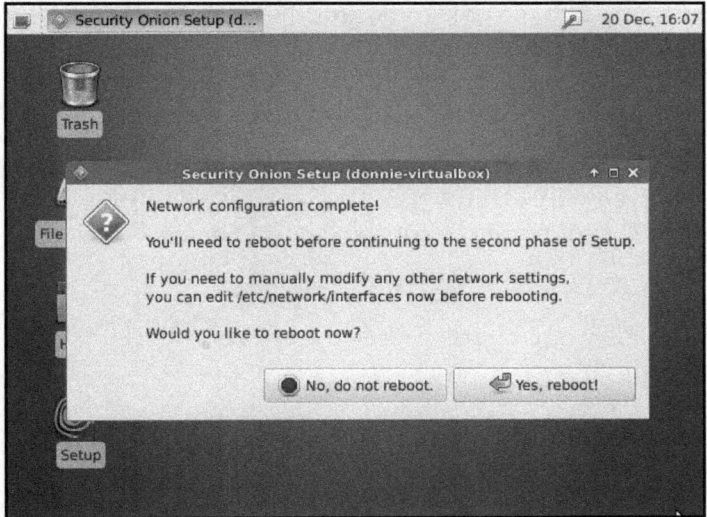

Once the machine has rebooted, double-click on the **Setup** icon again, but this time choose to skip the network configuration. For a first-time user of Security Onion, **Evaluation Mode** is quite helpful because it automatically chooses the most correct options for most stuff.

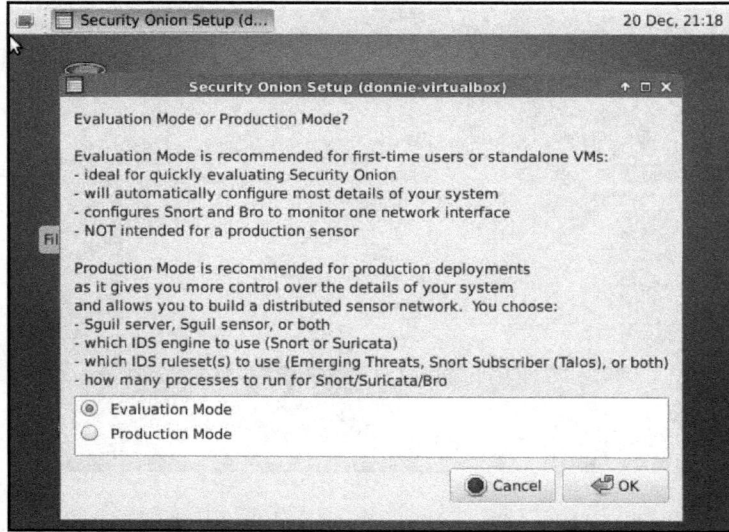

From here on out, it's just a matter of confirming which network interface will be the sniffer interface and filling in login credentials for the different graphical frontends. And then, after waiting a few moments for the setup utility to download Snort rules and perform the final configuration steps, you'll have your very own operational NIDS. Now I ask, what could be easier?

Security Onion comes with several different graphical frontends. My favorite is Squert, which is shown here. Even with just the default set of detection rules, I'm already seeing some interesting stuff. The following screenshot shows Squert:

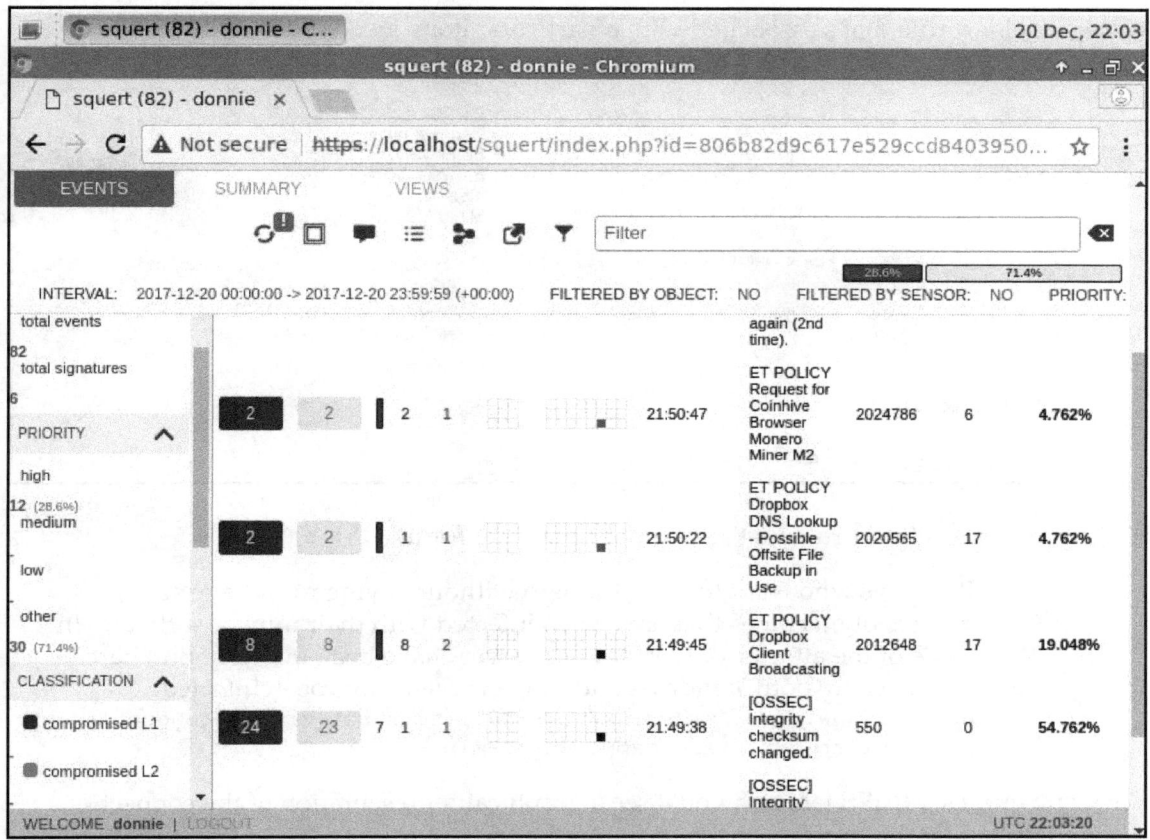

For one thing, I see that somebody on the network is mining some Monero cryptocoin. Well, actually, I'm the one who's doing it, so it's okay. But, that is a good thing to be able to detect because bad guys have been known to plant Monero mining software on corporate servers for their own benefit. Monero cryptocoin mining puts a big load on a server's CPUs, so it's not something that you want on your servers. Also, some sneaky website operators have placed JavaScript code on their web pages that cause any computer that visits them to start mining Monero. So, this rule is also good for protecting desktop systems.

Another thing I see is Dropbox client broadcasting, which again is okay because I'm a Dropbox user. But, that's something else that you may not want to have on a corporate network.

To see the Snort rule that's associated with a particular item, just click on it:

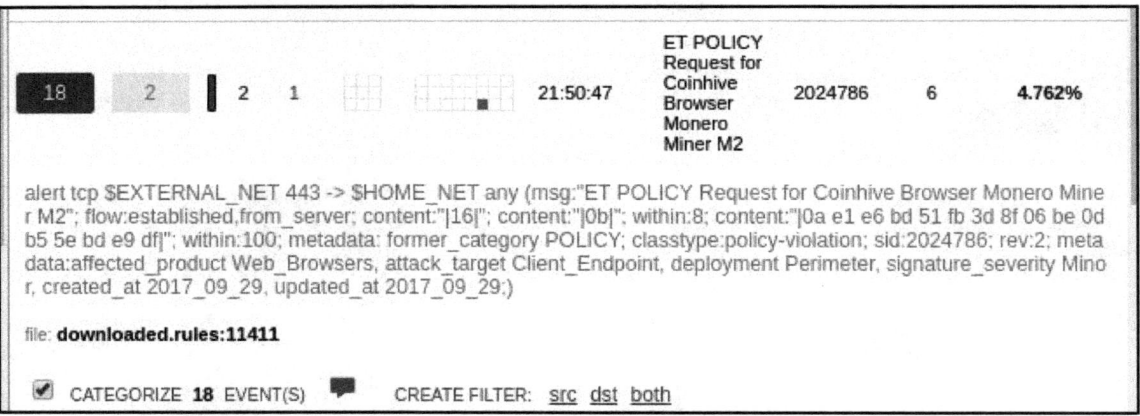

It's just a standard Snort rule that's already been set up for us.

TIP

Bad guys who want to mine Monero without paying for it have set up botnets of machines that have been infected with their mining software. In some of the attacks, only Windows servers have been infected. But, here's a case where both Windows and Linux servers have been infected: `https://www.v3.co.uk/v3-uk/news/3023348/cyber-crooks-conducting-sophisticated-malware-campaign-to-mine-monero`

Click on Squert's **VIEWS** tab, and you'll see a graphical representation of the connections that your machines have established:

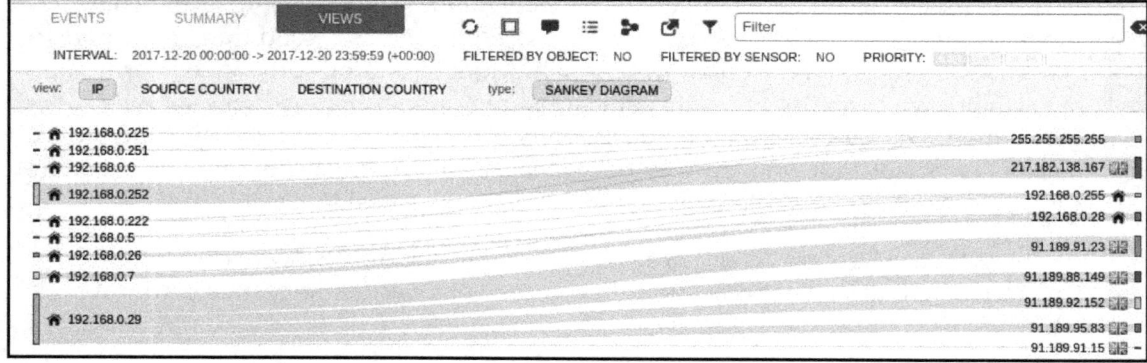

There's still a lot more than I could show you about both Security Onion and Snort, but alas, space doesn't permit. I've given you the gist of it, now go try it for yourself.

I know that I made this Snort/Security Onion thing look rather easy, but there's a lot more to it than what I've been able to show you. On a large network, you might see a lot of traffic that doesn't make a lot of sense unless you know how to interpret the information that Snort presents to you. You might also need to fine-tune your Snort rules in order to see the anomalies that you want to see, without generating false positives. Or, you might even find the need to write your own custom Snort rules to handle unusual situations. Fortunately, the Security Onion folk do provide training, both on-site and online. You can find out more about it at the following website:
`https://securityonionsolutions.com/`.

Scanning and hardening with Lynis

Lynis is yet another FOSS tool that you can use to scan your systems for vulnerabilities and bad security configurations. It comes as a portable shell script that you can use not only on Linux, but also on a variety of different Unix systems and Unix-like systems. It's a multipurpose tool, which you can use for compliance auditing, vulnerability scanning, or hardening. Unlike most vulnerability scanners, you install and run Lynis on the system that you want to scan. According to the creator of Lynis, this allows for more in-depth scanning.

The Lynis scanning tool is available as a free-of-charge version, but its scanning capabilities are somewhat limited. If you need all that Lynis has to offer, you'll need to purchase an enterprise license.

Installing Lynis on Red Hat/CentOS

Red Hat/CentOS users will find an up-to-date version of Lynis in the EPEL repository. So, if you have EPEL installed, as I showed you in `Chapter 1`, *Running Linux on a Virtual Environment*, installation is just a simple matter of doing:

```
sudo yum install lynis
```

Installing Lynis on Ubuntu

Ubuntu has Lynis in its own repository, but which version you get depends on which version of Ubuntu you have. The Ubuntu 16.04 LTS repository has a version that's fairly far behind what's current. The version in the Ubuntu 17.10 repository is newer, but still not completely up to date. In either case, the command to install Lynis is:

```
sudo apt install lynis
```

If you want the newest version for Ubuntu or if you want to use Lynis on operating systems that don't have it in their repositories, you can download it from the author's website.

 You can download Lynis from `https://cisofy.com/downloads/lynis/`. The cool thing about this is that once you download it, you can use it on any Linux, Unix, or Unix-like operating system. (This even includes MacOS, which I just now confirmed by running it on my old Mac Pro that's running with macOS High Sierra.)

Since the executable file is nothing but a common shell script, there's no need to perform an actual installation. All you need to do is to extract the archive file, `cd` into the resultant directory, and run Lynis from there:

```
tar xzvf lynis-2.5.7.tar.gz
cd lynis
sudo ./lynis -h
```

The `lynis -h` command shows you the help screen, with all of the Lynis commands that you need to know.

Scanning with Lynis

Lynis commands work the same regardless of which operating system that you want to scan. The only difference is that if you're running it from the archive file that you downloaded from the website, you would `cd` into the `lynis` directory and precede the `lynis` commands with a `./`. (That's because, for security reasons, your own home directory isn't in the path setting that allows the shell to automatically find executable files.)

To scan your system that has Lynis installed, follow this:

```
sudo lynis audit system
```

To scan a system on which you just downloaded the archive file, follow this:

```
cd lynis
sudo ./lynis audit system
```

Running Lynis from the shell script in your home directory presents you with this message:

```
donnie@ubuntu:~/lynis$ sudo ./lynis audit system
[sudo] password for donnie:


[!] Change ownership of /home/donnie/lynis/include/functions to 'root' or
similar (found: donnie with UID 1000).

    Command:
       # chown 0:0 /home/donnie/lynis/include/functions

[X] Security check failed

    Why do I see this error?
    --------------------------------
    This is a protection mechanism to prevent the root user from executing
user created files. The files may be altered, or including malicious pieces
of script.

    What can I do?
    ----------------------
    Option 1) Check if a trusted user created the files (e.g. due to using
Git, Homebrew or similar).
            If you trust these files, you can decide to continue this run
by pressing ENTER.

    Option 2) Change ownership of the related files (or full directory).

       Commands (full directory):
          # cd ..
          # chown -R 0:0 lynis
          # cd lynis
          # ./lynis audit system

[ Press ENTER to continue, or CTRL+C to cancel ]
```

That's not hurting anything, so you can just hit *Enter* to continue. Or, if seeing this message really bothers you, you can change ownership of the Lynis files to the root user, as the message tells you. For now, I'll just press *Enter*.

Running a Lynis scan in this manner is similar to running an OpenSCAP scan against a generic security profile. The major difference is that OpenSCAP has an automatic remediation feature, but Lynis doesn't. Lynis tells you what it finds and suggests how to fix what it perceives to be a problem, but it doesn't fix anything for you.

Space doesn't permit me to show the entire scan output, but I can show you a couple of example snippets:

```
[+] Boot and services
------------------------------------
  - Service Manager                                 [ systemd ]
  - Checking UEFI boot                              [ DISABLED ]
  - Checking presence GRUB                          [ OK ]
  - Checking presence GRUB2                         [ FOUND ]
    - Checking for password protection              [ WARNING ]
  - Check running services (systemctl)              [ DONE ]
        Result: found 21 running services
  - Check enabled services at boot (systemctl)      [ DONE ]
        Result: found 28 enabled services
  - Check startup files (permissions)               [ OK ]
```

The warning message shows that I don't have password protection for my GRUB2 bootloader. That may or may not be a big deal because the only way someone can exploit that is to gain physical access to the machine. If it's a server that's locked away in a room that only a few trusted personnel can access, then I'm not going to worry about it, unless rules from an applicable regulatory agency dictate that I do. If it's a desktop machine that's out in an open cubicle, then I would definitely fix that. (We'll look at GRUB password protection in Chapter 10, *Security Tips and Tricks for the Busy Bee*.)

In the File systems section, we see some items with the SUGGESTION flag:

```
[+] File systems
------------------------------------
  - Checking mount points
    - Checking /home mount point                    [ SUGGESTION
]
    - Checking /tmp mount point                     [ SUGGESTION
]
    - Checking /var mount point                     [ SUGGESTION
]
  - Query swap partitions (fstab)                   [ OK ]
  - Testing swap partitions                         [ OK ]
  - Testing /proc mount (hidepid)                   [ SUGGESTION
]
  - Checking for old files in /tmp                  [ OK ]
  - Checking /tmp sticky bit                        [ OK ]
```

```
    - ACL support root file system                      [ ENABLED ]
    - Mount options of /                                [ NON DEFAULT
]
    - Checking Locate database                          [ FOUND ]
    - Disable kernel support of some filesystems
       - Discovered kernel modules: cramfs freevxfs hfs hfsplus jffs2 udf
```

Exactly what Lynis suggests comes near the end of the output:

```
. . .
. . .

  * To decrease the impact of a full /home file system, place /home on a
separated partition [FILE-6310]
      https://cisofy.com/controls/FILE-6310/

  * To decrease the impact of a full /tmp file system, place /tmp on a
separated partition [FILE-6310]
      https://cisofy.com/controls/FILE-6310/

  * To decrease the impact of a full /var file system, place /var on a
separated partition [FILE-6310]
      https://cisofy.com/controls/FILE-6310/
. . .
. . .
```

The last thing we'll look at is the scan details section at the end of the output:

```
Lynis security scan details:

Hardening index : 67 [############        ]
Tests performed : 218
Plugins enabled : 0

Components:
- Firewall              [V]
- Malware scanner       [X]

Lynis Modules:
- Compliance Status     [?]
- Security Audit        [V]
- Vulnerability Scan    [V]

Files:
- Test and debug information     : /var/log/lynis.log
- Report data                    : /var/log/lynis-report.dat
```

For `Components`, there's a red `X` by `Malware Scanner`. That's because I don't have ClamAV or `maldet` installed on this machine, so Lynis couldn't do a virus scan.

For `Lynis Modules`, we see a question mark by `Compliance Status`. That's because this feature is reserved for the Enterprise version of Lynis, which requires a paid subscription. As we saw in the previous chapter, you have OpenSCAP profiles to make a system compliant with several different security standards, and it doesn't cost you anything. With Lynis, you have to pay for the compliance profiles, but you have a wider range from which to choose. In addition to the compliance profiles that OpenSCAP offers, Lynis also offers profiles for HIPAA and Sarbanes-Oxley compliance.

If you're based here in the United States, you most surely know what HIPAA and Sarbanes-Oxley are and whether they apply to you. If you're not in the United States, then you probably don't need to worry about them.

Having said that, if you work in the healthcare industry, even if you're not in the United States, the HIPAA profile can give you guidance about how to protect private data for patients.

The last thing I want to say about Lynis is about the Enterprise version. In this screenshot from their website, you can see the current pricing and the differences between the different subscription plans:

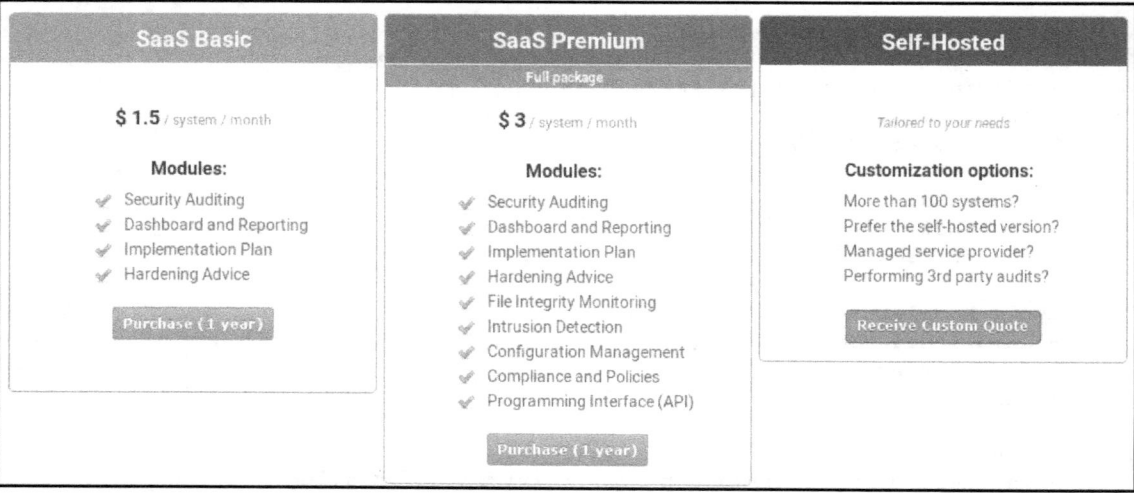

As you can see, you have choices.

 You'll find information about pricing at this website:
`https://cisofy.com/pricing/`.

That pretty much wraps it up for our discussion of Lynis. Next, let's look at an *external* vulnerability scanner.

Finding vulnerabilities with OpenVAS

The **Open Vulnerability Assessment Scanner (OpenVAS)** is something that you would use to perform remote vulnerability scans. You can scan a single machine, a group of similar machines, or an entire network. It's not included in the repositories of the major Linux distros, so the best way to get it is to install one of the specialty security distros.

The big three security distros are Kali Linux, Parrot Linux, and Black Arch. They're aimed at security researchers and penetration testers, but they contain tools that would also be good for just a normal security administrator of either the Linux or Windows variety. OpenVAS is one such tool. All three of these three security distros have their unique advantages and disadvantages, but as Kali is the most popular, we'll go with it for the demos.

 You can download Kali Linux from `https://www.kali.org/downloads/`.

When you go to the Kali download page, you'll see lots of choices. If you're like me and don't like the default Gnome 3 desktop environment, you can choose something else. I'm personally an LXDE guy, so I'll go with it:

Kali 64 bit LXDE	HTTP | Torrent	2.7G	2017.3	4dd54f9aeecbec612af3dab581485415d817ddd6db251c9c880ff2d14657497e

Kali is built from Debian Linux, so installing it is pretty much the same as installing Debian. The one exception is that the Kali installer lets you create a password for the root user, but it doesn't let you create a normal, non-root user account. That's because pretty much everything you do with Kali requires you to be logged in as the root user. I know that flies in the face of what I've been telling you about not logging in as `root` and about using `sudo` from a normal user account instead. However, most of the stuff you need to do with Kali doesn't work with `sudo`. Besides, Kali isn't meant to be used as a general-purpose distro, and you'll be okay logging in as a root as long as you only use Kali as it was intended to be used.

> OpenVAS is a rather memory-hungry program, so if you're installing Kali in a virtual machine, be sure to allocate at least three GB of memory.

The first thing you'll want to do after installing Kali is to update it, which is done in the same way that you'd update any Debian/Ubuntu-type of distro. Then, install OpenVAS, as follows:

```
apt update
apt dist-upgrade
apt install openvas
```

After the OpenVAS installation completes, you'll need to run a script that will create the security certificates and download the vulnerability database:

```
openvas-setup
```

This will take a long time, so you might as well go grab a sandwich and a coffee while it's running. When it's finally done, you'll be presented with the password that you'll use to log in to OpenVAS. Write it down and keep it in a safe place:

```
sent 757 bytes  received 46,858,055 bytes  1,217,112.00 bytes/sec
total size is 46,844,168  speedup is 1.00
/usr/sbin/openvasmd
User created with password '4c739e0f-1b84-4bf2-b71c-68d2adf106a8'.
root@kali:~#
```

You can control and update OpenVAS from the applications menu:

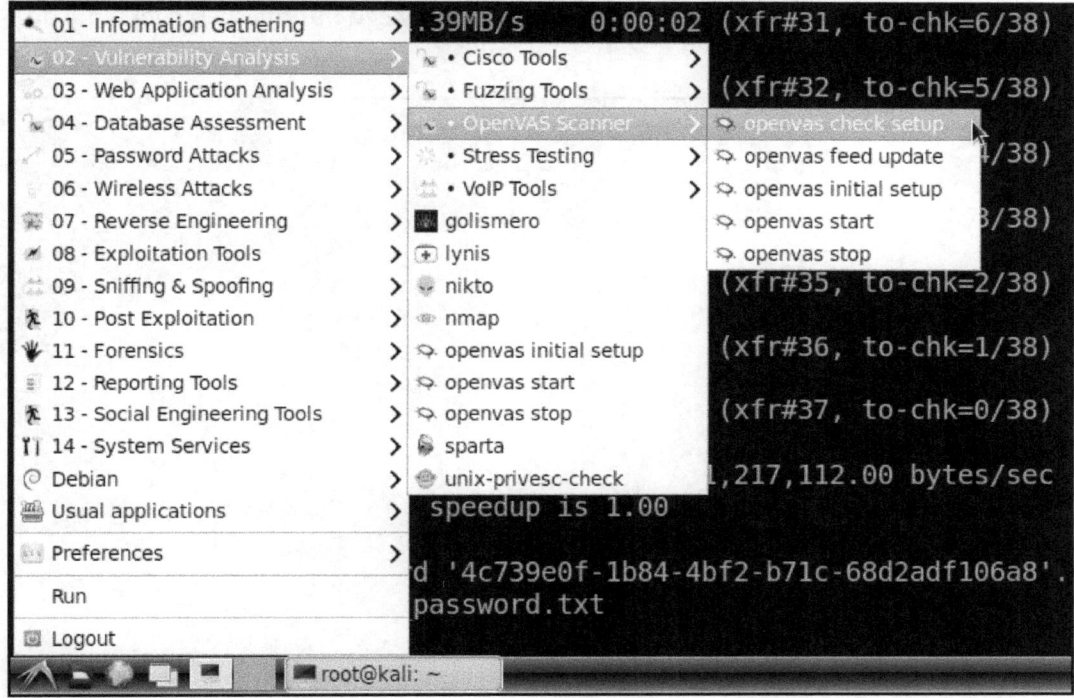

On that menu, click on **openvas start**. Then, open Firefox and navigate to `https://localhost:9392`. You'll get a security alert because OpenVAS uses a self-signed security certificate, but that's okay. Just click on the **Advanced** button, then click on **Add Exception**:

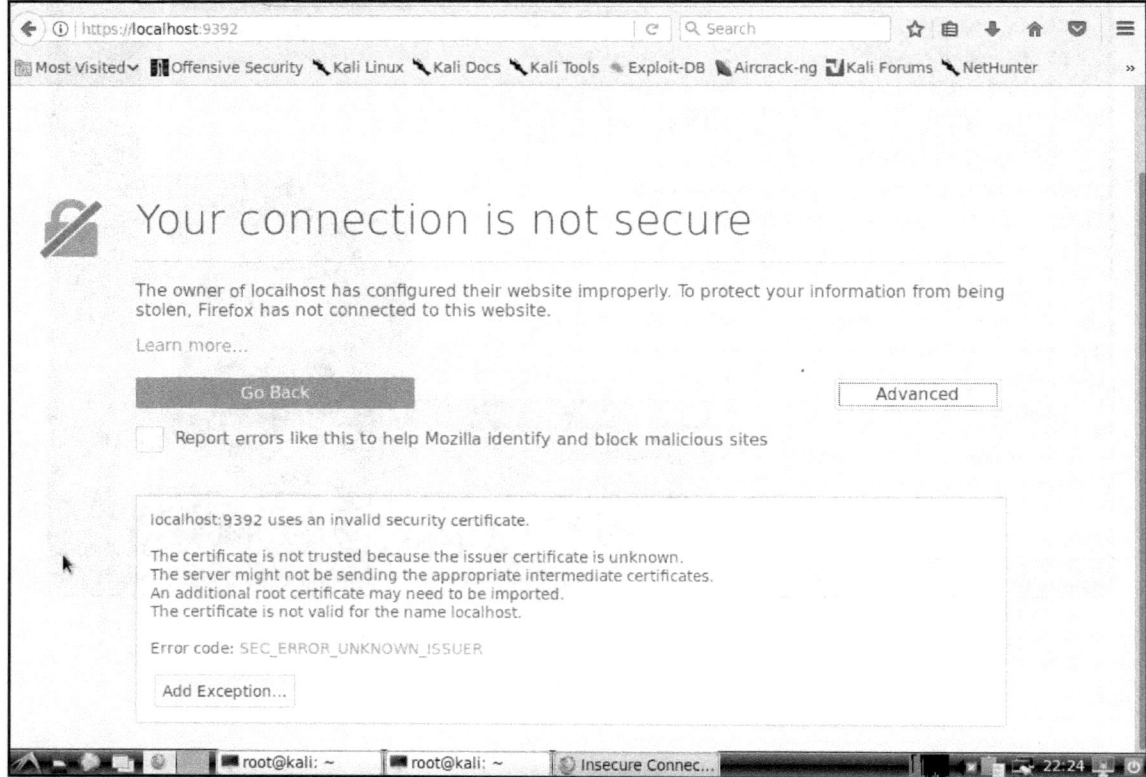

At the login page, enter `admin` as the user and then enter the password that got generated by the `openvas-setup` script.

Now, there's all kinds of fancy stuff that you can do with OpenVAS, but for now, we'll just look at how to do a basic vulnerability scan. To begin, select **Tasks** from the **Scans** menu on the OpenVAS dashboard:

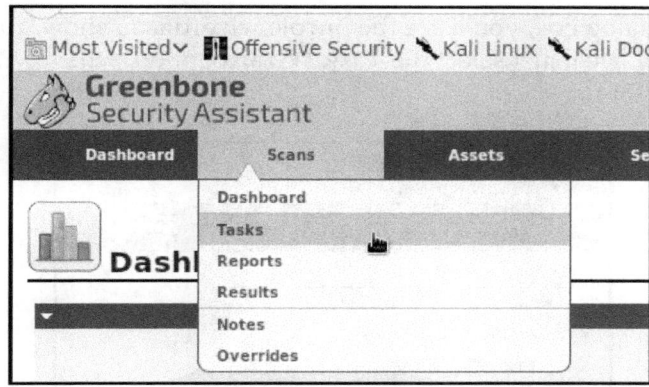

This makes this dialog box pop up, telling you to use the wizard. (Yes indeed, we're off to see the wizard.):

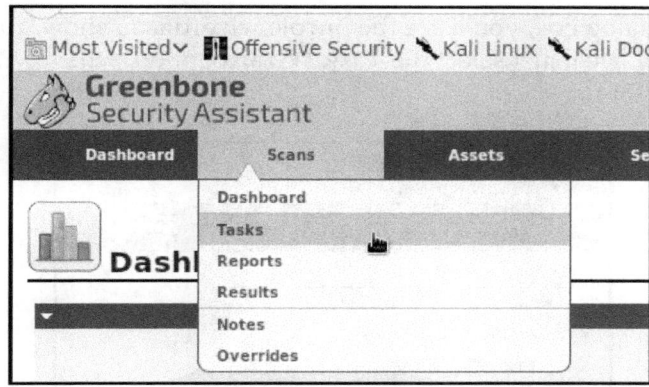

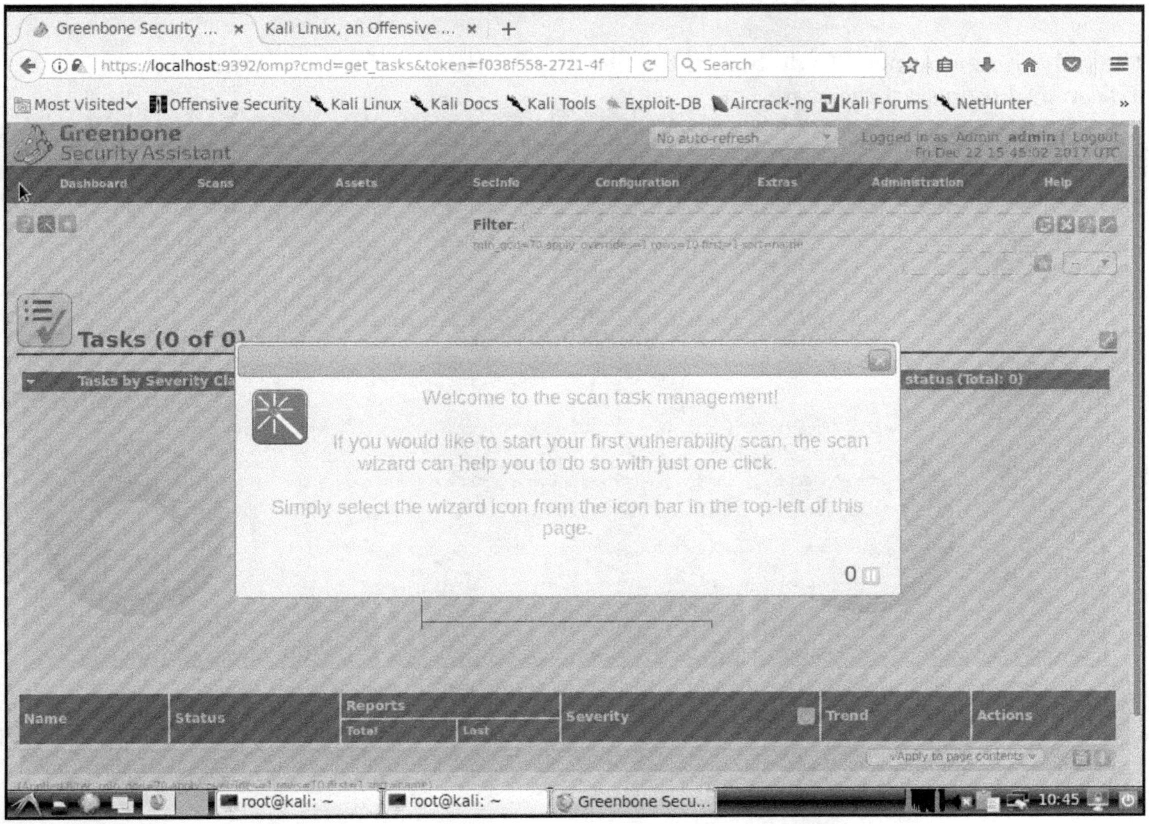

After you close the dialog box, you'll see the purple wizard icon show up in the upper left-hand corner. For now, we'll just select the **Task Wizard** option, which will choose all of the default scan settings for us:

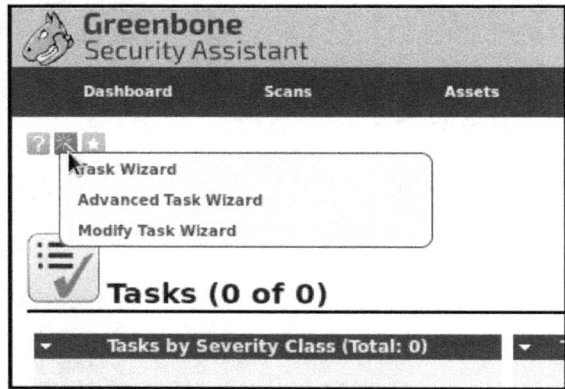

The only thing you need to do here is to enter the IP address of the machine that you want to scan and then start the scan:

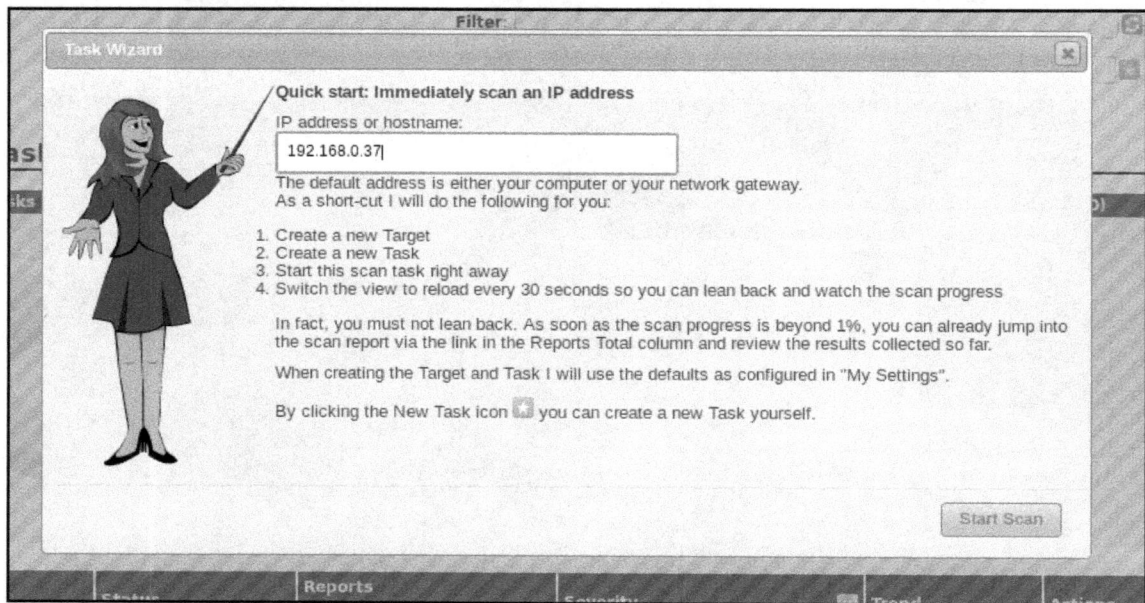

The scan will take some time, so you might as well go grab a sandwich and a coffee.

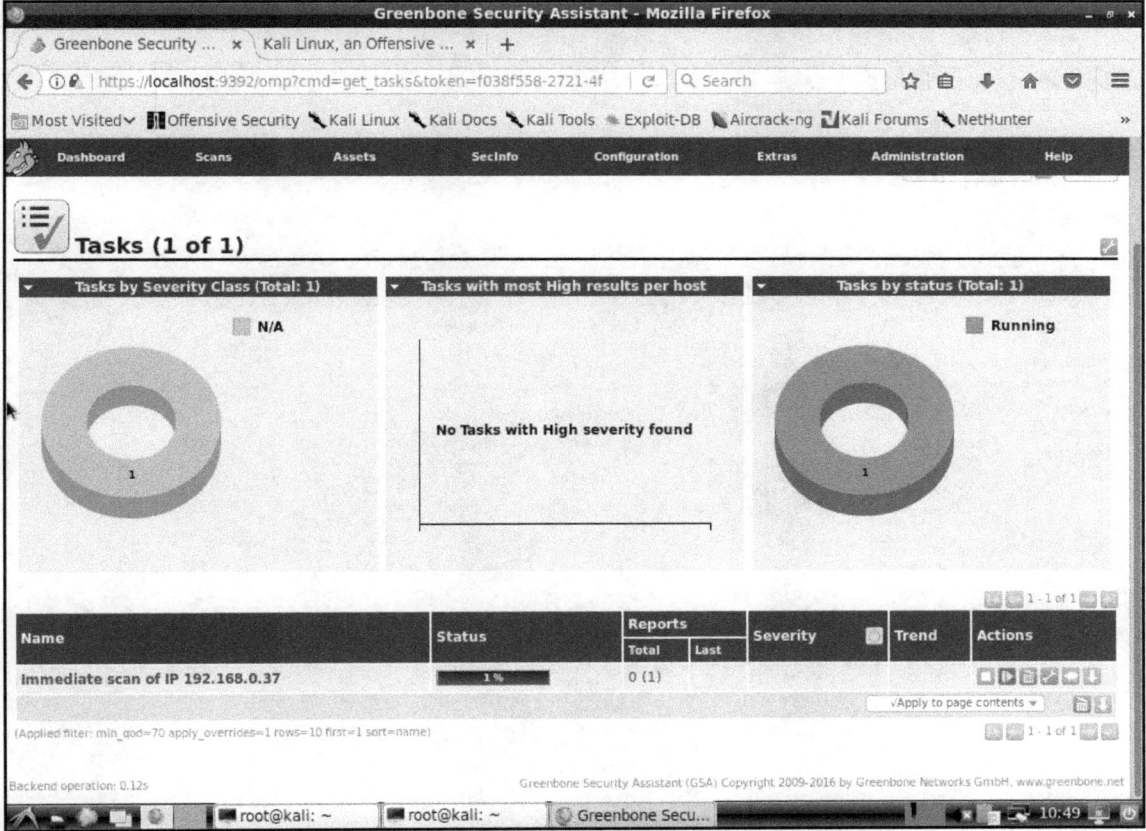

The type of scan that you're doing is named **Full and Fast**, which isn't the most comprehensive type of scan. To select another type of scan and to configure other scan options, use the **Advanced Task Wizard** as shown in the following screenshot:

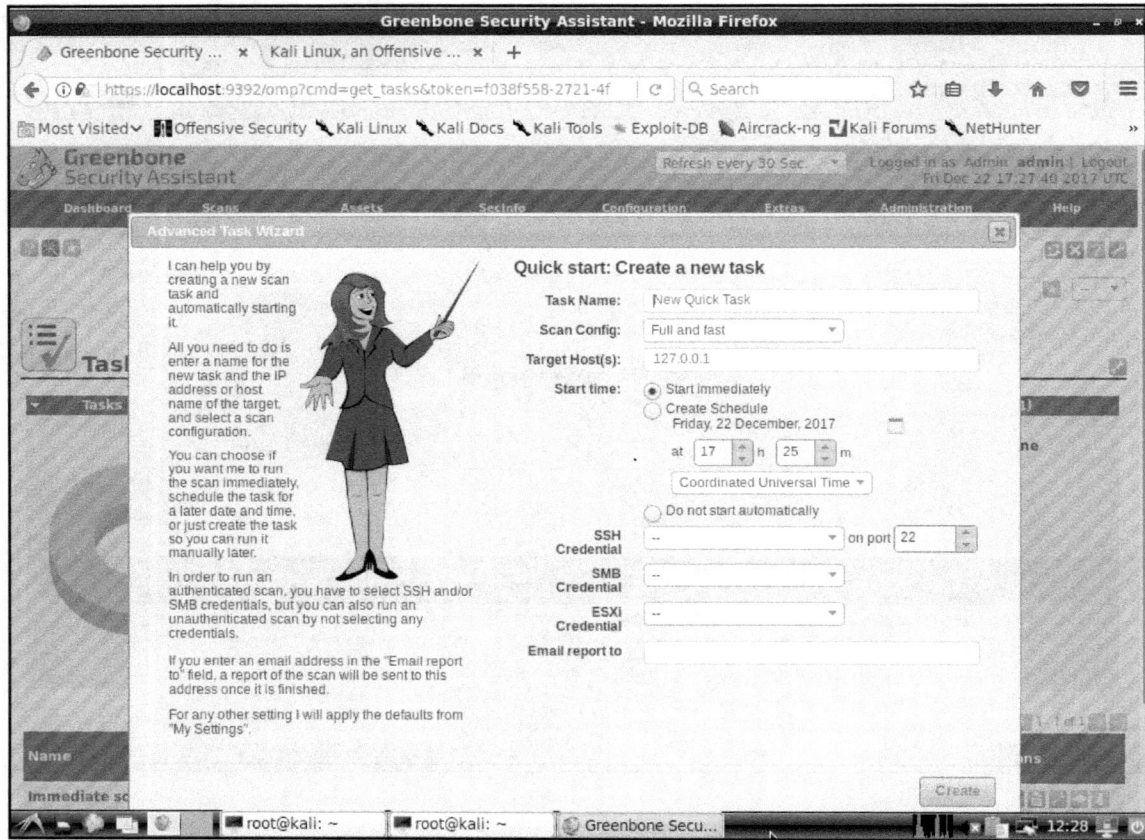

Here, you see the drop-down list of the different scan options:

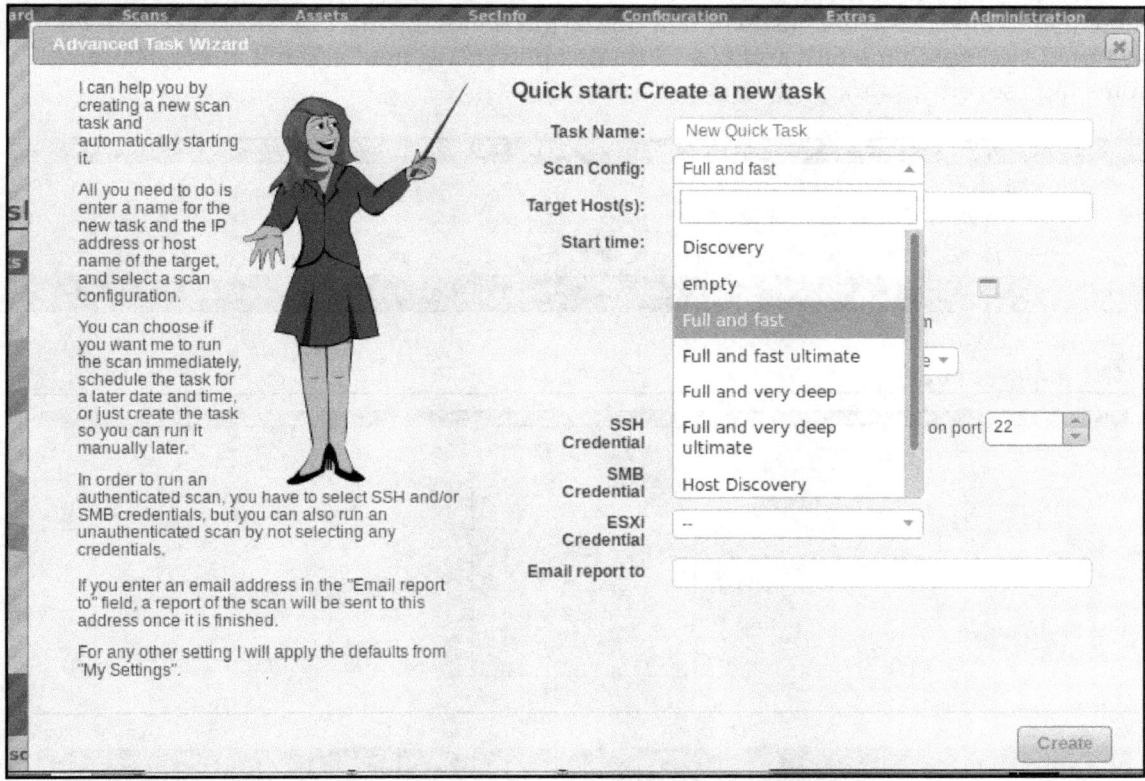

When I did the first scan with the default **Full and Fast** option, I didn't discover many problems. I had one of medium severity and 18 of low severity, and that was it. I knew that there had to be more problems than that due to the age of the machine that I was scanning, so I tried again with the **Full and fast ultimate** option. This time, I found more, including some high severity stuff:

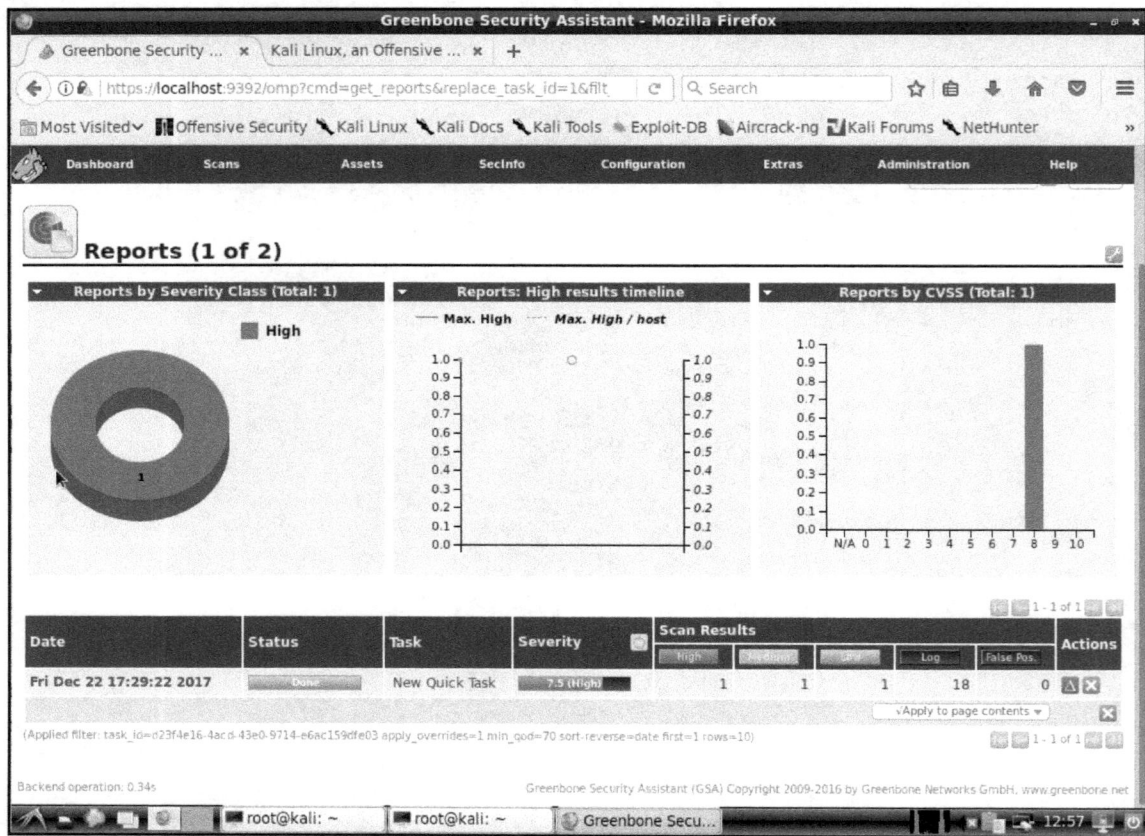

The report shows that my machine is using weak encryption algorithms for Secure Shell, which is classified as medium severity. It also has a print server vulnerability that's classified as a high-severity problem.

You also want to pay attention to the items that aren't flagged as vulnerabilities. For example, the **VNC security types** item shows that port 5900 is open. This means that the **Virtual Network Computing** (**VNC**) daemon is running, which allows users to remotely log in to this machine's desktop. If this machine were an internet-facing machine, that would be a real problem because there's no real security with VNC, the way there is with Secure Shell.

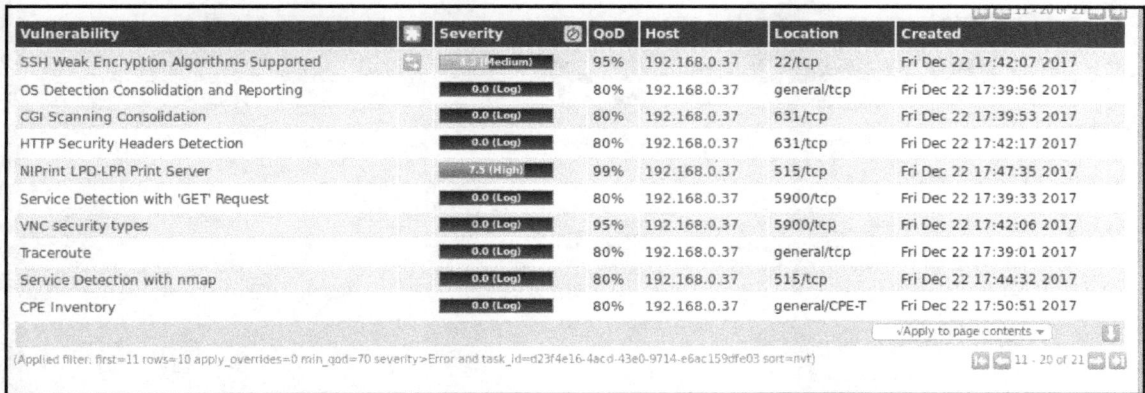

Vulnerability		Severity		QoD	Host	Location	Created
SSH Weak Encryption Algorithms Supported		4.3 (Medium)		95%	192.168.0.37	22/tcp	Fri Dec 22 17:42:07 2017
OS Detection Consolidation and Reporting		0.0 (Log)		80%	192.168.0.37	general/tcp	Fri Dec 22 17:39:56 2017
CGI Scanning Consolidation		0.0 (Log)		80%	192.168.0.37	631/tcp	Fri Dec 22 17:39:53 2017
HTTP Security Headers Detection		0.0 (Log)		80%	192.168.0.37	631/tcp	Fri Dec 22 17:42:17 2017
NIPrint LPD-LPR Print Server		7.5 (High)		99%	192.168.0.37	515/tcp	Fri Dec 22 17:47:35 2017
Service Detection with 'GET' Request		0.0 (Log)		80%	192.168.0.37	5900/tcp	Fri Dec 22 17:39:33 2017
VNC security types		0.0 (Log)		95%	192.168.0.37	5900/tcp	Fri Dec 22 17:42:06 2017
Traceroute		0.0 (Log)		80%	192.168.0.37	general/tcp	Fri Dec 22 17:39:01 2017
Service Detection with nmap		0.0 (Log)		80%	192.168.0.37	515/tcp	Fri Dec 22 17:44:32 2017
CPE Inventory		0.0 (Log)		80%	192.168.0.37	general/CPE-T	Fri Dec 22 17:50:51 2017

√Apply to page contents ▾

(Applied filter: first=11 rows=10 apply_overrides=0 min_qod=70 severity>Error and task_id=d23f4e16-4acd-43e0-9714-e6ac159dfe03 sort=nvt)   11 - 20 of 21

By clicking on the print server item, I can see an explanation of this vulnerability.

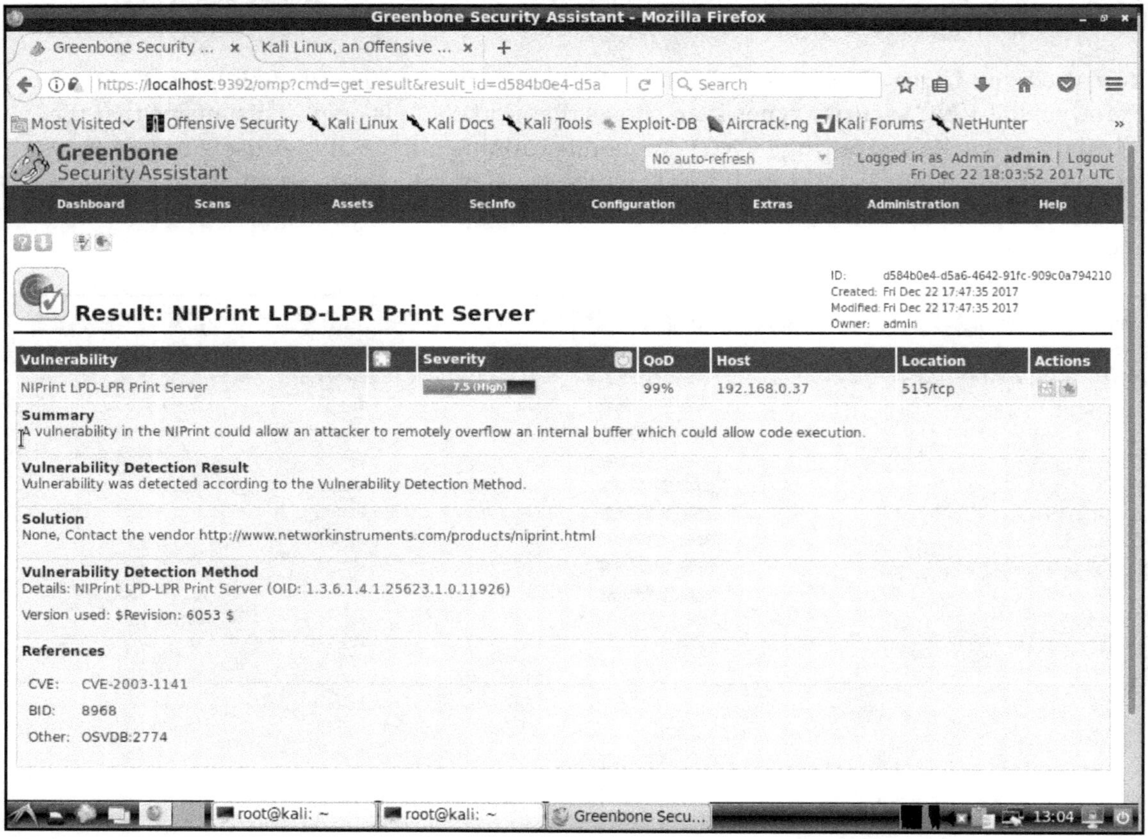

Keep in mind that the target machine, in this case, is a desktop machine. If it were a server, there's a good chance that we'd see even more problems.

And, that pretty much wraps things up for OpenVAS. As I said before, there's a lot of awesome stuff that you can do with it. But, what I've shown you here should be enough to get you started. Play around with it and try out the different scan options to see the difference in results.

> If you want to find out more about Kali Linux, you'll find a great selection of books about it at the Packt Publishing website.

Web server scanning with Nikto

OpenVAS, which we just looked at, is a general-purpose vulnerability scanner. It can find vulnerabilities for any kind of operating system or for any server daemon. However, as we've just seen, an OpenVAS scan can take a while to run, and it might be more than what you need.

Nikto is a special-purpose tool with only one purpose. That is, it's meant to scan web servers and only web servers. It's easy to install, easy to use, and capable of doing a comprehensive scan of a web server fairly quickly. And, although it's included in Kali Linux, you don't need Kali Linux to run it.

Nikto in Kali Linux

If you already have Kali Linux, you'll find that **nikto** is already installed under the **Vulnerability Analysis** menu:

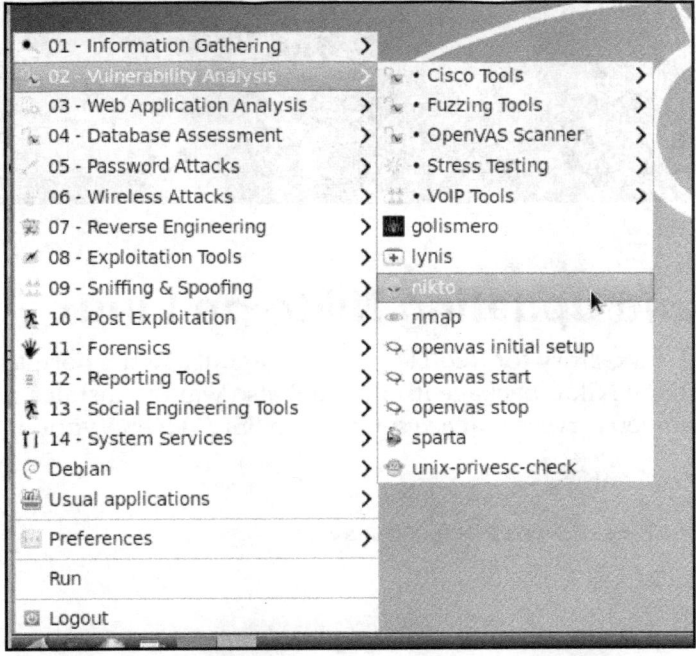

When you click on that menu item, you'll open a command-line terminal with a display of the Nikto help screen:

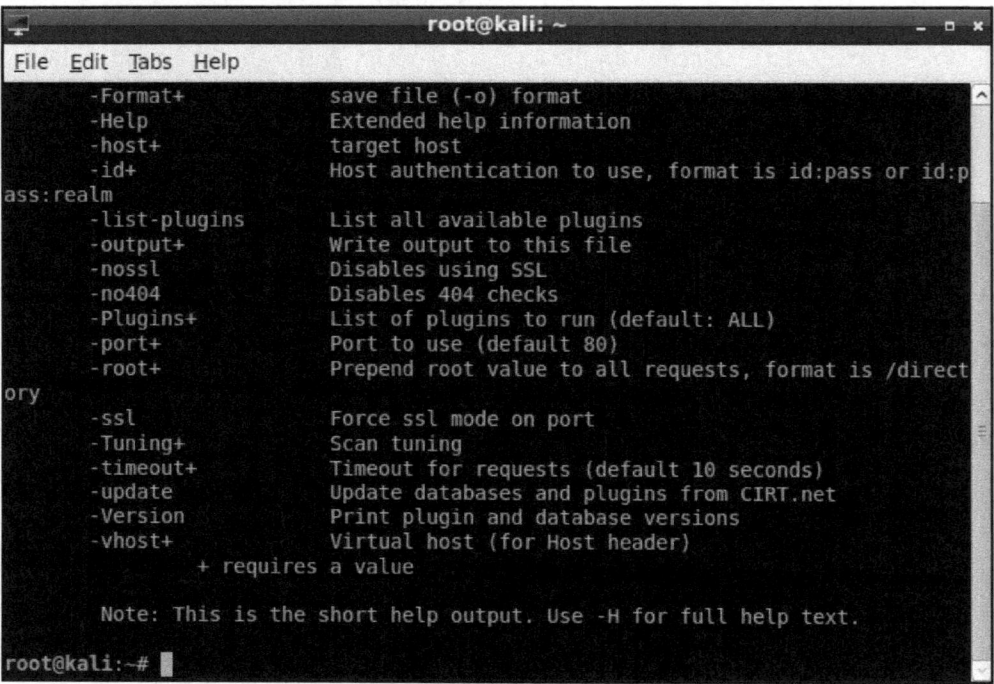

```
                    root@kali: ~                          _ □ ×
File  Edit  Tabs  Help
        -Format+           save file (-o) format
        -Help              Extended help information
        -host+             target host
        -id+               Host authentication to use, format is id:pass or id:p
ass:realm
        -list-plugins      List all available plugins
        -output+           Write output to this file
        -nossl             Disables using SSL
        -no404             Disables 404 checks
        -Plugins+          List of plugins to run (default: ALL)
        -port+             Port to use (default 80)
        -root+             Prepend root value to all requests, format is /direct
ory
        -ssl               Force ssl mode on port
        -Tuning+           Scan tuning
        -timeout+          Timeout for requests (default 10 seconds)
        -update            Update databases and plugins from CIRT.net
        -Version           Print plugin and database versions
        -vhost+            Virtual host (for Host header)
                + requires a value

     Note: This is the short help output. Use -H for full help text.

root@kali:~#
```

Installing and updating Nikto on Linux

Nikto is in the EPEL repository for Red Hat/CentOS, and it's in the normal repository for Ubuntu. Along with the Nikto package itself, you'll also want to install a package that allows Nikto to scan web servers that are set up with SSL/TLS encryption.

To install on Red Hat/CentOS:

```
sudo yum install nikto perl-Net-SSLeay
```

To install on Ubuntu:

```
sudo apt install nikto libnet-ssleay-perl
```

The next thing you'll want to do is to update the database of vulnerability signatures. But, at the time of writing this, there's a slight bug in the Red Hat/CentOS implementation. For some reason, the `docs` directory is missing, which means that the update functions won't be able to download the `CHANGES.txt` file to show you what changed with the new database updates. To fix that on your CentOS virtual machine, use this:

```
sudo mkdir /usr/share/nikto/docs
```

Keep in mind though that this could be fixed by the time you read this.

From here on out, things will work the same on either of your virtual machines. To update the vulnerability database, use this:

```
sudo nikto -update
```

Nikto itself doesn't require `sudo` privileges, but updating it does because it requires writing to a directory where normal users can't write.

Scanning a web server with Nikto

From here on out, you no longer need `sudo` privileges. So, you get a break from always having to type your password.

To do a simple scan, use the `-h` option to specify the target host:

```
nikto -h 192.168.0.9
nikto -h www.example.com
```

Let's look at some sample output:

```
+ Allowed HTTP Methods: POST, OPTIONS, GET, HEAD
+ OSVDB-396: /_vti_bin/shtml.exe: Attackers may be able to crash FrontPage
by requesting a DOS device, like shtml.exe/aux.htm -- a DoS was not
attempted.
+ /cgi-bin/guestbook.pl: May allow attackers to execute commands as the web
daemon.
+ /cgi-bin/wwwadmin.pl: Administration CGI?
+ /cgi-bin/Count.cgi: This may allow attackers to execute arbitrary
commands on the server
+ OSVDB-28260:
/_vti_bin/shtml.exe/_vti_rpc?method=server+version%3a4%2e0%2e2%2e2611:
Gives info about server settings.
+ OSVDB-3092:
/_vti_bin/_vti_aut/author.exe?method=list+documents%3a3%2e0%2e2%2e1706&serv
ice%5fname=&listHiddenDocs=true&listExplorerDocs=true&listRecurse=false&lis
```

```
tFiles=true&listFolders=true&listLinkInfo=true&listIncludeParent=true&listD
erivedT=false&listBorders=fals: We seem to have authoring access to the
FrontPage web.
+ OSVDB-250: /wwwboard/passwd.txt: The wwwboard password file is browsable.
Change wwwboard to store this file elsewhere, or upgrade to the latest
version.
+ OSVDB-3092: /stats/: This might be interesting...
+ OSVDB-3092: /test.html: This might be interesting...
+ OSVDB-3092: /webstats/: This might be interesting...
+ OSVDB-3092: /cgi-bin/wwwboard.pl: This might be interesting...
+ OSVDB-3233: /_vti_bin/shtml.exe/_vti_rpc: FrontPage may be installed.
+ 6545 items checked: 0 error(s) and 15 item(s) reported on remote host
+ End Time:            2017-12-24 10:54:21 (GMT-5) (678 seconds)
```

At the top, we see that there's an shtml.exe file present, that's supposedly for the FrontPage web authoring program. I have no idea why it's there, considering that this is a Linux server and that that's a Windows executable. Nikto is telling me that by having that file there, someone could possibly do a **Denial-of-Service (DOS)** attack against me.

Next, we see that there are various scripts in the /cgi-bin directory. You can see from the explanatory messages that that's not a good thing because it could allow attackers to execute commands on my server.

After this, we see that there's an author.exe file in the vti_bin directory, which could theoretically allow someone to have authoring privileges.

The final item of interest is the passwd.txt file that's in the wwwboard directory. Apparently, this password file is browsable, which is definitely not a good thing.

Now, before you accuse me of making these problems up, I will reveal that this is a scan of a real production website on a real hosting service. (And yes, I do have permission to scan it.) So, these problems are real and need to be fixed.

Here are a couple of other sample messages that I got from scanning a web server that's running WordPress:

```
HTTP TRACK method is active, suggesting the host is vulnerable to XST
Cookie wordpress_test_cookie created without the httponly flag
```

To make a long story short, both of these two problems could potentially allow an attacker to steal user credentials. The fix, in this case, would be to see if the WordPress folk have issued any updates that would fix the problem.

So, how can we protect a web server against these kinds of vulnerabilities?

- As we saw in the first example, you want to ensure that you don't have any risky executable files on your web server. In this case, we found two `.exe` files that might not hurt anything on our Linux server, since Windows executable files don't run on Linux. However, on the other hand, it could be a Linux executable that's disguised as a Windows executable. We also found some `perl` scripts that definitely would run on Linux and that could pose a problem.
- In the event that someone were to plant some malicious script on your web server, you would want to have some form of mandatory access control, such as SELinux or AppArmor, that would keep the malicious scripts from running. (See `Chapter 7`, *Implementing Mandatory Access Control with SELinux and AppArmor*, for details about that.)
- You might also consider installing a web application firewall, such as *ModSecurity*. Space doesn't permit me to cover the details of ModSecurity, but you'll find a book that covers it at the Packt Publishing website.
- Keep your systems updated, especially if you're running a PHP-based content management system such as WordPress. (If you keep up with the IT security news, you'll see stories about WordPress vulnerabilities more often than you'd like to.)

There are other scan options, which you can see by just typing `nikto` at the command line. For now though, this is enough to get you started with basic web server scanning.

Summary

We've reached yet another milestone in our journey, and we saw some cool stuff. We started with a discussion about the basics of setting up Snort as a NIDS. I then showed you how to seriously cheat by deploying specialty Linux distros that already have Snort set up and ready to go.

Next, I introduced you to Lynis and how you can use it to scan your system for various vulnerabilities and compliance issues. Finally, we wrapped things up with working demos of OpenVAS and Nikto.

In the next chapter, we'll wind up this whole journey with a look at some quick tips for busy administrators. I'll see you there.

10
Security Tips and Tricks for the Busy Bee

In this, our final chapter, I'd like to do a round-up of quick tips and tricks that don't necessarily fit in with the previous chapters. Think of these tips as time savers for the busy administrator.

We'll cover the following topics:

- Quick ways to audit which system services are running
- Password-protecting the GRUB2 configuration
- Securely configuring and then password-protecting UEFI/BIOS
- Use a security checklist when setting up your system

Auditing system services

A basic tenet of server administration, regardless of which operating system we're talking about, is to never have anything that you don't absolutely need installed on a server. You especially don't want any unnecessary network services running because that would give the bad guys extra ways to get into your system. And, there's always a chance that some evil hacker might have planted something that acts as a network service, and you'd definitely want to know about that. In this chapter, we'll look at a few different ways to audit your system to ensure that no unnecessary network services are running on it.

Auditing system services with systemctl

On Linux systems that come with systemd, the `systemctl` command is pretty much a universal command that does many things for you. In addition to controlling your system's services, it can also show you the status of those services. We have the following code:

```
donnie@linux-0ro8:~> sudo systemctl -t service --state=active
```

Here's the breakdown of the preceding command:

- `-t service`: We want to view information about the services—or, what used to be called **daemons**—on the system
- `--state=active`: This specifies that we want to view information about all the system services that are actually running

A partial output of this command looks something like this:

```
UNIT                                              LOAD   ACTIVE SUB
DESCRIPTION
accounts-daemon.service                           loaded active running
Accounts Service
after-local.service                               loaded active exited
/etc/init.d/after.local Compatibility
alsa-restore.service                              loaded active exited
Save/Restore Sound Card State
apparmor.service                                  loaded active exited
Load AppArmor profiles
auditd.service                                    loaded active running
Security Auditing Service
avahi-daemon.service                              loaded active running
Avahi mDNS/DNS-SD Stack
cron.service                                      loaded active running
Command Scheduler
. . .
. . .
systemd-sysctl.service                            loaded active exited
Apply Kernel Variables
systemd-tmpfiles-setup-dev.service                loaded active exited
Create Static Device Nodes in /dev
systemd-tmpfiles-setup.service                    loaded active exited
Create Volatile Files and Directories
systemd-udev-root-symlink.service                 loaded active exited
Rule generator for /dev/root symlink
systemd-udev-trigger.service                      loaded active exited
udev Coldplug all Devices
systemd-udevd.service                             loaded active running
```

```
udev Kernel Device Manager
systemd-update-utmp.service                        loaded active exited
Update UTMP about System Boot/Shutdown
```

You generally won't want to see quite this much information, although you might at times. This command shows the status of every service that's running on your system. What really interests us now is just the network services that can allow someone to connect to your system. So, let's look at how to narrow things down a bit.

Auditing network services with netstat

The following are two reasons why you would want to keep track of what network services are running on your system:

- To ensure that no legitimate network services that you don't need are running
- To ensure that you don't have any malware that's listening for network connections from its master

The netstat command is both handy and easy to use for these instances. First, let's say that you want to see a list of network services that are listening, waiting for someone to connect to them:

```
donnie@linux-0ro8:~> netstat -lp -A inet


(Not all processes could be identified, non-owned process info
 will not be shown, you would have to be root to see it all.)
Active Internet connections (only servers)
Proto Recv-Q Send-Q Local Address          Foreign Address    State
PID/Program name
tcp        0      0 *:ideafarm-door        *:*                LISTEN     -
tcp        0      0 localhost:40432        *:*                LISTEN
3296/SpiderOakONE
tcp        0      0 *:ssh                  *:*                LISTEN     -
tcp        0      0 localhost:ipp          *:*                LISTEN     -
tcp        0      0 localhost:smtp         *:*                LISTEN     -
tcp        0      0 *:db-lsp               *:*                LISTEN
3246/dropbox
tcp        0      0 *:37468                *:*                LISTEN
3296/SpiderOakONE
tcp        0      0 localhost:17600        *:*                LISTEN
3246/dropbox
tcp        0      0 localhost:17603        *:*                LISTEN
3246/dropbox
```

```
udp         0        0 *:57228              *:*
3376/plugin-contain
udp         0        0 192.168.204.1:ntp    *:*                      -
udp         0        0 172.16.249.1:ntp     *:*                      -
udp         0        0 linux-0ro8:ntp       *:*                      -
udp         0        0 localhost:ntp        *:*                      -
udp         0        0 *:ntp                *:*                      -
udp         0        0 *:58102              *:*
5598/chromium --pas
udp         0        0 *:db-lsp-disc        *:*
3246/dropbox
udp         0        0 *:43782              *:*
5598/chromium --pas
udp         0        0 *:36764              *:*                      -
udp         0        0 *:21327              *:*
3296/SpiderOakONE
udp         0        0 *:mdns               *:*
5598/chromium --pas
udp         0        0 *:mdns               *:*
5598/chromium --pas
udp         0        0 *:mdns               *:*
5598/chromium --pas
udp         0        0 *:mdns               *:*                      -
raw         0        0 *:icmp               *:*              7       -
donnie@linux-0ro8:~>
```

The breakdown is as follows:

- -lp: The l means that we want to see which network ports are listening. In other words, we want to see which network ports are waiting for someone to connect to them. The p means that we want to see the name and process ID number of the program or service that is listening on each port.
- -A inet: This means that we only want to see information about the network protocols that are members of the inet family. In other words, we want to see information about the raw, tcp, and udp network sockets, but we don't want to see anything about the Unix sockets that only deal with interprocess communications within the operating system.

Since this output is from the OpenSUSE workstation that I just happen to be using at the moment, you won't see any of the usual server-type services here. However, you do see a few things that you likely won't want to see on your servers. For example, let's look at the very first item:

```
Proto Recv-Q Send-Q Local Address      Foreign Address      State
PID/Program name
tcp       0      0 *:ideafarm-door    *:*                  LISTEN
-
```

The `Local Address` column specifies the local address and port of this listening socket. The asterisk means that this socket is on the local network, and `ideafarm-door` is the name of the network port that is listening. (By default, `netstat` will show you the names of ports whenever possible, by pulling the port information out of the `/etc/services` file.)

Now, because I didn't know what the `ideafarm-door` service is, I used my favorite search engine to find out. By plugging the term `ideafarm-door` into DuckDuckGo, I found the answer:

WhatPortIs   Browse Ports   Submit New Port   Statistics   Blog

Port 902 : TCP/UDP

Below is your search results for Port **902**, including both TCP and UDP
Click the ports to view more detail, comments, RFC's and more!

Search Results

Port 902	UDP	ideafarm-door
Port 902	TCP	ideafarm-door 902/tcp self documenting Door: send 0x...
Port 902	TCP	VMware Server Console (TCP from management console t...
Port 902	UDP	VMware Server Console (UDP from server being managed...

The top search result took me to a site named *WhatPortIs*. According to this, the `ideafarm-door` is in reality port `902`, which belongs to the VMware Server Console. Okay, that makes sense because I do have VMware Player installed on this machine. So, that's all good.

 You can check out the *WhatPortIs* site here: `http://whatportis.com/`.

Next on the list is:

```
tcp       0      0 localhost:40432    *:*        LISTEN
3296/SpiderOakONE
```

This item shows the local address as `localhost` and that the listening port is port `40432`. This time, the `PID/Program Name` column actually tells us what this is. *SpiderOak ONE* is a cloud-based backup service that you might or might not want to see running on your server.

Now, let's look at a few more items:

```
tcp 0       0 *:db-lsp               *:*        LISTEN        3246/dropbox
tcp 0       0 *:37468                *:*        LISTEN
3296/SpiderOakONE
tcp 0       0 localhost:17600        *:*        LISTEN        3246/dropbox
tcp 0       0 localhost:17603        *:*        LISTEN        3246/dropbox
```

Here, we see that Dropbox and SpiderOak ONE are both listed with the asterisk for the local address. So, they're both using the local network address. The name of the port for Dropbox is `db-lsp`, which stands for *Dropbox LAN Sync Protocol*. The SpiderOak ONE port doesn't have an official name, so it's just listed as port `37468`. The bottom two lines show that Dropbox also uses the local machine's address, on ports `17600` and `17603`.

So far we've looked at nothing but TCP network sockets. Let's see how they differ from UDP sockets:

```
udp       0      0 192.168.204.1:ntp      *:*
-
udp       0      0 172.16.249.1:ntp       *:*
-
udp       0      0 linux-0ro8:ntp         *:*
-
```

The first thing to note is that there's nothing under the `State` column. That's because with UDP, there are no states. They actually are listening for data packets to come in, and they're ready to send data packets out. But since that's about all that UDP sockets can do, there was really no sense in defining different states for them.

In the first two lines, we see some strange local addresses. That's because I have both VMware Player and VirtualBox installed on this workstation. The local addresses of these two sockets are for the VMware and VirtualBox virtual network adapters. The last line shows the hostname of my OpenSUSE workstation as the local address. In all three cases, the port is the Network Time Protocol port, for time synchronization.

Let's now look at one last set of UDP items:

```
udp           0      0 *:58102          *:*
5598/chromium --pas
udp           0      0 *:db-lsp-disc    *:*
3246/dropbox
udp           0      0 *:43782          *:*
5598/chromium --pas
udp           0      0 *:36764          *:*
udp           0      0 *:21327          *:*
3296/SpiderOakONE
udp           0      0 *:mdns           *:*
5598/chromium --pas
```

Here, we see that my Chromium web browser is ready to accept network packets on a few different ports. We also see that Dropbox uses UDP to accept discovery requests from other local machines that have Dropbox installed. I assume that port `21327` performs the same function for SpiderOak ONE.

Of course, since this machine is my workhorse workstation, Dropbox and SpiderOak ONE are almost indispensable to me. I installed them myself, so I've always know that they were there. However, if you see anything like this on a server, you'll want to investigate to see if the server admins know that these programs are installed, and then find out why they're installed. It could be that they're performing a legitimate function, and it could be that they're not.

A difference between Dropbox and SpiderOak ONE is that with Dropbox, your files don't get encrypted until they've been uploaded to the Dropbox servers. So, the Dropbox folk have the encryption keys to your files. On the other hand, SpiderOak ONE encrypts your files on your local machine, and the encryption keys never leave your possession. So, if you really do need a cloud-based backup service and you're dealing with sensitive files, something like SpiderOak ONE would definitely be better than Dropbox. (And no, the SpiderOak ONE folk aren't paying me to say that.)

If you want to see port numbers and IP addresses instead of network names, add the n option. We have the following code:

```
donnie@linux-0ro8:~> netstat -lpn -A inet

(Not all processes could be identified, non-owned process info
 will not be shown, you would have to be root to see it all.)
Active Internet connections (only servers)
Proto Recv-Q Send-Q Local Address      Foreign Address      State
PID/Program name
tcp        0      0 0.0.0.0:902        0.0.0.0:*            LISTEN    -
tcp        0      0 127.0.0.1:40432    0.0.0.0:*            LISTEN
3296/SpiderOakONE
tcp        0      0 0.0.0.0:22         0.0.0.0:*            LISTEN    -
tcp        0      0 127.0.0.1:631      0.0.0.0:*            LISTEN    -
tcp        0      0 127.0.0.1:25       0.0.0.0:*            LISTEN    -
tcp        0      0 0.0.0.0:17500      0.0.0.0:*            LISTEN
3246/dropbox
tcp        0      0 0.0.0.0:37468      0.0.0.0:*            LISTEN
3296/SpiderOakONE
tcp        0      0 127.0.0.1:17600    0.0.0.0:*            LISTEN
3246/dropbox
tcp        0      0 127.0.0.1:17603    0.0.0.0:*            LISTEN
3246/dropbox
udp        0      0 192.168.204.1:123  0.0.0.0:*                      -
udp        0      0 172.16.249.1:123   0.0.0.0:*                      -
udp        0      0 192.168.0.222:123  0.0.0.0:*                      -
udp        0      0 127.0.0.1:123      0.0.0.0:*                      -
udp        0      0 0.0.0.0:123        0.0.0.0:*                      -
udp        0      0 0.0.0.0:17500      0.0.0.0:*
3246/dropbox
udp        0      0 0.0.0.0:50857      0.0.0.0:*
5598/chromium --pas
udp        0      0 0.0.0.0:43782      0.0.0.0:*
5598/chromium --pas
udp        0      0 0.0.0.0:44023      0.0.0.0:*
10212/plugin-contai
```

```
udp       0       0 0.0.0.0:36764      0.0.0.0:*                        -
udp       0       0 0.0.0.0:21327      0.0.0.0:*
3296/SpiderOakONE
udp       0       0 0.0.0.0:5353       0.0.0.0:*
5598/chromium --pas
udp       0       0 0.0.0.0:5353       0.0.0.0:*
5598/chromium --pas
udp       0       0 0.0.0.0:5353       0.0.0.0:*
5598/chromium --pas
udp       0       0 0.0.0.0:5353       0.0.0.0:*             -
raw       0       0 0.0.0.0:1          0.0.0.0:*        7    -
donnie@linux-0ro8:~>
```

All you have to do to view the established TCP connections is to leave out the l option. On my workstation, this makes for a very long list, so I'll only show a few items:

```
donnie@linux-0ro8:~> netstat -p -A inet
(Not all processes could be identified, non-owned process info
 will not be shown, you would have to be root to see it all.)
Active Internet connections (w/o servers)
Proto Recv-Q Send-Q Local Address      Foreign Address       State
PID/Program name
tcp        1      0 linux-0ro8:41670   ec2-54-88-208-223:https CLOSE_WAIT
3246/dropbox
tcp        0      0 linux-0ro8:59810   74-126-144-106.wa:https ESTABLISHED
3296/SpiderOakONE
tcp        0      0 linux-0ro8:58712   74-126-144-105.wa:https ESTABLISHED
3296/SpiderOakONE
tcp        0      0 linux-0ro8:caerpc  atl14s78-in-f2.1e:https ESTABLISHED
10098/firefox
. . .
. . .
```

The Foreign Address column shows the address and port number of the machine at the remote end of the connection. The first item shows that the connection with a Dropbox server is in a CLOSE_WAIT state. This means that the Dropbox server has closed the connection, and we're now waiting on the local machine to close the socket.

Because the names of those foreign addresses don't make much sense, let's add the n option to see IP addresses instead:

```
donnie@linux-0ro8:~> netstat -np -A inet
(Not all processes could be identified, non-owned process info
 will not be shown, you would have to be root to see it all.)
Active Internet connections (w/o servers)
Proto Recv-Q Send-Q Local Address        Foreign Address      State
PID/Program name
```

```
tcp        0       1 192.168.0.222:59594   37.187.24.170:443    SYN_SENT
10098/firefox
tcp        0       0 192.168.0.222:59810   74.126.144.106:443   ESTABLISHED
3296/SpiderOakONE
tcp        0       0 192.168.0.222:58712   74.126.144.105:443   ESTABLISHED
3296/SpiderOakONE
tcp        0       0 192.168.0.222:38606   34.240.121.144:443   ESTABLISHED
10098/firefox
. . .
. . .
```

This time we see something new. The first item shows a `SYN_SENT` state for the Firefox connection. This means that the local machine is trying to establish a connection to the foreign IP address. Also, under `Local Address`, we see the static IP address for my OpenSUSE workstation.

If I had space to display the entire `netstat` output here, you'd see nothing but `tcp` under the `Proto` column. That's because the UDP protocol doesn't establish connections in the same way that the TCP protocol does.

Something to keep in mind is that rootkits can replace legitimate Linux utilities with their own trojaned versions. For example, a rootkit could have its own trojaned version of `netstat` that would show all network processes except for those that are associated with the rootkit. That's why you want something like Rootkit Hunter in your toolbox.

If you need more information about `netstat`, see the `netstat` man page.

Auditing network services with Nmap

The `netstat` tool is very good, and it can give you lots of good information about what's going on with your network services. The slight downside is that you have to log in to every individual host on your network in order to use it.

If you'd like to remotely audit your network to see what services are running on each computer, without having to log in to each and every one, then you need a tool like Nmap. It's available for all the major operating systems, so even if you're stuck having to use Windows on your workstation, you're in luck. An up-to-date version is built into Kali Linux, if that's what you're using. It's also in the repositories of every major Linux distro, but the version that's in the Linux repositories is usually quite old. So if you're using something other than Kali, your best bet is just to download Nmap from its creator's website.

 You can download Nmap for all of the major operating systems from https://nmap.org/download.html.

In all cases, you'll also find instructions for installation.

You'll use Nmap the same way on all operating systems, with only one exception. On Linux and Mac machines, you'll preface certain Nmap commands with sudo, and on Windows machines, you won't. Since I just happen to be working on my trusty OpenSUSE workstation, I'll show you how it works on Linux. Let's start by doing a SYN packet scan:

```
donnie@linux-0ro8:~> sudo nmap -sS 192.168.0.37

Starting Nmap 6.47 ( http://nmap.org ) at 2017-12-24 19:32 EST
Nmap scan report for 192.168.0.37
Host is up (0.00016s latency).
Not shown: 996 closed ports
PORT STATE SERVICE
22/tcp open ssh
515/tcp open printer
631/tcp open ipp
5900/tcp open vnc
MAC Address: 00:0A:95:8B:E0:C0 (Apple)

Nmap done: 1 IP address (1 host up) scanned in 57.41 seconds
donnie@linux-0ro8:~>
```

Here's the breakdown:

- -sS: The lower-case s denotes the type of scan that we want to perform. The uppercase S denotes that we're doing an SYN packet scan. (More on that in a moment.)
- 192.168.0.37: In this case, I'm only scanning a single machine. But, I could also scan either a group of machines, or an entire network.
- Not shown: 996 closed ports: The fact that it's showing all of these closed ports instead of filtered ports tells me that there's no firewall on this machine. (Again, more on that in a moment.)

Next, we see a list of ports that are open. (And, more on that in a moment.)

The MAC address of this machine indicates that it's an Apple product of some sort. In a moment, I'll show you how to get more details about what kind of Apple product that it might be.

Let's now look at this more in detail.

Port states

An Nmap scan will show the target machine's ports in one of three states:

- `filtered`: This means that the port is blocked by a firewall
- `open`: This means that the port is not blocked by a firewall and that the service that's associated with that port is running
- `closed`: This means that the port is not blocked by a firewall, and that the service that's associated with that port is not running

So, in our scan of the Apple machine, we see that the Secure Shell service is ready to accept connections on port 22, that the print service is ready to accept connections on ports 515 and 631, and that the **Virtual Network Computing** (**VNC**) service is ready to accept connections on port 5900. All of these ports would be of interest to a security-minded administrator. If Secure Shell is running, it would be interesting to know if it's configured securely. The fact that the print service is running means that this machine is set up to use the **Internet Printing Protocol** (**IPP**). It would be interesting to know why we're using IPP instead of just regular network printing, and it would also be interesting to know if there are any security concerns with this version of IPP. And of course, we already know that VNC isn't a secure protocol, so we would want to know why it's even running at all. We also saw that no ports are listed as `filtered`, so we would also want to know why there's no firewall on this machine.

One little secret that I'll finally reveal, is that this machine is the same one that I used for the OpenVAS scan demos. So, we already have some of the needed information. The OpenVAS scan told us that Secure Shell on this machine uses weak encryption algorithms and that there's a security vulnerability with the print service. In just a bit, I'll show you how to get some of that information with Nmap.

Scan types

There are lots of different scanning options, each with its own purpose. The SYN packet scan that we're using here is considered a stealthy type of scan because it generates less network traffic and fewer system log entries than certain other types of scans. With this type of scan, Nmap sends a SYN packet to a port on the target machine, as if it were trying to create a TCP connection to that machine. If the target machine responds with a SYN/ACK packet, it means that the port is in an open state and ready to create the TCP connection. If the target machine responds with an RST packet, it means that the port is in a closed state. If there's no response at all, it means that the port is filtered, blocked by a firewall. As a normal Linux administrator, this is one of the types of scans that you would do most of the time.

The -sS scan shows you the state of TCP ports, but it doesn't show you the state of UDP ports. To see the UDP ports, use the -sU option:

```
donnie@linux-0ro8:~> sudo nmap -sU 192.168.0.37

Starting Nmap 6.47 ( http://nmap.org ) at 2017-12-28 12:41 EST
Nmap scan report for 192.168.0.37
Host is up (0.00018s latency).
Not shown: 996 closed ports
PORT        STATE            SERVICE
123/udp     open             ntp
631/udp     open|filtered ipp
3283/udp    open|filtered netassistant
5353/udp    open             zeroconf
MAC Address: 00:0A:95:8B:E0:C0 (Apple)

Nmap done: 1 IP address (1 host up) scanned in 119.91 seconds
donnie@linux-0ro8:~>
```

Here, you see something a bit different. You see two ports listed as open|filtered. That's because, due to the way that UDP ports respond to Nmap scans, Nmap can't always tell whether a UDP port is open or filtered. In this case, we know that these two ports are probably open because we've already seen that their corresponding TCP ports are open.

ACK packet scans can also be useful, but not to see the state of the target machine's network services. Rather, it's a good option for when you need to see if there might be a firewall blocking the way between you and the target machine. An ACK scan command looks like this:

```
sudo nmap -sA 192.168.0.37
```

You're not limited to scanning just a single machine at a time. You can scan either a group of machines or an entire subnet at once:

```
sudo nmap -sS 192.168.0.1-128
sudo nmap -sS 192.168.0.0/24
```

The first command scans only the first 128 hosts on this network segment. The second command scans all 254 hosts on a subnet that's using a 24 bit netmask.

A discovery scan is useful for when you need to just see what devices are on the network:

```
sudo nmap -sn 192.168.0.0/24
```

With the -sn option, Nmap will first detect whether you're scanning the local subnet or a remote subnet. If the subnet is local, Nmap will send out an **Address Resolution Protocol (ARP)** broadcast that requests the IPv4 addresses of every device on the subnet. That's a reliable way of discovering devices because ARP isn't something that will ever be blocked by a device's firewall. (I mean, without ARP, the network would cease to function.) However, ARP broadcasts can't go across a router, which means that you can't use ARP to discover hosts on a remote subnet. So, if Nmap detects that you're doing a discovery scan on a remote subnet, it will send out ping packets instead of ARP broadcasts. Using ping packets for discovery isn't as reliable as using ARP because some network devices can be configured to ignore ping packets. Anyway, here's an example from my own home network:

```
donnie@linux-0ro8:~> sudo nmap -sn 192.168.0.0/24

Starting Nmap 6.47 ( http://nmap.org ) at 2017-12-25 14:48 EST
Nmap scan report for 192.168.0.1
Host is up (0.00043s latency).
MAC Address: 00:18:01:02:3A:57 (Actiontec Electronics)
Nmap scan report for 192.168.0.3
Host is up (0.0044s latency).
MAC Address: 44:E4:D9:34:34:80 (Cisco Systems)
Nmap scan report for 192.168.0.5
Host is up (0.00026s latency).
MAC Address: 1C:1B:0D:0A:2A:76 (Unknown)
Nmap scan report for 192.168.0.6
Host is up (0.00013s latency).
MAC Address: 90:B1:1C:A3:DF:5D (Dell)
. . .
. . .
```

We see four hosts in this snippet, and there are three lines of output for each host. The first line shows the IP address, the second shows whether the host is up, and the third shows the MAC address of the host's network adapter. The first three pairs of characters in each MAC address denote the manufacturer of that network adapter. (For the record, that unknown network adapter is on a recent model Gigabyte motherboard. I have no idea why it's not in the Nmap database.)

The final scan that we'll look at does four things for us:

- It identifies open, closed, and filtered TCP ports
- It identifies the versions of the running services
- It runs a set of vulnerability-scanning scripts that come with Nmap
- It attempts to identify the operating system of the target host

The scan command that does all of these things looks like this:

```
sudo nmap -A 192.168.0.37
```

I guess that you could think of the -A option as the *all* option, since it really does do it all. (Well, almost all, since it doesn't scan UDP ports.) Here are the results of the scan that I did against my target:

```
donnie@linux-0ro8:~> sudo nmap -A 192.168.0.37

Starting Nmap 6.47 ( http://nmap.org ) at 2017-12-24 19:33 EST
Nmap scan report for 192.168.0.37
Host is up (0.00016s latency).
Not shown: 996 closed ports
PORT STATE SERVICE VERSION
22/tcp open ssh OpenSSH 5.1 (protocol 1.99)
|_ssh-hostkey: ERROR: Script execution failed (use -d to debug)
|_sshv1: Server supports SSHv1
515/tcp open printer?
631/tcp open ipp CUPS 1.1
| http-methods: Potentially risky methods: PUT
|_See http://nmap.org/nsedoc/scripts/http-methods.html
| http-robots.txt: 1 disallowed entry
|_/
|_http-title: Common UNIX Printing System
5900/tcp open vnc Apple remote desktop vnc
| vnc-info:
| Protocol version: 3.889
| Security types:
|_ Mac OS X security type (30)
1 service unrecognized despite returning data. If you know the
```

```
service/version, please submit the following fingerprint at
http://www.insecure.org/cgi-bin/servicefp-submit.cgi :
SF-Port515-TCP:V=6.47%I=7%D=12/24%Time=5A40479E%P=x86_64-suse-linux-gnu%r(
SF:GetRequest,1,"\x01");
MAC Address: 00:0A:95:8B:E0:C0 (Apple)
Device type: general purpose
Running: Apple Mac OS X 10.4.X
OS CPE: cpe:/o:apple:mac_os_x:10.4.10
OS details: Apple Mac OS X 10.4.10 - 10.4.11 (Tiger) (Darwin 8.10.0 -
8.11.1)
Network Distance: 1 hop
Service Info: OS: Mac OS X; CPE: cpe:/o:apple:mac_os_x

TRACEROUTE
HOP RTT ADDRESS
1 0.16 ms 192.168.0.37

OS and Service detection performed. Please report any incorrect results at
http://nmap.org/submit/ .
Nmap done: 1 IP address (1 host up) scanned in 213.92 seconds
donnie@linux-0ro8:~>
```

There are several interesting things here. First, there's the Secure Shell information:

```
22/tcp open ssh OpenSSH 5.1 (protocol 1.99)
|_ssh-hostkey: ERROR: Script execution failed (use -d to debug)
|_sshv1: Server supports SSHv1
```

Version 5.1 is a really old version of OpenSSH. (At the time of writing, the current version is version 7.6.) What's worse is that this OpenSSH server supports version 1 of the Secure Shell protocol. Version 1 is seriously flawed and is easily exploitable, so you never want to see this on your network.

Next, we have amplifying information on the print service vulnerability that we found with the OpenVAS scan:

```
515/tcp  open  printer?
631/tcp  open  ipp      CUPS 1.1
| http-methods: Potentially risky methods: PUT
|_See http://nmap.org/nsedoc/scripts/http-methods.html
| http-robots.txt: 1 disallowed entry
|_/
|_http-title: Common UNIX Printing System
```

In the `631/tcp` line, we see that the associated service is `ipp`, which stands for **Internet Printing Protocol**. This protocol is based on the same **Hypertext Transfer Protocol (HTTP)** that we use to look at web pages. The two methods that HTTP uses to send data from a client to a server are **POST** and **PUT**. What we really want is for every HTTP server to use the POST method because the PUT method makes it very easy for someone to compromise a server by manipulating a URL. So, if you scan a server and find that it allows using the PUT method for any kind of HTTP communications, you have a potential problem. In this case, the solution would be to update the operating system and hope that the updates fix the problem. If this were a web server, you'd want to have a chat with the web server administrators to let them know what you found.

Finally, let's see what Nmap found out about the operating system of our target machine:

```
Running: Apple Mac OS X 10.4.X
OS CPE: cpe:/o:apple:mac_os_x:10.4.10
OS details: Apple Mac OS X 10.4.10 - 10.4.11 (Tiger) (Darwin 8.10.0 -
8.11.1)
Network Distance: 1 hop
Service Info: OS: Mac OS X; CPE: cpe:/o:apple:mac_os_x
```

Wait, what? Mac OS X 10.4? Isn't that really, really ancient? Well yeah, it is. The secret that I've been guarding for the past couple of chapters is that the target machine for my OpenVAS and Nmap scan demos has been my ancient, collectible Apple eMac from the year 2003. I figured that scanning it would give us some interesting results to look at, and it would appear that I was right. (And yes, that is eMac, not iMac.)

Password-protecting the GRUB 2 bootloader

People sometimes forget passwords, even if they're administrators. And sometimes, people buy used computers but forget to ask the seller what the password is. (Yes, I've done that.) That's okay, though, because all of the major operating systems have ways to let you either reset or recover a lost administrator password. That's handy, except that it does kind of make the whole idea of having login passwords a rather moot point when someone has physical access to the machine. Let's say that your laptop has just been stolen. If you haven't encrypted the hard drive, it would only take a few minutes for the thief to reset the password and to steal your data. If you have encrypted the drive, the level of protection would depend on which operating system you're running. With standard Windows folder encryption, the thief would be able to access the encrypted folders just by resetting the password. With LUKS whole-disk encryption on a Linux machine, the thief wouldn't be able to get past the point of having to enter the encryption passphrase.

With Linux, we have a way to safeguard against unauthorized password resets, even if we're not using whole-disk encryption. All we have to do is to password-protect the **Grand Unified Bootloader (GRUB)**, which would prevent a thief from booting into emergency mode to do the password reset.

Whether or not you need the advice in this section depends on your organization's physical security setup. That's because booting a Linux machine into emergency mode requires physical access to the machine. It's not something that you can do remotely. In an organization with proper physical security, servers—especially ones that hold sensitive data—are locked away in a room that's locked within another room. Only a very few trusted personnel are allowed to enter, and they have to present their credentials at both access points. So, setting a password on the bootloader of those servers would be rather pointless, unless you're dealing with a regulatory agency that dictates otherwise.

On the other hand, password-protecting the bootloaders of workstations and laptops that are out in the open could be quite useful. But, that alone won't protect your data. Someone could still boot the machine from a live disk or a USB memory stick, mount the machine's hard drive, and obtain the sensitive data. That's why you also want to encrypt your sensitive data, as I showed you in Chapter 4, *Encrypting and SSH Hardening*.

To reset a password, all you have to do is to interrupt the boot process when the boot menu comes up and change a couple of kernel parameters. However, resetting passwords isn't the only thing you can do from the boot menu. If your machine has multiple operating systems installed—for example, Windows on one partition and Linux on another partition—the boot menu allows you to choose which operating system to boot up. With the old-style legacy GRUB, you could prevent people from editing kernel parameters, but you couldn't prevent them from choosing an alternate operating system on multiboot machines. With the new GRUB 2 that's in newer versions of Linux, you can choose which users you want to be able to boot from any particular operating system.

Now, just so you'll know what I'm talking about when I say that you can edit kernel parameters from the GRUB 2 boot menu, let me show you how to perform a password reset.

Resetting the password for Red Hat/CentOS

When the boot menu comes up, interrupt the boot process by hitting the down-arrow key once. Then, hit the up-arrow key once to select the default boot option:

```
CentOS Linux (3.10.0-693.11.1.el7.x86_64) 7 (Core)
CentOS Linux (3.10.0-693.5.2.el7.x86_64) 7 (Core)
CentOS Linux (3.10.0-693.el7.x86_64) 7 (Core)
CentOS Linux (0-rescue-2eda73dbd53444c5b4f8d6e607d581d5) 7 (Core)




Use the ↑ and ↓ keys to change the selection.
Press 'e' to edit the selected item, or 'c' for a command prompt.
```

Hit the *E* key to edit the kernel parameters. When the GRUB 2 configuration comes up, cursor down until you see this line:

```
        linux16 /vmlinuz-3.10.0-693.11.1.el7.x86_64 root=/dev/mapper/centos-ro\
ot ro crashkernel=auto rd.lvm.lv=centos/root rd.luks.uuid=luks-2d7f02c7-864f-4\
2ce-b362-50dd830d9772 rd.lvm.lv=centos/swap rhgb quiet LANG=en_US.UTF-8
```

Delete the words `rhgb quiet` from this line and then add `rd.break enforcing=0` to the end of the line. Here's what these two new options do for you:

- `rd.break`: This will cause the machine to boot into emergency mode, which gives you root user privileges without you having to enter a root user password. Even if the root user password hasn't been set, this still works.
- `enforcing=0`: When you do a password reset on an SELinux-enabled system, the security context for the `/etc/shadow` file will change to the wrong type. If the system is in enforcing mode when you do this, SELinux will prevent you from logging in until the `shadow` file gets relabeled. But, relabeling during the boot process can take a very long time, especially with a large drive. By setting SELinux to permissive mode, you can wait until after you've rebooted to restore the proper security context on just the `shadow` file.

When you've finished editing the kernel parameters, hit *Ctrl* + *X* to continue the boot process. This will take you to the emergency mode with the `switch_root` command prompt:

```
Entering emergency mode. Exit the shell to continue.
Type "journalctl" to view system logs.
You might want to save "/run/initramfs/rdsosreport.txt" to a USB stick or /boot
after mounting them and attach it to a bug report.

switch_root:/# _
```

In emergency mode, the filesystem is mounted as read-only. You'll need to remount it as read-write and enter a `chroot` mode before you reset the password:

```
mount -o remount,rw /sysroot
chroot /sysroot
```

After you enter these two commands, the command prompt will change to that of a normal bash shell:

```
switch_root:/# mount -o remount,rw /sysroot
switch_root:/# chroot /sysroot
sh-4.2# _
```

Now that you've reached this stage, you're finally ready to reset the password.

If you want to reset the root user password, or even if you want to create a root password where none previously existed, just enter:

```
passwd
```

Then, enter the new desired password.

If the system has never had a root user password and you still don't want it to have one, you can reset the password for an account that has full sudo privileges. For example, on my system, the command would look like this:

```
passwd donnie
```

Next, remount the filesystem as read-only. Then, enter `exit` twice to resume rebooting:

```
mount -o remount,ro /
exit
exit
```

The first thing you need to do after rebooting is to restore the proper SELinux security context on the `/etc/shadow` file. Then, put SELinux back into enforcing mode:

```
sudo restorecon /etc/shadow
sudo setenforce 1
```

Here's a before and after screenshot of the context settings for my `shadow` file:

```
[donnie@localhost ~]$ cd /etc
[donnie@localhost etc]$ ls -Z shadow
----------. root root system_u:object_r:unlabeled_t:s0 shadow
[donnie@localhost etc]$ sudo restorecon shadow
[sudo] password for donnie:
[donnie@localhost etc]$ ls -Z shadow
----------. root root system_u:object_r:shadow_t:s0     shadow
[donnie@localhost etc]$ _
```

You can see that resetting the password changed the type of the file to `unlabeled_t`. Running the `restorecon` command changed the type back to `shadow_t`.

Resetting the password for Ubuntu

The procedure for resetting a password on an Ubuntu system is quite a bit different and quite a bit simpler. Start out the same as you did with the CentOS machine, by pressing the down-arrow key once to interrupt the boot process. Then, press the up-arrow key once to select the default boot option. Hit the *E* key to edit the kernel parameters:

```
                    GNU GRUB  version 2.02~beta2-36ubuntu3.14

 *Ubuntu
  Advanced options for Ubuntu




         Use the ↑ and ↓ keys to select which entry is highlighted.
         Press enter to boot the selected OS, `e' to edit the commands
         before booting or `c' for a command-line.
```

When the GRUB 2 configuration comes up, cursor down until you see the `linux` line:

```
        linux        /vmlinuz-4.4.0-104-generic root=/dev/mapper/ubuntu3\
--vg-root ro _
```

Change the `ro` to `rw` and add `init=/bin/bash`:

```
        linux        /vmlinuz-4.4.0-104-generic root=/dev/mapper/ubuntu3\
-vg-root rw init=/bin/bash_
```

Press *Ctrl* + *X* to continue booting. This will take you to a root shell:

```
Begin: Running /scripts/init-bottom ... done.
bash: cannot set terminal process group (-1): Inappropriate ioctl for device
bash: no job control in this shell
root@(none):/# _
```

Since Ubuntu doesn't normally have a password assigned to the root user, you would most likely just reset the password of whoever had full sudo privileges. See the following example:

```
passwd donnie
```

When you're in this mode, the normal reboot commands won't work. So, once you've finished with the password reset operation, reboot by entering:

```
exec /sbin/init
```

The machine will now boot up for normal operation.

Preventing kernel parameter edits on Red Hat/CentOS

Ever since the introduction of Red Hat/CentOS 7.2, setting a GRUB 2 password to prevent kernel parameter edits is easy. All you have to do is to run one command and choose a password:

```
[donnie@localhost ~]$ sudo grub2-setpassword

[sudo] password for donnie:
Enter password:
Confirm password:
[donnie@localhost ~]$
```

That's all there is to it. The password hash will be stored in the `/boot/grub2/user.cfg` file.

Now, when you reboot the machine and try to do a kernel parameter edit, you'll be prompted to enter a username and password:

```
Enter username:
root
Enter password:
_
```

Note that you'll enter `root` as the username, even if the root user's password hasn't been set on the system. The `root` user, in this case, is just the superuser for GRUB 2.

Preventing kernel parameter edits on Ubuntu

Ubuntu doesn't have that cool utility that Red Hat and CentOS have, so you'll have to set a GRUB 2 password by hand-editing a configuration file.

In the `/etc/grub.d/` directory, you'll see the files that make up the GRUB 2 configuration:

```
donnie@ubuntu3:/etc/grub.d$ ls -l
total 76
-rwxr-xr-x 1 root root  9791 Oct 12 16:48 00_header
-rwxr-xr-x 1 root root  6258 Mar 15  2016 05_debian_theme
-rwxr-xr-x 1 root root 12512 Oct 12 16:48 10_linux
-rwxr-xr-x 1 root root 11082 Oct 12 16:48 20_linux_xen
-rwxr-xr-x 1 root root 11692 Oct 12 16:48 30_os-prober
-rwxr-xr-x 1 root root  1418 Oct 12 16:48 30_uefi-firmware
-rwxr-xr-x 1 root root   214 Oct 12 16:48 40_custom
-rwxr-xr-x 1 root root   216 Oct 12 16:48 41_custom
-rw-r--r-- 1 root root   483 Oct 12 16:48 README
donnie@ubuntu3:/etc/grub.d$
```

The file you want to edit is the `40_custom` file. However, before you edit the file, you'll need to create the password hash. Do that with the `grub-mkpasswd-pbkdf2` utility:

```
donnie@ubuntu3:/etc/grub.d$ grub-mkpasswd-pbkdf2
Enter password:
Reenter password:
PBKDF2 hash of your password is
grub.pbkdf2.sha512.10000.F1BA16B2799CBF6A6DFBA537D43222A0D5006124ECFEB29F5C
81C9769C6C3A66BF53C2B3AB71BEA784D4386E86C991F7B5D33CB6C29EB6AA12C8D11E0FFA0
```

```
D40.371648A84CC4131C3CFFB53604ECCBA46DA75AF196E970C98483385B0BE026590C63A1B
AC23691517BC4A5D3EDF89D026B599A0D3C49F2FB666F9C12B56DB35D
donnie@ubuntu3:/etc/grub.d$
```

Open the file `40_custom` file in your favorite editor and add a line that defines who the superuser(s) will be. Add another line for the password hash. In my case, the file now looks like this:

```
#!/bin/sh
exec tail -n +3 $0
# This file provides an easy way to add custom menu entries. Simply type
the
# menu entries you want to add after this comment. Be careful not to change
# the 'exec tail' line above.

set superusers="donnie"

password_pbkdf2 donnie
grub.pbkdf2.sha512.10000.F1BA16B2799CBF6A6DFBA537D43222A0D5006124ECFEB29F5C
81C9769C6C3A66BF53C2B3AB71BEA784D4386E86C991F7B5D33CB6C29EB6AA12C8D11E0FFA0
D40.371648A84CC4131C3CFFB53604ECCBA46DA75AF196E970C98483385B0BE026590C63A1B
AC23691517BC4A5D3EDF89D026B599A0D3C49F2FB666F9C12B56DB35D
```

 The string of text that begins with `password_pbkdf2` is all one line that wraps around on the printed page.

After you save the file, the last step is to generate a new `grub.cfg` file:

```
donnie@ubuntu3:/etc/grub.d$ sudo update-grub

Generating grub configuration file ...
Found linux image: /boot/vmlinuz-4.4.0-104-generic
Found initrd image: /boot/initrd.img-4.4.0-104-generic
Found linux image: /boot/vmlinuz-4.4.0-101-generic
Found initrd image: /boot/initrd.img-4.4.0-101-generic
Found linux image: /boot/vmlinuz-4.4.0-98-generic
Found initrd image: /boot/initrd.img-4.4.0-98-generic
done
donnie@ubuntu3:/etc/grub.d$
```

Now when I reboot this machine, I have to enter my password before editing the kernel parameters:

```
Enter username:
donnie
Enter password:
_
```

There's only one problem with this. Not only does this prevent anyone except the superuser from editing the kernel parameters, it also prevents anyone except for the superuser from booting normally. Yes, that's right. Even for normal booting, Ubuntu will now require you to enter the username and password of the authorized superuser. The fix is easy, although not at all elegant.

The fix requires inserting a single word into the /boot/grub/grub.cfg file. Easy enough, right? But, it's not an elegant solution because you're not really supposed to hand-edit the grub.cfg file. At the top of the file, we see this:

```
# DO NOT EDIT THIS FILE
#
# It is automatically generated by grub-mkconfig using templates
# from /etc/grub.d and settings from /etc/default/grub
#
```

This means that every time we do something that will update the grub.cfg file, any hand-edits that we've made to the file will be lost. This includes when we do a system update that installs a new kernel, or when we do a sudo apt autoremove that removes any old kernels that we no longer need. The supreme irony though is that the official GRUB 2 documentation tells us to hand-edit the grub.cfg file to deal with these sorts of problems.

Anyway, to fix things so that you no longer need to enter the password to boot normally, open the /boot/grub/grub.cfg file in your favorite text editor. Look for the first line that begins with menuentry, which should look something like this:

```
menuentry 'Ubuntu' --class ubuntu --class gnu-linux --class gnu --class os
$menuentry_id_option 'gnulinux-simple-f0f002e8-16b2-45a1-bebc-41e518ab9497'
{
```

Before the opening curly brace at the end of the line, add the text string, --unrestricted. The menuentry should now look like this:

```
menuentry 'Ubuntu' --class ubuntu --class gnu-linux --class gnu --class os
$menuentry_id_option 'gnulinux-simple-f0f002e8-16b2-45a1-bebc-41e518ab9497'
--unrestricted {
```

Save the file and test it by rebooting the machine. You should see that the machine now boots up normally on the default boot option. But, you'll also see that a password will still be required to access the **Advanced options for Ubuntu** submenu. We'll fix that in just a bit.

Password-protecting boot options

For any given Linux system, you'll have at least two boot options. You'll have the option to boot normally and the option to boot into recovery mode. Red Hat-type and Ubuntu-type operating systems are unique, in that they don't overwrite the old kernel when you do an operating system update. Instead, they install the new kernel along with the old one, and all the installed kernels have their own boot menu entries. On Red Hat-type systems, you'll never have more than five installed kernels because once you have five kernels installed, the oldest kernel will automatically get deleted the next time a new kernel is available in a system update. With Ubuntu-type systems, you'll need to manually delete the old kernels by running `sudo apt autoremove`.

You might also have a dual-boot or a multiboot configuration, and you might want for only certain users to use certain boot options. Let's say that you have a system with both Windows and Linux installed, and you want to prevent certain users from booting into either one or the other. You can do that by configuring GRUB 2, but you probably won't. I mean, a password and user account are required for logging in to an operating system anyway, so why bother?

The most realistic scenario I can think of where this would be useful would be if you have a computer set up in a publicly accessible kiosk. You would surely not want for the general public to boot the machine into recovery mode, and this technique would help prevent that.

This technique works mostly the same on both Red Hat-type and Ubuntu-type distros, with only a few exceptions. The major one is that we need to disable the submenu on the Ubuntu machine.

Disabling the submenu for Ubuntu

Theoretically, you can disable the Ubuntu submenu by placing `GRUB_DISABLE_SUBMENU=true` into the `/etc/default/grub` file and then by running `sudo update-grub`. However, I couldn't get that to work, and according to the results of my DuckDuckGo searches, neither can anyone else. So, we'll manually edit the `/boot/grub/grub.cfg` file to fix that.

Look for the `submenu` line that appears just after the first `menuentry` item. It should look like this:

```
submenu 'Advanced options for Ubuntu' $menuentry_id_option 'gnulinux-
advanced-f0f002e8-16b2-45a1-bebc-41e518ab9497' {
```

Comment out that line to make it look like this:

```
# submenu 'Advanced options for Ubuntu' $menuentry_id_option 'gnulinux-
advanced-f0f002e8-16b2-45a1-bebc-41e518ab9497' {
```

Scroll down until you see this line:

```
### END /etc/grub.d/10_linux ###
```

Just above this line, you'll see the closing curly brace for the submenu stanza. Comment out that curly brace so that it looks like this:

```
# }
```

Now when you reboot the machine, you'll see the whole list of boot options instead of the just the default boot option and a submenu. However, as things now stand, only the designated superuser can boot into anything except the default option.

Password-protecting boot option steps for both Ubuntu and Red Hat

From here on out, the steps are the same for both the CentOS and the Ubuntu virtual machines, except for the following:

- On your Ubuntu machine, the `grub.cfg` file is in the `/boot/grub/` directory. On your CentOS machine, it's in the `/boot/grub2/` directory.
- On Ubuntu, the `/boot/grub/` and `/etc/grub.d/` directories are world-readable. So, you can `cd` into them as a normal user.
- On CentOS, the `/boot/grub2/` and `/etc/grub.d/` directories are restricted to the root user. So, to `cd` into them, you'll need to log in to the root user's shell. Alternatively, you can list the contents from your normal user shell with `sudo ls -l`, and you can edit the files you need to edit with `sudo vim /boot/grub2/grub.cfg` or `sudo vim /etc/grub.d/40_custom`. (Substitute your favorite editor for vim.)
- On Ubuntu, the command to create a password hash is `grub-mkpasswd-pbkdf2`. On CentOS, the command is `grub2-mkpasswd-pbkdf2`.

With these slight differences in mind, let's get started.

If you're working with a server that's just running with a text-mode interface, you'll definitely want to log in remotely from a workstation that has a GUI-type interface. If your workstation is running Windows, you can use Cygwin, as I showed you in `Chapter 1`, *Running Linux in a Virtual Environment*.

The reason for this is that you'll want a way to copy and paste the password hashes into the two files that you need to edit.

The first thing you'll do is to create a password hash for your new users:

- On Ubuntu:

    grub-mkpasswd-pbkdf2

- On CentOS:

    grub2-mkpasswd-pbkdf2

Next, open the `/etc/grub.d/40_custom` file in your text editor and add a line for your new user, along with the password hash that you just created. The line should look something like this:

```
password_pbkdf2 goldie
grub.pbkdf2.sha512.10000.225205CBA2584240624D077ACB84E86C70349BBC00DF40A219
F88E5691FB222DD6E2F7765E96C63C4A8FA3B41BDBF62DA1F3B07C700D78BC5DE524DCAD9DD
88B.9655985015C3BEF29A7B8E0A6EA42599B1152580251FF99AA61FE68C1C1209ACDCBBBDA
A7A97D4FC4DA6984504923E1449253024619A82A57CECB1DCDEE53C06
```

Note that this is all one line that wraps around on the printed page.

What you're supposed to do next is to run a utility that will read all of the files in the `/etc/grub.d/` directory along with the `/etc/default/grub` file and that will then rebuild the `grub.cfg` file. But, on CentOS, that utility doesn't work correctly. On Ubuntu, it does work correctly, but it will overwrite any changes that you might have already made to the `grub.cfg` file. So, we're going to cheat.

Open the `grub.cfg` file in your text editor:

- On Ubuntu:

    sudo vim /boot/grub/grub.cfg

- On CentOS:

    sudo vim /boot/grub2/grub.cfg

Scroll down until you see the `### BEGIN /etc/grub.d/40_custom ###` section. In this section, copy and paste the line that you just added to the `40_custom` file. This section should now look something like this:

```
### BEGIN /etc/grub.d/40_custom ###
# This file provides an easy way to add custom menu entries.  Simply type the
# menu entries you want to add after this comment.  Be careful not to change
# the 'exec tail' line above.
password_pbkdf2 "goldie"
grub.pbkdf2.sha512.10000.225205CBA2584240624D077ACB84E86C70349BBC00DF40A219
F88E5691FB222DD6E2F7765E96C63C4A8FA3B41BDBF62DA1F3B07C700D78BC5DE524DCAD9DD
88B.9655985015C3BEF29A7B8E0A6EA42599B1152580251FF99AA61FE68C1C1209ACDCBBBDA
A7A97D4FC4DA6984504923E1449253024619A82A57CECB1DCDEE53C06
### END /etc/grub.d/40_custom ###
```

Finally, you're ready to password-protect the individual menu entries. And here, I've discovered yet another difference between Ubuntu and CentOS.

In all of the menu entries for CentOS, you'll see that the `--unrestricted` option is already there for all menu entries. This means that by default, all users are allowed to boot every menu option, even if you've set a superuser password:

```
menuentry 'CentOS Linux (3.10.0-693.11.1.el7.x86_64) 7 (Core)' --class
centos --class gnu-linux --class gnu --class os --unrestricted
$menuentry_id_option 'gnulinux-3.10.0-693.el7.x86_64-advanced-f338b70d-
ff57-404e-a349-6fd84ad1b692' {
```

So on CentOS, you don't have to do anything if you want all users to be able to use all available boot options.

Now, let's say that you have a `menuentry` that you want to be accessible to everybody. On CentOS, as I just pointed out, you don't have to do anything. On Ubuntu, add `--unrestricted` to the `menuentry`, as you did previously:

```
menuentry 'Ubuntu' --class ubuntu --class gnu-linux --class gnu --class os
$menuentry_id_option 'gnulinux-simple-f0f002e8-16b2-45a1-bebc-41e518ab9497'
--unrestricted {
```

If you want for nobody but the superuser to boot from a particular option, add `--users ""`. (On CentOS, be sure to remove the `--unrestricted` option first.)

```
menuentry 'Ubuntu, with Linux 4.4.0-98-generic (recovery mode)' --class
ubuntu --class gnu-linux --class gnu --class os $menuentry_id_option
'gnulinux-4.4.0-98-generic-recovery-f0f002e8-16b2-45a1-bebc-41e518ab9497' -
-users "" {
```

If you want for only the superuser and some other particular user to boot from a certain option, add `--users`, followed by the username. (Again, on CentOS, remove the `--unrestricted` option first.):

```
menuentry 'Ubuntu, with Linux 4.4.0-97-generic' --class ubuntu --class gnu-
linux --class gnu --class os $menuentry_id_option 'gnulinux-4.4.0-97-
generic-advanced-f0f002e8-16b2-45a1-bebc-41e518ab9497' --users goldie {
```

If you have more than one user that you want to access a boot option, add an entry for the new user in the `### BEGIN /etc/grub.d/40_custom ###` section. Then, add the new user to the `menuentry` that you want for him or her to access. Separate the usernames with a comma:

```
menuentry 'Ubuntu, with Linux 4.4.0-97-generic' --class ubuntu --class gnu-
linux --class gnu --class os $menuentry_id_option 'gnulinux-4.4.0-97-
generic-advanced-f0f002e8-16b2-45a1-bebc-41e518ab9497' --users goldie,frank
{
```

Save the file and reboot to try out the different options.

Now that we've gone through all this work, I need to remind you again that any manual edits that you've made to the `grub.cfg` file will be lost any time that a new `grub.cfg` gets generated. So, any time you do a system update that includes either installing or removing a kernel, you'll need to manually edit this file again to add back the password protection. (In fact, the only real reason I had you add the users and their passwords to the `/etc/grub.d/40_custom` file is so that you'll always have that information available to copy and paste into `grub.cfg`.) I wish that there were a more elegant way of doing this, but according to the official GRUB 2 documentation, there isn't.

You'll find the security section of the official GRUB 2 documentation at `http://www.gnu.org/software/grub/manual/grub/grub.html#Security`.

Before we leave this topic, I'd like to share my personal thoughts about GRUB 2.

It was necessary to create a new version of GRUB because the old legacy version doesn't work with the new UEFI-based motherboards. However, there are things about GRUB 2 that are very disappointing.

In the first place, unlike legacy GRUB, GRUB 2 isn't implemented consistently across all Linux distros. In fact, we've just seen in our demos how we have to do things differently when we go from CentOS to Ubuntu.

Next is the fact that the GRUB 2 developers gave us some good security options, but they haven't given us an elegant way of implementing them. I mean, really. The whole idea of telling us to implement security features by hand-editing a file that will get overwritten every time we do an operating system update just doesn't seem right.

And finally, there's the sad state of GRUB 2 documentation. I don't mean to sound like I'm tooting my own horn because I know that that's unbecoming. However, I think it's safe to say that this is the only comprehensive write-up you'll find anywhere for using the password-protection features of GRUB 2.

Securely configuring BIOS/UEFI

This topic is different from anything we've looked at thus far because it has nothing to do with the operating system. Rather, we're now going to talk about the computer hardware.

Every computer motherboard has either a BIOS or a UEFI chip, which stores both the hardware configuration for the computer, and the bootstrap instructions that are needed to start the boot process after the power is turned on. UEFI has replaced the old-style BIOS on newer motherboards, and it has more security features than what the old BIOS had.

I can't give you any specific information about BIOS/UEFI setup because every model of the motherboard has a different way of doing things. What I can give you is some more generalized information.

When you think about BIOS/UEFI security, you might be thinking about disabling the ability to boot from anything other than the normal system drive. In the following screenshot, you can see that I've disabled all SATA drive ports except for the one to which the system drive is connected:

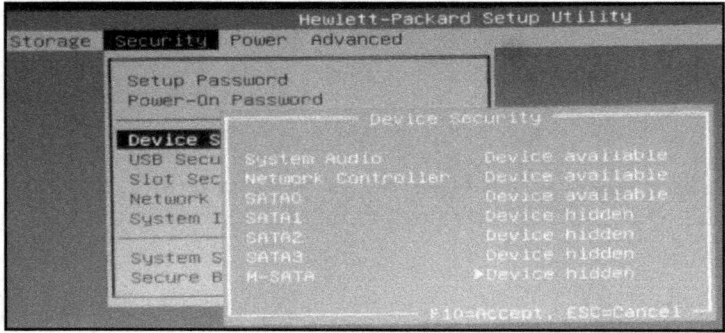

When computers are out in the open where the general public can have easy physical access to them, this might be a consideration. For servers that are locked away in their own secure room with limited access, there's no real reason to worry about it, unless the security requirements of some regulatory body dictate otherwise. For machines that are out in the open, having whole disk encryption would prevent someone from stealing data after booting from either an optical disk or a USB device. However, you might still have other reasons to prevent anyone from booting the machine from these alternate boot devices.

Another consideration might be if you work in a secure environment where supersensitive data are handled. If you're worried about unauthorized exfiltration of sensitive data, you might consider disabling the ability to write to USB devices. This will also prevent people from booting the machine from USB devices:

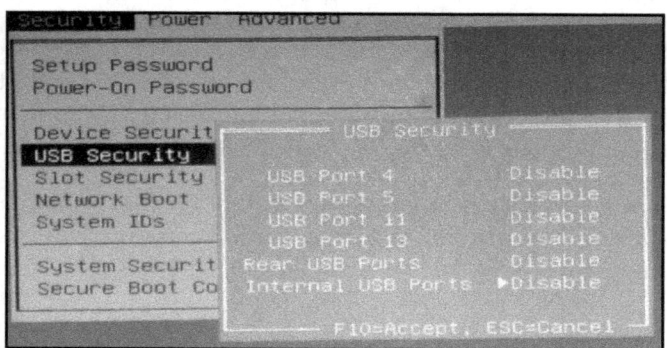

However, there's more than just this to BIOS/UEFI security. Today's modern server CPUs come with a variety of security features to help prevent data breaches. For example, let's look at a list of security features that are implemented in Intel Xeon CPUs:

- Identity-protection technology
- Advanced Encryption Standard New Instructions
- Trusted Execution Technology
- Hardware-assisted virtualization technology

AMD, that plucky underdog in the CPU market, have their own new security features in their new line of EPYC server CPUs. These features are:

- Secure Memory Encryption
- Secure Encrypted Virtualization

In any case, you would configure these CPU security options in your server's UEFI setup utility.

You can read about Intel Xeon security features at: `https://www.intel.com/content/www/us/en/data-security/security-overview-general-technology.html`.

And, you can read about AMD EPYC security features at `https://semiaccurate.com/2017/06/22/amds-epyc-major-advance-security/`.

And of course, for any machines that are out in the open, it's a good idea to password-protect the BIOS or UEFI:

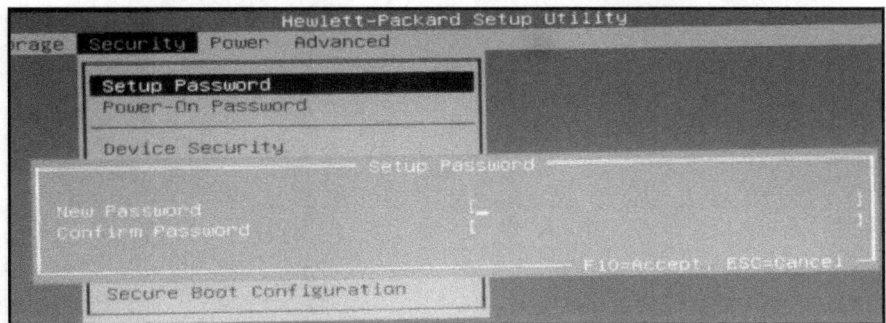

If for no other reason, do it to keep people from monkeying around with your settings.

Using a security checklist for system setup

I've previously told you about OpenSCAP, which is a really useful tool to lock down your system with just a minimum amount of effort. OpenSCAP comes with various profiles that you can apply to help bring your systems into compliance with the standards of different regulatory agencies. However, there are certain things that OpenSCAP can't do for you. For example, certain regulatory agencies require that your server's hard drive be partitioned in a certain way, with certain directories separated out into their own partitions. If you've already set up your server with everything under one big partition, you can't fix that just by doing a remediation procedure with OpenSCAP. The process of locking down your server to ensure that it's compliant with any applicable security regulations has to begin before you even install the operating system. For this, you need the appropriate checklist.

There are a few different places where you can obtain a generic security checklist if that's all you need. The University of Texas at Austin publishes a generic checklist for Red Hat Enterprise 7, which you can adjust if you need to use it with CentOS 7, Oracle Linux 7, or Scientific Linux 7. You might find that some checklist items don't apply to your situation, and you can adjust them as required:

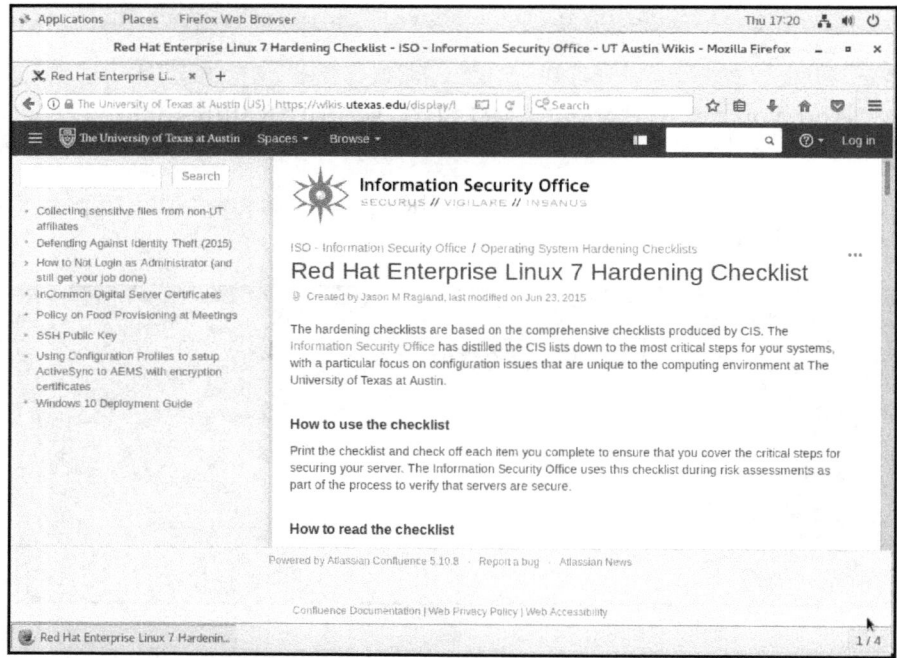

For specific business fields, you'll need to get a checklist from the applicable regulatory body. If you work in the financial sector or with a business that accepts credit card payments, you'll need a checklist from the Payment Card Industry Security Standards Council:

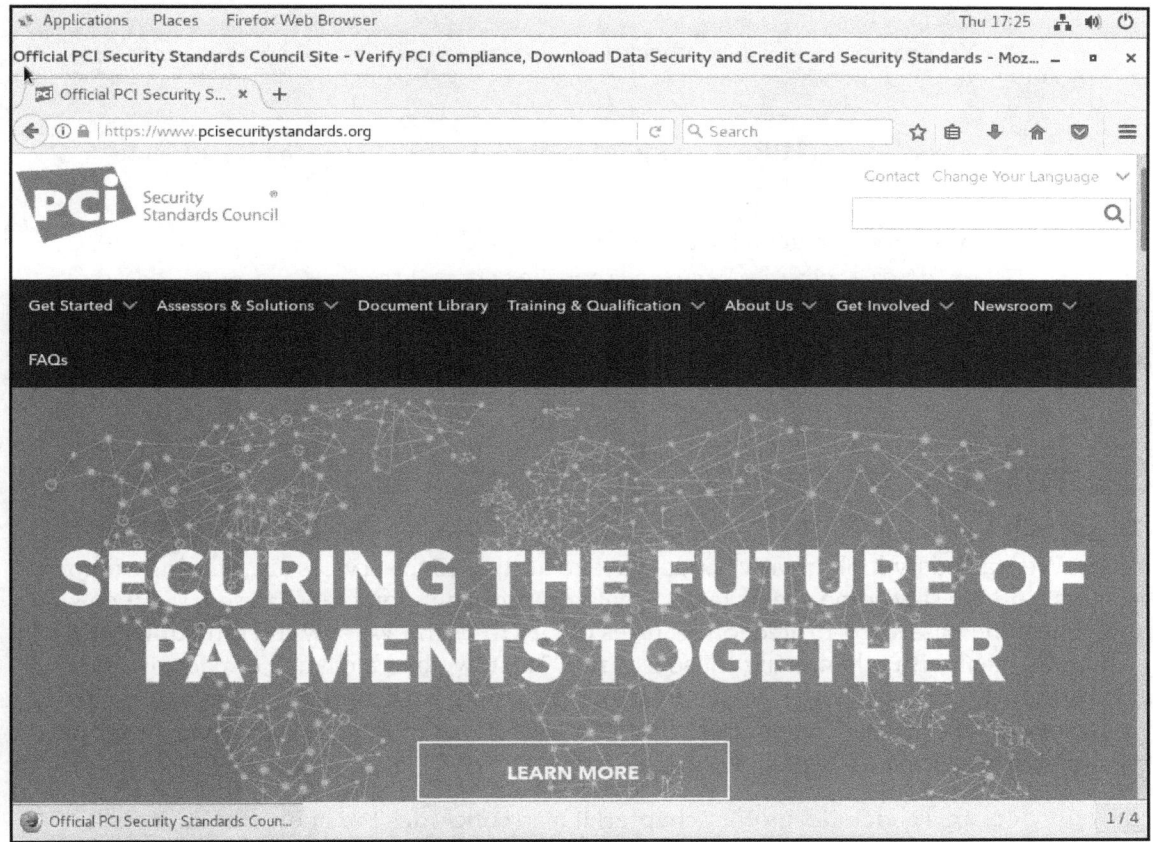

And, for healthcare organizations here in the U.S., there's HIPAA with its requirements. For publicly-traded companies here in the U.S., there's Sarbanes-Oxley with its requirements:

You can get the University of Texas checklist from at: `https://wikis.utexas.edu/display/ISO/Operating+System+Hardening+Checklists`.

You can get a PCI-DSS checklist at: `https://www.pcisecuritystandards.org/`.

You can get a HIPAA checklist at: `https://www.hipaainstitute.com/security-checklist`.

And, you can get a Sarbanes-Oxley checklist at: `http://www.sarbanes-oxley-101.com/sarbanes-oxley-checklist.htm`.

Other regulatory bodies may also have their own checklists. If you know that you have to deal with any of them, be sure to get the appropriate checklist.

Summary

Once again, we've come to the conclusion of another chapter, and we covered a lot of cool topics. We started by looking at various ways to audit which services are running on your systems, and we saw some examples of what you probably don't want to see. We then saw how to use the password-protection features of GRUB 2, and we saw the little quirks that we have to deal with when using those features. Next, we had a change of pace by looking at how to further lock down a system by properly setting up a system's BIOS/UEFI. Finally, we looked at why we need to properly begin preparations to set up a hardened system by obtaining and following the proper checklist.

Not only does this conclude another chapter, it also concludes the book. But, it doesn't conclude your journey into the land of *Mastering Linux Security and Hardening*. Oh, no. As you continue this journey, you'll find that there's still more to learn, and still more that won't fit into the confines of a 300-page book. Where you go from here mainly depends on the particular area of IT administration in which you work. Different types of Linux servers, whether they be web servers, DNS servers, or whatever else, have their own special security requirements, and you'll want to follow the learning path that best fits your needs.

I've enjoyed the part of the journey on which I've been able to accompany you. I hope that you've enjoyed it as much as I have.

Other Books You May Enjoy

If you enjoyed this book, you may be interested in these other books by Packt:

Linux Device Drivers Development
John Madieu

ISBN: 978-1-78528-000-9

- Use kernel facilities to develop powerful drivers
- Develop drivers for widely used I2C and SPI devices and use the regmap API
- Write and support devicetree from within your drivers
- Program advanced drivers for network and frame buffer devices
- Delve into the Linux irqdomain API and write interrupt controller drivers
- Enhance your skills with regulator and PWM frameworks
- Develop measurement system drivers with IIO framework
- Get the best from memory management and the DMA subsystem
- Access and manage GPIO subsystems and develop GPIO controller drivers

Mastering Linux Kernel Development
Raghu Bharadwaj

ISBN: 978-1-78588-305-7

- Comprehend processes and files—the core abstraction mechanisms of the Linux kernel that promote effective simplification and dynamism
- Decipher process scheduling and understand effective capacity utilization under general and real-time dispositions
- Simplify and learn more about process communication techniques through signals and IPC mechanisms
- Capture the rudiments of memory by grasping the key concepts and principles of physical and virtual memory management
- Take a sharp and precise look at all the key aspects of interrupt management and the clock subsystem
- Understand concurrent execution on SMP platforms through kernel synchronization and locking techniques

Leave a review – let other readers know what you think

Please share your thoughts on this book with others by leaving a review on the site that you bought it from. If you purchased the book from Amazon, please leave us an honest review on this book's Amazon page. This is vital so that other potential readers can see and use your unbiased opinion to make purchasing decisions, we can understand what our customers think about our products, and our authors can see your feedback on the title that they have worked with Packt to create. It will only take a few minutes of your time, but is valuable to other potential customers, our authors, and Packt. Thank you!

Index

CPSIA information can be obtained
at www.ICGtesting.com
Printed in the USA
LVHW020357170822
726060LV00006B/221

9 781788 620307